A HISTORY OF KERALA
1498-1801

A HISTORY OF KERALA
1498-1801

by

K. M. Panikkar

GYAN

Published by

Gyan Publishing House
5, Ansari Road
Daryaganj, New Delhi-110002
Phone: 011-47034999, 9811692060
E-mail: books@gyanbooks.com

Distribution Network
gyanbooks.com
India, USA, Canada, UK, Australia

ISBN: 978-81-212-5545-5 (HB)
First Published, 1960

2nd Impression 2024

Printed at: Gyan Press, Delhi.

A HISTORY OF KERALA 1498-1801
Author: K. M. PANIKKAR

A HISTORY OF KERALA

1498-1801

by

K. M. PANIKKAR

INTRODUCTION

Over a quarter of a century ago I published my first serious historical study entitled *Malabar and the Portuguese.* It was followed soon afterwards by a companion volume on *Malabar and the Dutch.* It was, however, many years later that I picked up the thread of Kerala history again, in order to round off the period by dealing with the Mysorean invasion of Kerala. The present volume combines the three works, and may be said to cover the history of Kerala from 1498 to 1801.

A singular feature of Kerala history during this entire period is its lack of political unity. There was no central point from which the evolution of Kerala could be viewed. It is for this reason that I thought it best to weave the history of Kerala around the Portuguese, Dutch and Mysorean relations, for these outside powers were, during each succeeding period, connected with every part of Kerala. A unity of treatment was possible on that basis.

When the period opens Kerala is seen at the height of its feudal anarchy. There were no less than four kings, forty-six territorial chieftains and innumerable lesser barons. At the end of the period only the states of Travancore and Cochin existed and they also were under the paramountcy of the English East India Company while the rest was incorporated in the British district of Malabar. The historic kingdom of the Zamorins which had so heroically defended Kerala independence for over 250 years fell to the Mysorean assault. The principalities to the south of Cochin were incorporated in Travancore by Martanda Varma and Cochin itself escaped only by a timely surrender to Mysore. Thus the division of Kerala into British Malabar, Cochin and Travancore which was to endure for nearly 150 years came into existence.

The story is in many ways a fascinating one. The history of the period assumes a significance far beyond its territorial limitation because of the major forces at play in the shaping of events. From the arrival of Vasco da Gama, the story of Kerala is translated into a chapter in world history. Some of the leading personalities whose activities are connected with Kerala are men of international stature: Vasco da Gama, Cabral, Affonso Albuquerque among the Portuguese, Van Imhoff and Van Rheede among the Dutch and Hyder Ali and Tippu among the Mysoreans. Nor were the Kerala rulers who were pitted against them men of ordinary calibre. The great Zamorins are, alas, fated to remain anonymous, known to us only by their title, with only their heroic deeds to celebrate their glory. But Martanda Varma, Paliyathu Komi Achan, Rama Raja of Travancore and Keshava Das are men whose personalities stand out in bold relief on the canvas of history.

From the point of view of culture also, this was the period marked by notable developments. It saw the rise of Malayalam as a great literature. Cherusserry and Punam in the north, Ezuthachan, Kunjan Nambiar and Unnayi Warrier in central Kerala, the Niranam Panikkars in central Travancore, in fact all the great figures of classical Malayalam, lived during this period. The *Kathakali* both as literature and as a dance form originated and matured at this time. In the field of Sanskrit scholarship and letters also the contribution of Kerala was outstanding. Melpathur Narayana Bhattathiri, Mazhamangalom Nampudiri and Aswati, Prince of Travancore and numerous others in the field of letters, the Payyoor Patteris and others in the field of *Mimamsa* and Bala Rama Varma in music and arts, made Kerala one of the centres of all-India culture. The court of the Zamorin was famed all over South India for its patronage of Sanskrit Letters in the 16th and 17th centuries and later Travancore under Rama Raja stepped into that position. From the point of view of painting also, the murals in the Padmanabhapuram and Mattanchery Palaces and the Vaikom and Ettumanoor temples testify to an efflorescence of Kerala genius.

A period of such significance in the political, social and cultural development cannot fail to be attractive to the historian. Since the publication of *Malabar and the Portuguese* in 1928, some interesting monographs relating to this period have been published by Malayali scholars. Of these the most important is a pioneer work on the history of *The Zamorins of Calicut* by Mr. K. V. Krishna Ayyar which is a mine of information on Calicut History. Mr. P. K. S. Raja's *Medieval Kerala* is another work of interest. Mr. O. K. Nambiar's *Portuguese Pirates and Indian Seamen* is a popular version of the struggle on the sea between the Zamorin and the Portuguese. The period of Dutch relations has been the subject of a major study by Dr. Poonnen. An exhaustive biography by Mr. Puthezhathu Raman, Menon of Saktan Thampuran, one of the Cochin Rajas who played a notable part in the time of Tippu, sheds light on the social conditions at the close of the period. Officially sponsored publications of the former Travancore Government, it need hardly be said, present a very biassed view of the development of that state. Literary history has been the subject of two authoritative works one by R. Narayana Panikkar, entitled *Bhasha Sahitya Charitram* and the other by Ulloor Parameswara Iyer under the title of *Kerala Sahitya Charitram.*

Malabar and the Portuguese contained a very valuable introduction by Sir Richard Temple (Baronet). Sir Evan Cotton had similarly contributed a learned foreword to *Malabar and the Dutch*. As both these are interesting in themselves I have included them as an appendix at the end of the book.

Finally, I take this opportunity to express my gratitude to the authorities of the Annamalai University for undertaking the publication of this work. I am also greatly indebted to Mr. C. K. Srinivasan, M.A., B.L., M. Litt., the author of the *Maratha Rule in the Carnatic* who was for a time working as my Secretary, for his interest in this book and in its publication. It was his persistence that compelled me to recast the two earlier volumes and to complete the story of the period by including the Chapters on Kerala and Mysore.

K. M. PANIKKAR.

New Delhi,

March 1960.

CONTENTS

Section I

Chapter		Page
I.	Kerala—The Background ...	1
II.	Kerala on the eve of Portuguese Arrival ...	18
III.	Vasco Da Gama's Voyage ...	28
IV.	Vasco Da Gama ...	35
V.	The Fight for Land Power ...	53
VI.	Almeida and The Naval Fight ...	61
VII.	Albuquerque and the Stabilisation of of Portuguese Power ...	68
VIII.	Trouble in Calicut, Cochin and Quilon ...	86
IX.	Trouble in Calicut, Cochin and Quilon (Contd.) ...	93
X.	Fall of the Kunjalis ...	122
XI.	Last days of Portuguese Power ...	131
XII.	Portuguese Policy in Kerala—General ...	143
XIII.	Portuguese Religious Policy in Kerala.	160
XIV.	The Causes of Portuguese Failure ...	171
XV.	Kerala at the End of The Portuguese Period ...	177

Section II

I.	Arrival of The Dutch in Kerala ...	185
II.	Plight of the Cochin Rajah ...	198
III.	The Dutch War with The Zamorin ...	209
IV.	Internal Intervention ...	221
V.	Rise of Travancore ...	231
VI.	Expansion of Travancore ...	244

Chapter			Page
VII.	Eclipse of The Dutch	...	260
VIII.	Disappearance of The Dutch	...	268
IX.	Dutch policy in Kerala	...	277
X.	Dutch Administration and Trade	...	294
XI.	Kerala at the end of the 18th Century.		307

Section III

I.	Kerala and Mysore	...	324
II.	Mysore invasion of Kerala	...	331
III.	Hyder's second attempt on Malabar	...	346
IV.	Tippu and Kerala	...	356
V.	Resistance of Travancore	...	363
VI.	Expulsion of Tippu	...	393
VII.	Mysore and Cochin	...	398
VIII.	Kerala Settlement	...	404
IX.	Political and Economic Results of Mysore Invasion	...	412
X.	Kerala Culture	...	426
	Appendix I	...	435
	Appendix II	...	443
	Appendix III	...	448
	Appendix IV	...	453
	Appendix V	...	455

CHAPTER I.

SECTION I

KERALA—THE BACKGROUND

Traditionally Kerala extended from Gokarnam to Cape Comorin, but in historical times its area was confined to the Malayalam speaking territories on the coast. It is a narrow strip of coastal area bounded by the Western Ghats on one side and by the sea on the other, tapering towards the south where the ghats meet the sea near Cape Comorin. The low lands nowhere extend more than a few miles from the sea. The mountain ranges—monsoon area with a high degree of rainfall, have at all times been covered with rich primaeval forests creating an impenetrable wall separating the plains of the East Coast from the hilly tracts of the West. Only at Palghat at the centre and at Aramboly near the Cape do the ghats provide natural openings to the eastern side.

Thus ensconced, the Kerala littoral would seem from the beginning to have lived a life of its own, isolated to a large extent from the developments in Peninsular India. But though her historic association with the East Coast except in the extremities was sporadic, her connection across the seas with the countries bordering on the Arabian Sea was continuous and of particular importance. Malabar teak was found in the ruins of Ur. At least from the earlier centuries of the first millennium B. C. the Kerala ports seem to have been frequented by merchant ships from the Red Sea and the Persian Gulf ports in search of spices and other valuable products of Kerala. This tradition as we shall see continued till the arrival of the Portuguese in the last years of the fifteenth century.

We have however no authentic record relating to Kerala till the 3rd centrury B. C. The first direct allusion to the kings of this area is found in an inscription of Asoka mentioning Keralaputra as one of the borderland kings of the south. Apart from references in Tamil, early Sanskrit literature has also allusions to Kerala indicating that at least by the 3rd century B. C. Kerala was fairly well known to writers in the north. Kautalya's *Arthasastra* mentions the Kerala River Choornika as one of the places where pearls were available. Vatsyayana also knew of Kerala. By the time of Kalidasa there was more intimate knowledge of the area; for there are apt descriptions of the area in *Raghuvamsa* in the *digvijaya* of Raghu.

Though it became a recognised part of Bharata Varsha by the 2nd century B. C., it is strange that no record relating to its early history has yet been discovered in Kerala itself. The earliest record discovered in Kerala relating to its own history is the Bhaskara Ravi Varman inscription of the 8th century A. D. That document however reveals a monarchy in an advanced state of feudal disruption, indicating many centuries of historical evolution. But nothing definite can be postulated as no evidence of an earlier period has come down to us. Briefly the history of the period before the 8th century can be summarised as follows:—

Some time before the third century B. C., a small trickle of Brahmins seems to have reached the country. The process of migration is not clear; but it would appear that they were settled in the area by a powerful monarch; for the geographical distribution, the organisation of the community and their special customs show clear-sighted planning which could not have been the result of unregulated migration. The Nampudiris or the emigrant Brahmins have since then formed the apex of Kerala society.

Prior to the advent of the Nampudiris, a fierce warlike tribe whose racial origins are shrouded in obscurity, worshipping nagas, and deriving from them the eponymic of Nakar (later Nayar), occupied the country, enslaving the original inhabitants and keeping them bound to land. Though there is some evidence of a conflict between the Nampudiris and the Nayars, a social adjustment seems to have been worked out early enough which left the Nayars in effective occupation of the land, with more or less exclusive local political power, while the Nampudiris, allying themselves with the leading Nayar families, maintained a social and religious pre-eminence. With minor exceptions the feudal chiefs of Kerala were Nayars, most of whom were closely allied to Nampudiris, while religious authority and the control of temples were vested in the latter.

The introduction from Polynesia via Ceylon of the cocoanut and the open rigged canoe seem to have brought with it the other major section of the population, the Ezhavas, some time before the Christian era.

With the annexation of Egypt to the Imperial domains by Augustus, trade with Rome developed on an extensive scale, especially as the Roman sailors, learning from "the discovery" of Hippalos of the seasonal character of the monsoon were able to take advantage of these winds for the navigation of the Arabian Sea. The great hoards of Roman coins discovered in Kerala bear ample witness to the extensive character of this trade.

The main port in Kerala which was the centre of this trade, as Pliny says, was Muziris or Cranganore. It was known in Kerala as Muyirikkodu—it is so mentioned in the so-called Christian plates. The earlier Tamil poets allude to it as Musiri. The *Periplus* mentions that "Muziris is a city at the height of prosperity frequented as it is by ships from Ariake and by Greek ships from Egypt." The exports of Kerala consisted mainly of "pearl, in considerable quantity and of superior quality; pepper in larger quantities and gems of every variety." The imports were mainly coral, lead, tin, stibium, etc. It will be noticed that the trade which the Romans carried on with Kerala was practically in the same commodities as those in which the Portuguese traded at a later time.

It is as a result of this close connection with Arabia, Egypt and the West that Kerala came to have in its midst a community of Jews and St. Thomas Christians. Of the exact time of the arrival of the Jews and the Christians, we have no definite information. We have evidence that they were flourishing in Kerala in the 7th century. Besides these communities, there was a powerful trade guild of Chetties, which carried on commerce with Arabia and Egypt as well as with the far east, called Manigramam which, on no evidence at all, has been claimed to have consisted of Christians. The only reason for such an assumption is that when Gen. Macaulay discovered the plates awarding rights to Manigramam, he thought they belonged to the Christians and handed them over to the Syrian Church. The Tanu Ravi plate specially mentions that it was granted to Eravi Korttan, the head of the Manigramam. That the Mangramam was a Hindu guild is clear from the fact that the temple and tank of Sri Narayana in Takopa in Siam is, according to an inscription found there, placed under the protection of the Manigramam. The inscriptions of Tiruvellerai, near Trichinopoly, point to the same fact. What is of importance to us here is that the Manigramam was a powerful trading association whose activities extended all over Kerala.

According to reliable tradition, St. Thomas the Apostle landed in India in A. D. 49, and converted a number of local families to the Christian religion. While there is no positive evidence to prove this, it is difficult to deny its truth as we have the recorded statements of Pantaenus, the head of the Alexandrian school, who visited India in the second century, that he found a flourishing Christian community there. Later in the fifth century a Syrian merchant named Thomas of Kana visited Malabar and his name is associated with a small-scale settlement of emigrants from the Levant. Some time at the beginning of the Christian era, a small Jewish community also reached the Malabar Coast and made their home there.

By the first century A. D. the Kerala country seems to have been united under a powerful dynasty, known to history as the Cheras. Their capital was at Tiruvanchikkulam near the present town of Cranganore (Muziris). Karikala Chola is said to have defeated the Chera King entering the Kerala country from the south, but was satisfied with a nominal over-lordship strengthened by a matrimonial alliance by which the Chola victor gave his daughter to the Chera King. The issue of this marriage is the renowned Cheran Senguttuvan who crossed the Palghat gap and conquered the Coimbatore territory.

A traditional list of Perumals covering the period from the second to the ninth century is available in books, but nothing is known about them beyond their mere names. No inscriptions, coins or other evidences of their work have come down to us to enable us to reconstruct the political history of the period. Of the twenty-one Perumals beginning with Keya, Harischandra and Kulasekhara who are said to have lived in the fifth century, are the most famous.

Buddhism and Jainism gained considerable popularity in Kerala and seemed to have been in the ascendant till about the 6th century A. D. The *Vihara* at Srimula Sthana was internationally famous and seems to have been a great centre of

Buddhist learning. By the sixth century these religions lost their hold in Kerala.

Sea communications with China from the port of Quilon became very important, especially after Roman trade with China began to develop to considerable proportions. Quilon became a great international emporium, and so late as the 15th century we have allusions to Chinese Junks in the harbours of the coast. Direct sailings from Quilon to the Chinese ports were a regular feature of the communications of the period.

In the 8th century Kerala witnessed a great revival of Hinduism and we have the immortal name of Sankara illuminating the pages of Indian history. This may well be claimed to be first appearance of Kerala on the stage of Indian history.

Political history is shrouded in obscurity, till the middle of the 9th century, when the Pandyan King, Varaguna, entered Kerala in 864 and established a short-lived suzerainty. The revolt against Pandyan occupation was led by a prince who has become a legendary figure in Kerala history, under the name Cheraman Perumal.

The Pallavas made no attempt on Malabar, but the Chola monarchs penetrated into Kerala on a number of occasions and annexed the area to the south of Trivandrum to their imperial domains. Chola inscriptions bear witness to the effectiveness of their conquest.

By about the 8th century the political contours of Kerala became fairly clear. Viraraghava Chakravarti's grant to the Jews is attested by the great feudatories and the Nampudiri gramams of Panniyur and Chovvara. Though the date of this grant is not finally established, it is claimed by most scholars to belong to this period. The grants made there were attested to by the Chiefs of Venad, Vambilanad, Ernad, Valluvanad and Nedumpurayoor. These feudal nobles with whose knowledge and approval the grant is made represent the families of Travancore, Vadakkumkur, Calicut and Valluvanad, and Nedunganad, who evidently had by this time attained practical independence. The Venad Rajas controlled the southern extremity and were related to the rulers of Desinganad (Quilon) and Otanad (Kayamkulam). The Vembilanad Chiefs controlled the territory lying between Cochin and Tiruvella. The Zamorin's authority centred round Ernad. In this manner in the period between the 9th and 12th centuries a feudal Kerala grew up, making the tradition of unity no more than a distant and lingering memory.

No political event of any significance emerges during this period till the meteorlike rise of Vira Ravi Varma Sangrama Dhira of Desinganad (Quilon). This ruler carried Kerala arms into Chola and Pandya countries. Inheriting nothing more than a small principality, Ravi Varma (born circa 1266) built up a military power in Kerala, conquering the neighbouring chiefs, and began intervening in the family quarrels of the Pandyan kings. In the period between 1299 and 1312 he defeated the Pandya and Chola kings and had himself crowned at Kanchi (1309-10). For a brief period he seems to have had political sway over South India. But the imperial pretensions disappeared with him, and the Quilon kings after Vira Ravi Varma reverted to the position of local rulers.

Two significant changes had taken place in Kerala in the period between 1000 and 1360 A. D. The decay of Cranganore following the disappearance of the imperial tradition enabled Calicut develop into a major port. The Zamorin whose family domains in Ernad gave him no elbow room was desirous of finding an outlet to the sea. By stratagem he occupied the coastal strip which belonged to the Kadathanad Porlatheri Raja and founded there in 1042 a city, which from the royal citadal took the name of Kovil Kotta (Kozhikkode) or palace fortress. Thus was the first stone laid of the imposing structure of Zamorins' power which was to dominate Kerala for four centuries and write its name into world history.

In 1341 a geographical change took place which was destined to have considerable importance in the history of Kerala and India. The Periyar which which was, till it was dammed in its upper reaches, a river of sorrows owing to the heavy floods to which it was subject surpassed its own past records. So great was the pressure of the flood that changing its mouth, it forced a way into the sea opposite the present town of Ernakulam and thereby brought into existence the Cochin Harbour. The new port affording protection inside the backwaters during the monsoon and Calicut having achieved prominence under the patronage of the Zamorins, Cranganore fell into decay.

From the earliest times Kerala had been in contact with the Arabian coast and traders especially from Muscat and other centres of the Arabian Peninsula used to frequent the Malabar ports. When Islam swept over Arabia, its influence was felt immediately in Kerala also. In fact according to a fairly ancient tradition the last Perumal himself became a convert to Islam, abdicated his throne and left on a pilgrimage from which he did not return. There is no inherent improbability in the story. But the further details about his partitioning the land of Kerala and distributing portions to his feudatories and relations are obviously apocryphal. That Islam began to spread in Malabar early enough both by conversion and by the settlement of Arab traders is clear from a Muslim inscription in Pantalayini Kollam in North Malabar dated Hejira 166. With the growth of Arab commercial activity under the Khalifs, Malabar ports became popular with the traders of Muslim capitals. Numerous Arabian travellers, the most notable among whom are Ibn Khurdadbeh (869-885) and Abu Zaid of Zirag (916) speak of Malabar ports. Ibn Hankal writing in the 10th century speaks of mosques in Kerala where Muslims offered their prayers.

The Muscat traders seem to have been the first to establish themselves firmly at Calicut. An old tradition preserved in the *Keralotpatti* tells the story of a Muslim merchant from that place who deposited with the Zamorin boxes of gold, pretending they were only pickles. The Zamorin on discovering that the boxes contained gold recalled the merchant and handed him back his hoard and the merchant who was greatly impressed by this honesty decided to settle down there. Whatever be the truth of the story, from the 12th century at least the Zamorins' relations with the Arab traders became intimate and Calicut slowly attained a pre-eminence in the trade of pepper and other spices which made it the greatest emporium on the West Coast. Gradually the Moslems monopolised the external trade of the coast. It should be remembered that as a result of the *Pax Islamica* in the Middle East the trade with the West in spices and other luxury goods had increased to unprecedented proportions. From the Indonesian Archipelago there was an unending flow of what in Europe was considered more precious than gold and gems and Calicut was the great intermediate port for this trade. Naturally Malabar's own pepper and cardamom and the textiles which were also in great demand were shipped from this port. As a result the Zamorin became one of the wealthiest rulers in India, and easily the most powerful on the West Coast. He claimed for himself the title of Kunnalaikkon, the lord of the mountains and the sea and by slow degrees reduced the neighbouring princes to a position of subordination.

With the gradual penetration of Islam in the coastal areas, the social structure of Kerala attained its present form. It was a social system of parallel societies. The Hindu society with local rulers at its head formed the orthodox *pays legal*. Parallel to it was a Christian community, perhaps not more than five per cent of the population at the time living under their own *Metrans*, (bishops) around their churches. A small Jewish community lived in Cranganore, living the life prescribed by the *Torah*. From Cannanore to the South along the coast, principally in towns, Arab Muslim traders had their warehouses and settlements. A local Muslim community grew up around these settlements.

The Hindu community which formed the preponderant element of the population consisted of a sumberged base of slave and untouchable classes with a gradually ascending feudal structure at the top. The social pre-eminence belonged to the Nampudiri Brahmins, whose spiritual head was Azhuvanchery Tamprakkal. Most of the temples and a considerable portion of the land belonged to them. Devoted to learning and scholarship, the Nampudiris maintained a high literary tradition and in the period between the twelfth and the fifteenth centuries contributed a great deal to Sanskrit and Malayalam literatures. Especially in the field of *Mimamsa* their contribution could be said to have been unique.

Below them came the Nayars. The Nayars were not a caste; they were a race. Every kind of caste, with varying social pretensions, existed among them. At the top were the Samantas who were the ruling families of Kerala. The great feudal nobles all over the area from the borders of South Canara to Cape Comorin came from them. Their titles varied according to places. Known as Nambiars, Kaimals, Mannadiars, Karthas, Panikkars, Unnithans, Valiathans and Kurups, they excercised local political power, based both on a feudal holding of land and a compulsory military service. The Nayar gentry was more like the Samurais of Japan, hereditarily attached as fighting men to the great feudal nobles. Their military organisation was under a system known as the *Kalaris*. In every *desom* and village, there were families with the title of Panikkar or Kurup who were the heads of *Kalaris* to which every Nayar family was attached for the purpose of training and mobilisation. Descriptions of these *Kalaris* and the training given in them have come down to us from foreign observers. According to Duarte Barbosa: "When these Nayars are 7 years of age, they are immediately sent to school to learn all manner of feats of agility and gymnastics for the use of their weapons. First they learn to dance, and then to tumble and for that purpose they render supple all their limbs from childhood, so that they can bend them in any direction. And after they had experience in this they teach them to manage the weapons which suit each one most, that is to say, bows, club dances, and most of them are taught the use of the sword and the buckler which is of more common use among them. In this fencing there is much agility and science and there are very skilful men who teach this art who are called Panikkars. They are captains in war[1]". Johnston in his *Relations of the most famous kingdoms of the World* (1611) describes the *Kalari* training in the following words: "It is strange to see how ready the soldier of this country is at his weapons; they are all gentlemen and termed Naires. At seven years of age they are put to school to learn the use of their weapons, where, to make them nimble and active their sinews and joints are stretched by skilful fellows, and anointed with oil sesamas. By this anointing they became so light and nimble that they can wind and turn their bodies as if they had no bones, casting them backward, forward, high and low even to the astonishment of beholders. Their continuous delight is in their weapon, persuading themselves that no nation goeth beyond them in skill and dexterity."

---

1. Duarte Barbosa p. 128.

The *Kalaris* varied in size and importance. Some like the *Kalari* of Dharmmothu Panikkar, the hereditary commander-in-chief of the Zamorin, trained thousands of men, while the village *Kalaris* had attached to them an average of fifty families. The Nayars thus provided a national militia. Attached to the local feudal lords, they were, according to contemporary witnesses, arrogant, quick to pick up quarrels and oppressive towards the lower classes.

In many areas they were organised into *changathams* or sworn companies which carried on vendettas and stood by each other in trouble. Some rulers also maintained Nayar companies known as *chavers* who swore to die in the protection of their masters. *Chavers* generally acted as body-guards of important rulers.

The Nayar social organisation was based on the marumakkathayam system or matrilineal descent. They lived in impartible joint families, known as *tharavads,* under their own *Karnavan,* the oldest male member of the family. The *Karnavan* enjoyed absolute power over the younger members, similar to the *patria potestas* of the Roman family. Women enjoyed social freedom and marriage ties were loose. There is some evidence that among the lower orders polyandry was not uncommon, but among the higher classes, who were allied by a system of common law marriage with Nampudiris, moral conduct, though perhaps lax, according to modern standards, was by no means promiscuous.

The commonalty among the Nayars were cultivators of land. Education was fairly well spread among them, for along with the Brahmins they contributed a great deal to the growth of Malayalam literature from the beginning. To the *Kalaris* giving instruction in warfare were also attached village schools. The Menons (and Pillais in the south) who were the clerks at the royal courts were Nayars and the service of the monarch required a standard of education not only in Malayalam but in Sanskrit and Tamil.

Next below the Nayars were the Ezhavas, known as Thiyas in the north, a community which like the Nampudiris and the Nayars was spread evenly all over Kerala. They were basically a cultivating class, traditionally associated with the growing of cocoanut and with the tapping of trees. Possibly of Polynesian origin they arrived in Kerala from Ceylon, as their name Ezhavas indicates, and introduced cocoanut cultivation on the coast. In a copper plate inscription of the 8th century their privileges in regard to tapping cocoanut trees and collecting pepper are specifically mentioned. Zeenuddin describes their occupation as being "to climb the cocoanut trees, gather the fruit and extract the juice from its branches which becomes a fermented liquor of an intoxicating nature".

The majority of the Ezhavas follow matrilineal descent, though the patrilineal descent is also followed by considerable sections of the people. Before the middle of the 19th century they were considered an untouchable class and many social prohibitions were extended to them. But many families among them enjoyed honours and the tradition of some of them excelling themselves in the arts of war has come down through bardic literature. The story of Aromal Chevakar, though perhaps belonging to the 16th century, clearly shows that there were Ezhava families who had an established position in the martial hierarchy of Kerala. But the community as a whole was in a state of social and economic depression.

Apart from these major communities Hindu society also included a small sprinking of Tamil Brahmins, attached to courts and palaces, and a very flourishing community of Konkanis engaged in coastal trade. The latter was established mainly in port towns and lived an isolated life, having very little social relations with others. There were also small castes of artisans and craftsmen attached to each village and receiving communal payment, an integral part of the village society.

The submerged base of all this apparently flourishing community was the vast body of agricultural labour kept outside the contact of the upper classes by very rigid caste rules. In fact the absurdity to which caste oppression could go was best exemplified in Kerala where the gradations of untouchability were marked by distances of approach. Some castes like the Pulayas, who constituted the main body of agricultural labour could not, it would appear, be seen by Nampudiris without polluting them. They could not approach a Nayar: the proper distance for the Pulaya to keep was sixty feet away from a Nayar. Old Portuguese records declare that when Nayar noblemen came out in the streets, some one went in front of them shouting "po, po", get away, get away, so that they may not be polluted by the proximity of untouchables.

In the parallel community the most numerous were the Christians, and the most influential, the Muslims. The Christians, unlike the Nampudiris, Nayars and Ezhavas, were concentrated in certain areas. They were not to be found to the north of Kunnamkulam, or to the south of Quilon. Within this area they had many places with historic churches around which there were flourishing settlements. Their main occupation was agriculture, oil milling and petty trade. Some families among them also had taken to warlike occupations. Originally they seem to have been under the Patriarchate of Babylon. This church which was Nestorian in doctrine changed its headquarters in A.D. 762 to Baghdad. "The power of the Nestorian Patriarch," says Neale in the *History of the Holy Eastern Church* "culminated in the beginning of the 11th century when he had twenty five Metropolitans, who ruled (Christian communities) from China to the Tigris and from the Lake Baikal to Cape Comorin".

With the fall of the Patriarch of Baghdad, the authority over the Malabar church seems to have passed to the Jacobite Patriarchate of Antioch, which connection is still upheld by a considerable section. But Rome also did not neglect this area. A Bull of John XXII dated 5th April 1330, addressed to the Christians of Quilon intended to be delivered to them by Friar Jordanus whom the Holy See had nominated the Bishop of Quilon, called on the Nascarini (Nabrene Christians) to abjure their schism and to enter the Roman Church. Jordanus seems to have met with some success for when John de Marignolli, visited Quilon on his way to China he reported: "There is a church of St. George here (in Quilon) of the Latin communion at which I dwell and I adorned it with fine paintings and there taught the holy law".

But whatever be the success that Jordanus had and the teaching of Marignolli, the church of Malabar as a whole continued to be in communion with the Patriarchate of Antioch till the time of the arrival of the Portuguese.

The Muslim community, as stated before, was confined to the coastal towns. Their leadership was in the hands of the Arab merchant princes who had established themselves mainly at Calicut and Cannanore. Their influence was mainly with the rulers of these two States, whose prosperity depended mostly on the export trade in pepper and spices. Their prosperity is attested to by all authorities. Ibn Batuta declares that the Moors of Malabar were extremely rich, that one of their leading merchants "could purchase the whole freightage of such vessels as put in there and fit out others like them." The Mamalis and Khoya Musas whom the Portuguese encountered on the coast were merchant princes to whom Cairo and Damascus were as familiar as Calicut and Cannanore.

Though they wielded considerable influence with the Kerala rulers, Zeenuddin noted that the Muslims of Malabar refrained from political influence. "I would have it understood" says he "that the Mahommedans of Malabar lived in great comfort and tranquillity in consequence of their abstaining from exercising any oppression towards the people of the country as well as from the consideration which they invariably evinced for the ancient usages of Malabar."[1] The Nayars and the Arabs got on well. *Tofutul-Mujahideen* adds[2]: "Notwithstanding that the rulers and their troops were all pagan, they (Muslims) paid much regard to their prejudices and customs and avoided any act of aggression on the Mahommedans except on extraordinary provocation, this amicable policy being the more remarkable from the circumstances of the Mahommedans not being a tenth part of the population."

In fact, the most significant feature of Kerala life from the earliest times has been the wide sense of the tolerence and mutual respect between the different communities who had made their home there. Christians and Moslems, Jews and Konkanis lived side by side with the Kerala Hindus in a state of perfect understanding and amity, respecting each other's customs and prejudices and scrupulously avoiding all interference.

Before closing this survey allusion may be made to the knowledge which the Western countries had of Kerala before the arrival of the Portuguese. Stray Europeans seem to have visited the country at different times. Marco Polo travelled in Kerala and has left us a brief description. Archbishop Monte Corvino stayed in Malabar for a year in the second half of the 13th century on his way to the court of Kublai Khan. We have already alluded to the appointment of Jordanus by the Pope to the See of

1. *Tofutul Mujahideen* p. 103.
2. *Ibid* p. 76.

Quilon in 1330 and to the visit of John de Marignolli. In the 15th century a decade before Vasco da Gama arrived in Calicut, an ambassador from the Portuguese king carrying letters of credence to Prester John (Emperor of Ethiopia) had arrived in Cannanore. Pero de Covilham, the envoy, was no ordinary man. He was a linguist, scholar and diplomat who had seen service in many areas. Disguised as a Moslem, Covilham travelled in an Arab dhow and reached the Malabar coast. This is how his visit to Calicut is described by Bishop Mathews in his *Quest of Prester John*:

"He saw more over Calicut, strange gorgeous city of thatched houses and half naked men, of cocoa palms besides the beach, of gold and jewels, of elephants and pepper. Especially pepper! Pepper may not mean much to us, but in that age, it ranked with precious stones. Men risked the perils of the deep and fought and died for pepper."

Kerala was to the Europeans therefore no unknown country. Many men of position had visited and reported on it. The merchants of Venice and Genoa, no less than the financiers of Amsterdam, had a considerable amount of information about the country, its products and its people. To reach India had been their dream and the dream was on the point of realisation.

CHAPTER II.

POLITICAL CONDITIONS IN KERALA ON THE EVE OF PORTUGUESE ARRIVAL

The political conditions of Kerala at the end of the 15th century immediately before the arrival of the Portuguese presented a complex feudâl scene. The whole area from the Netravati River to Cape Comcrin was divided into a number of petty principalities over each of which ruled a Raja or some less pretentious chief who vaguely acknowledged the suzerainty of one of the major rulers. Both Indian and foreign authorities agree that at the close of the 15th century only the Kolathiri or the King of Cannanore, the Zamorin or the King of Calicut and the Tiruvadi—as the Portuguese authorities call him —the King of Venad had what we may call full sovereign rights[1]. Apart from these rulers, there were the minor Rajahs of whom the chief were the Rajahs of Tanur, Cranganore, Cochin, Mangät, Idappalli, Vadakkumkur, Procaud, Kayamkulam and Quilon. The effective power in the land was in the hands of the Kaimals and Kartavus, independent nobles who maintained armies of their own, and owed allegiance sometimes to more than one sovereign. The major rulers, like the Zamorin, often claimed and exacted many rights over these lords; but as the strength of the great rulers was dependent on the willing subordination of the smaller Chiefs, the policy pursued by the suzerains was to leave them to themselves as far as possible. Kerala law did not recognise the right of the sovereign either to depose a rebellious Chief or to confiscate his property. The *Tofutul Mujahideen* mentions, with regard to the Zamorin, that "whenever he commenced hostilities with any of the considerable Chiefs of Malabar after subduing them, it was his practice to return to them their possessions, and the

1. Duarte Barbosa, page 150.

restitution; although sometimes delayed for a long time, he made always in the end."[1] It should be remembered that the obligation the Chiefs owed was mainly for military support in time of war. The suzerain could not interfere in their internal affairs, or stop them from going to war against each other. In fact, there was, strictly speaking, nothing in the nature of royal power in Kerala. The difference between the political organisation in Kerala and the feudal system which it resembles superficially lies in this fundamental fact. In many ways, the Nayar lords resembled feudal Barons, especially in that they had to provide soldiers when their suzerain went to war with another ruler. But the feudal principle was entirely absent from Kerala, because the lords were themselves the owners of the land and did not hold it even nominally of the King. There is in fact every reason to believe that the political organisation of Kerala developed from small local communities, each holding independently of the other.

Though the lords and minor Rajahs of Kerala had the rights of private war, of entering into alliances and treaties with others and of levying customs, yet social opinion did not permit any but the Kings of Cannanore (Kolathiri), Calicut and Travancore to wear crowns, to coin money or to hold ceremonial umbrellas over their heads. These were considered the insignia of royalty. At the time when the Portuguese reached India, the Rajah of Cochin had none of these dignities[2]. The Rajah of Cochin claimed a superior social status, he being a Kshatriya while the Zamorin belonged to the Nayar caste. This was felt as an indignity and much of the history of the Portuguese in Kerala can be understood only in the light of this fact.

1 *Tofutul Mujahideen*, page 59.

2. Duarte Barbosa, p. 107; *Kerala Charitam*, 113.

Of the position of Calicut at the time of the arrival of the Portuguese we have ample records, both Indian and foreign. Indian records, literary and historical, are unanimous that it was a great city and a flourishing port, one of the most important in India, which carried on trade with all parts of the world. Abdur Razzak, the Ambassador of Shah Rukh, noted in 1443 that Calicut was so flourishing a port "that merchants from every city and every country came together there. In it are to be found abundance of precious articles brought thither from maritime countries ...... Security and justice are so firmly established in the city that the most wealthy merchants bring thither from maritime countries considerable cargoes which they unload and unhesitatingly send into the markets and bazaars without thinking in the meantime of any necessity of keeping watch over their goods". Nicolo Conti described it as "a noble emporium for the whole of India". Ludovico de Varthema writing between 1503—1508 describes the country of Calicut at great length and confirms the view of the earlier writers of the great prosperity of the town and the general security of its government.

Calicut was a town about 8 miles in circumference. The population consisted mostly of Hindus, but there was a considerable number of Mahommedans from Ormuz, Cairo, Abyssinia and even Tunis. They had built two mosques in the city where they met for their Friday prayers. The foreign trade of Calicut was practically in their hands. The Arab traders never interfered in the politics of the state and for this reason were held in high esteem by the rulers of Calicut. Besides, through them the State of Calicut was able to equip its army with better arms and secure Arab horses; and much of the power of Calicut as against the other states rested on this. The city was visited by the fleet of Cheng Ho, the Chinese admiral during his many voyages in the Indian ocean and MaHuan, his chronicler, describes it as a great emporium frequented by traders from all parts of the world.

The Zamorin Rajahs claimed a vague supremacy in the area lying between the territories of Kolathiri in the North to Tiruvella in the south. Though originally their supremacy in Kerala was questioned by the Valluvanad Rajah, by about the 13th century the Zamorin became the leading ruler on the West coast. The area south of Quilon was held by the Rajah of Travancore who never acknowledged the sovereignty of the Zamorin. The Kolathiri Rajah of Cannanore was also independent; but the area between the Kingdoms of Cannanore and Travancore obeyed the command of the ruler of Calicut.

The government of Calicut was an autocracy tempered on the one hand by the power of the semi-independent vassal chiefs who were perpetually in revolt, and on the other, by the sacerdotal power of the Nampudiri Brahmins, who, like the Catholic Church in the middle ages, constituted a supra-national power. The great Nayar Chiefs, who were independent in their territory, also functioned as hereditary officials of the state while others were merely vassal rulers. These often fought among themselves and sometimes combined to defy the authority of their suzerain.

The administration of Calicut was carried on under the direct orders of the Zamorin and his ministers. Duarte Barbosa notes that the King of Calicut "keeps many clerks in his palace. They are all in one room, separate and far from the King, sitting on benches and there they write all the affairs of the King's revenue and his alms and the pay which is given to all and the complaints which are presented to the King, and at the same time the accounts of the collection of taxes. There are seven or eight who always stand before the King with pens. These clerks always have several leaves subscribed by the King in blank and when he commands them to despatch any business, they write it on these leaves."[1] The city of Calicut had a separate Governor and a customs officer.

The Kingdom of Kolathiri which lay to the north of Calicut had, as its principal city, the port of Cannanore. This port also carried on great commerce with Mecca and Surat.[2] The country that lay inside was fertile and produced much fruit, aromatics and spices. The Rajas who ruled the country traced their claims to the alleged partition by the last Perumal. The first authentic information we have of this country is from Marco Polo who declares that the Kingdom of Ely was tributary to nobody. Pepper and ginger grow there and other spices in quantities. Kolathiri's territory extended from the Netravati river to Korappuzha in the south which was the boundary between his and the Zamorin's territories. But as in the case of other Kerala Kings the area was divided up into many principalities under semi-independent rulers. The most important of those were the Ali Rajas of Cannanore, Randathara, Kottayam, Kadathanad, with numerous feudal barons under them. Ali Raja of Cannanore was a Mussalman prince who followed matrilineal descent. The family is said to be originally a branch of Kolathiri, a princess from the royal house having married Arya Kulangara Nayar, embraced Islam to avoid excommunication and was given the area as her share. The Rajas of Cannanore conquered the Maldives in the 12th century and the Kolathiri who was the sovereign of the Laccadives leased out the islands to Ali Raja on an annual payment. Authority over Randathara was vested in the hands of a number of Nayar Barons, who owed only nominal allegiance to the Kolathiri who was their liege lord. The Raja of Kadathanad originally held the area around Calicut, but when the Zamorin expelled him from the coastal

1. Duarte Barbosa, p. 110.
2. *Noticias da India*—Vol. I, p. 221, *et seq.*

tract, he accepted the protection of the Kolathiri and held the Kadathanad territory as a feudatory.

The Kolathiri Rajahs were seldom on friendly terms with the rulers of Calicut and the rivalry between these two Royal Houses formed one of the permanent features of Kerala history. The Kolathiri Kings claimed a higher social status, though they were not Kshatriyas like the Rajas of Cochin.

The other important Kingdom was Travancore. This state extended from the city of Quilon down to Cape Comorin. *Tofutul Mujahideen* states that the King "who possessed the greatest number of soldiers was Tiruvadi, Rajah of Quilon and Kumaree[1], whose country lay between and to the east of those towns and whose territories were of considerable extent." Ansteley's *Collection of Voyages* also alludes to the Rajah of Travancore as a powerful and independent ruler. The original history of the state is shrouded in mystery, but from about 1250 we have authentic records by which to trace the growth of its power, In that year the family of Quilon was left with only a princess who married a prince of the Chirava family named Jayasimha who thereupon assumed royal power. From him the territory took the name of Jayasimha Nad—or Singanatti as the Portuguese call it. His son Ravi Varma was as we have seen, an important figure in the history of South India. He conquered the Pandya and Chola Kingdoms and had himself crowned at Kanchivaram where he had his victories inscribed on stone. Many branches of this family, each reigning over small tracts, are mentioned in Malayalam books. Of these the most important are Trippappur and Attungal. In the latter place only women had the right to rule, the males being considered, according to seniority, as head or members of one of the other branches. This custom is still preserved in the Travancore family, the Senior Maharani of Travancore being always styled the Princess of Attungal.

1. Zeenuddin, p. 58—59.

Of the minor princely families the most important was that of Cochin. This family belongs to the Kshatriya caste and claims descent from the last Perumal or Emperor of Malabar. But, whatever might have been their claims to independence in earlier times, these had entirely disappeared by the end of the 13th century. The Zamorin as has been pointed out was lord and master; and, even in the domains immediately surrounding Cochin, authority was shared between the Rajah and the different Nayar barons. The Cochin Rajahs had the curious custom, found among other important families of Malabar also, of forcing the eldest person into retirement on the pretext of desiring religious meditation. As a result of this, there were always two parties, one taking orders from the abdicated ruler and the other from the reigning Raja, a position which almost invited the interference of the powerful King of Calicut.

North of Cochin on the backwaters was the principality of Cranganore, whose rulers were subject to the authority of the Zamorin. The *Noticias da India* mentions that the territory of Mangat lies to the east of Cranganore. Further up the river, adjoining Mangat, was the principality of Parur the ruler of which was a Nampudiri Brahmin. In the territory of the Zamorin which lay to the north of these the Nayar barons had less power.

To the east of Cochin on the other side of the backwater lay the land of Idappalli, also ruled by a Brahmin Chief. The rulers of Idappalli were the friends of the Zamorin and served him as an advance guard against the Raja of Cochin. It was in Idappalli that the great battles, in which Duarte Pecheco won his fame, were fought. Idappalli provided for the Zamorin the base for operations against Cochin, and the campaigns, in the period we have to describe in the chapters to follow, always opened with an invasion into the very heart of Cochin from the side of Idappalli.

South of the territories of the Rajah of Idappalli lay the important territory of Vadakkumkur. Its capital was the town of Kaduthirithi, a few miles to the south-east of Vaikom. The Portuguese alluded to Vadakkumkur as "the pepper country", as the finest pepper produced further inland had to come to them through this state. The Rajahs of this place are Nayars by caste and are alluded to in ancient documents as "Vadakkumkur Nayar." Though nominally subordinate to the Rajah of Cochin to whom they were allied by marriage, the Vadakkumkur Rajahs enjoyed full ruling authority and had very considerable military strength, which the Portuguese found out on more than one occasion. Another branch of the same family ruled further south.

The marshy land consisting of the present Taluq of Ambalapuzha and the eastern portion of Changanacherry was under the rule of a Brahmin Rajah who bore the hereditary name of Deva Narayanan. This Chief had a considerable naval force under him which was commanded by a family of Arayars. Between Procaud and Quilon lay the state of Kayamkulam or Kallikoilon. Though the Chief of Kayamkulam was not very powerful, his state enjoyed considerable importance from the commercial point of view, as it was the natural outlet for the fertile country which lay to the interior. Politically the interior was split up even more than the territories of Cochin or Calicut. In the small district of Tiruvella alone there were 10 Brahmin families who ruled with equal authority.

The absence of royal authority, which was thus the main characteristic of Kerala polity, had early in the 15th century begun to undergo a slow change. The establishment of the great Hindu Empire of Vijayanagar whose authority extended to the borders of Cannanore had its influence on the political conditions of Kerala. Besides, Calicut had become by this time the great centre of Western trade and the Zamorin was easily the wealthiest and the most powerful ruler on the coast. He had assumed the style and dignity of a great King. His naval forces were strong enough to scour the coast from Gujarat to Ceylon. Even more than this, the Zamorin had the support of the Moorish settlers who contributed largely to the prosperity and power of his kingdom. With their help he was extending his power in such a way that in the century immediately preceding the arrival of the Portuguese he had practically become the King of all Kerala from Cannanore to Procaud and exercised royal power in a way that no other Kerala ruler had done.

Besides the local traditions, what stood in the way of the Zamorin setting himself up as an auto-cratic monarch in the manner of the Kings of Vijaya-nagar or the other rulers of the east coast was the curious religious polity of Kerala. Politically divided into small principalities, Kerala was a single entity from the point of view of social and religious organisation. The very fact that there were no kingdoms and states but only Rajahs and Chiefs, who had often rights and properties in each other's territory, helped the growth of an extra-political social unity. In the temples of Cochin and even of Travancore the Zamorin had many rights. In the territories directly under the sway of the Zamorin there were many temples in which minor Chiefs who did not owe allegiance to him exercised authority. The Rajah of Kayamkulam had special rights in the temple of Kutalmanikyam in Irinjalakuda in the territory of the Cochin Rajah. Besides this, the position of the Nampudiri Brahmins was also definitely ex-territorial. Like the Catholic Church before the Reformation, the Nampudiri Brahmins did not recognise political boundaries; and what was more, the Rajahs themselves had no such territorial nations as to expect powerful religious or social organisations within their area to yield unitary obedience to them. Most of the temples with their enormous revenues were in the hands of the Brahmins. Even the Sri

Padmanabha pagoda at Trivandrum, which is one of the most ancient foundations in Kerala and one of the richest, was governed by a body of eight members, and the Rajah, whose family temple it was, had only half a vote.

With the power of the territorial magnates so well established, and the authority of the religious organisations placed clearly above political divisions, it was impossible to develop in Kerala a central government with all-embracing authority, except by a process of slow evolution. The expansion of the Zamorin's power, based on the support of the Moors, had begun to do this with some success and his authority had slowly penetrated down to the borders of Procaud when the Portuguese arrived on the scene.

Thus, at the end of the 15th century, Kerala was leading a comparatively happy, though politically unsettled life. In many ways, her organisation was primitive; but she had evolved a system in which trade flourished, different communities lived together without friction, and absolute religious toleration existed. The wars of the Chieftains did not materially affect the tranquillity of her life, and in town and country alike law and order were enforced. The weakness of the system was that though there were many Kings and Rajahs there was no such thing as royal authority, no central power capable of uniting the Nayars into a single confederacy. Undoubtedly, the course of Kerala history during the two centuries previous to the arrival of the Portuguese was in the direction of an increase of the Zamorin's power and the establishment of Kerala confederation under his authority. But this very process gave rise to jealousies and feuds. It is this fact that should be clearly borne in mind in the study of the period following the arrival of the Europeans in India.

CHAPTER III

VASCO DA GAMA'S VOYAGE

In the navigating activities of the 15th century, which were mainly conceived with the object of circumventing the Mahommedan control of the Red Sea route to India, Portugal played an important part. The desire for maritime exploration and discovery was given a great and lasting impetus in that country by the adventurous spirit and career of Dom Henry, Duke of Viscau, better known to the world as Prince Henry the Navigator. This subject is dealt with in fuller detail in the present writer's *Asia and Western Dominance,* (London 1953). It was Prince Henry who conceived the idea of reaching India by rounding the southern point of Africa. In his expeditions Prince Henry was loyally supported by his father and later on by his brother. Besides this royal encouragement, he had at his command the immense resources of the Order of Christ of which he was the Grand Master. That the wealth of this religious Order should be used for the purpose of exploration was nothing strange, because Prince Henry, like a devout Christian, regarded his discoveries as the conquest of new worlds for Christ. It is important to remember this because the policy of the Portuguese in the East becomes intelligible only in the light of the firm belief which they entertained, till the very end of their supremacy in the Indian seas, that their work was the work of God and, therefore, as against them, no body of men, unless they be Christians had any rights.

Prince Henry's discoveries encouraged him in the project of claiming for Portugal the right of sovereignty over all the new lands in Africa and Asia. In 1441 he made a request to the Pope to grant to the Crown of Portugal such territories as may be discovered beyond Cape Bojador. Dom Henry did not fail to point out that as a Christian prince he considered it his first duty that the heathen peoples of the lands discovered should be claimed for Christ. The Curia agreed to grant his request, and a Papal Bull was issued giving the crown of Portugal the exclusive rights of sovereignty in Africa and Asia.

Information about the seas on the other side of Africa was by this time slowly trickling down to Europe. The Venetians had presented to Dom Pedro, the brother of Prince Henry, a copy of Marco Polo's *Travels* with a map of the world as the Venetian traveller knew it. In a map made for King Affonso in 1460, the eastern coast of Africa was traced and marked by Fra Mauro, a Venetian friar. Dom Joao II was as enthusiastic as his predecessors and even more determined. His first attempt in this direction was to select Joao Peres de Covilhao, a fidalgo who knew Arabic well, for a journey to India by land. Accompanied by Affonso de Paiva, Covilhao started from Lisbon in the first week of May 1487. Leaving Paiva at Aden, he took a boat to Malabar reaching Cannanore by the traditional route of Greek and Roman trade. He stayed for a considerable time both at Cannanore and at Calicut and gathered valuable information about Indian trade. On his return journey, Covilhao, however, was forced to stay in Abyssinia where he died after many years of service.

The maritime expeditions that Joao II organised were even more successful. Two ships of 50 tons each were fitted out in 1486 and their command was entrusted to Bartholomeo Diaz. Diaz rounded the Cape of Good Hope and thus the way was opened for an expedition to India. Joao II recognised the importance of the discovery in opening up the passage to India, and it is in recognition of this fact that he gave to the promontory the name of the Cape of Good Hope. Dom Joao thereupon took up with enthusiasm the organisation of a more ambitious expedition which was to reach India direct. He began the preparations immediately. He had already received valuable information about the route to India from the King of Benin during the latter's visit to Portugal in 1484. Before his project could materialise, Dom Joao died (1496). Dom Manuel who succeeded him, though of a less idealistic nature, inherited in full the enthusiasm of his family for maritime discovery and took up the project with zeal. In this he had the advice of the Hebrew Astronomer, Abraham Ben Zakut. In consultation with him, the necessary preparations were made. Three ships were specially constructed with a view to stand a prolonged voyage on the high seas and all due care was taken to provide for contingencies and unforseen circumstances. The ships were built on the plans of Bartholomeo Dias, and their construction took over a year. The accumulated experience of over half a century of exploration and voyage, and the information systematically gathered from various sources from the time of Dom Pedro were utilised[1] fully in the methodical preparation of the great undertaking. The armada was ready in 1497 and the King, to the surprise of all, entrusted its command to an unknown courtier, a fidalgo of his Household, Vasco da Gama.

Vasco da Gama was the third son of Estevao da Gama and his wife Isabel Sodre. On both sides he was descended from noble stock. The da Gamas were a well-known family tracing their descent to a knight who accompanied Quialdo the Fearless. Another da Gama was a famous general in the time of Affonso III, and yet another, Alvaro da Gama, fought with Affonso IV in the battle of Salado.[2] The Sodres, of whom we shall hear a great deal in connection with India, were an equally well-known family.

---

1. Reade *in the Journal of the Royal Asiatic Society*, 1898, p. 589.
2. Estevao himself was the Controller of the Household of King Affonso.

The family seat of the da Gamas was in the town of Sines where the church built by Vasco can still be seen. Here it was that the future navigator was born in 1469. Vasco became a Gentleman of the Household of the King, Dom Manuel. It was when he was in that position that he was selected to command the expedition. The reason for this selection is obscure. There was nothing in the previous life of Vasco as a courtier to entitle him to the command of an armada. The reason that Barros gives is that the original idea was that of Estevao da Gama, the father of Vasco, and Dom Manuel nominated Vasco as a recognition of his dead father's claims.

The ships were fully equipped, provisioned, and were ready to set sail. The voyage was blessed by ecclesiastical dignitaries. The voyagers were absolved of all sins by virtue of a Bull which.Prince Henry the Navigator had obtained for the benefit of those who may die without the comforts of religion in the middle of the sea. On July 8th the whole crew heard Mass and then from Balem the armada sailed. On which ship Vasco da Gama himself was is not definitely known. Correa, who wrote his history with the help of the diary of a priest, who accompanied the Captain-Major, states that the flag-ship was San Rafael, while Barros who is more reliable as a historian, states that San Gabriel was the ship on which Vasco himself sailed. The generally accepted view is that San Gabriel was the flag-ship. According to modern conceptions these were hardly more than small sailing vessels. San Gabriel was not more than 120 tons while San Rafael was even of less capacity. But they were heavily armed for their size—San Gabriel carried no less than 20 guns. The rigging consisted of 3 masts with six sails. It is on a ship like this that the voyage to India was undertaken.

Rounding the Cape after a stormy voyage, the armada reached Mozambique in March 1498. There Vasco da Gama captured an Indian named Davane.

After many adventures, the ships reached Melinde at the end of April. The Portuguese captain was received with honour. After an exchange of presents, ceremonial visits, etc., the King who was well disposed towards the Portuguese offered da Gama pilots who knew the seas well and could direct him to Calicut. Between the African Coast and Calicut there was a regular trade in spices; and it was at the King of Melinde's suggestion that the decision was taken to sail to Calicut instead of to Cambay. With the help of the pilot said to be a Gujarati, who was lent by the King of Melinde, the Arabian Sea was crossed without difficulty in 20 days' time. The land first sighted was near Cannanore, but the Portuguese did not anchor there. Sailing down the coast, they anchored off Kappat, a few miles to the north of Calicut on May 17th[1].

The discovery of the sea-route to India was a great event from the point of view of the results that followed from it. But as a feat of exploration, or even of nautical adventure, it was of no importance.

The historical results that flowed from the direct contact of European Powers with India and the commerce and wealth which the control of the Indian seas gave to Europe, have shed an exaggerated light on Vasco's achievement. It should be remembered that the project of a voyage to India round the Cape did in no sense originate with Vasco da Gama. He had in fact nothing to do with the conception or the planning of the project. It had already been planned by Dom Joao following the traditional policy of Dom Henry; and in this Dom Joao had at his disposal the expert advice of Abraham Ben Zakut. Even the instructions to Gama were drawn up in consultation with him. The discovery of the Cape of Good

---

1. It is characteristic of Portuguese historians that they are not agreed even as to the month in which Vasco da Gama reached India.

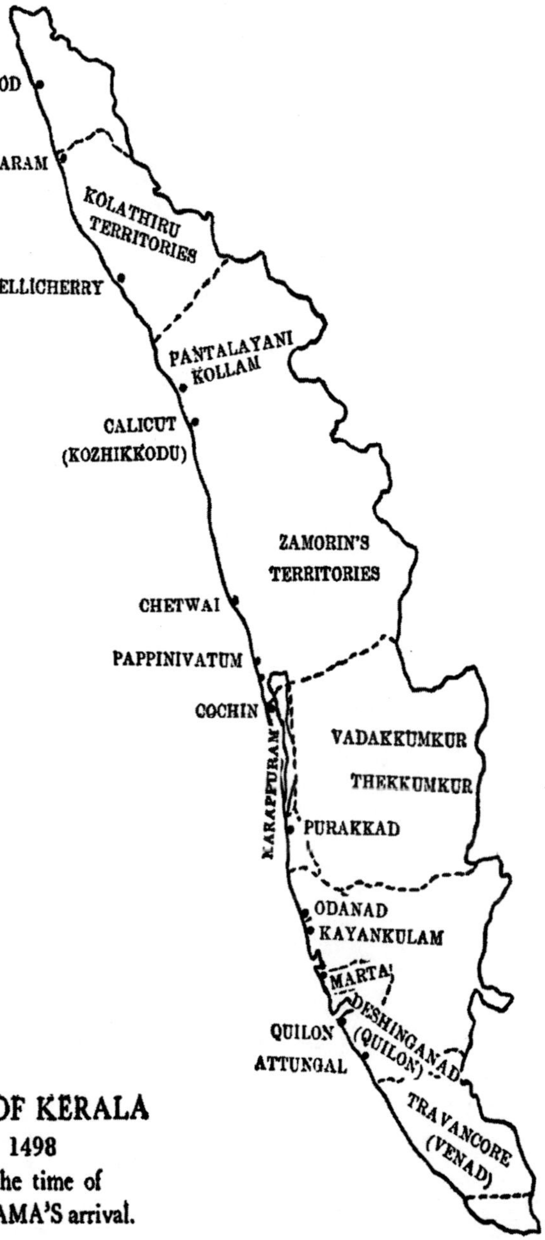

MAP OF KERALA
1498
at the time of
DA GAMA'S arrival.

Hope by Diaz had partially fufilled the dream of Dom Joao; and the plan itself was matured and its organisation undertaken by Dom Manuel, on the basis of authentic information gathered by the court during half a century of exploration. Moreover, India was in no sense a *terra incognita.* It was in close contact with Europe, through the Venetians and the Moors. Besides, the sea-faring people on the Coast of Africa, consisting mainly of Arabian settlers, knew the routes and the winds, and da Gama had the help of competent Indian pilots supplied to him by the King of Melinde. He was not sailing in uncharted seas like Columbus or Magellan, but sailing along recognised routes to a country which was situated at a known distance from the African coast. There is nothing in Vasco da Gama's discovery which entitles him to the claim of a great explorer or navigator. His glory is based entirely on the historical results that followed, for which he was hardly responsible.

The real importance of the new "discovery" lay in the fact that it broke the monopoly which the Venetians and the Egyptians had so long enjoyed in the trade with India. Before that time no European nation since Alexander's time had come into direct contact with India. Egypt, by its natural position, had stood as the intermediary between India and the west. The arrival of da Gama with his two ships at Calicut was the end of India's political isolation from Europe. Till then her intercourse with outside peoples was confined to those that lived on her north-west frontier. Indian rulers had not realised the possibilities of sea power and the political strength that it can bring. Vasco da Gama created for India a new frontier and with it new political and commercial problems.

The effect of this was not immediately recognised in India. Indian Powers, accustomed to look only to dangers from land forces, did not realise the menace to their security implied in the two ships which had reached the Kerala shore. The only people who realised the far-reaching significance of this event were the Moors who saw that their trade supremacy was endangered and fought desperately against the newcomers. Both the Egyptians and the Turks saw the true extent of the danger and were prepared to meet it. But internal cmoplications, resulting mainly from the conquest of Egypt by the Turks, gave the Portuguese a short respite during which they were able to consolidate their naval position, from which, even if they did not advance, they were never fully dislodged till the Dutch entered the field.

CHAPTER IV.

VASCO DA GAMA

Da Gama arrived at Kappat or Capucad, a few miles north of Calicut. A large number of people gathered on the shore to see the vessels which were of a kind different from those usually navigating the coast. It was decided by the Portuguese, after a consultation, not to go on shore without hostages. Da Gama also circulated the story through some fishermen that his ships were merely the advance guard of a numerous armada with which he had parted company. Communications were opened with the Zamorin's officers who were extremely friendly. The Zamorin's pilots took the ships inside the harbour at Pantalayini Kollam where they were safe from storms. The Portuguese captain and his friends were invited to land. Da Gama, with a number of his officers, landed on shore and travelled inland to where the Zamorin was at the time. A curious incident happened on the way. Seeing a Hindu temple where the priest was conducting a religious ceremony, da Gama and his companions, mistaking it for a Christian Church, went in and worshipped.

The Zamorin received the party in a special durbar. Da Gama was careful to let it be known widely that he represented a very powerful King. Besides, as Correa himself says, there were many Moors at the Calicut court who were well acquainted with the conditions and politics of Europe and who must have informed the ruler as to who these foreigners were and where they came from. Gama presented himself at court dressed "in a long cloak, coming down to his feet, of tawny coloured satin, lined with smooth brocade and underneath a short tunic of blue satin and white buskins and on his head a cap with lappets of blue velvet with a white feather fastened with a splendid medal; and a valuable enamel collar on his shoulders and a rich sash with a handsome dagger."[1] He was accompanied by a page dressed in red satin, and in front of him went the men in single file.[2] The King watched their arrival from a balcony. Gama was received at the gate of the palace by the commander of the bodyguard, without whose permit no one could enter the palace. The King received them "seated on a rich bed set out with silk and gold in a room arranged with silk stuffs of various colours and of white canopy which was of subtle workmanship and covered the whole room."[3] The Zamorin was clothed "in white cotton strewed with branches and roses of beaten gold[4] but wore many ornaments of great value." Correa says, "He had on his left arm above the elbow a bracelet which seemed like three rings together, the middle one larger than the others, all studded with rich jewels particularly the middle one which bore large stones which could not fail to be of very great value; from this middle ring hung a pendant stone which glittered; it was a diamond of the thickness of a thumb. Round his neck was a string of pearls about the size of hazel-nuts; the string took two turns and reached to his middle. Above it, he wore a thin round gold chain which bore a jewel of the shape of the heart,[5] surrounded with larger hearts and all full of rubies; in the middle was a green stone of the size of a large bean, which, from its showiness, was of great price, which was called an emerald." The Zamorin was attended by his chief officers. Behind him stood a page boy armed with a drawn sword, "a red shield with a border of gold and jewels, and a boss in the centre, of a span's breadth of the same materials, and the rings inside for the arm were of gold."

---

1. Correa—Three voyages, page 192.
2. *Ibid* page 193.
3. Faria y Sousa, page 47.
4. Faria y Sousa, page 47.
5. Evidently a pathakkam which is an insignia of royalty in Malabar.

After the presents were placed before the King, da Gama was ushered in. Compliments were exchanged and the Captain-Major made a speech explaining his mission and the desire of the Portuguese King to open commercial relations with India. He also presented to the King kneeling, the letter of Dom Manuel. The letter was received with great courtesy, but beyond that the negotiations did not proceed. The Zamorin's answer to the request for commercial facilities was vague, and da Gama was asked to communicate to the Treasurer of the King what commodities he wanted. The parting was cordial, and the Portuguese and the people of the town met in friendly intercourse. But da Gama was not satisfied. The kind of stuff he had brought from Lisbon for exchange in India was not suited to the Indian market and there was no demand for it from the Indian side. The Portuguese attributed this to the intrigues of the Moors and complained to the Zamorin that the goods were not being sold. Whatever the cause was, there was but little trade done between the Portuguese and the local inhabitants.

Soon, the Zamorin, who was residing a few miles out of Calicut, sent for da Gama in order to have another interview with him. The Portuguese, always suspicious that others were intriguing against them, were particularly nervous, and in this feeling they were confirmed by certain words which a Castilian resident at Calicut dropped in a low tone to da Gama when he was starting on the journey. Portuguese historians, with that genius for seeing in every incident a miracle and every skirmish a battle, have regaled their countrymen with stories of treachery and patient endurance in the face of misfortune. Nothing in fact had happened to justify the fears the Portuguese entertained. The Zamorin had merely asked for the goods to be unloaded. In fact, for the inconvenience that da Gama had suffered in coming so far into the interior, the Zamorin expressed his regret.

When the monsoon season was over, da Gama made preparations for returning to Portugal. He requested the Zamorin for permission to leave a factor at Calicut in charge of the merchandise which he was not able to sell. The Zamorin required customs to be paid according to the regulations of the port; but this da Gama refused to do. It was this controversy that embittered the relations of da Gama with the Zamorin and helped to convince the latter that the newcomers were bent not merely on commercial pursuits. Da Gama sailed away from Calicut as soon as the monsoon season was over, taking with him a few low caste captives whom he had held as hostages.

Leaving Calicut on the 29th August 1498, da Gama sailed north and reached the port of Cannanore. At the invitation of the Kolathiri Rajah who had a hereditary feud with the Zamorin who was always attacking his country and threatening his independence, Gama landed there. The Rajah was naturally anxious to be on friendly terms with the Portuguese and offered them all facilities for trade. The Zamorin had already warned the other rulers of Malabar about the Portuguese, but this did not deter the Kolathiri from entering into an informal agreement with them and helping them to load their ships. From Cannanore they set sail on the 20th of November. The ships put in at Anjediva, a group of small islets on the Malabar coast, where some time was spent in repairing and refitting the vessels. Here Gama also came across a Jew from Grenada who had become a Mahommedan, and carried him to Lisbon. This Mahommedan was converted to Christianity under the name of Gaspar da India.

Da Gama reached Lisbon on the 29th of August, 1499. The successful return of the armada caused great rejoicings in Portugal. The fleet had been absent for over two years. The whole court gathered at the port of Belem near where the great cathedral of St. Jeronymus now raises its stately head. The nobility, the clergy, the ladies of the court, all mingled to get a sight of the "hero" who had made the greatest sea-voyage of the age and discovered the sea-route to India. The King, Dom Manuel, was himself awaiting him attended by the Household. As the ship drew near and anchored at the harbour, Jorge de Vasconcelos, a chief noble of the Household, was sent by the King to convey the greetings to the Admiral. When Vasco got down from the ship, his appearance was indeed striking. His majestic figure was made more striking by the flowing beard which had never been shaved or trimmed since leaving Portugal. Dressed in a close-fitting silk jacket, but with no ornaments, he walked straight up to where the King was. Dom Manuel stood up to receive him. After a long audience, during which da Gama described his adventures in detail, he drove with the King to the palace where he was presented to the Queen. Honours and titles were showered upon him. The title of "Dom" along with the perpetual right of 200 Cruzados a year was given to him.

From the commercial point of view, da Gama's voyage was a great success. The cargo he brought with him was worth 60 times the cost of the expedition and the King was naturally anxious that the resources which were thus opened out to him should be exploited in full. A new expedition was fitted up with Pedro Alvarez Cabral as commander. The instructions given were to persuade the Zamorin to drive out the Moors, and if unsuccessful in that to proceed to Cannanore. His armada consisted of 33 ships and carried 1500 men. Among those who were associated with Cabral were Bartholomeo Diaz and Nicolas Coelho. After a very eventful voyage, in which chance led him to the coast of Brazil, which was thus "discovered and taken possession of" by the Portuguese, Cabral reached India with only 6 ships.

The Portuguese King could not have selected a worse officer if he wanted to establish peaceful relations with the Indian rulers and carry on trade. Cabral had neither tact nor foresight. He had an overweening pride which suspected an insult in every innocent movement, and was short-tempered. On arriving at Calicut, he sent on shore, dressed in Portuguese costume, a low caste fisherman whom Gama had taken to Europe, with a message to the sovereign. In a country like Malabar which is caste-ridden this was the greatest possible insult. Though the Zamorin would not see the messenger, an interview with Cabral was arranged. On September 18th the Zamorin met Cabral, but the interview broke up owing to a misunderstanding. Cabral, thinking that his person was in danger, returned in a hurry to the ship, leaving the cargo and the Portuguese who accompanied him on the shore. Negotiations were then resumed between the Zamorin's plenipotentiaries and Aires Correa, as the agent of Cabral. After prolonged discussions extending over 2½ months a settlement was reached which gave the Portuguese the right of having a factory in Calicut.

The Portuguese in the meantime began to claim extraordinary rights on the sea. Their idea is thus put by Barros:

"It is true that there does exist a common right to all to navigate the seas and in Europe we acknowledge the rights which others hold against us; but this right does not extend beyond Europe; and therefore the Portuguese as Lords of the Sea are justified in confiscating the goods of all those who navigate the seas without their permission."[1]

Under cover of this convenient theory Cabral seized a ship belonging to the Arabs that was at

1. arros, Vol. I. Bk. I.

anchor in the harbour. His complaint was that the Arab ships were able to load pepper which he wanted for himself. The Portuguese were already putting forward claims of monopoly; but the local traders sold naturally to those who paid them the best price. Cabral complained of this to the Zamorin who replied that they were welcome to buy as much as they could pay for. But Arab competition was keen; and Cabral being dissatisfied with the method of bidding and buying in the open market, hit upon the easy way of attacking the Arab vessels within his reach and taking possession of them. Up to this, the Nayars on the coast were friendly with the Portuguese. They treated them with courtesy and did business with them. In fact, the Portuguese themselves recognised the friendliness of the inhabitants and had only a few weapons with them in their camp on shore. But the news of Cabral's unwarranted aggression caused anger and consternation to the people of Calicut who had, for many centuries, complete security of property and person. So they were roused to fury, and destroyed the factory in the riot that ensued. More than half the Portuguese on land were wounded.[1]

Cabral retaliated in his brutal fashion. He massacred the crew of all the boats he could lay hands on in the harbour and in some cases burnt the ships with the men in them. The coast area of Calicut is occupied mostly by low caste fishermen in thatched huts and consequently the action of the Portuguese did not cause much material damage, though the bombardment struck terror in the minds of the people in general. It confirmed in the minds of the Nayars of Calicut that the intruders were uncivilised barbarians, treacherous and untrustworthy. It made the Zamorin an enemy and the most determined opponent of Portuguese connection as Affonso Albuquerque found out later on.[2]

1. *Kerala Caritam*, p. 21.
2. *Cartas of Albuquerque*, p. 130.

Cabral soon discovered that further stay in Calicut would be of no use and might probably become dangerous. The coast was unknown to him and the monsoon was about to set in. At the suggestion of the converted Jew, Gaspar da India, he decided to sail to Cochin. He reached that port on Christmas Eve 1500. There was with him in his boat a Malayali Christian, named Michael Jougue, belonging to the Syrian church, who had embarked with a view to go to Palestine. Cabral sent him along with a Portuguese to seek an interview with the Rajah of the place. The residence of this prince was at Kalpathi, separated from the mainland and the seashore. They interviewed the Rajah [1] who was greatly pleased to hear about the quarrel between the newcomers and the Zamorin. Permission was immediately granted to the Portuguese to buy whatever they wanted, and Cabral found in Cochin, unlike in Calicut, a docile ally whose submission to his plans was likely to be of great importance to Portuguese power in the East.

Cabral himself visited the Rajah and presented him with a variety of things which he had especially brought from Portugal. An informal treaty was arranged by which permission was granted to the Portuguese to build a factory in Cochin. As the experience of popular fury in Calicut had taught him to be cautions, Cabral requested the Rajah that some leading Nayars might be sent to the ship as hostages. This was agreed to. With the whole-hearted support of the ruler, the ships were loaded without difficulty in a very short time. At the same time, messengers arrived from Cannanore and Quilon inviting the Portuguese to those towns and promising them satisfactory trade arrangements.

The warmth with which the Cochin Rajah welcomed Cabral, and the ease with which negotiations were concluded, were all due to the humiliation which

---

1. Correa: *Lendas da India*—Tome I—Chanter IX.

the Rajah felt in his being a subordinate to the Zamorin. Cochin was at that time a very small principality dependent on Calicut. It was the privilege of the Zamorin to settle even the succession to the Musnad. The Cochin Rajah had no right of coinage, and the Zamorin even interfered in matters of administration. The chief noblemen in the state, especially the Anchi Kaimals who held the territory on the coast, were the supporters of the Zamorin and defied the Cochin Rajah's authority with his help. This was a humiliating position for the Rajah, and, for some considerable time past, he was intriguing to throw off this galling yoke. In the Portuguese adventurers, an exaggerated version of whose exploits he had heard through Michael Jougue as well as through the Mahommedan merchants, he thought he found allies and with their help he would be able to free himself from the control of the Zamorin. But Unni Rama Varmah who made the alliance little foresaw the misfortunes and humiliations which awaited this change of allegiance. The Portuguese Governor became in a short time his lord and master, and made the Cochin Rajah drink to the very dregs the cup of humiliation in exchange for the ready help he had given the newcomers.

In the meantime the Zamorin did not remain idle. In the short period of a fortnight, he equipped a fleet of about 80 ships carrying about 1500 men. When they were sighted off Cochin, Cabral's courage deserted him. At night, he fled taking along with him even the Nayar hostages who were on the ship.[1] One of them, a relation of the Rajah, was treated with special honour by Cabral and was presented to Dom Manuel who took a great liking for him. He was made a noble of the court and given vast estates

---

1. He abandoned even those Portuguese who were on land numbering about 30, including Duarte Barbosa, the writer.

in the country. He was carefully educated in Portuguese, and later on converted to Christianity, when he took the name of Manuel. He was employed to draft the King's letters to Malabar Princes. He lies buried in the Cathedral at Evora where his tomb may still be seen.

Sailing hurriedly, Cabral anchored at Cannanore, in the country of the Rajah of Chirakkal who helped him to load some further cargo. Thence he left for Portugal.

The first naval encounter with the Indians did not end in favour of the Portuguese. This was due to the incapacity of the commander. We have sufficient evidence to show that the people of Malabar were as good seamen as the Portuguese. But events were soon to prove that on sea, as on land, equipment is the deciding factor. The equipment of the Portuguese ships was the best of the time, excluding perhaps the ships of the Turkish navy. The fire-arms which the Portuguese used were a novelty in India; and it is these facts that settled the fate of India's command of the sea. But, in spite of all this, for a very long time, in fact till 1599 when the fort of the Kunjalis was taken, Indian ships continued to harass Portuguese trade and cause them great damage.

Besides the five ships, which were all that were left of the armada of thirteen, laden with the spices and the merchandise of the East, Cabral took with him a letter from the Rajah of Cochin to the King of Portugal, and many valuable presents for the Queen. The royal letter was written on gold leaf, and professed friendship to the royal family of Portugal and expressed the Rajah's pleasure at the trade relations which were established. The presents for the Queen included ornaments studded with precious stones and a large quantity of the best silk.

The alliance with Cochin was important in two ways. The Rajah of Cochin, being a discontented and powerless prince, was a willing tool of Portuguese ambition. He saw in the new power of the foreigners an easy way of gaining his independence. The Zamorin's interference with the affairs at Cochin, which mainly took the form of deposing the ruler at the time of the accession of the Zamorin and installing a new one, and of compelling all Cochin products to be sold through the port of Calicut, had the result of creating a smouldering discontent in the hearts of Cochin Rajahs. They were therefore glad that an opportunity had come by which they could profit.

Secondly, the Cochin harbour, unlike the port of Calicut, provided a base which could be defended from the sea. What the Portuguese wanted was not a trading factory, but a port in which they could establish themselves. The factory in Calicut which was on the mainland and surrounded by the Zamorin's men, could not be defended against hostile attack. Cochin is on a small island, separated from the mainland by the backwaters and so narrow that every part of it could be shelled from the sea. Its acquisition gave the Portuguese a strong foothold from which no land power could expel them. Besides, Cochin was in the centre of Kerala, a suitable point for controlling the politics and trade of the country. Behind it lay what the newcomers called "the great pepper country", and the backwaters provided an excellent line of communication. Moreover, from a political point of view, Cochin was especially suited for the exercise of their power. Around the town were a number of small chieftains, all fighting against one another. The *Noticias da India*[1] mentions the chief of Mangat, a few miles to the east of Cochin, and the chief of Parur, a few miles to the north, as rulers of importance; it also states that the

---

1. pp. 225—230.

country surrounding Cochin was in the hands of Kaimals. To the south-east lay the small but important principality of Vadakkumkur. A few miles to the east of Cochin was the Brahmin principality of Edappalli, and to the south the peninsula of Shertallay was divided up between 73 petty lords. There was no prince powerful enough to resist the aggression of the Portuguese and the result was that, with Cochin as their centre, they were able to intimidate and domineer over the neighbouring areas.

The long absence of Cabral made the Portuguese King send out a small fleet of 4 ships under Joao de Nova. On the way he got full information as to what happened to Cabral at Calicut and Cochin. On seeing the disasters of both da Gama and Cabral at Calicut, de Nova avoided going to Calicut and sailed to Anjediva where he was met by the emissaries of the King of Cannanore. Before going to Cannanore he tried to find out what happened to his compatriots at Cochin. Nova found that, at Cochin, the merchants refused to exchange goods and insisted on cash. As he was not plentifully supplied with gold, he left for Cannanore in the hope that he might be able to realise money by selling European goods at that port. But the Mahommedan merchants organised a successful boycott. Finally, through the help of the Rajah who stood guarantee, he was able to load his ships and return to Europe.

The return of Cabral dissipated the earlier optimism about India. It was now recognised that even the sovereignty of the seas which the Portuguese King had claimed for himself as "the Lord of the navigation, conquest and commerce of Ethiopia, Arabia, Persia and India," would be keenly contested. But Dom Manuel was prepared for any sacrifice and fitted up a new armada to be sent to the Indian waters for the purpose of retaliating against the Zamorin and of effectively asserting the authority of the Portuguese in the Arabian Sea. Cabral was first nominated as admiral. But the King showed a lack of confidence in him, and da Gama then volunteered to go.

The new armada consisted of 15 ships. The captains who accompanied da Gama whom Barros mentions by name were Luis Coutinho, Francesco de Cunha, Joao Lopes Perestillo, Affonso d'Aguiar, Ruy de Castenhada, Diago Fernandez Correa who was nominated as captain of the factory of Cochin, and Antonio de Campo. The flag-ship San Jeronymo, in honour of the patron saint, was under the command of Vincent Sodre, a relative of da Gama. Of the 15 sails six were large vessels including San Jeronymo and Lionarda commanded by Coutinho, and five were lateen-rigged caravels fitted with heavy artillery, They carried 800 men in arms. The soldiers who had joined the expedition were paid 3 cruzados a month besides two quintals of pepper for every 18 months they spent outside Portugal.

On the 30th of January 1502, the King heard Mass at the Cathedral of San Jeronymo, and in a speech made da Gama admiral of the Indian, Persian and Arabian Seas. The fleet sailed from Belem on the 10th of February. The King himself went out on his barge. Out of the fifteen vessels, ten under the admiral were to return after taking effective measures to secure the whole commerce of the Indies for Portugal and after punishing the Zamorin. The other five under Vincent Sodre were to form a permanent Eastern squadron stationed in the Indian seas. A month and a half later another squadorn of five vessels under Estavo da Gama left for India. This armada is probably the biggest that went out to India before the 19th Century. It was equipped and sent out with a view to conquest, because the Portuguese King had finally realised that a monopoly of the trade of India could not be achieved except by an effective control of the sea.

On the way, the Portuguese fleet committed numerous acts of piracy. A ship belonging to a brother of Khoja Kassim of Calicut was returning from Mecca. Da Gama stopped it and plundered the goods. "The Captain-Major", says the admiring author of *Lendas da India*, "after making the ships empty of goods, prohibited any one from taking out of it any Moor, and then ordered them to set fire to it." No pleading could assuage the thirst of the Portuguese for blood; and though the Moors offered all they possessed, the order was given to set fire. This is a typical example of the inhuman and almost demoniacal cruelty of the Portuguese adventurers, and we shall meet with many more as we proceed further. What is astonishing is that the Portuguese historians have no word of disapproval for this horrible and cruel massacre, and even Camoens passes over it.

Da Gama reached Anjediva and made it the base of operations. In order to fulfil the first part of the orders to him, which was to establish a monopoly of trading in the Indian seas, the ships separated and began capturing all merchant vessels seen on the high seas. They gathered a rich harvest. On reaching Cannanore, the King of Chirakkal came with 4,000 Nayar swordsmen to see him. An interview took place on a scaffolding on the sea side.[1] The Rajah was given various presents including a sword of gold and enamel. A commercial treaty was discussed but it was not possible to settle the prices as the merchants said that the King had only the right to the duties. Finally, it was agreed that they should receive the same prices in Cannanore as in Cochin. Vincent Sodre was left behind in Cannanore with instructions "to buy and gather in the warehouse rice, sugar, honey, butter, oil, cocoanuts and dried fish, and to make cables of coir."[2]

---

1. Correa says it took place in a house.

2. *Three voyages*, page 325.

From Cannanore, da Gama sailed to Calicut. He found the harbour cleared. According to Barros, the Zamorin sent four messages to the Captain-Major, the final one being when da Gama was only two leagues from Calicut. In these messages, he pointed out that, if any one had a complaint, it was he and he was however prepared to make an agreement. Gama insisted as a preliminary of peace that all Mahommedans in the city should be expelled. The Zamorin refused to consider so impossible a demand. Gama immediately began to bombard the city. The Zamorin had huge barricades erected with palm trees, but considerable damage was done by fire. The Nayars of the shore also attempted to reply with the help of two guns. The rice vessels that arrived during these days were plundered and their crew captured. The Captain-Major ordered his men "to cut off the hands, the ears, the noses of all the crews and put them all into one of the small vessels in which he ordered them to put the friar (a Brahmin envoy of the Zamorin who came with a Portuguese safe-conduct) also without ears nor nose nor hands, which he ordered to be strung round his neck with a palm for the King on which he told him to have a curry made to eat of what the friar brought him."[1] The vessel was then set on fire. The Zamorin, on hearing of this outrage for which it is impossible to find a parallel in history, swore "to expend his whole kingdom" to fight the Portuguese.

After a futile bombardment for 3 days, da Gama sailed to Cochin. He reached that port on November 7. The Portuguese there, whom Cabral in his haste had left behind, met him and described to him how the Cochin Rajah had saved them from the enmity of the Moors and even allowed them to sleep in his own palace. The Rajah also sent envoys to greet him. The next day, the Captain-Major went on shore and presented the Rajah the various gifts

1. *Three voyages*, vol. I. page 331.

which he had brought from Portugal in return for the letter and presents that the Rajah had sent. These included 2,000 gold Cruzados enclosed in a large silver cup. The Rajah was well pleased and allowed the Portuguese to load their ships with merchandise. After a few days, during which five large vessels and two small ones were laden with pepper, cardamom and other spices, da Gama appeared in his true colours. He presented his terms of alliance to the Rajah. The first was that all pepper, cardamom and other spices must be sold to the Portuguese at a price to be fixed by the Captain-Major and the Raja, and the second was that the Portuguese should be given the right of building factories and keeping garrisons in places of their choice and that no one else should be allowed to do so. The Rajah was, at this, taken aback. He had welcomed the Portuguese as if they were friends, but now he found out that they had gone there as masters. In his chagrin, Unni Rama Varmah wanted time to consider the demands. Gama rose in anger and left the conference demanding that an answer should be given then and there. The poor Rajah followed him and begged his forgiveness. He promised to agree to whatever the Portuguese desired. That was the very point da Gama aimed at. The Rajah was given many valuable presents including a gold crown.

In the meantime, the Zamorin made great preparations. He collected a large naval force under Koja Kassim with a view to attack da Gama off Cochin. He asked the Rajah of Cochin whether he wanted the friendship of the foreigner or the friendship of Calicut.[1] Da Gama's anxiety was to escape with his booty to Europe; so leaving Diogo Fernandez Correa as the factor in Cochin he sailed off to Portugal. When he was about to leave, the Rajah of Cochin appealed to him not to go, explaining the precariousness of his position, how the Zamorin was

1. *Kerala Pazhama,* page 35.

organising a great expedition against him, and how members of his own family, the nobles of his state and even a part of his army were ready to side with the Zamorin against the Portuguese. To all this appeal by the Rajah of Cochin, da Gama turned a deaf ear and had his ships laden. But before he could leave in safety, he had to meet the Calicut fleet, which under Khoja Ambar lay ready for him. The battle was indecisive; and Gama was able to sail away in safety. This is how admiral Ballard describes the action.

"A most notable clash of arms followed of great historical interest. In estimating the strength of the contending forces we have no records for guidance except those of the old Portuguese chroniclers, who were naturally biassed; but Correa's statement that the Red Sea fleet comprised seventy dhows and the Malabar coast flotilla one hundred small craft, does not seem impossible. All were strongly manned—some carrying 600 men—and the larger vessels mounted a mortar battery as ship's armament, useful at short ranges. The Red Sea division was commanded by Khojambar, an Arab seaman of great repute in the east, and the Malabar flotilla by Cassim, another leader well known on that coast. Everything was in favour of the oriental Armada therefore in material essentials, except on one point. The Portuguese ships alone carried long range ordnance—by the standards of the day—and if only da Gama could manoeuvre so as to fight at his own range his success was reasonably assured. To get to close quarters and swamp the enemy by sheer weight was the whole object therefore of the Asiatics; to allow the enemy to get just close enough for annihilation by superior gunnery the object of the Europeans."

One thing of special interest which happened while da Gama was at Cochin was the interview which took place between him and the representatives of the local Christians. These men, believing that with the arrival of the Christian Portuguese, the time of good fortune and greatness had come for them, approached him and offered their allegiance to the King of Portugal. They suggested that, if a fort was built by the Portuguese in the area where they were strong, the whole of Kerala could be conquered. They little knew what persecutions, miseries and outrages they would have to suffer at the hands of these Christian Portuguese, whom they thus invited to conquer Kerala.

CHAPTER V

THE FIGHT FOR LAND POWER

The warm welcome which the Cochin Rajah gave the Portuguese and the treaty he made with Cabral wrought upon him the wrath of his overlord. The secret clause of Cabral's treaty was that the Portuguese would make the Cochin Rajah independent of the Zamorin and instal him as the chief ruler of Malabar. Twelve years later, when the great Albuquerque succeeded in making peace with the Zamorin by abandoning this ambition of placing a puppet King of the Portuguese as the sovereign of Kerala, the King of Cochin, Unni Rama Varmah, who signed the treaty with Cabral, wrote to the King of Portugal in the following words:

> "After all this had taken place they came to me at this my port and I assisted them with all they asked me for, both in cargoes for their ships and all the other things ...... It has from that time appeared to all my friends and enemies that the friendship existing between Your Highness and myself could not be severed on any account and this they knew for certain that I was crowned the chief-king and your chiefest friend."[1]

The Zamorin saw the danger which lay in the alliance between his vassal and the Portuguese. It was clear that, if the Portuguese were allowed to establish themselves in Cochin, the independence of the Kerala princes was not safe. The Zamorin was fully aware of the cruelty and treachery of the newcomers. He asked for their surrender, or, in case the Cochin Rajah's honour forbid that, for their expulsion from Cochin. The Rajah, proud of his new alliance, and believing in the promise of the Portu-

1. Biker's *Treaties.* Vol. I.—Torre de Tombo *Corpo Chronologico* P. 1. Maco 14.

guese to make him the ruler of Malabar, refused to agree against the wishes of his own officers, nobles and leading generals.

At this, the Zamorin moved south with his army. His main allies were the Rajah of Idappalli, whose, state was but a few miles away from the town of Cochin and the Patingettedam Nampudirippad, a Brahmin nobleman who held the environs of Trichur. With their help, he marched into the heart of Cochin without any resistance. At this time, Vincent Sodre with his squadorn arrived at Cochin; but, in spite of the earnest request of the Portuguese in the fort and of the Rajah, he refused to help them and sailed away under the pretext that it was the best time of the year to plunder Mahommedan ships in the Red Sea. But he met there with a tragic fate, his squadron and most of the men being destroyed in a terrible gale near the Curia Muria Islands. On March 1, 1503, the war between Calicut and Cochin began. In the early skirmishes, success lay with the Cochin Rajah. This was mainly due to the efforts of Lorenco Moreno with whose help the Cochin forces defended the fort at Idappalli with great courage. But the Zamorin, attacking both from the sea and from the land, carried the day and the Cochin forces drew back and in the battle that ensued the Cochin army was annihilated, and three Cochin Princes, including the heir apparent who was the commander-in-chief, were killed. The Cochin Rajah gathered another army and attempted to stem the tide of invasion and failing to do so, took sanctuary along with his Portuguese allies, in a temple.

The Zamorin again sent envoys to the Rajah of Cochin with the message that he only wanted that the Portuguese should be expelled. This was again refused. At this the Zamorin carried fire and sword into the enemy's territory, and, after establishing a strong garrison at Cochin, returned to Calicut.

The monsoon interfered with the course of the campaign and the Zamorin stayed at his capital for the next three months. But the time was not wasted. The Ruler of Calicut recognised that, if the foreigners were to be successfully resisted, it could be done only with their own superior weapons. For this purpose, he employed in his service two Italians. Pero Antonio and Joa Maria, who undertook to cast cannon for him and to teach his soldiers the use of it. From that time warfare with the Zamorin took a new turn; and during the whole period that the Portuguese had power on the sea, they were never able to subdue him, though by stratagem and by policy they gained some temporary advantages.

By the end of the monsoon time, three small squadrons from Portugal arrived in Indian waters. The first to reach was the squadron under Francesco d'Albuquerque who was followed by his cousin Affonso Albuquerque (later on Governor) with three ships, while a similar force under Antonio de Saldhana arrived a few weeks afterwards. Francesco Albuquerque heard of the whole course of events in Cochin while in Cannanore and sailed immediately southwards with a view to bring help to Cochin. Francesco drove out the Zamorin's garrison from Cochin and built there, on the pretext of helping the Rajah, the first Portuguese fortress. The Rajah supplied the necessary material and the foundations for the fort were laid on the 27th of September, 1503. The structure was in the form of a square of 183 yards surrounded by a deep moat. The Rajah himself came and encouraged the builders, little knowing that he was loading the pistol against his own breast. The fort was named after Dom Manuel. The Rajah of Cochin was indemnified by a gift of 10,000 Cruzados and the Portuguese captain extolled the great generosity and wonderful loyalty with which the Rajah had defended the Portuguese refugees in the days of their greatest trial.

The Zamorin's forces had retired from the immediate neighbourhood and the allies lost no time in taking revenge. One incident in this otherwise uninteresting campaign deserves mention illustrating the methods of the Portuguese in carrying on war. Near Cochin there was a Chieftain by the name of Cheruvaippil Kaimal who was lord of 3,000 Nayars. The Portuguese captain, with the help of the Rajah, surrounded his castle and, after defeating his troops, set fire to the town killing men, women and children. The Rajah of Idappalli was especially the object of their inhuman revenge. They burnt his villages, desecrated the temples, and carried off women and children into slavery. They mercilessly laid waste whole tracts through which they passed and ravaged the population like a plague.

After the retirement of the Zamorin to his own territory, the Portuguese pointed out to the Rajah the necessity of dealing with his own Chiefs. The first agreement of importance that he made with his own barons was the treaty with the Anchi Kaimals, the powerful lords who held the territory on the mainland side of the Cochin river. By this treaty, which may be said to lay the foundation of the Cochin Rajah's effective sovereignty in his own state, the Kaimals accepting definitely the Rajah's suzerainty over them, swore allegiance to him and his family, and agreed to hold their estates of him. This treaty is of great importance because it is the first testimony of the course, which the Portuguese attempted to follow as a part of their policy, that of aggrandising their power with the small Chieftains under the cover of the nominal suzerainty of the Cochin Rajah.

A truce with the Zamorin was arranged, but the Portuguese did not keep it for long. They attacked some of the boats carrying pepper and other merchandise belonging to the subjects of Calicut and war was again declared. Information regarding the preparations the Zamorin was making was brought to Albuquerque by a Mahommedan spy. The Portuguese captain was anxious to stay and fight the Zamorin's forces, but his soldiers were bent on reaching home. Leaving Duarte Pacheco with about 90 effective men to defend the fortress of Cochin, the work on which was by this time completely finished, and after provisioning it to stand a siege, the Albuquerques left for Lisbon. Francesco and his ship never reached Portugal.

The Zamorin prepared his attack with great care. He knew that on account of the ravages of the Portuguese, no cultivation had taken place in the area around Cochin, and that rice, the staple food of the people, was scarce. In the circumstances rice had to be imported from the Carnatic coast. The Zamorin persuaded the Mahommedan merchants to desist from this, and Ismail Marakkar, the head of the Mahommedan community, issued orders prohibiting the trade in rice with Cochin. But Duarte Pacheco was an able and resourceful man. He had the leading Muslim merchant of Cochin and his family kidnapped and helped as hostages for rice supply and the crisis was averted.

The military campaign began favourably for the Zamorin. He advanced with a large army into Cochin territory and came as far as Idappalli. The river at Idappalli becomes shallow and fordable over a considerable length. But the approach to it is narrow and near the banks it is somewhat deep. Up to the ford the Zamorin's army marched without opposition. But there he had to meet the Portuguese captain, Duarte Pacheco, who takes his place in point of military ability, resourcefulness and skill, with Clive, de Bussy and Wellington in the history of Indo-European relations. Pacheco had made a careful study of the military topography of the area, in which he was called on to fight and had made elaborate preparations which were unknown to the Zamorin. He had with him also 100 Portuguese with the best military equipment of the age, besides a large force belonging to the Cochin Rajah. He erected a stockade in the middle of the river, in its fordable part, without either his allies or his enemies suspecting it. When the Zamorin's army approached the ford and encamped on the other side, it found the passage strongly guarded and a caravel with artillery supporting enemy action from the deep end of the ford.

An effort was however immediately made to break through the defence. The Zamorin's plan was to attack with boats on both flanks and try to cut down the stockades by a frontal attack. Both these attempts failed. Pacheco defended the ford with heroic gallantry for over 3½ months, at the end of which the Zamorin retired to his own territory. It is certainly one of the most glorious feats of arms which Indian soldiers under European command have performed in India. Though Portuguese historians celebrate it, Pacheco received neither reward nor honour. Only the Cochin King created him a "Dom."[1] The war was continued in a desultory fashion. The arrival of Lopo Soares with 14 ships gave additional strength to the Portuguese and their allies, and after some abortive pourparlers, Calicut itself was bombarded for two days. After that, Soares attacked Cranganore, the capital of a principality under the Zamorin. Cranganore is situated at the head of the creek and had once been an excellent port. This was the base of Zamorin's operations against Cochin. Mammali, the admiral of the Zamorin's fleet, made it his chief port and carried on depredatory expeditions against Cochin. Supporting

---

1. The grant to Pacheco runs thus:

"We, Kerala Unni Rama Koil Thirumulpad, King of Cochin, sovereign of Adavil Cherriveppel, Nedungad, in remembrance that when the Zamorin Rajah attacked us, in Meenam month 679 (Malayalam Era) Pacheco defended us and brought victory to our arms; therefore we grant to him and to his descendants in perpetuity engraved on his shield the five crowns indicative of the five Kings he defeated and seven weapons to indicate the seven battles with the Zamorin. In the handwriting of Chirikandan" (*Kerala Pazhama,* pages 65—66).

him and waiting for the departure of the Portuguese was the general of Calicut with a large army. The Cochin Rajah informed Soares of these preparations and invited him to attack the Zamorin's sea forces. Soares planned and carried out a surprise attack, destroying many of the Calicut sloops and capturing all the rest. Mammali himself with his two sons died fighting. The Portuguese landed on the shore and were given permission to plunder the houses, but as the Nayars made a stout resistance, order was given to burn the town. The Jews who had made Cranganore their headquarters for many centuries considered this the destruction of their own holy city and left that town and settled at Cochin and the surrounding areas.[1]

Besides this fight at Cranganore, the fleet under Lopo Soares carried out another important naval operation. At Pantalayini Kollam, the Moors had gathered 17 ships to carry them across to Cairo and Mecca. They had guarded them with guns and kept a force of 4,000 men to defend it against attack. The ships were laden with merchandise. Lopo Soares attacked it with two caravels and 15 boats. After a long and hard-fought battle the Portuguese gained the victory and the ships were sunk or burnt (1506).

The first round of the contest for the trade of India may be said to end with this. The Portuguese at this time were fighting not for political supremacy nor even for the command of the sea, but for the right to trade with Kerala. The Zamorin who was the most powerful ruler on the coast opposed it. The Moors whose vested interests were threatened and who were able to realise the significance of the advent of the Portuguese, not only opposed them but used every possible method to drive them out. But the cupidity of the Cochin Rajah, his rivalry with the Zamorin, and his deisre to become the leading ruler of Kerala were exploited by the Portuguese who

---

1. *Kerala Pazhama*, page 104.

found in him a willing ally and a convenient tool. In the first round of the fight, the Portuguese were not able to establish themselves as a Kerala power. But it became clear that there was no possibility of driving them away from the Indian coast. They had gained the right to trade; and by the relations entered into with Cochin, Quilon and Cannanore, they had secured considerable commercial interests. Neither on sea, nor on land were they the masters; but the Moors, the Zamorin and the other Indian powers recognised after 4 years of fight, that a new and incalculable factor had been added to the already complicated politics of India.

CHAPTER VI.

ALMEIDA AND THE NAVAL FIGHT

When Cabral returned to Lisbon, the Portuguese King realised that the problem was either to send a large force and hold the seas or to give up the dreams of Indian trade.[1] This, as we saw, was attempted with partial success. But, in the meantime, Portuguese interests in India grew. The policy so far followed was to send out a fleet every year in the hope that it would be able to destroy Indian shipping and enable the Portuguese to secure the monopoly of Indian trade. This was soon found impossible; and it was represented to Dom Manuel that without a permanent representative in India with authority to initiate a continuous policy and keep constant watch, even the trade interests in the country would suffer. Manoel Tilles, the factor at Cochin, wrote to the King dated January 8, 1504 that, without the appointment of a fully powered officer, the Portuguese in India would not be able to hold their own. The necessity for such organisation was recognised by the King and Dom Francesco d' Almeida sailed to India as the first Viceroy. He was, however, not to take the title without having first built fortresses at Anjediva, Cannanore Cochin and Malacca. The policy of the Portuguese is made clear by this instruction. It was to build fortresses and hold the strategic centres from which they could command the seas. Each of these fortresses was to be put on a permanent basis with a captain, a staff and a garrison, and the Viceroy was to be the head of the whole organisation. He was also asked to destroy the power of the Moors on the sea, to get the Mahommedan merchants of Calicut expelled and, what is more, to cripple the power of the Sultan of Egypt. What the Portuguese Government discovered early enough

1. Faria y Sousa, *Asia*, page 63.

was that the power of the Zamorin and his opposition to their schemes had the support of the Sultan of Egypt with whom he was in close alliance. What was of the highest importance, if the power of the Portuguese was to be unchallenged in Kerala, was to break the communications existing between Egypt and Calicut. The necessity for a strategic base at Anjediva arose from this consideration.

Almeida, after erecting a fort at Anjediva, went to Cannanore where also arrangements were made for the immediate erection of a fortress; after this, Almeida took the title of Viceroy. At Cochin, he had to face a political crisis on which the future of the Portuguese policy depended. By one of the many curious customs of the Cochin Royal family, the eldest member took the title of Perumpatappu Muppil and retired into religious seclusion. Thus it was the second member who always ruled as the sovereign. The Muppil died in 1505 and the ruler Unni Rama Varmah, who had welcomed the Portuguese and was in fact their only avowed friend, had now retired from his throne. The heir-apparent, who, according to the matrilineal law in force in the ruling families of Kerala, was the eldest male member counting descent through the female line, was openly against the Portuguese connection. If this prince was to succeed Unni Rama Varmah, the friendly relations established with Cochin would immediately come to an end. The Zamorin as the overlord whose right it was to see that succession laws were obeyed, supported the prince, both from the point of view of policy and from that of law. Popular opinion also was strongly in his favour. Even the Rajah did not want to set aside the dynastic law. But Almeida saw that, if the Portuguese had to continue their trade relations, decisive action should be taken. After heavy pressure, he made the Rajah agree to supersede the heir-apparent and nominate a more docile prince as the ruler. The new prince was installed and crowned with a golden crown sent from Portugal and he was made to take the oath of fealty and allegiance to the King of Portugal. Cochin thus became not only a subordinate state, but a fief of the Kingdom of Portugal; and its Rajah was henceforth alluded to in correspondence by the Viceroy and others as the faithful servitor of Portugal. Almeida also used the opportunity to secure from the Rajah the right to build a new and strong fortress at Cochin. The immediate result of this arrangement was to plunge the whole country into civil war.

With the Portuguese power thus well established both by the new fort that was built and the complete control established over the Rajah himself, Almeida took in hand the second part of his instructions, which was the destruction of Arab trade and of the relations existing between the Zamorin and the Sultan of Egypt. His main effort lay in two directions. The first was to close the way through the Maldives, to which line the Arab trade route had been diverted. The Portuguese did not know of the Maldives and to close this line Lorenco Almeida, the son of the Viceroy, was sent with a fleet. He missed the Maldives but reached Ceylon. The second step taken by Almeida was to destroy the naval forces of the Zamorin. The Italian Varthema, who was living in Calicut and who therefore knew the affairs of the Zamorin from internal sources, conveyed to the Portuguese camp the news that a large naval force was equipped at Calicut consisting of two hundred small vessels, carrying guns cast by the Italians, which was meant as a convoy for a cargo fleet going to Egypt. The Portuguese navy under Lerenco Almeida met this fleet and, in a grimly fought battle lasting two days, destroyed the Zamorin's ships. It is the superior equipment of the Portuguese navy that gained for Lorenco his victory. The Zamorin, though thus defeated on the sea in the fight against the Portuguese, continued to harass effectively by his ships the trade of those who were their allies. Loyalty was not one of the strong points of the Portuguese captains then in India, and the ships of the allies were abandoned to the fury of the Zamorin.

The King of Calicut was also politically active. He was pressing forward a league of Kerala princes against the Portuguese. Those who had allied themselves with Portuguese were his hereditary enemies, the King of Cannanore and the Rajah of Cochin. The Zamorin was now able to point out the humiliating servitude to which the Rajah of Cochin had been reduced as an argument to persuade the Rajah of Cannanore to abandon the Portuguese. Other causes also favoured him. The old Rajah of Cannanore who had welcomed the foreigners was dead. The new ruler was not committed to the policy of his predecessor. Moreover, the action of the Portuguese captain Ganzalo Vaz, in violating the safe-conducts issued to the ships of the leading Mahommedan merchant of Cannanore, plundering the cargo and murdering the crew, caused great anger.

The alliance between the Zamorin and the Kolathiri, as the Rajah of Cannanore was called, was a reversal of traditional policy. But the new circumstances of Portuguese power necessitated it. The Kolathiri laid siege immediately to Cannanore. The fortress held out for four months, though the garrison had to undergo terrible privations. When the entire stock of food and everything edible had been exhausted and the Portuguese were on the point of surrendering, the ships of Tristao da Cunha arrived. The garrison was saved; but the treaty made with Kolathiri showed that the Portuguese realised the danger that lay in the alliance between Cannanore and Calicut.[1]

After putting an end to the trouble at Cannanore, destruction of the naval power of the Zamorin was again attempted. With the new reinforcements that da Cunha had brought, the Viceroy felt that he was sufficiently strong to attack the Calicut

1. Varthema, page 281.

forces at their base. All the Portuguese vessels on the Indian Seas were brought together, With this large force commanded by the Viceroy in person together with Tristao da Cunha and Lorenco d'Almeida, the Calicut forces were attacked and totally defeated.

But the Zamorin had yet another card to play. He invoked the aid of the Sultan of Egypt, with whom he was in alliance, through the Marakkars or his Muslim admirals. The Egyptian merchants in Calicut put pressure on the Sultan, who needed no persuasion as the incessant depredations of the Portuguese were causing Egyptain trade great harm. A fleet was soon fitted up and despatched to the Indian waters under Mir Husayn, an officer of experience and ability. It carried no less than 1,500 men and was equipped with the latest weapons. The idea was to cross to Gujarat and, with the island of Diu as base, operate against the Portuguese fleet. Husayn reached Diu just after the monsoon. The rumour of the Egyptians coming in strength to support the Zamorin had already spread in India. In fact, from the earliest days of their advent to India, the Portuguese always dreaded a strong Egyptian attack. But they had by this time got so far accustomed to this fear that the rumour was not credited. Lorenco d'Almeida sailed north to meet the Egyptian vessels, half disbelieving in their existence. Even when the fleet was sighted, the Portuguese mistook them for the ships of Affonso Albuquerque who was known to be on his way to India from Ormuz.

The two fleets met at Chaul. It was mainly a war of artillery, as the Portuguese attempt to board the Egyptian vessels was repulsed. After two days of cannonading the Portuguese decided to flee, but the flag-ship of Lorenco d'Almeida was hit and the captain himself was killed. Even up to his last breath, he kept on encouraging his men to fight and it was only after a very hard struggle that the Egyptians were able to board the ship.

The number of Portuguese killed amounted to 140. An almost equal number was wounded. Mir Husayn also lost heavily, but the victory was his. For the time, the Portuguese had lost the command of the sea, and it looked as if they had to abandon the Indian trade and retire to their homeland.

The superiority of the Portuguese fleet against the naval forces of the Zamorin lay in better gunnery and more efficient equipment. When it came face to face with the Egyptian fleet which was its equal in every way, the advantage did not lie with the Portuguese. Their easy victories over the Zamorin's ships had made them underestimate the strength of the enemy and when the guns from Mir Husayn's ships opened and artillery fire was directed with accuracy and skill, the Portuguese were surprised. The lesson of the victory was clear to Indian rulers, that without equal equipment and efficient gunnery it was impossible to defeat the Portuguese on the sea.

Almeida realised the gravity of the disaster that had overtaken Portuguese power. He knew that the most urgent necessity was to recover the command of the seas which he had lost. He collected all the ships, men and arms which were available. No time was lost. The Viceroy started north with this new armada which consisted of 18 ships and 1,200 men. He reached Diu on the 2nd of February, 1509. He had, even before he started, bought off the Governor of Diu, Malik Aiyaz, a Russian convert who had accepted employment under the king of Gujarat. Treachery had thus weakened the Indo-Egyptian force. The Egyptians had only 10 ships as against the Viceroy's 18. As Malik Aiyaz had secretly joined the Portuguese, Mir Husayn's supplies depended upon the 100 sailing vessels which the Zamorin had sent. The battle which ensued on February 3rd, 1509 was inconclusive, in spite of the tremendous odds in favour of the Portuguese. But the Egyptian ships retired leaving the command of the seas again in the hands of the Portuguese.

The first round in the naval fight was thus over. It was as indecisive in its results as the land fight. The sovereignty of the sea, which the Portuguese claimed, was unstable. Their authority had not been established in spite of all the fighting that had taken place during the last ten years. The Egyptian adventure showed that with proper handling and efficient gunnery, the Portuguese naval power could be crushed. On land their position was still more insecure. Except the Rajah of Cochin, their old ally, who had now been reduced to a servitor, they had neither friends nor supporters on shore. From this perilous position the Portuguese power was saved by the unaided genius, extraordinary resourcefulness and unflinching courage of Affonso Albuquerque, afterwards styled the Great.

CHAPTER VII

ALBUQUERQUE AND THE STABILISATION OF PORTUGUESE POWER

Affonso Albuquerque had, along with his cousin, previously visited India in 1503. He was again sent out in April 1506 in command of a convoy consisting of 4 vessels which accompanied a cargo fleet under Tristao da Cunha. Albuquerque was nominated Governor of India from Gujarat to Cape Comorin. The Viceroyalty which was created for Almeida in 1505 included all the possessions and areas over which the Portuguese claimed authority. This was altered in the appointment by the provision made in the case of Albuquerque who was nominated Governor only for the area between Gujarat and Cape Comorin, while Jorge d'Aquiar was appointed for the area between the Cape of Good Hope and Gujarat, and Diogo Lopes de Sequiera was to be Governor of the area east of Cape Comorin. All the three Governors had equal and co-ordinate authority within their respective areas.

Albuquerque commenced his regime as Governor under circumstances which reflect the greatest discredit on the political loyalty of the Portuguese. On his way to India, he anchored at Ormuz and demanded that the King of Ormuz should become a tributary of Portugal. As the King refused to do it, Albuquerque destroyed the ships in the harbour and landed his men. Thereupon the King agreed to the terms, undertook to pay an annual tribute and granted the Portuguese a site to build a fortress. A bitter quarrel arose between Albuquerque and his captains on the question of the distribution of the booty. Taking advantage of this quarrel, the ministers at Ormuz refused to ratify the treaty; and when Albuquerque bombarded the town and attempted to blockade it, the captains opened direct negotiations with the enemy and went away to India. Albuquerque had to raise the blockade and retire.

The disobedient captains reached Cochin and represented to the Viceroy, Dom Francesco d'Almeida, that Albuquerque had acted in a high-handed manner and done many things in Ormuz which were irregular and arbitrary. The Viceroy, acting on their advice, wrote to the King of Ormuz disapproving of the action of Albuquerque and promised the King to punish him on his arrival. It should be mentioned here that the appointment of Albuquerque as Governor was to take effect only after the expiration of Almeida's full three years' term of Viceroyalty, and therefore, the Governor-designate had to be legally under Almeida's orders if he happened to be in Indian waters. Albuquerque, therefore, did not hurry on his voyage to the Indian coast and reached Cannanore only on the 5th of December, 1508. The Viceroy was on his way to Diu to meet the Egyptian navy and Albuquerque was asked to wait till his return from that expedition. Albuquerque went to Cochin and awaited the return of Almeida. Almeida returned on the 8th of March, 1509, but refused to hand over charge on the frivolous pretext that the particular ship on which he had been ordered to return had not arrived. Albuquerque protested against this, but Almeida refused to listen. The faction against the new Governor grew in strength and even drew up a petition asking Almeida not to surrender his charge to Albuquerque. The retired Rajah of Cochin, whom Albuquerque had known personally during his previous visit in 1503 and with whom he was on terms of friendship, was approached by him privately. The Rajah sent word to Almeida that as King Manuel's letter had appointed Albuquerque his representative, goods can be handed over only to him.[1] On this, Albuquerque

1. *Kerala Pazhama,* pages 104—106,

was accused of intriguing with the Rajah and imprisoned in Cochin and later on sent to Cannanore[1].

For more than 6 months, Albuquerque was subjected to this kind of indignity. It was only in September, 1509, with the arrival of a new fleet under Marcheal Dom Ferdinando Cutinho who was a relative of Albuquerque, that Almeida surrendered his authority and left for Portugal. However he was not destined to reach it, as he was killed along with many others in his attempt to plunder an African village. Albuquerque's ill luck did not end with the departure of Almeida. The Marcheal who had now assumed military and naval command was a rash and reckless warrior to whom political considerations made no appeal. He insisted on an immediate attack on Calicut. Albuquerque had other views. He had already made up his mind that the only safe policy for the Portuguese was to make honourable peace with the Zamorin. To this end he was already in correspondence with the heir-apparent of Calicut. But the Marcheal was insistent on attacking the Zamorin declaring that the King had specially sent him out for that purpose. Albuquerque agreed half-heartedly. The Cochin Rajah was consulted. The purpose of this was to get the Rajah to attack the Zamorin on the land side as a diversion, and to utilise the Brahmin spies in the Rajah's service to find out the nature and extent of the enemy's preparations[2].

At the council of war that was held at which the Cochin Rajah was present, the latter reported that the Zamorin was in the interior fighting one of his rebel chieftains, that the garrison in the city

1. The full story of the intrigues against Albuquerque which is an illuminating commentary on the Portuguese politics of the time many be read in the *Commentaries*. It shows the political character of contemporary Portuguese at its worst.

2. *Commentaries*, page 54.

of Calicut consisted only of a few hundred Nayars, and that no considerable defence works had been erected on the coast. The fleet started immediately for Calicut and reached that town on the 3rd of January, 1510. Albuquerque landed and captured the jetty. The Marcheal was furious that this success did not go to him, and wanted immediately to press on to the palace, conquer the city and destory it, as he had gaily promised the King. His temerity led to a terrible disaster.

In spite of Albuquerque's remonstrances, the Marcheal marched into the city and overpowered the guards at the palace. The men with him began to pillage, loot and desecrate the whole place. The news of the defeat of the palace guards roused the Nayar militia which soon surrounded the place. Only a small party with Albuquerque at its head escaped. Even they were harassed and pursued up to the sea-shore and the Governor himself was badly wounded. The Marcheal, with his chief officers, were cut off from the rest; but he fought like a lion, and ordered the palace to be set on fire. In spite of their heroic efforts, the Portuguese, who had violated the sanctity of the Zamorin's palace could not escape the Nayars. Among those who died on that fateful day, besides the Marcheal, were Vasco de Silveira, Lionel Coutinho and Fillippe Rodriguez. More than 70 fidalgoes died in the fight. The Marcheal's banner remained with the Zamorin's commander and Albuquerque's own flag was captured in his presence by a Nayar soldier. The pompous boast of the Marcheal that he would bring back to his King a door of the Zamorin's palace ended in the greatest disaster that overtook Portuguese arms in the East.

This defeat decided the course of the Portuguese policy in Kerala. So far the attempt was to subdue the Zamorin and reduce him to the position of a dependent like the Rajah of Cochin. Albuquerque had begun to see even before the disaster at Calicut, that to reduce the power of the Zamorin was an impossible undertaking with the forces at the disposal of the Portuguese, and that the only wise thing to do was to make peace with the Zamorin, abandoning the Cochin policy which, from the time of Duarte Pacheco, the Portuguese had accepted as their own. This defeat also rendered it necessary to find another and more convenient base for naval operations. Albuquerque decided upon Goa as the most suitable place for this purpose. It was impregnable against land attacks and could easily be defended from the sea. The Hindu Kings of Vijayanagar desired to have a port, free from the Mahommedan control, through which they could get their supplies of arms, ammunition and horses, and therefore their Governor, Timoja, helped in the project. The place was easily taken; but Adil Shah, in whose territory it was, roused himself to activity and recaptured it with the help of the Mahommedans in the town. Albuquerque had again failed. He had been driven out of Goa, as he had been out of Calicut. All the three expeditions he had so far undertaken at Ormuz, Calicut and Goa had failed miserably. But Albuquerque's greatness was best displayed when he was in adversity. He immediately set to work to gather another force. Many were the obstacles he had to overcome; but his iron will refused to accept defeat, and on October 3rd 1510, he started from Cannanore to drive Adil Shah's forces out of Goa. After a very stiff battle the island was again occupied and defence works were raised immediately with a view to enable the garrison to hold out against any land attack. From the first, Albuquerque decided to make it the centre of the Portuguese activity in India, and now he took his measures in accordance with this plan.

Almost immediately after settling the affairs of Goa and making arrangements for its development, Albuquerque had to leave for Malacca whence he returned to Cochin only in February 1512. The port of Cochin was grossly neglected ever since Almeida left India. Albuquerque had other views and was almost continuously employed away from the nominal capital of Portugal in the East, so that anarchy almost reigned there. Civil war broke out in the Cochin state. Unni Rama Varmah, who had retired from the position of the ruler to the titular dignity of Perumpatappu Muppil, died, which meant that the ruler then in authority had to take his place. The Portuguese did not want the continuance of this system; and though the Rajah himself was willing and his people were unanimously insistent, Nuno, the captain at the Cochin fort decided that the custom was to be abolished and that the Rajah was to continue as ruler. Fearing that he might be persuaded by the members of his family and by the priests, the captain actually imprisoned him within the area under the direct control of the Portuguese. Nuno insisted that the Rajah cannot even abdicate without the permission of Albuquerque. The result of this was a civil war in Cochin, in which the Zamorin intervened to support the claim of the people. Albuquerque himself arrived on the scene and fought for a short time with the Zamorin, but his policy gave him no time to interfere effectively in the internal affairs of the state.

During the short visits he paid to what was even then the chief establishment of the Portuguese in India, Albuquerque devoted his energies to putting its affairs on a sound basis. When he took charge of Portuguese affairs, not only was indiscipline rife, but the elements of an efficient organisation were absent. In a letter to the King dated 10th of October 1510, wrote:

> "It appears to me, Senhor, that it is not right to have such a standing as you have at Cochin without an auditor for house and factory not for a winding up of accounts but that your business be always stimulated and not be trusted to men who say 'I

will render an account when I go to Portugul' and meanwhile would have in their possession two or three thousand cruzados or as much as they liked."

Besides this, the officials were all intriguing and fighting against one another. "What reigns here now", he complains in another letter, "is the wish to acquire authority before your Highness, by the defeats of others taking delight in the failures and discomfiture that occur to each other."

The affairs of Cochin during the absence of Albuquerque in Malacca did indeed go wrong. The principal ships of the fleet were broken up. Many leading people whom the Governor trusted were sent away from Cochin. The blockade of Calicut, which was the principal point of Portuguese policy up to that time, was slackened. From Calicut, six ships laden with cargoes had left while the Governor was in Malacca.

The situation in Cochin was summed up in the following way by Albuquerque in a letter to the King:

"Your factors at Cochin reveal to the King of Calicut the secrets of Portugal and they intrigue with him to cast discredit on your Governor."[1]

In fact, Antonio Reall and Lorenco Moreno were in league with Calicut.[2] The whole system fell

1. Cartas, 24—dated November 30th 1513.

2. These two officers hated Albuquerque; but though his subordinates he was powerless against them. They had the ear of the King. While Albuquerque was away in Malacca, they used their power to persecute all who were in favour of the Governor and wrote to the King misrepresenting the actions of the Governor. They never obeyed his orders. In fact, Albuquerque complained to the King that when after taking Goa, the second time he wrote to the Cochin men "Advising them what it was expedient for them to do in order to strengthen my position in Goa if the Moors were to attack again" he did not receive a reply for three months. (Letter 24, dated November 30th 1513.)

into disorganisation. Albuquerque's efforts in Cochin were directed mainly to bring back the efficiency of the factory and to make the fortress stronger.

As the fortress of Cochin appeared to him rather small and of little shelter, he erected a rampart on the side where the ships anchor.[1] It was in the shape of a quadrangle lengthening towards the spot where the ships lie, and came right on to the wall of the fortress itself. It had an entrance towards the sea and another for the ships. Other improvements were also effected in order to make the fortress easily defensible against land attack. He delimited the boundaries between the fortress area and the town, and expelled from the former all who were not Christians. The reason for this act, which Albuquerque gives in a letter to the King[2] is that there were "houses which befriended the outside Gentiles and Moors and these traded in deceiving slaves to rob their masters and escape."

The war with the Zamorin continued its weary course. The injury to Calicut was small. After the retreat of the Egyptians and the defeat of his own navy, the Zamorin changed his tactics. He gave up building ships with which he had hoped to fight against the Portuguese, but built instead a large fleet of fast paraoes and kept on harassing Portuguese commerce. Of this new attempt, Albuquerque speaks thus in one of his letters:

> "He had now had 60 caturis made in his land and as the ships of Cochin enter they sally out endeavouring to capture them. Calicut greatly oppressed us with them, because the factor of Cannanore did not dare to send coir or supplies in paqueres and paraoes to Cochin for fear of being

---

1. Letter dated 1st of August 1512.
2. Letter dated 1st of April 1512.

> captured. The Calicut men watched from the mountain heights and any atalaya or parao they saw coming, they at once pounced upon them."[1]

It was becoming clearer every day to Albuquerque that the fight with Calicut was not in the interests of Portugal, but merely in the interests of the Rajahs of Cochin and Cannanore. "I know," he writes to the King, "why the King of Cochin having 30,000 Nayars and the King of Cannanore having 60 thousand do not go to destroy Calicut; because they want to keep this dispute (between the Zamorin and the Portuguese) till the end of time. They do not wish to make war, but that we should do so." Albuquerque realised that it was impossible to reduce the power of the Zamorin by open war. "If your wish is to destroy it by stern war," he wrote, "it will require a fleet always in occupation on her and the fleet of India is not so large that it can be divided into two squadrons."

Besides, the policy of blockade, by which it was hoped to destroy the commerce of Calicut, completely failed. Albuquerque informed the King that it was a vain endeavour to guard Calicut in such a way as to cut off its supplies, "because there is much rice in the land, Dharma Patanam and Cannanore will always supply it in large quantities and this cannot be stopped except by stopping the navigation of Cannanore."[2] "Moreover, when your vessels which sail round Calicut are small and furnished with a few hands, they (the Calicut people) rise against them and some are in the risk of being taken. When they escape this danger, they would withdraw outside. They launch their ships into the sea and load them; and your caravels and small

---

1. Torre de Tombo—*Corpo Chronologico,* p. 1—Maco 11—Document 50.

2. Torre de Tombo—*Corpo Chronologico,* p. 1—Maco 13—Document 106—Letter dated November 30th, 1513.

vessels do not dare to send out their boats, while they have a hundred paraoes laden with merchandise around one ship and freight her in two hours and with the right wind the ship goes the round of the sea and your vessels remain at anchor. One goes out of Ponnani, another from Pandarini, some others from Cranganore and others from Chalea while others depart from Dharma Patanam with safe-conducts issued from Cannanore. They have always done navigation and will continue unless you have those ports occupied with some very good ships and some rowing vessels to be close upon the shore."[1]

Realising that the policy of blockade had failed and that the war with Calicut was being continued purely in the interests of the Rajahs of Cochin and Cannanore, Albuquerque opened negotiations with the Zamorin. Though the circumstances, as Albuquerque himself admits, were in the Zamorin's favour, the terms which the Portuguese wanted to impose were those of conquerors. One of them was that Zamorin should give permission to build a fortress in Calicut which was to be garrisoned by Portuguese soldiers. As the Governor himelf admitted, this meant the destruction of the power of the Zamorin. "If these terms would be accepted," Albuquerque wrote to his King, "you could better bridle and master it and make of Calicut what you desired than by all your campaigns; for it is now 15 years that you have been fighting and yet very little damage has been done."[2] Naturally, the Zamorin, who had by this time fully realised the inner motive of Portuguese policy, did not consent to this. As a result Albuquerque began to intrigue with the heir-apparent of Calicut and pressed him to poison the reigning Zamorin. Albuquerque did not hesitate to confess his crime. "I hold it for

1. Torre de Tombo—*Corpo Chronologico*, p. 1. Maco 13—Document 106—Letter dated November 30th, 1513.
2. Ibid.

certain," he wrote to the king, "that the Nampiadiri slew the Zamorin with poison, because in all my letters I bid him to kill the Zamorin with poison, and that in a peace treaty I will come to an agreement with him."[1]

The King of Portugal was averse to a treaty with Calicut. He had vowed to destroy the Zamorin and had even sent successive armadas for that specific purpose. A marcheal of Portugal, who had publicly undertaken to conquer Calicut for him, had been killed in the city and the Portuguese force drvien out. To make peace with the Zamorin without exacting reparations or winning even a victory was to accept defeat. His point of view was strongly supported by the Cochin clique, Antonio Reall and Lorenco Moreno, who had set themselves to work against the policy of the Governor. They persuaded the Rajah of Cochin to write a long letter to the King of Portugal strongly protesting against the proposed peace with Calicut. He complained that the negotiations were undertaken without consulting him, and that, though the Zamorin was the greatest of their enemies, peace had been made with him without destroying his power. "This peace," he added, "was done for no other reason than that of dishonouring me. Your Highness should not put aside my friendship to take up that of Calicut."

Albuquerque was bound to the new Zamorin, by secret agreement, to make peace; and therefore he did not give the least attention to the Cochin Rajah's complaints, but advised his King to put away his sensitiveness on the matter of making peace with Calicut as it was the Portuguese who were to blame for the war. He also pointed out that, as long as peace was not made with Calicut,

1. Ibid. In spite of 15 years' war "Calicut is the largest city in this part of India and the richest" (Cartas).

foreign intrigues would continue. "It is the hostility of Calicut to us," wrote he, "that makes Venezia so confident of all things of India and put such trust in her former trade; and it is that which makes Cairo equip fleets trusting to eject your ships and men out of India. As long as Calicut continues in its present state, so long will Cairo and Venezia continue to foster their project."

Besides, he promised the King that he would secure by treaty what the Portuguese had so far failed to gain by war. "I do not see what advantage can accrue from the war of Calicut since you do not conquer it. I should state more; if what you wish is to stop her commerce with Mecca you could better effect it by peace than by warfare; I can also obtain all the ginger of Calicut, and I will obstruct all their navigation with Mecca."[1]

It was with these objects in view that Albuquerque entered into negotiations with the new Zamorin who was amicably disposed towards him. The threat of a Turkish invasion of Indian waters, which was one of the alarming rumours then current in India, made him realise the necessity of opening up the Red Sea; and for this purpose he started with a large fleet on February 17th, 1513. The expedition, however, achieved nothing. An attempt to take Aden ended in disaster, and after a fruitless voyage up the Red Sea, the Portuguese fleet returned to Goa in September. The negotiations with the Zamorin, which were conducted by Dom Garcia de Noronha, a nephew of the Governor, had proceeded satisfactorily, and a definitive treaty was signed dated Cannanore 24th December 1513.[2]

---

1. *Corpo Chronologico,* p. 1, Maco 22—Document 64.
2. *Corpo Chronologico,* p. 1, Maco 13—Document 63.

By this treaty, it was agreed:

(1) That the Zamorin should sell to the King of Portugal all spices and drugs that may be in the land;

(2) That the Portuguese would pay the usual dues to the Zamorin for the things bought;

(3) That, if the Portugese buy horses or elephants, they shall pay the usual dues;

(4) That the Portuguese would issue safe-conducts to the ships of Calicut.

The other commercial clauses in the treaty were that the Portuguese factor was not to purchase merchandise except in the presence of the King's clerk, so that the King's dues might be collected; that ginger was to be purchased direct from the cultivators and that the price of pepper should be the same as that paid at Cannanore. By another clause, it was agreed "that justice be divided this wise. That any Nayar or native of the land or Moor who shall have any strife or contention with the Portuguese, no harm shall be done to him by the Portuguese, only he shall be taken to the King to be punished and justice done to him. And in the same manner, Portuguese men, when they are found in acts which entail the penalties of justice, the crime being with the Nayars or the natives, they shall be brought to the captain of the fortress for him to punish and have justice done." The Portuguese also undertook to help the Zamorin in his wars except against Cochin or Cannanore.

The Portuguese received permission to build a fort near Calicut. The construction of it was immediately undertaken and was placed under the charge of Thomas Fernandez, the master builder. Francesco Noqueira was nominated captain.

Though this treaty was not long in force and war soon broke out again, it is an event of considerable importance in the history of Portuguese relations with Kerala. It marked the failure and the consequent abandonment of the policy of conquering Kerala. What was originally attempted was to establish a Portuguese hegemony of Kerala from Cape Comorin to Mangalore, in the same way as Almeida had established it in Cochin. "Cochin is like another of your towns, like Lisboa," wrote the subservient Rajah of Cochin. The aim of the Portuguese was to establish their power on the coast working through the Rajahs of Cannanore and Cochin. This policy could not succeed so long as the Zamorin remained independent; and so Albuquerque looked beyond Kerala and found in Goa a base from which he could command the Arabian Sea. The treaty with the Zamorin also marked the decline in the importance of Cochin and Cannanore. "Do not trouble," wrote Albuquerque, "about the traffic of Cannanore, which is profitless. It has neither port, nor river for the ships, nor galleys, nor merchandise, nor precious stones, nor merchants, to trade in your factory." With the founding of Goa, Cochin lost its importance, and the Portuguese ceased to interest themselves in any very serious way in the politics of Kerala.

The peace, thus established between the Zamorin and the Portuguese, was naturally unwelcome to the Moors. They knew that the previous Zamorin had been poisoned at the instigation of the Portuguese, and that the new King would probably dance to Albuquerque's tune. Though their apprehensions on this score were soon falsified, the Moorish merchants felt aggrieved at the Zamorin's action. "The King of Calicut," bewails a Mahommedan historian, "rolled up the carpet of destruction and pursued the path of friendship with the Feringies."[1]

In the states which were subject to Portugal, Albuquerque interfered forcibly. At Cochin, when

1. "Nawab Muhabat Khan: Akbar i Muhabat"—Elliot's *History*.

the Rajah said that his priests had declared that his doings were wrong, Albuquerque quietly replied that he was bound to obey not the priests, but the King of Portugal. At Cannanore, his interference was even more decisive. The magistrate of that place was said to be friendly towards Mussulmans, and Albuquerque asked the King to dismiss him. Naturally enough, the King demurred to such a demand. The Governor immediately drew up a long list of charges, all of which pointed to the same conclusion, namely that the officer was not favourably inclined towards the Portuguese. The King promised to enquire into the charges, but Albuquerque insisted on immediate action, threatening to withdraw protection from Cannanore ships if the King did not yield.[1] The relations with Cannanore continued to be strained during the whole period. The officer was supported in his attitude of hostility towards the Governor by Portuguese officers. The trade of Cannanore was much neglected and the factory lost its importance during the time of Albuquerque. Duarte Barbosa was much troubled by this state of affairs, and wrote to the King, thus:

"Let Your Highness order relief to be sent to this factory in merchandise, and by an especial order command that they be unloaded here, because they all pass on to Cochin and they leave us nothing here, nor do they come to remain here three days."[2]

All these representations from various quarters had their effect. Especially, Antonio Reall who had the ear of the King kept up a relentless campaign of hatred and calumny. When the Governor was in Ormuz, orders from Portugal reached Goa that he was superseded, and that Lopo Soares was appointed instead. Albuquerque, who had been very ill, heard

1. Letter of October 11th, 1512.
2. Volume I of India Office transcript. *Corpo Chronologico* 281,

of the appointment and died just as his ship was anchoring at Goa on return from Ormuz.

Albuquerque was deservedly called the Great. He had a high sense of duty and stern discipline, and an eye for everything political and strategic. Otherwise he could not have created a Portuguese "Empire", because, as will be shown, the Portuguese had neither the resources nor the administrative ability required for it. Nor could he, for any length of time, have put vigour into their affairs in the East. The importance of his Governorship lies in the general principles which he followed in his regime, and the policy which he initiated. More than even Dupleix or Clive, he was the man who discovered that Indians trained on European methods to use European arms provided a most effective instrument for imperialist aggression. But he was wise enough to realise that Portgual had not the resources either in men or in money to cherish any such territorial ambition in India. What he wanted was to establish a complete monopoly of the Indian trade, to break up the combinations that Venice and Egypt were engineering, and further to place the sea power of Portugal, on which all this depended, on an unshakable footing. The basis of this scheme consisted in having a chain of fortresses from Aden to Malacca, at Ormuz, Diu, Goa, Cannanore, Cochin and Quilon, each one of which could be easily defended from the sea. But even this required a permanent squadron, and a central base where ships could be repaired, provisions accumulated and central direction maintained. It was for this purpose that he conquered Goa. In a passionate letter to a friend, he described how Goa afforded all the facilities which did not exist in Cochin, how it was large enough to hold a fairly big population, how foodstuffs were plentiful, and how it was easily defensible against attacks.

This scheme of a chain of fortresses needed a regular military force in each place, and a permanent squadron on the seas. But the King was not inclined to send "either arms or men or any equipment of war. He even wanted to withdraw the squadrons." Albuquerque's appeal was for men and money. In every letter, he represented to the King that without adequate forces, the Portuguese would not be able to establish themselves even as traders. He pointed out that "only good strongholds and men will keep the people at peace; by this manner alone will the traffic of merchandise be effected in India without warfare and too many quarrels."[1] His demand in the way of either men or money was not great. He wanted only 3,000 effective soldiers with whom he offered to place the entire trade of India in the hands of Portugal. The only way to avoid war expense and trade losses in India, in his opinion, was by maintaining a good army. "Once more, I repeat," he wrote to the King, "that if you wish to avoid war in India and be at peace with all her Kings, then you should send men and good arms, or that you should hold the principal places on the shore of India."

As the supply of men from Portugal could not always be depended upon, Albuquerque decided on the plan of making his Portuguese men marry the Indian women whom he took as prisoners. By this plan he hoped to bring in course of time into existence a body of people to whom could be entrusted the defence of the fortresses. Another way in which he hoped to strengthen the Portuguese position in these fortresses was by permitting only Christians to live within the area. In Cochin, all non-Christians were expelled from within the fortress.

What Albuquerque had to contend with all through his life in India was the intrigue carried on by the Portuguese officials against him. Every factor had the right of communicating directly with the King, and the officials misused this privilege to misrepresent and calumniate one another. They had

1. Cartas, 1st of April 1512.

no feeling of patriotism or loyality. The factors of Cochin were in communication with the Zamorin when he was fighting against Albuquerque. The officers always lived in disorder, and even the strict habits of the Governor had no influence on them. "Keep away from the letters of your officers," Albuquerque warned the King many times. Moreover, many of the officers had money dealings with the Moors, and were in their pay. Albuquerque attempted to introduce discipline in their ranks but in vain. The quarrel between Hastings and Francis is indeed nothing, when compared to the quarrel between him and Antonio Reall. He dismissed and sent back to Portugal a good many officers. He fined or otherwise punished those who were guilty of irregularities. He tried to introduce even business habits into the administration. But his success was only partial, even during his stay at Cochin or at Goa, wherefrom he was frequently absent in Malacca or Ormuz. After his supersession, the whole administration again drifted into confusion. Private gain, personal aggrandisement, gross corruption and base intrigue again became the most striking features of the Portuguese administration in India.

CHAPTER VIII

TROUBLE IN CALICUT, COCHIN AND QUILON

By the conquest of Goa, Albuquerque made Portugal one of the minor powers in India, in direct relations with the Vijayanagar and Bahmini kingdoms. As Goa was the main commercial outlet of these prosperous kingdoms, its trade had great prospects of development. But from a political point of view, Portuguese power did not in the least advance from the point at which Albuquerque left it. His successors in the Governorship of Portuguese affairs in the East were mostly men interested in amassing wealth by private trade. They had neither political ability, nor loyalty to national interests. Besides, it was not so easy as it was at the time of Duarte Pacheco to win victories against Indian rulers. As Albuquerque confessed in a letter dated November 30th 1513, "the people with whom we wage war are no longer the same; and artillery, arms and fortresses are all now according to our usage." In fact, these conditions effectively prevented any extension of Portuguese authority in India.

The Governor who superseded Albuquerque was Lopo Soares, who was formerly sent to India as the admiral of the annual fleet. With him came back all those whom Albuquerque's stern discipline had expelled. The main activity of the Governor seems to have been to undo systematically whatever his predecessor had done. Albuquerque had suppressed private trade which was injurious to national interests, and led to the disloyalty of officials. Soares, as soon as he took charge, gave permission to his officers to engage in trade on their own account. After this, he left for an expedition against the Egyptians in the Red Sea, but disaster awaited him at every turn. The heat of the Red Sea took a terrible toll, more than 800 Europeans dying of thirst.

All his military adventures ended in failure. The internal administration of Cochin and Goa had also broken down. High officials tried to engage in plunder and piracy on their own account, which brought on the settlement considerable trouble and loss. One such raid into Adil Shah's territory cost more than 150 lives. Piracy by Portuguese officials was rife on the sea, and the men who took to it never honoured the Cartas of the Governors. The *Kerala Pazhama* or the Chronicles of Kerala, which we had occasion to quote before, describes the atrocities of the Portuguese on the seas thus:

> "Besides these cruelties perpetrated on the land, the Portuguese were also responsible for unmentionable atrocities on the sea. The Feringi ships alone did not keep the peace. The Mahommedan ships were the special objects of their fury. Every ship had to carry safe-conduct issued by the Portuguese captain. But even with that they were not safe. The Portuguese seamen demanded heavy bribes and bakshish, and if whatever they asked for was not given the ships would be confiscated."[1]

The only political event of importance in Kerala during the time was the treaty made with Quilon. The Queen of Quilon had invited Vasco da Gama to open a factory there; and in the time of Almeida a factory and a stone-house capable of defence had been built. But when Antonio de Sao was captain, a quarrel had broken out which led to the destruction of the factory. The quarrel took place in this manner: Joao Homem, a captain of the Portuguese fleet, arrived in Quilon and he, finding some Mahommedan vessels loading pepper, immediately took possession of them. When the captain left, the people of the town under Bala Pillai rose up in arms,

1. Pages 164 and 165.

pulled down the Portuguese factory and set fire to the house. The Portuguese garrison died in the fight. Albuqerque had the good sense to see that the blame lay on the Portuguese. Though negotiations were carried on from the Cochin factory, no agreement was reached in his time. After Lopo Soares became Governor, a new treaty with Quilon was made[1] by which the Queen agreed to erect the fort of San Thome in the same manner and in the same spot, and to compensate for the death of Antonio de Sao by giving the Portuguese King 500 bharas of pepper. The Quilon state also agreed not to export pepper but to sell it only to the Portuguese at the Cochin rates. No dues were to be paid for the use of the port, and the Queen agreed not to receive or favour the enemies of Portugal. The treaty with Quilon contained a number of interesting clauses about the local Christians. The Queen was asked to treat them with favour, and it was agreed that the Christian traders in the land were to pay dues to the Portuguese. Freedom of conversion was to be guaranteed.

After this, the relations with Quilon were friendly. The general public of the state was against Portuguese, and the Queen, realising it, entered into a secret agreement with the captain of the Portuguese factory, Hector Rodrigues. The Portuguese wanted to build a fortress with stone, and they, on bribing the Queen with 2,000 silver pieces, got permission from her in 1519 without the knowledge of the public. In 1520, a new agreement was made with Quilon by which the captain agreed that private Portuguese traders should pay dues. With the consent and connivance of the Queen who was thus bribed, Rodrigues began to plunder the traders who carried on a great land commerce between Tinnevelly and Kayamkulam. This had the effect of stopping the land route which lay through the

1. Treaty of the 25th of September 1516.

Quilon territory and through the Aramboly pass to the East Coast.

The high-handedness of the Portuguese caused trouble in Cochin also. With the permission of the factor of the place, Diogo Mendez de Vasconcellos, a Portuguese fidalgo by the name of Gasper de Silva went out to Cochin territory and shot one of the peacocks sacred to a temple deity. The result was that the people of the neighbourhood rose in revolt, and in the riot that ensued four of the Portuguese were killed. It had, however, the effect of making the Rajah of Cochin issue a prohibitory order against the shooting of these birds in his State.

The effect of Lopo Soares' Governorship of 3 years is thus described in a letter of Gaspar Gonsalves to the King[1] "I make known to Your Highness that Lopo Soares in an evil hour came to India, both he and as many of his captains who came with him, because his whole care and mind is no other than traffic and no longer in the service of your Highness. Before he came, the whole world was at peace; wherever the breath of your Portuguese went it was obeyed; and now you have India all in revolt and no one will obey us and even the most obedient people in India who are the Mukkuvas (low-caste fishermen) want to oust us......Now, they attack us, kill us and rob us. And this, they say, is due to your esteemed and loved Fidalgo of the Household, Antonio Reall of Cochin who, it is said, is in league with the robbers."

Soares was recalled, and in his stead Diogo Lopez de Sequiera was sent out. Diogo was hardly better than his predecessor and he too proved a failure. His orders were to capture and fortify Diu, and to [illegible] the Red Sea in which he failed. The im[illegible] this period for Malabar lay in the fight [illegible]een the Zamorin and the Rajah

[illegible] No. 51.

Due to the antiquity and rarity of the book, some text is unfortunately absent on pages 89 and 90, impacting the overall legibility of the original content.

of Cochin. The Rajah of Cochin did not like the peace that was established between his hereditary enemy and the Portuguese, and made successive attempts to embroil them. In 1514, he provoked a war with Calicut at Cranganore, and went even to the extent of sending a message to the Zamorin that it was done at the instance of the Portuguese. In this, the Rajah was of course encouraged by Antonio Reall and Lorenco Moreno. But Dom Garcia de Noronha happened to be at Cochin and made it perfectly clear that the Portuguese had no hand in the affair.

The motives which led the Rajah of Cochin to embroil the Portuguese with the Zamorin are not far to seek. He saw that his ambition of destroying the power of Calicut with the help of the Portuguese, in the vain hope of which he had humiliated himself before his own people by accepting the crown from the foreign King, had no longer any chance of success. Even the material prosperity, which came to Cochin as a result of Portuguese connection, was menaced by the alliance with Calicut. As he complained, "merchants of Calicut all along the coast who had come to ask of me safe-conducts for navigating now proceed to ask for them of the King of Calicut......All the merchants of the port of Calicut navigate with his safe-conducts." All this meant loss of money and prestige to Cochin. The Rajah was also anxious to wreak vengeance on Calicut for the death of many of his relatives on the battlefield. His intrigues in 1514 being foiled, the cunning ruler awaited a better opportunity. At about the time that Diogo Lopez was leaving, the Cochin Rajah again declared war on the Zamorin, and asked the Portuguese captain for his help. The Cochin factory sent 40 soldiers, of whom 30 were matchloc[illegible]
The Rajah put in the field about 50,[illegible]
prepared to invade Calicut [illegible]
Zamorin forestalled hi[illegible]
wholly in favour of [illegible]

Due to the antiquity and rarity of the book, some text is unfortunately absent on pages 89 and 90, impacting the overall legibility of the original content.

a military sense, the war went against Cochin, the Rajah succeeded in embroiling Calicut with the Portuguese. The Zamorin's relations with the Portuguese began to cool down as a result of the help given to Cochin in time of war. The *Tofutul Mujahideen* even mentions that in 1517 a perfidious attempt was made against the Zamorin's life. He was invited to the Portuguese fort by the captain with the intention of imprisoning him there; but one of the Portuguese officers, who disapproved of the perfidy, betrayed the plot to him by a signal, and he escaped.[1] Soon, there was again open hostility between Calicut and the Portuguese.

The Portuguese affairs in India were steadily deteriorating. Private gain was the only motive of the Governors, and corruption and intrigue became the chief characteristics of their government. The defence of Cochin had already fallen into decay. Cannanore was practically abandoned. The incompetent Governors had forgotten the principles and policy of Albuquerque. "One thing I require to remind Your Highness," writes one official to the King, "is that there are no gunners, most of them being shoemakers who know nothing......Likewise arms......we have left our arms where the Moors can take them. The captain scattered the men about and no place was effectively guarded. Naval men were deserting for service in the ships of private traders. In fact, private trade is eating into the very vitals of Portuguese commercial administration. I never witnessed one thing so opposed to the service of Your Highness as this."[2] The private traders, most of whom were of course Government officials, were competing with the royal factories with results that could be imagined. They raised the prices, got the best commodities for themselves and took away

1. *Tofutul Mujahideen* Page 114.
2. *Corpo Chronologico*, Part I—Maco 27, Document No. 69.

from service the ablest seamen. A curious letter, written by Gandangora (Kandankoran) who is described as the Governor of the King of Cochin, addressed to the King of Portugal shows how notorious the matter had become."

'Senhor, I, Gandangora, the Governor of the King of Cochin and overseer of the treasury, on account of the desire I have of serving Your Highness, have resolved upon writing this letter to you in order to give you an account of the things that relate to your service. Your Highness is aware that the merchants of Cochin had always resolved upon serving you with pepper and with other things that may be had. They have now become discontented through the unworthy action of your factors.

"They do not pay regularly; and even more, do positive injury to the traders. Besides, your captains purchase pepper outside at a rate higher than Your Highness pays. The Gentiles will not sell pepper except at that price now. Hence the merchants have besought me to write to Your Highness. Kochali Marakkar, who is the principal merchant, declares that Your Highness should send Lorenco Moreno to Cochin in order to serve you as you desire. He enjoys great credit with the Moors as well as others......" The King's revenue was in fact neglected and Governors and other officers cared only for their own profit.

CHAPTER IX

TROUBLE IN CALICUT, COCHIN AND QUILON (*contd.*)

Matters became even worse, in the time of Dom Duarte de Menzes who came to India with the title of Governor in January 1522. He was extremely corrupt and engaged in private trade, and openly took brides. The main activities of the Portuguese at this time were directed against Ormuz and Malacca. The relations with Calicut were very unsatisfactory and for a long time there was trouble between the Portuguese authorities and the Zamorin. Albuquerque hoped that the blackade of Calicut which the Portuguese ships were not able to undertake successfully as an act of war, could be enforced by a trade treaty which secured for the Portuguese Captain the right of issuing passes. He, himself, stated in his letter that this was the object of the peace with Calicut, and that by the treaty he could obstruct all other navigation. But in this Albuquerque did not succeed. The Zamorin's ships and the merchantmen of the Moors refused to take the least notice of the safe-conducts of the Portuguese, and sailed the seas in open defiance. A continuous commercial intercourse was maintained with the Red Sea, and the Portuguese claim of the lordship of the sea was hardly more than a pompous boast.

The result of all this was decreased revenues and diminished prestige. An effort was made by the new King, Dom John,to set matters right, and for this purpose Vasco da Gama who lived an retirement, was commissioned to go out as the Viceroy. Da Gama was the second Viceroy,[1] Almeida being the

1. The title of Viceroy was given by royal patent and was supposed to carry almost royal dignity. No one but nobles could sit in the presence of the Viceroy and even grandees could only sit on stools. All others had

first. Da Gama, who had been raised to the dignity of the Count of Videguiera, was living in retirement at Evora, having incurred the displeasure of the court. The reason of this estrangement was that Da Gama wanted the lordship of his birthplace, and, though the Order of St. Thiago to which it belonged refused to part with it, he proceeded to build a palace and live there. The Order complained to the King, who commanded him to quit the place in 30 days. This was in 1507[1] The death of Dom Manuel restored him to the favour of the Court and in 1524 he was sent out with the most extensive powers to reform the administration and correct abuses. Twenty years of forced inactivity had altered the character of the man. It was not the hardy adventurer that came out as Viceroy. Even Correa describes him as haughty, proud and disdainful:

"Dom Vasco brought with him great state and was served by men bearing silver maces, by a major-domo and two pages wearing gold neck chains, many equerries and body servants very well clothed and cared for. He also brought rich vessels of silver and rich tapestry of Flanders, and for the table at which he sate brocade cloths. They brought to him at table large dishes, as if to the King, with his napkin bearer bringing him the ewer and all the forms of precedence of a King......He had a guard of two hundred men with gilt pikes, clothed with his livery......He was a very disdainful man and ready to anger, very rash, much feared and respected. He brought as his secretary Vincento Pegado a noble gentleman who in the office spoke to him with one knee on the ground."

Da Gama's fleet, which consisted of nine ships and five lateen caravels arrived at Goa on the 23rd

---

to speak standing. No one could sit at the same table nor would the Viceroy visit anyone. Law concerning titles, Memorandum about the Viceroys, *Noticias da India* Vol. I, p. 518, Part II.

1. Prestage: *Geographical Society's Journal*, 1925 *Jan.*

of September. He assumed the government, without awaiting the arrival of Dom Duarte, and proceeded in a most high-handed fashion. He prohibited private trade and issued a proclamation that, if anyone was found to navigate the seas without his permission, the ship would be confiscated and the owner banished to Portugal. Correa describes his reforms thus:—

"He took away pay and rations from married men who were not to receive them unless there was a war or unless they went on board the fleet. He had an enquiry made into the peculations and robberies which the officers had committed in the revenue of the mainland and ordered them all to be arrested and strict accounts to be taken from them......He ordered it to be proclaimed, under pain of death and confiscation that any person who had got any of the King's artillery should send and deliver it to the magazine without any penalty, even though they might have stolen it anywhere, and this within the space of one month, after which they would incur the penalty."[1]

After effecting these preliminary reforms, Da Gama sailed for Cochin. Here he was soon made to feel that 25 years of Portuguese effort had not secured for them the mastery of the sea. The Calicut ships sailed everywhere without any acknowledgment of Portuguese authority. Their ships were light and very fast. They appeared in all directions under the very nose of the Viceroy's ships, like street urchins throwing stones at a stronger man and running away. Francesco de Mendoca was supposed to be guarding the coast with a fleet of 8 ships; but his vessels were heavy and slow, and the Calicut vessels showed their contempt for him openly. Gama stayed three days at Cannanore, where the Kolathiri received him with great honour. He passed Calicut at night and reached Cochin. Almost the first thing he did was to

---

1. *Three Voyages.* Pages 397 & 8.

order fast light ships to be built which could fight on equal terms with Zamorin's vessels. With the help of a Goanese boat builder named Vyne the matter was immediately taken in hand. Before anything could be accomplished, Gama fell seriously ill, and died in Cochin on the 24th of December 1524. He was buried in the principal chapel of St. Antonio in Cochin, from where his body was removed in 1538; and now he lies buried in the great Cathedral of St. Jeronymus in Belem, which was built almost entirely with the money from India.

Vasco da Gama was hardly a great man. He was neither a great explorer like Magellan, nor a man of ideas and imagination like Columbus. Of statecraft, he had but little. As between Affonso Albuquerque and himself, there was the difference between a statesman who had the vision of great things and knew how to carry them out, and an adventurer whose ideas were crude and whose imagination was only in the matter of personal luxury. Though money and honours were heaped upon him by Dom Manuel, he was not satisfied and took the order of the King to leave Sine, where he had put forward pretensions of feudal authority, with bad grace. Inordinately vain of his achievement, he was jealous of the good name of other navigators and bore a special hatred towards Magellan.[1] Even in that age of cruelty, his demoniacal inhumanity, of which many examples we have had occasion to give, was such as to create horror. Regarding the discovery of the sea route to India, little credit as navigator can be given to him, as the Cape of Good Hope had already been rounded. Even the plan of exploring a new way to India was not his. Therefore there is nothing that points to any greatness in him. From Melinde he was accompanied by competent pilots who knew every inch of the sea between Africa and Calicut. That he was rash, tactless and over-

1. *Three Voyages,* Introduction p. XXIV.

bearing will easily be granted. A mere accident made him the first European explorer to visit India by a route which was not commanded by the Moors. The event is pregnant with history, not because a new and unknown country had been discovered but that a way was found for evading the monopoly of the Venetian merchants and the control which the Sultan of Egypt had on the line communications.

Gama was uncultivated and ignorant. Even Camoens does not hide this. Courage, of course, he had. But that quality he shared with the meanest adventurer that sailed with him. It is indeed strange that this inhuman, greedy and uncouth sailor should have, in the popular imagination of Europe, become one of the heroes of his age, greater in the estimation of his countrymen and the world than Henry the Navigator, Affonso Albuquerque, Magellan, Cameons or Duarte Pacheco.

Da Gama's third visit to India as Viceroy was merely an unimportant incident. He was not able to check the decay that had set in. His successor was Dom Henrique de Meneses. His period of government is important for Malabar, because during his time Malabar became a scene of warfare, and the struggle for naval supremacy reopened.

The Zamorin, who was bribed by Albuquerque to murder his uncle, was dead. The traditional policy of the Kings of Calicut was to encourage trade with Egypt, Cambay and Arabia, and to maintain the proud title of the Lord of the Seas. The Portuguese pretension of being sole masters of maritime traffic was a sufficient cause of trouble. Nor did the rulers of Calicut look with favour on the small fortress that the Portuguese had built on the shore of Calicut. As was expected, the trouble, which was brewing for a long time, came to a head in the matter of rival claims on the sea. In 1524 the leading Mahommedan merchants of Cochin, Ahmed Marakkar, his brother Kunjali Marakkar and their maternal uncle Mahommed Ali Marakkar, left Cochin because of the oppresssion of the Portuguese, and settled down at Calicut. Enraged by this, Henrique de Meneses and Lope Vaz de Sampayo attacked Ponnani[1], the naval station of the Zamorin, and stormed it. In this campaign the Portuguese secured the help of the Arayan of Procaud, the naval commander of the Chief of that place. Dom Henrique de Meneses, who suspected the Arayan of half-heartedness in the latter part of the campaign, ordered his men to shoot his ally. The Arayan was seriously wounded. On account of this treacherous conduct of the Portuguese, Procaud declared war. After much desultory fighting on the sea, the Arayan was defeated in 1525, and Procaud itself was plundered in 1528. In the plunder the Portuguese took, besides large quantities of gold and silver, a number of cannon and 13 vessels.

The naval war with the Zamorin was all this time going on without any decisive engagement. After the destruction of Ponnani by Francesco d'Almeida in 1507, the Kunjali Marakkars, who were the hereditary admirals of the Zamorin's fleet shifted their headquarters to Kottakkal. Under Kutti Ali, in 1524, a large and effective fleet began to operate and did great damage to Portuguese trade. Lope Vaz de Sampayo came into action against Kutti Ali off Cannanore but the results were not decisive. Kutti Ali's prowess on the sea was such as to strike terror into the hearts of the Portuguese; and for over two years he practically cut off all connection between Cochin and Goa. Finally, the Governor made a supreme effort to destroy his power, and in a fight in 1528 Kutti Ali was taken prisoner. This however did not affect the growth of Zamorin's sea power; for Kunjali II, the son of Kutti Ali, soon followed in his father's footsteps with greater success.

---

1. Faria I, 284.

On land also, the fight was carried on with vigour. The Zamorin's forces besieged the Calicut factory. Dom Joao de Lima who was the factor of the place defended it stubbornly, but the Zamorin pressed the enemy hard. Antonio Rabello, who took part in the fight, describes it thus in a letter to the King.[1] "On one side of the fortress they made deep trenches and ditches and placed artillery, and on the other sides Nayars made entrenchments. They bombarded the fort for many days, but perceiving that they were not causing much damage they erected flat mantlets. One day Captain Dom Joao ordered us to sally out against one of these, and we set fire to it. The enemy also erected wooden castles and filled them with musketeers. The Nayars then made an attempt to starve the fortress by setting all their forces on the side of the sea so as to prevent disembarkation and the entry of supplies. Message was sent to the Governor who at once despatched Christoam Infante with two caravels and supplies for the fortress. He landed at fall of day between the two towers with 30 men......The Governor himself came with all his fleet to Calicut where he remained for 15 days holding a council as to whether he should land. He resolved upon getting down and sent Francesco Antonio da Silviera with 400 men. This was accomplished only with great difficulty because the boats could not be brought near the shore. A council was then held to decide as to the best way of attacking the entrenchments. The plan adopted was to give signal to the fort for a sortie to clear the shore and then the captain in chief was to land. This was successful. The siege was raised."

Negotiations were immediately opened by the Zamorin, but they came to nothing as the Portuguese wanted the fortress to be rebuilt. War was therefore renewed, and the Portuguese were forced to abandon their foothold on Calicut land and withdraw.

---

1. *Corpo Chronologico*, Part I Maco 33, Document 59.

The effort to subdue Calicut by building a fort in the capital failed. This was the fourth time the Portuguese had to acknowledge defeat in twenty-five years and to withdraw after prolonged conflict with the Zamorin. It is generally claimed by Portuguese historians that the war inflicted heavy damages on the King of Calicut. As Rabello points out, it is true that they were able to sink a number of Calicut ships, but the losses of the Portuguese were greater. The income from cartas alone was 1500 cruzados every year. That, together with the very profitable trade that was carried on, was lost by the Portuguese. "The whole evil came through us," bewails Rabello.

Dom Henrique de Meneses died in 1526, and was succeeded by Lope Vaz de Sampayo as Governor. The war with the Zamorin continued almost exclusively on the sea. Under the leadership of Kutti Ali, who was assisted by the Arayan of Procaud, the fight went on as mentioned but in 1528 Kutti Ali was taken prisoner, and Procaud was captured and plundered. The Zamorin, however, fitted up another fleet under Pachachi Marakkar, a relation of Kutti Ali, With him was sent Kunjali, the son of Kutti Ali, who was destined to become the greatest of the Zamorin's admirals. A portion of the fleet was under the command of Ali Ibrahim. The first attempt of the combined fleet was against the Portuguese settlement in Ceylon. In Ceylon, the quarrels between the reigning King Bhuveneka Bahu and his brother Mayadunna helped the Portuguese to re-establish their authority on the pretext of helping the ruler. The Zamorin took the side of Mayadunna, and his fleet under Pachachi Marakkar appeared at Kotte. The fight between the naval powers in the Ceylon seas continued till 1535, when the Portuguese had to withdraw their forces to face a new and more powerful enemy, who made his appearance on the Indian seas—the Turkish Admiral Suleiman Pasha.

Lope Vaz de Sampayo was extremely high-handed in his dealings with his subordinates. He imprisoned the Rajah of Cochin, interning him in his own palace.

The trouble with Cochin leading to the imprisonment of the Rajah arose from that ruler's claim for port dues. In a letter to the King of Portugal[1] he complained:

"Albeit that I cannot deny having received many favours of Your Highness, nevertheless I cannot desist from reminding you of this favour guaranteeing me of the duties from the port of Cochin, on all the junks, ships, and all other things whatever that may come here from Malacca, Bengala and any other part. These dues are not at present paid and I do not dare to grieve any one by demanding them, albeit that these duties belong to me as they belonged to my ancestors. Your Highness has also agreed that any fidalgo, captain or any one else of any rank who brings goods here should pay me the said duties because it is these men who have in their hand most part of the trade. Let your Highness write to the Captain in Chief, the Controller of the Exchequer to have it done, because unless they pay me I could not sustain a great part of my expenditure."

The Portuguese authorities in Cochin steadily refused to give the Rajah's dues to him on one pretext or another. Affonsio Maxia, the Controller, in spite of pressure from officials, refused to yield on this point. Writing to the King of Portugal on January 15, 1530, he states:

"Antonio Saldana when he arrived here at once came to ask me to give up to the King of Cochin the duties owing to him. I did not want to tell him before the factor and the clerk of the treasury that

1. *Corpo Chronologico*, Part I, Maco 52, Document. 32.

this had nothing to do with him. I asked him to desist from arguing, but he continued to bring messages from the King of Cochin until I told him secretly that I did this by commission from your Highness."

With the other rulers, in alliance with Portugal, he was equally tyrannical in behaviour. His position as Governor was, however, irregular, as the successor to de Meneses, by the order of the King, was Pero Mescarenhas, who at that time was away in Malacca. In the meantime new orders were received from Lisbon appointing Lope Vaz as Governor. Though tyrannical and arbitrary, he was a good soldier. He kept the fleet in a high state of efficiency, and the forts under repair and with ample munitions. He was superseded by Nuno da Cunha.

Almost the first act of the new Governor was to reopen the war with Zamorin on the sea. Diogo de Silveira with thirty ships was ordered to engage the Zamorin's fleet and to maintain a close blockade of the Calicut coast. This he did most effectively, capturing no less than 27 large ships richly laden with merchandise. He also suggetsed that a fortress at the mouth of the Beypoor River at Chaliyam was necessary if the naval power of the Zamorin was to be annihilated. The Beypoor River runs through the middle of the Zamorin's territory dividing it into equal halves. If a fortress and naval station could be established at the mouth of the river, lighter craft would operate in the interior and harass the internal trade of the Zamorin. The feudatory Chief who owned the area around Chaliyam was the Rajah of Tanur who was favourably disposed towards the Portuguese. Negotiations were opened with him. After some hesitation the Chief of Tanur agreed, and the Portuguese built a fortress in which a strong garrison was stationed. The best available artillery was brought to this place and no pains were spared to make it impregnable.

The strategical value of the Chaliyam fort was such that it was like a pistol held at the Zamorin's throat.[1] It affected his whole trade and threatened his communications, in case he attacked Cochin. It gave the Portuguese a base from which they could carry war into the Zamorin's territory. Zeinuddin, who had an eye for military considerations, declares that the Portuguese official who negotiated the agreement with the Rajah of Tanur was a "master of the greatest subtlety, cunning, and capable of deep stratagem." For 40 years the effort, towards which the Zamorin directed all his strength, was to expel the Portuguese from this port, in which undertaking he succeeded only in 1571.

The naval fight continued. Kutti Ahmed Marakkar who was the leading captain on the Calicut side, was killed in 1531, and his place was taken by Kunjali II, whose ability and knightly manners evoked admiration even from the Portuguese writers. Kunjali had learnt naval warfare in the new school. He, therefore, had no hesitation in paying the Portuguese back in their own coin. Whenever he captured a Portuguese ship—and he captured no less than 50 in one year—he slew the entire crew. The result was that warfare in Kerala waters was intensified, and the Portuguese as well as the Indians suffered heavy losses.

Even were, however, taking a new turn. Portuguese power at this time was faced with a hostile combination, more dangerous than any it had to face before. An alliance was made between Cambay and Calicut, and an effort was made to obtain the help of the Turks, who had now become the masters of Egypt. In pursuance of a common scheme the Zamorin attacked the Portuguese in Cranganore. With the help of the Rajah of Cochin, the fort was defended; but the Portuguese, in spite of their ad-

1. See Cochin Rajah's letter dated 1533. Dec. 18. *Corpo Chronologico,* Part I Maco 52. Document 23.

vanced position at Chaliyam, could not take the offensive against the Zamorin.

Martim de Sousa, who was in charge of the Malabar squadron, realised that, if the Zamorin's power for offence was to be seriously curtailed, the enemies nearer Cochin, on whom the Calicut Ruler depended for support, should first be subdued. The classic reply of the Zamorin to any offensive directed against his State was to get the Rajah of Idappalli who, from his position on the rear of Cochin and from his command of the nodal pints, was a standing menace to the safety of the Portuguese and their ally, to make a diversion from his side. De Sousa decided, therefore, to attack the Rajah of Idappalli. A powerful force under Antonio Brito invaded the territory of that Brahmin Chief and laid the country waste. His capital was sacked, and the ruler, himself, was reduced to great straits. The Zamorin immediately came to his rescue. With a large force he started south. At the ford of Kumbalam, which was defended by a Portuguese force, his army was held up. To divert the attention of the Portuguese and to get them to withdraw their forces from Idappalli, the Zamorin's fleet under Kunjali appeared before Cochin and began successfully intercepting Portuguese convoys. This ruse succeeded as Martim de Sousa had to withdraw all his forces from land in order to meet Kunjali. Idappalli Rajah was saved, and the Zamorin withdrew.

The fight on the sea was not interrupted. Kunjali rounded Cape Comorin and attacked the Portuguese establishment at Nagapatam. But they were there overtaken by a Portuguese squadron and the fight went against the Calicut forces. Kunjali himself had to escape in disguise to Calicut. In 1537, however, a new Calicut fleet appeared on the sea, which conducted a very successful campaign against Portuguese merchant vessels. Martim de Sousa tried to chase the vessels, but the Marakkars eluded him, and continued their adventurous career on the sea inflicting serious loss on the trade as well as the naval prestige of the enemy. It was only on the 20th of February 1538, that Martin de Sousa was able to fight a great battle against the Marakkars and to get the sea cleared for a short time. The success was in the nick of time, because the Portuguese had soon to mobilise their whole strength to meet the Turkish expedition under Suleiman Pasha Al Khadim.

It was early in 1537, that Suleiman Pasha, the Turkish Governor of Egypt, began the preparations for an attack on Portuguese power in Indian seas. The instructions which the Pasha received from Sultan Suleiman the Magnificent were as follows.[1]

"You who are the Beglerbeg of Egypt, Suleiman Pasha immediately on receipt of my orders will get ready your bag and baggage and make preparations in Suez for a holy war and having equipped and supplied a fleet and collected a sufficient army you will set out for India and capture and hold those Indian ports: cutting off the road and blocking the way to Mecca and Medina you will avert the evil deeds of the Portuguese infidels and remove their flag from the sea."

The arrival of Suleiman Pasha off the Gujarat Coast made the concentration of all available Portuguese ships necessary to ward off that attack. The Turkish adventure, however, proved abortive, as Suleiman merely made a naval demonstration and returned to Egypt without actually engaging the Portuguese.

The retirement of the Turks came as a great blow to the Zamorin. Fifteen years of uninterrupted struggle had exhausted his treasury. Not one but

1. *Tarjuna Nuzhat as Sunna*-British Museum MSS. Add 7846 pp. 66a.

four fleets of his had been sunk, and the trade of Calicut was languishing. The Portuguese had established themselves at Chaliyam which gave them a unique position to carry on the war against him. Moreover, his old enemy, Unni Rama Kovil, the *roi faineant* of Cochin who had been placed on the throne by Almeida, died in 1537. As a result, the Zamorin agreed to negotiate a new treaty of peace. Kutti Ali, a relation of Kunjali the admiral, was sent to Goa, where he was received with pomp by the Viceroy, Garcia de Noranha, who had in the previous year succeeded the Governor Nuno da Cunha. Garcia de Noronha, who was the third Portuguese Viceroy in the East, was a nephew of Affonso Albuquerque and had served with him in India. The treaty was negotiated between the Zamorin and Dom Alvaro, who was sent to Calicut, on the basis of a preliminary set of terms which the Zamorin had sent through his ambassador.

The treaty was signed on the Galleon *S. Mathews* at the bar of Ponnani on the first of January 1540. The transcript dated December 6, 1539[1] runs as follows:

"Dom Garcia de Noronha, of the Council of the King, our Lord, Viceroy, Captain in Chief, and Governor of India, makes known to all......that the Zamorin sent him ambassadors by whom his desire for peace was communicated. He sent Dom Garcia notes on which he was prepared to act. These notes were read in the Council of Captain and other notables and they agreed that peace should be made on that basis. As he (Dom Garcia) had S. Mathews made ready to go to Calicut but fell ill, Dom Alvaro de Noronha his son, Dom Joao de Castro, his brother-in-law (later Viceroy), Pedro Lopez de Sousa, Captain in chief of the fleet and Dr. Pernao Rodrignes de Castillo Branquo, Controller of the Treasury and

1. *Tomob de Estadoda*, India Folio 216.

Joao de Coasta as secretary were sent to negotiate. The following letter was addressed to the Zamorin:

"I beseech as a favour of the most high and very powerful lord the Zamorin King of Calicut that whereas I am unable owing to my indisposition to go personally to effect the said peace that he should establish it with the aforesaid......and swear to them as is his custom because I shall keep to and fulfil as entirely as though this had been made by me."

It was agreed by the treaty—

(1) that the Zamorin should sell all the pepper that might be in his lands to the King of Portugal at the rates prevailing in Cochin, and that ginger in the land should also be sold to the Portuguese at 92 fanams per bhara, the price including the dues which the Zamorin should have;

(2) that the Zamorin should be entitled to send to Portugal pepper to be sold at the same price as that at which the Portuguese King sold his. For each 100 bharas which the Portuguese King sells the Zamorin should be entitled to send 3½ bharas of his own, bought with his money to be sold in Portugal at 15 cruzado per quintal. It was further agreed that the money so made should be sent back to the Zamorin by the Portuguese King in shape of merchandise so that "he could double his money"; and that the merchandise should be quicksilver, vermillion and coal;

(3) that the transportation, sale etc., of the Zamorin's pepper was to be entirely at the risk of the Portuguese King. The Zamorin was to lose nothing if the ships were damaged, or goods lost; and

(4) that a part of the Portuguese merchandise should always be sold at Calicut, in order that the Zamorin might have the customary dues.

The Zamorin also agreed to accept from the Portuguese cartas for the navigation of Moorish vessels. He agreed not to make war on the friends of the Portuguese (meaning the Rajah of Cochin), but if he did make war, the conditions of the treaty were not to be disturbed.

This treaty secured for the Zamorin great advantages. It gave him a settled income from Portuguese trade without any risk, and it revived the trade of Calicut. He also secured for himself complete freedom of action against the Cochin Rajah. The Portuguese on their side also gained considerably. The Zamorin agreed to accept the cartas for Moorish ships, and to sell pepper and ginger exclusively to them. There is no doubt that considerable relief was felt by the Portugeuse at the satisfactory conclusion of this treaty. The war with the Zamorin had not gone in their favour, and had caused them great loss both in trade and in men. Peace with the Zamorin meant for them freedom of action with other Kerala Princes, as the Cochin Rajah and others soon discovered.

The first to feel the effect of this treaty was the Rajah of Procaud, whose capital had been plundered in 1528. The Rajah, with the help of one of the Karappuram Kaimals attacked a Portuguese squadron and captured it. Dom Christovao da Gama immediately demanded satisfaction of the Rajah, who disclaimed all responsibility and declared it to be the work of the Kaimal. Da Gama attacked that Chieftain's territory and laid it waste. The Kaimal was slain in the fight. The Rajah of Procaud, considering discretion to be the best part of valour, made a treaty of friendship and alliance with the Portuguese.

Estava da Gama who was Governor for two years (1540-1542) was succeeded by Martin Affonso de Sousa, who shares with Duarte de Meneses the odium of being the worst Portuguese Governors who came out to India. He reduced the plunder of temples and sacred cities to a system and made it worse by hardened and inhuman cruelty. Even in 1540, two years before Martim de Sousa came to India, the King of Portugal had issued orders that all Hindu temples in Goa should be destroyed. De Sousa went a step further. He considered it evidently a part of his duty to his Christian sovereign, that the temples of the idolators, wherever found, should be razed to the ground, and their hoarded wealth plundered, in order to fill the purse of Christian adventurers. The following description from Whiteway (taken from Barros) pictures the activity of the new Governor in this direction.

"The Conjeevaram temples stand some 40 miles inland from Madras and were, at the time of which we are writing, in the territory of the Rajah of Vijayanagaram. They were visited regularly by the Rajahs themselves......Kanchi, as it is called in sacred writings, is one of the holy places of India...... Enriched by the annual stream of pilgrims and endowed by the munificence of the Hindu Rajahs of Vijayanagaram, the wealth of the temples was very great".

De Sousa, in the rains of 1543, organised an expedition to pillage the temples. As such an attack would rouse the whole coast, preparations were made to carry off the remains of St. Thomas (supposed to be buried at Mylapore near Madras). The fleet which sailed early in September was scattered and delayed by a storm. Though the preparations were made secretly, enough had leaked out to make the Rajah of Vijayanagaram uneasy. When, therefore, the Portuguese rounded Cape Comorin, they found so large a force collected, that any attack was out of the question. Therefore De Sousa returned with his forces to Kayamkulam.

On this coast, between Cochin and Quilon, the Portuguese had settled for over 40 years, and they depended upon the goodwill of the residents for the supply of the merchandise which was the bait that drew them to the East. This did not prevent De Sousa from leading an expedition to attack the temple of Tevelakkarai, a few miles inland, which local information reported to be enormously wealthy. There were two Jungadas (companies) attached to this temple; but one of the captains with almost all the guards had gone to the south when the movements of the Portuguese first attracted atention. "An offer of £ 12,000 down failed to turn the Governor from his intention and before nightfall the temple was reached. The building was of the usual design, surrounded by a wall with a few straw huts outside. The Governor and his immediate following went inside the temple and shut the door; those outside the building passed a miserable night, a prey to every imaginable horror—the fall of a shield nearly caused a stampede. Inside, the Governor and his friends spent the time in torturing the Brahmins of the temple and in digging up the floor. It was never known exactly what was found; a gold paten worth £. 50 was all that was ever shown; but as two barrels of matchlock powder were emptied, and the barrels passed in, and as afterwards they each required 8 slaves in relays to carry them, scandal was busy. When, in the morning, they started on their return journey, a Nayar, dressed with scrupulous care, with all his ornaments, followed by 10 or 12 others, flung himself on the Portuguese ranks. It was the remaining Jungada, with his relatives whom he could collect, who thus tried to wipe out by their deaths the stain upon their honour. During their retreat, the Portuguese were harassed by the country people, and suffered a loss of 30 killed and 150 wounded; but on the way, they sacked another temple whence they obtained some small amount in silver coins to distribute among the soldiery."

De Sousa's treachery also brought him into conflict with the Rajah of Chirakkal the Kolathiri—the oldest ally of the Portuguese in India. Abu Bakr Ali, a nephew of the great Mammali Marakkar of the time of Albuquerque, was foully murdered by Bastio de Sousa, a relative of the Governor, who was sent to Cannanore for the purpose of extorting money from him. Of the merchants of Cannanore, the Mammali family was the richest and most influential, and the murder of Abu Bakr Ali was an outrage equalling in brutality the action of Gonzalo de Vaz in murdering on sea, in defiance of a Portuguese safe-conduct, another nephew of Mammali. The result was an immediate declaration of war by Cannanore.

Martim de Sousa also negotiated a new treaty with Quilon on the 25th of October 1544.[1] It is declared that the treaty was negotiated with "the Adhikari Kaimal, Cate Nambiar, and with the Pillas, Nayars and Rulers of the said land." The treaty provided that in the event of a Portuguese or a native Christian being guilty of any crime he was to be sent to the captain for trial and punishment. The Portuguese were to be exempt from all dues. The Church of St. Thomas was to be specially protected. The Portuguese on their side, promised not to kill cows in Quilon territory.

In 1545 Dom Joao de Castro came out as Governor. The new Governor made peace with Cannanore and, in fact, generally tried to set right the mischief done by his predecessor. The importance of his Governorship (which was later on converted into a Viceroyalty) lay in the development of Portuguese religious policy. For some time past, the

---

1. *Tombo de Estado de India* Fol. 37.

Portuguese authorities were thinking seriously about the problem of Christianising those areas over which they had control. Their lack of power alone stood in the way of systematic persecution and wholesale conversion, as we shall show later. In the time of Joao de Castro the matter was taken in hand in earnest. The King of Portugal was especially anxious, and wrote to him a letter dated Lisbon, 8th of March in which he asked the Viceroy to take the most vigorous steps to put down heathen practices.

He also wrote that the King of Cochin should be asked to grant privileges and show favour to Christians.[1] An attempt was made even to convert some of the Malabar Rajahs. The only success they had was with the Rajah of Tanur, who was a rebellious feudatory of the Zamorin. This Chief had sold Chaliyam to the Portuguese hoping to benefit by the Portuguese connection at the expense of the Zamorin. When negotiations about his conversion were going on, the Viceroy, Dom Joao de Castro died. In the time of Garcia de Sa, the Rajah was again pressed, and a Jesuit, by the name of Antonio Gomez, was sent to instruct him in the Faith. The Rajah went to Goa, and was there admitted with great pomp into the Church. But this apostacy was of short duration. After a few months of trial, when he found that the benefits he had expected did not materialise he reurned to the religion of his ancestors

For ten years now there had been peace between the Zamorin and the Portuguese. The friendship of the Zamorin had given the Portuguese freedom to attack and reduce the smaller Rajahs of the coast; and this high-handed policy caused hostilities to break out once again between the Zamorin and the Portuguese, who as usual put the Cochin Rajah forward to fight their btatles. The cause of war was a dispute which arose between the Rajah of

1. *Life of Castro,* p. 46.

of Vadakkumkur—the Nayar Chief who controlled the market of pepper produced in the hills in the interior—and the Rajah of Cochin. When the dispute came to a head, the Vadakkumkur Rajah offered to abide by the arbitration of the Portuguese Captain. The Cochin Rajah also was not averse to this; but Francesco de Silva thirsted for war, and insisted that if the Vadakkumkur Rajah did not surrender unconditionally, he would invade the territory. War broke out in 1550. In the first battle that ensued at Vaduthalai, the Vadakkumkur Rajah died on the field, and his troops, as a result fled in confusion. Encouraged by this the Portuguese marched on, entered his capital and set fire to the palace. The defeated army had, however, rallied and attacked the Portuguese forces with vigour, which in turn fled with much loss, and the captain, Francesco de Silva, was himself killed. The Vadakkumkur army followed up this advantage, invaded Cochin and ravaged the territory. The Portuguese and their ally, the King of Cochin, had to take refuge in the fort.

The action against Vadakkumkur, who was a feudatory of the Zamorin, brought the King of Calicut into the field. Even the Rajah of Tanur, who was a friend of the Portuguese and had become a temporary Christian, marched at the head of his forces at the call of the Zamorin. The Captain of Cranganore blocked his way to the Cochin territory, but, by marching through the lands of the Chief of Kavalappara who was one of his generals, he was able to reach Trichur. All his important feudatories, including the Chief of Kavalappara and the Rajah of Mangat, were with him. The Zomorin's army occupied Vaduthalai, and though for a short time the Portuguese established a blockade, they were unable to make any impression. The Governor, Georges Cabral, was in the meantime superseded and his successor, Dom Affonso de Noronha, made no effort to press the war to a conclusion. The Zamorin's forces maintained their supremacy on land. The following is the reference that Diogo Botelho makes about this war in his letter to Baron d'Alvito: "There was war with the King of Calicut. The reasons were the quarrel between the King of Cochin and the Zamorin and because pepper was not coming through. Enrique de Sousa was the Captain at Cochin but Manuel de Supedveda was sent from Goa with orders to relieve him. Supedveda immediately proceeded to attack Vaduthalai and opened negotiations with the Rajah of Tanur who was the ensign-in-chief of the Zamorin."[1]

The history of the Portuguese after the time of Dom Affonso Noronha is a tale of ineptitude and corruption. The war on the sea continued, for, though by the treaty of 1540 the Zamorin had agreed to take out the safe-conducts, the conduct of the Portuguese in disregarding these on flimsy pretexts soon gave rise to quarrels. Luiz de Mello, who was the captain of the fleet, endeavoured unsuccessfully to come to action with the Calicut fleet. A squadron of the Zamorin's fleet with 15 vessels attacked Punney Kayal which was under the command of Manoel Rodriques. The Portuguese were put to flight, and the town was occupied and plundered by the Calicut men. Under Kunjali Marakkar the Calicut forces began to take to guerilla warfare on the sea, attacking convoys, destroying merchant ships and generally harassing the trade. These tactics met with much success. Kunjali avoided the Portuguese fleets and fought pitched battles only when he was forced to do so by circumstances. Luiz de Mello was, therefore, unable to get the Calicut fleet into action till 1558. Kunjali had the support of the naval commander of Cannanore, whose ruler, though traditionally the ally of the Portuguese, had, owing to the rudeness of Dom Payo de Noronha, become their inveterate enemy.

---

1. *Corpo Chronologico,* Part I. Maco 84. Letter dated July 15, 1551.

The battle was fought off Cannanore. The flagship of Kunjali was sunk in the fight, and the Portuguese captured three other ships. Though the losses of the Calicut fleet were thus heavy, the victory of De Mello was no more than nominal, as nine out of the thirteen Calicut vessels retired unpursued and continued their depredations. De Mello, who had gone to Goa to celebrate the victory, had to return immediately to cope with this danger. This time he came determined to destroy altogether the offensive power of the Zamorin's fleet on the sea. The Viceroy supported him in this, and gave him an additional force of 27 ships and 600 men. With this armada he appeared on the Kerala coast. The Portuguese Commander decided on a change of plan. The traditional strategy of the Portuguese was to chase the Kerala fleet and force it to fight a decisive action. This time De Mello decided to split up his forces and guard the main river mouths with a view to intercepting all egress and ingress. The Commander himself sailed up and down in his flagship, burning cities and ravaging the coast mercilessly. This policy met with considerable success and was carried on vigorously in 1559 and 1560.

Luiz de Mello was recalled in 1560 and the Kerala ships again appeared on the sea. The war with Cannanore was still going on, and the Zamorin's ships were helping the Kolathiri Rajah in harassing the enemy's transport. Dom Francesco de Mascarenhas who was sent by the Viceroy to bombard Cannanore and carry on the fight vigorously was attacked by the Kerala vessels, and one of the ships commanded by Jeronymo de Meneses had to fly hastily before the enemy. In reply to this the Viceroy, Conde De Rodondo, fitted up a fleet under a captain by the name of Domingas de Mesquita with express orders to kill all the men whom he could capture on the Malabar coast. De Mesquita, who was charged with this task, accomplished it with a very easy conscience. He was able, within the next few months, to capture 24 vessels, the men in which, in obedience to Viceregal orders, were either beheaded or sewn in sails and thrown overboard. It is estimated that no less than 2,000 men suffered this cruel fate. The Zamorin complained to the Governor Joao de Mendoca, but he refused to take any action. Enraged at this condonation of the barbarities perpetrated against his subjects, the Ruler of Calicut denounced the treaty of 1540 and declared war.

The hostilities between Cannanore and the Portuguese, which had started in 1558 as a result of Payo de Noronha's rudeness, were still going on, and when the Zamorin was openly on the side of the enemies, the Portuguese in Kerala were faced with such a situation as they had never met before. In 1564 the allies besieged the Fort of Cannanore and destroyed the Portuguese ships in the harbour. A relief force was sent from Goa under Andre de Sousa, who was later on superseded by Goncalo Pereira Marmanaque. The troops in the fort were also reinforced, and both sides prepared to carry on the war with vigour.

The campaign started in earnest on the sea. The Malabar fleet of the Portuguese was divided into three squadrons. Maramanaque, with the larger portion of it, blockaded Cannanore and scoured the seas in front of Calicut. Dom Paulo de Lima Pereira was stationed to the north of it, while the general work of patrolling was done by a fleet of seven ships under Pedro da Silva. The last named commander fell in with a fleet of Calicut paraoes which he attacked. The paraoes were chased down the coast, but at Pudupattanam, a naval station of the Kunjali's, the Kerala fleet received reinforcements and turned on the enemy, who fled after an indecisive conflict. Kunjali, the Calicut admiral himself, was ready with a large and well equipped fleet. Venturing north he attacked Dom Paulo in the Bay of

Bhatkal and gained a complete victory. Dom Paulo, who was on his way to Cannanore to help the beleagured garrison in that city, turned tail and returned to Goa, wounded in body and humiliated in spirit.

The continuous war in Kerala was seriously affecting the trade in pepper and other spices. Neither from Cannanore nor from Calicut was there anything to be had. Even in Cochin the trade was equally depressed owing to the hostility of the Rajah of Vadakkumkur and others. The Viceroy was, therefore, anxious to come to terms with Cannanore, where, though the siege had been raised after a stiff fight, the Portuguese position was by no means safe. The Rajah was, however, wearied of fighting and agreed to treat, and peace was again restored. This enabled the Portuguese to pursue the naval war with greater vigour. Alvaro Santomayor, with the fleet that was previously blockading Cannanore, turned his attention to Kunjali, whose campaign of guerilla warfare was doing great harm to Portuguese trade. So far it had been found impossible to chase him to his lair; and though Santomayor had as many as 20 ships under him, Kunjali still escaped his vigilance and continued his career of warfare. His depredations became so intolerable that the Viceroy, Dom Luiz de Atayde Conde de Atouqueria, despatched Martino Affonso de Miranda in 1569 with a large fleet of 36 vessels. This expedition met with no greater success. Kunjali eluded the vigilance of the Portuguese vessels, attacking them only under favourable conditions. Exasperated by these tactics, the Portuguese captain forced an engagement from a disadvantageous position; the battle ended in a victory for the Kerala fleet. De Miranda was wounded, and was carried to Cochin where he died. Another attempt to bring Kunjali to action was made the next year with no greater success. After these unsuccessful attempts, the Portuguese gave up, for the time, the idea of destroying Kunjali's power, and began a policy of attacking and destroying the coastal towns of Kerala. Dom Diogo de Meneses, who was in charge of the Malabar squadron, had under him about 40 vessels, and wherever he went he burnt, pillaged, and massacred without mercy. Among the ports which suffered from his devastating activities were Pantalayini Kollam, Tirokode and Ponnani. Kunjali, on his side, carried the war into the enemy's own territory sailing as far north as Diu. His forces also gained a victory over some Portuguese ships commanded by Ruy Dias Cabral and Henrique de Meneses, 1569. In this battle the Portuguese lost 70 men including the captain Ruy Cabral, while his companion Dom Henrique de Meneses was taken captive.

Though the Zamorin expressed willingness to cease hostilities, the Portuguese did not agree, as they had made up their minds to revenge for Kunjali's actions. But they had soon to repent their mistake. At the failure of his overtures for peace, the Zamorin entered into an alliance with Adil Khan and "Nizamulcao," Murtaza Nizam ul Shah the Mad. Adil marched on Goa, Nizam ul Khan on Chaul, and the Zamorin attacked the fortress of Chaliyam which was an eyesore to him. The Zamorin's fleet gained an initial victory. At the end of February 1570, he despatched a fleet under one of the Marakkars to help Nizamul Khan who was besieging Chaul. The fleet passed the Portuguese ships in the port and reached Chaul, but after a stay of twenty days the Marakkar returned without directly engaging the Portuguese ships. On his way back, the Calicut admiral made an unsuccessful attempt on Mangalore. He was soon overtaken and defeated off Cannanore by the squadron of Diogo de Meneses.

The Zamorin's attack by land on the fortress of Chaliyam was completely successful. The siege lasted for four months (June to September), when owing to the monsoon, the Portuguese ships were not in a position to bring reinforcements or otherwise render help. The *Tofutul Mujahideen* gives a graphic description of the siege.[1] "Early in July the Zamorin sent a large force under one of his commanders to attack the Fort. The people of Tanur and Parappanangadi joined in large numbers and a great battle took place outside the walls in which the Portuguese suffered heavy defeat. They then returned to their citadel and took refuge in it. But the troops of the Zamorin surrounded it, and throwing up trenches around it blockaded it with the greatest vigilance. In carrying on this siege the Zamorin expended vast sums of money. About two months after its commencement, he came down himself from Kunan to conduct the operations; and with such extreme vigour and activity did he pursue his measures, intercepting all supplies, that the stock of provisions of the Franks became entirely exhausted, and they were compelled to devour dogs and to feed on animals of a similar vile, impure nature. In cosequence of this scarcity there came out of the fort every day large bodies of their servants, both male and female, who were not molested by the besiegers. Now although the Franks sent supplies to their countrymen shut up in Chaliyam from Cochin and from Cannanore, yet these never reached them, their convoys having been attacked and destroyed. During the blockade, the besieged sent messengers to the Zamorin offering to capitulate and deliver up to him certain large pieces of cannon which were in the fort and also to indemnify him for the expenses of war, besides some other concessions. But he refused to consent to these terms, although his ministers were satisfied with them. Shortly after when the Franks perceived their condition desperate from failure of their provisions and that they could make no easier terms, they sent messengers to the Zamorin, offering to deliver up the fort with its arsenal and all its cannon, provided a safe passage was

1. *Tofutul Mujahideen*, p. 166.

afforded them and protection for their personal property guaranteed and he accepting these terms, the garrison marched out at midnight on the 10th of Jamadialakhur." The Zamorin demolished the fort "leaving not one stone upon another."

With their expulsion from Chaliyam, it may be said that the Portuguese effort to control Kerala came to an end. The war with the Zamorin, which began with the invasion of Calicut by Marcheal Countinho, ended, after 65 years of incessant struggle, in the signal defeat of the Portuguese. They had hoped to put down the power of the Zamorin by blockade of Calicut, but this after 12 years of trial had to be abandoned as a costly failure. They had tried to break his power by building a fortress at Calicut and holding it as a pistol at his throat, a policy which had succeeded eminently at Cochin. This also ended in failure. The Zamorin agreed to the construction of a fort, but when the factor made an attempt to assert political authority, the Calicut Ruler collected his forces and drove the Portuguese into the sea. The next attempt was to hold the strategic position at Chaliyam, and from there attack and harass the trade of Calicut. Great hopes were entertained of this scheme. When the fort was built, the King of Cochin had written jubilantly to the King of Portugal thus: "It seems to me that a great service was rendered to Your Highness by the Governor by building the fortress at Chaliyam because this tempers the Zamorin down so much that he will do what Your Highness may require of him."[1] This was in fact what the Portuguese had hoped for. But these dreams failed to materialise. For forty years the fight continued and it ended only with the withdrawal of the Portuguese from the mainland.

1. Letter dated 1533. Dec. 18. *Corpo Chronologico,* Part 1. Maco 52 Document 23.

It is true that even after this the Portuguese continued to be in possession of Cochin for another 70 years. But their political power, and the ambition to control Kerala and maintain effective authority over its rulers, ceased with this. They maintained a precarious foothold at Cannanore, Cochin Cranganore, Procaud and Quilon; but in the territories over which the Zamorin ruled they had no factory or commercial house. Seventy years of conflict had come to nothing, and the victory in this prolonged struggle lay decisively with the Ruler of Calicut.

CHAPTER X

FALL OF THE KUNJALIS

The continuous naval fight kept up by the Kunjalis on behalf of the Zamorin was extremely exasperating to the Portuguese. With the reconquest of Chaliyam, the power of Kunjali on the coast became practically irresistible. Kunjali III, who was the head of the family, had already won his laurels in many a fight, and now, after the Portuguese base on the Calicut coast was destroyed, it became possible for him to consolidate his power. From the grateful Zamorin whom he had served so well, he obtained permission to build fortresses and dockyards at Pudupattanam. Within two years after the Portuguese defeat at Chaliyam, Kunjali built for himself the Marakkar Kotta and established himself there as a feudatory of the Zamorin. His power grew considerably and, on land, he exercised privileges and authorities enjoyed by Nayar Chiefs.[1]

The Portuguese, though driven out from the mainland, did not give up the fight on the sea. A large naval force was despatched from Goa which harried and plundered the coastal towns. In 1572, a Portuguese force landed at Parappanangadi, pillaged the town and set fire to the mosques and temples. The main ports of the territory of Calicut, Trikodi, Kapakad and Ponnani suffered heavily from these marauding expeditions. But even worse than this, the Portuguese ships began intercepting the rice trade with Tulunad, causing thereby a famine in the land. Zeinuddin mentions that in 1577 they captured 50 Arab vessels carrying rice, with the result that much distress was caused among the poor people. The town of Nileshwaram was attacked and reduced to ashes.

---

1. *Vadakkan Pattu*—The Nair Ballads—mentions this.

In 1578 the Portuguese Viceroy sent ambassadors to negotiate with Calicut. But the Zamorin was away then at a temple performing a religious ceremony. The negotiations were, however, carried on by his ministers on his behalf. But they came to nothing, because the Portuguese demanded the right to build a fort at Funam. The Portuguese negotiators were, therefore, sent back; but the Zamorin, who did not want to renew hostilities, sent an embassy of his own to Goa which was received with great pomp and courtesy. The negotiations were reopened and, though they dragged on for some weeks, no agreement was reached.

Tired of useless diplomacy, the Portuguese again decided on war. In this course, they had the support of the King of Cochin, who was particularly anxious that the Portuguese and the Zamorin should not become friends. The Rajah of Cochin took the field with a large army, and a Portuguese contingent was sent to help him, while a naval attack, meant as a diversion, was made on the coast. The Zamorin's forces marched down south, and the Allies—the Cochinites and the Portuguese—attacked him with vigour, but were defeated.[1] "Exasperated by this defeat, the galliots of the Franks sailed out from Cochin" for the purpose of harassing the trade of the Zamorin. An attack was made on Chaliyam in the hope of recovering that strategic position, but it met with no success. The same tactics of chasing the ships and destroying the ports and villages on the sea coast, were continued by Mathias d' Albuquerque. It did not seriously affect the Zamorin, especially as the fight on the sea did more harm to Portuguese trade than it did to him.

In the meantime there was trouble brewing in Cochin. The port dues of Cochin were shared bet-

1. *Tofut ul Mujahideen*, p. 177.

ween the Rajah and the Portuguese authorities. 9 per cent ad valorem duty was charged by the Portuguese and 3½ per cent by the Rajah. We have noticed how, under orders from the King, Dom Manuel, the Portuguese tried as early as 1530 to evade payment. As the Rajah protested vigorously the payments were renewel. In 1583 the Governor persuaded the ruler to give up that right. The people rose in revolt at this surrender of an important source of revenue. The captain of the fort appealed to Goa. The garrison in Cochin was reinforced, but the people refused to be cowed down. The position was extremely grave, as an attack on Cochin by the local population openly in revolt against their own Rajah and against the Portuguese Governor would have meant immediate disaster. Realising the gravity of the situation the Portuguese authorities withdrew their claim.

One result of the agitation in Cochin was that negotiations were reopened with the Zamorin. The main object of the Portuguese was the erection of a fort at Ponnani which is an important centre for internal trade. Ruy Gonsalves de Camara, the uncle of the Governor, was sent on this mission, but the Zamorin was in no hurry. On one excuse or another, he refused to proceed with the negotiations for a considerable time, and agreed to the construction of a fort only with bad grace. Kunjali did not like this concession, especially as he felt that a Portuguese fort at Ponnani would be a constant menace to him. In 1586 he fought a battle with the Portuguese and defeated them. In 1589 Khwaja Musa, the nephew of Kunjali, fell in with a Portuguese squadron. Musa had with him more than twenty galleys. After a stiff fight the Portuguese ships were put to flight. These two victories gave the Kunjalis the command of the Kerala seas. Musa captured many Portuguese ships and caused much damage to their trade. For over two years Portuguese navigation was practically intercepted on the Kerala coast. Musa even contemplated attacking Colombo.

A powerful fleet consisting of over 20 ships under Andre Furtado was sent by Mathias d'Albuquerque, the Viceroy, to destroy Musa's power. Musa was overtaken, and in the battle that took place all his ships were destroyed, and he, himself, escaped with great difficulty by swimming to the shore. The destruction of Musa's fleet did not dishearten Kunjali. He took to the sea immediately with another fleet and swept the Portuguese ships off the Kerala coast. As his attacks were causing much damage, the Portuguese were willing to make peace, and, at the intercession of a Catholic priest, negotiations were opened which ended in a satisfactory settlement in 1591.

As usual peace did not last long, because the Zamorin would not accept the *cartas*, and the Portuguese insisted on treating all ships navigating without their authority as pirates. This action on their part led to reprisals on the part of the Zamorin, though the official attitude of peace was maintained on both sides. Kunjali was especially lucky. A richly laden galley returning from China was attacked and dsetroyed. To take revenge for this, a very powerful force was specially fitted up and sent down to the Kerala coast under Andre Furtado who had defeated Khwaja Musa in 1591. He captured 3 of the Zamorin's vessels with rich booty. The Kerala fleet which he attacked, though defeated in battle, escaped intact.

In 1595 Kunjali IV succeeded as Chieftain of Marakkar Kotta at Pudupattanam, and admiral of the Zamorin's fleet. He strengthened the fortifications, erecting towers heavily armed with cannon. He was even more successful against the Portuguese than his father. But in his success he became proud and haughty and forgot his allegiance to the Zamorin. He cut off the tail of one of the Zamorin's elephants, and humiliated a Nayar. The enraged

Zamorin resolved to humble the pride of his overgrown subject and entered into an alliance with the Portuguese. The Viceroy sent Dom Alvaro de Abranches to negotiate the agreement. In the meantime Mathias d'Albuquerque was recalled, and Francisco da Gama Conde de Vidiguera, a grandson of Vasco da Gama, was sent in his stead. As a result the agreement was delayed till 1597.

This agreement between the Zamorin and the Portuguese caused the Cochin Rajah great dissatisfaction. By various methods he tried to make the allies quarrel. He circulated the rumour that the Zamorin was actually in league with his rebellious officer, and that the agreement was only a ruse to get the Portuguese into his power. This rumour spread fast and made the Portuguese suspect the attitude of their ally. The Zamorin, however, advanced on Pudupattanam with a large army from the land side, while the Portuguese attacked it from the sea coast.

The Marakkar Kotta was at the mouth of the river, on a promontory, easily defensible and difficult of attack. It was strongly fortified and held by a trained and well armed garrison. The attack from the seaside had also been foreseen, and Kunjali had gathered a powerful force to meet the naval attack of the Portuguese. The attack began by the Portuguese taking up a position at the mouth of the river from which they opened fire on the fort. The Zamorin's forces, which were attacking from the other side, were stiffened by a Portuguese contingent. With all these preparations, the first attack ended in disaster. Belcheor Ferreira's attack from the landside was easily repulsed. The attack of Luiz de Gama from the seaside also miscarried, resulting in heavy losses. The first effort, therefore, ended in failure as there was no co-ordination between the military and naval forces.

A new agreement was made in December 1599 with the Zamorin by Andre Furtado who was sent to take charge of the operations. The treaty provided that the princes of Tanur and Chaliyam were to be given as hostages and they were to remain in Cochin. In return the Portuguese were to give as hostages Dom Pedro de Noronha, Jeronymo Botelho, Antonio Matoso and two Fathers of the Society of Jesus. The Zamorin was to provide 1000 labourers, fifteen elephants and all the carpenters together with the wood necessary for the fight. The contingent that the Zamorin was to bring was to consist of 5000 Nayars, 2000 of whom were to be under the orders of the Portuguese commander. It was also agreed that if the fight was not over by the 20th of January, when the Zamorin would have to proceed to the Feast of Mamankam, the Rajah of Tanur was to be sent back. The Portuguese also agreed to give to the Zamorin half of the money, goods, artillery and ships captured.

Furtado, learning from the mistakes and defeat of his predecessor, proceeded with caution. First of all he cleared the river and erected batteries from which it would be possible to attack the enemy effectively. The attack was pressed with vigour. Kunjali, finding his position untenable, opened negotiations with the Zamorin requesting only that his men's lives should be spared. The Zamorin would not agree to this without consulting his ally, and Furtado was bent on destroying Kunjali's power. A new attack from both sides destroyed the Marakkar's power of resistance, and Kunjali surrendered on the condition that his life would be spared. He surrendered his sword to the Zamorin who yielded him to the Portuguese. Breaking their plighted word, the Portuguese put him to death at Goa.

Thus ended the power of the Kunjali Marakkars. It has been the custom of European writers, following Portuguese historians to call them "pirates." The Portuguese gave them this name, because it was their claim that they alone had the right to navigate the seas in virtue of the title that the King of Portugal took for himself . To them, any person who questioned their right on the sea was a pirate. Barros, in fact, goes to the extent of saying that, though the right of navigating the seas belonged to all nations equally in Europe, in Asiatic countries it was the exclusive privilege of the Portuguese. Only on this basis could the Kunjalis be considered "Pirates." They were the admirals of the Zamorin. They held their land and authority from and under him. Even the title Kunjali Marakkar was his grant. They enjoyed a position and prestige equal to Nayar Chieftains. They had to pay duties to the Zamorin[1] and take their orders from him, as the Portuguese found out. To call an opponent a pirate may be an easy way of discrediting him; but a family of hereditary naval commanders, who fought with success against the Portuguese for a century under orders from their King, could not be dismissed in that summary manner.

We have no detailed information of the amount of losses which they were able to inflict. The Portuguese historians themselves agree that the activities of the Marakkars caused them incalculable harm. Every year they had to fit out new fleets to deal with the Marakkars' encroachments. Remy Defeynes de Monfot mentions that in one year the Kerala sailors captured 160 caravels from the Portuguese.[2] Finch says that in "one year the Malabars took six Portuguese vessels, captured one Ormuz ship and three frigates. Soon after they took 16 out of a fleet of 25 vessels from Cochin and had 50 frigates and galliots on cruise. They carry in each frigate 100 soldiers and in their galliots 200."[3]

1. Pyrard I—338, 344.
2. Somers—*Collection of Travels*
3. Foster's *Early Travels.*

Of their enterprise, energy and valour it is impossible to speak too highly. Though successive misfortunes overtook them, and the superior equipment of the Portuguese ships was sure to destroy them in open conflict, every year the Kunjalis fitted up new fleets. Time after time, their fleets were sunk and the crew mercilessly slain, but the varying fortunes of war did not deter them from further effort. Their flag flew from Colombo to Cutch. They knew no fear, and there is not a single instance of a Kunjali or his relation surrendering to the Feringhee. Even on the last occasion the Marakkar surrendered to his sovereign, whose authority he had defied, and not to the Portuguese Commander. Like true seamen, they took to the sea with its dangers and its fortunes. Their tactics against the Portuguese, which were evolved after the retreat of the Egyptian forces in 1507, were to intercept trade, harass the enemy and avoid pitched battles. As a rule their vessels were faster, as Vasco da Gama discovered when he came out as Viceroy. Their armament, though less heavy than what the Portuguese ships carried, was effective and they used it with great skill.

It may be a matter of surprise that the Zamorin should have allied himself with the Portuguese to destroy the power of the Marakkars, who had served him so well for centuries, especially against the Portuguese during the previous one hundred years. The reasons are simple. The expulsion of the Portuguese from Chaliyam had removed the menace which had hung over his head like a sword of Damocles; and he was thereby relieved of the necessity of the withdrawal of the Portuguese, Kunjali's power depending upon a strong naval force. Secondly, with the withdrawl of the Portuguese, Kunjali's power had increased and he began to claim for himself authority and position, which conflicted with the sovereignty of the Zamorin. In fact, he had become an overgrown subject. The fortresses and base he had constructed at Kottakkal gave him the belief that he was an independent Chieftain and no longer dependent on the Zamorin. Thirdly, there was the growing antagonism of the Nayar population whose privileges and rights he ignored. Of this we have ample evidence in the popular ballads which are still extant.

The tombs of the Kunjalis can even now be seen at Kottakkal where the family still lives. They are held in great veneration by the Mahommedan population. There can be no doubt that the lives of these Chiefs reflect glory and honour on all Kerala, for their achievements against the naval tyranny of the Portuguese form indeed a great chapter in the history of Kerala.

CHAPTER XI

LAST DAYS OF PORTUGUESE POWER

The destruction of the sea power of the Marakkars did not help the Portuguese in maintaining their supremacy unquestioned on the sea. A new and more dangerous rival had already entered the arena. In 1594, at a meeting of the leading merchants held at Amsterdam, it was decided to send a Dutch fleet to India. A company was formed, and a fleet of 4 vessels left for India the next year. Soon, other private companies followed. By 1599 the Dutch were firmly established in Eastern trade; and the English followed in their wake. The monopoly of India's trade with Europe, which the Portuguese had enjoyed for just a hundred years, ended with this. Even the trade slowly disappeared, while the forts and factories which they had established on the coast were gradually captured by the Dutch.

The nominal authority of the Portuguese in Kerala waters and their control of Kerala trade, through Cochin, Quilon and Cannanore continued for another half a century. But their political power in Kerala had vanished and the command of the sea was contested by the Dutch. Even the trade in pepper and spices, which had given them great profit in early days, languished. The continuous quarrels with the Chiefs and the hostility of the Syrian Christians whom the Portuguese had alienated by their religious persecution combined with the inveterate hatred of the Moors ruined their trade. Moreover, the traditional fight between the Zamorin and the Rajah of Cochin had broken out again, destroying the hopes of a revival in the trade with the Ruler of Calicut which the Portuguese had entertained.

While the fight against Kunjali was going on, the Cochin Rajah attacked Koratty Kaimal, one of the feudatories of the Zamorin, in the hope of embroiling Calicut with the Portuguese. As soon as the campaign against the Marakkar was over, the ruler of Calicut marched against his enemy, and, though the Cochin Rajah was driven out of the lands he had invaded, the Zamorin himself was wounded by a stray shot. A truce was arranged but did not last long. The new Zamorin, who succeeded the destroyer of Kunjali, recognised that the invasion of Cochin could not succeed so long as the line of communication with that state was threatened by the fort of Cranganore. The Rajahs of Cranganore had been feudatories of the Zamorin for many centuries. But after the Portuguese had established themselves there, the Chief of Cranganore took advantage of the continued hostility between them and the Zamorin to declare his independence. With that extraordinary persistency which characterised the policy of the Rulers of Calicut, the Zamorin had never forgiven this defection. In 1536 he attacked and conquered Cranganore and re-established his own sovereignty. But the Chief, with the help of the Portuguese who had built a fort in his capital, again revolted. The establishment of the Portuguese at Chaliyam seriously prejudiced the Zamorin's claims against his feudatory and checked his activities in this quarter; but with its destruction the way was again open to him to attack Cranganore. When the new war with Cochin opened at the beginning of the century, the Zamorin called upon the Chief of Cranganore to help him with soldiers. As that Chief did not want to offend either the Portuguese who were helping the Rajah of Cochin, or the Zamorin who was his suzerain, he remained inactive. The result was that, as soon as the Ruler of Clicut was free, he attacked Cranganore and annexed its northern part to his own State. After this the Zamorin made preparations to attack the town and fortress of Cranganore, which were in the possession of the Portuguese. A contemporary description of the fortress of Cranganore is to be found in a Portuguese manuscript *Noticias da India* "Its fort," says the writer, "was built by Dom Miguel Bolin who defended it against many attacks from Calicut......The fortress is provided with a Cathedral and an Archbishop appointed by the Holy See. The fortress has a captain for its maintenance with the garrison and artillery required for its defence, a misericordia and a hospital and a house of the Fathers of the Company of Jesus and another of St. Francis. The fortress is 100 fathoms in length from bastion to bastion and 3 in height and 6 spans in width. The settlement which is near the fortress contains a hundred married couples, forty Portuguese and the rest natives. The wall which surrounded the settlement is sixty fathoms and fifteen spans in height."[1]

The Zamorin decided to attack this fortress and was, in that effort helped by the Rajah of Parur, a Brahmin Chief who was ill disposed towards both the Portuguese and the King of Cochin. At this time, even the King of Cochin was not on friendly terms with the Portuguese though he did not dare to openly show his hostility. The Viceroy was, therefore, anxious not to embroil himself with the Zamorin, and sent an embassy to Calicut offering to open negotiations. The Zamorin knew that this was meant as a dilatory move, and, while accepting the large presents sent and receiving the embassy with courtesy, went forward with his preparations for the attack. Early next year he sent an army which surrounded the fortress and besieged it. The garrison was reduced to great straits. Enough provisions, however, continued to reach Cranganore from Cochin, and the fort held out until the next year when relief arrived under Dom Barnardo de Noronha. The Dutch ships, which were hastening to the help of the Zamorin, were intercepted and the siege was raised.

---

1. *Noticias da India*—India Office Manuscript, Portuguese translations Vol. I. Page 225.

But the minor Chiefs of Kerala had learned the lesson. They saw that a new force had entered the Arabian Sea, with whose help it would be possible for them to free themselves from the hated yoke of the Portuguese. The Dutch also realised that in Kerala the position of the Portuguese was precarious because of the hostility of the Princes; and for the next 30 years the attempt of the Dutch captains on the coast was mainly directed towards maintaining friendly relations with the Chiefs. This was in fact the end of the Portuguese power in Malabar. In the years that followed, they exercised little or no sway on land as they had to fight both the English and the Dutch on the sea. In 1616 Captain Kealing, an English sailor, reached Cranganore; and the Zamorin agreed to sign a treaty with England by which he promised to give the English facilities for trade, if they, on their side, helped him to reconquer Cochin.[1] With the Dutch also the Zamorin had entered into negotiations about the reconquest of Cochin.

The Portuguese, on their side, were handicapped in this struggle for naval supremacy, by the indifference with which the Spanish monarchy viewed Portuguese concerns in the East. Every since Philip II had brought Portugal under his control, the interest which the Portuguese Kings had personally taken in the development of Eastern trade had vanished. Neither reinforcements nor instructions were received regularly from Portugal. Challenged on the sea both by the Dutch and the English, and hated by the Indian Powers, the Portuguese fought a losing battle and in spite of heavy odds maintained their position for a time. But, neither from the point of view of Kerala history, nor from that of the history of India in general, is the struggle worth recording.

---

1. Letters received by the East India Company from its servants. Vol. V—1616.

The opposition of even the minor Kerala Rulers increased when it became evident that the Portuguese power was weakening.

The condition of the Portuguese in India at this time was most deplorable. Public coffers were empty; the soldiers were not paid; and the rivalry between the religious Orders and the State hampered all effective action. The Jesuits and other religious bodies had become all-powerful. They took no notice of the orders of the Viceroy and usurped Royal jurisdiction and revenues. The Viceroy, writing in 1631 to the King, complained that in certain areas of Travancore, the Jesuits had become the real masters. The religious Orders were heavily subsidised from State revenues; and it is said that thert were twice as many Portuguese priests as there were laymen of the same nationality in each city. As monks were given large allowances from the State, and as soldiers had often to go for months without pay, it became the common practice in the army to take holy Orders or go into a monastery. A great portion of the revenues of the State went for the upkeep of large bodies of priests.

A curious custom had also developed of sending out girls from the orphanage in Lisbon with dowries provided for in the form of orders of appointment for their husbands. One such girl brought with her an order for the Governorship of Cranganore. This scandal grew to such an extent that in 1627 an order was promulgated that all such dowry appointments should be limited to three years.

The decay of Portuguese power was most visible in the towns. The Conde de Vigueira, the Viceroy, wrote to the King in 1622, that Cochin which was the centre of spice trade had ceased to have any trade at all. Even before this time Cannanore had been neglected. Quilon also had become unimportant. These fortresses, the King was told by the Viceroy, were without guns or other effective means of defence. The revenue system was mainly based on duties and on the sale of *cartas*. With the loss of trade the revenue from the first diminished. With the loss of power the revenue from the second ceased. The area of land that the Portuguese held was very small and was farmed out bringing in but little revenue. Thus it became impossible even to keep the fortresses in ordinary repair.

Even the Viceroyalty fell into disrepute. The Conde de Vigueira, when he was appointed Viceroy in 1621, wrote to the King reminding him that the appointment had been offered to three other people who had refusd it, suggesting thereby that in going out to India as Viceroy he was doing a favour to his King. The home government also was negligent of what was going on in India; and, though successive Viceroys asked to be supplied with sufficient reinforcements, hardly any came from Portugal. In the meantime the Dutch had entered the Indian Ocean and begun to challenge Portuguese authority.

Every since the Dutch Company entered into the competition for Eastern trade, there was between them and the Portuguese unceasing and relentless war. The Portuguese continued to look upon the Dutch as intruders, and attempted to drive them out of the Indian seas by force. This policy brought them into continuous conflicts, which swallowed up their revenue and ruined their trade. It is outside the purpose of this book to trace the fight between these two Powers. It is sufficient for our purpose to remember that, after consolidating their power in the Eastern Archipelago, the Dutch attacked the Portuguese in Ceylon in alliance with Rajah Simha. In 1638 three Dutch ships under Wilhelm Jacobs Coster made their first attack. After considerable fighting the Portuguese were expelled from the island in 1658. The Dutch established themselves in strength at Colombo, and turned their attention to the Portuguese establishments on the Malabar coast.

The first place to be attacked was Quilon. In December 1658 Ryklof Van Goens[1] captured that fort and, after establishing a strong garrison there, cruised the Kerala coast and returned to Colombo. The Portuguese, with the help of the Rani of Quilon, made a counter-attack, and the Dutch Governor withdrew the garrison to Colombo on the 14th of April 1659. The very next year Van der Meyden started again for the Kerala coast with a large force, reaching Azhikode, near Cranganore, on February 10, 1661. There the Dutch Governor entered into negotiations with the Zamorin who had sent his heir-apparent as ambassador, and an agreement was reached, by which the contracting parties undertook to cooperate in order to drive out the Portuguese.

The first attack of the Allies was on Pallipporto—Pallipuram. The importance of this fort lay in the fact that it provided an excellent base for attacking Cochin. After a determined resistance, the fort was stormed by the Dutch who handed it over, according to their treaty, to the Zamorin. No effort was made immediately to attack Cochin. The Portuguese at once proceeded to strengthen their defences and to make preparations for withstanding a siege. The Dutch also kept this object in view, and entered into negotiations with the leading Chiefs on the coast.

The Kingdom of Cochin was then in a state of civil war. The cause of this lay in a series of conflicting adoptions which gave rise to rival claims to

1. Ryklof Van Goens was a man who had experience of Indian seas and of Indian conditions from his childhood. At the age of 10 he came out to the East with his father. Two years later he visited the Coromandel Coast. When he was appointed to the Malabar expedition he was an Extraordinary Member of the Council at Batavia.

the throne.[1] It will be remembered that, early in the 16th century, the Portuguese under Albuquerque had interfered and dispossessed a senior branch of the family on the ground that the claimant belonging to that branch was a supporter of the Zamorin. The junior branch which was reigning became extinct in 1646, and adoptions were made both from the elder dispossessed branch and a collateral branch living at Palliviritti. Between these two branches, family feud broke out immediately, and, with the help of the Portuguese, the members adopted from the elder branch were again expelled. In 1650 the Gadi became vacant, and, without considering the claims of the elder branch, five princes from Tanur, who were traditional friends of the Portuguese, were adopted in 1658 and given the right to succeed.

The dispossessed princes of the branch appealed to the Zamorin who immediately took up their cause. With the intervention of the Zamorin, the nobles became divided into two parties, one supporting the Tanur adoptees, and the other the exiled princes. The leading supporters of the dispossessed princes were Adityavarman, Rajah of Vadakkumkur, and the Chief of Idappali... The new adoptees found support in the Rajahs of Procaud and Valluvanad. The principals in the fight were, of course, the Zamorin, on behalf of the elder branch, and the Portuguese, on behalf of the new line.[2] The Nayar Chief of Paliyam, who was the most powerful of the nobles of Cochin and the hereditary Prime Minister of the State, secretly supported the cause of the exiled princes. In 1661, when after the capture of Cranganore the Dutch admiral Van Goens was in Pallipuram, the Chief visited him and entered into a

1. There is an extremely interesting Malayalam book recently discovered and published by the government of Travancore which deals in detail with these adoptions and the wars that followed. *Padappattu*—Vol. 5 of the Srimulam Library, published at Trivandrum.

2. *Padappattu*, P. 14.

secret agreement. It was in the form of a request for protection which was granted by the pleasure of the Company. The following in the text of that agreement.

"I, Palietter Come Menone, Chief of the Island of Veipeen, being in difficulties on account of the Portuguese and other enemies named having done great harm to my land and my subjects, and caused trouble to me, for which reasons, finding myself powerless to resist such enemies, I am compelled to look out for a powerful nation which will maintain and protect my land and my subjects. With this object in view, I pray for and accept the protection of the Honourable Netherland East India Company in order that they may protect me against the enemies of my State. And at the same time I yield and surrender to the same Honourable Company my person, territory and subjects".[1]

This request was agreed to; and the Dutch, thereby, got their first foothold in Cochin. On the advice of the Paliyam Chief, the claimant to the Cochin State, Vira Kerala Varma, who was in exile at Vadakkumkur, visited Colombo, and invited the Dutch Governor to help him to drive out the Portuguese. We know the details of the proceedings in connection with this, not only from Portuguese and Dutch sources but also from a contemporary Malayalam Chronicle, the *Padappattu* already referred to. The plan, agreed to, was that the Zamorin should invade Cochin from the North, and Vira Kerala Varma, with the help of his allies, the Vadakkumkur and Thekkumkur Rajahs, should attack Cochin from the South, while the admiral was to attack it from the sea.

In the autumn of 1661 the Supreme Government at Batavia fitted out another expedition, with Jacob

1. Selections from the records of the Madras Government (Madras 1911). No. 13-P. 124.

Hustart, Councillor, as Civil Chief and Admiral Van Goens as Commander. Captain Nieuhoff, the explorer and writer, was on one of the ships. The fleet took a heavy train of artillery from Colombo on the 7th of October, and sailed for the Kerala coast. Meeting the ships of Commodore Roodhas at Manapare on the 15th of November, the expedition arrived before Quilon on the 7th of December. Immediately, a powerful body of soldiers was landed, and on the 8th they marched "in battle array into the country."[1] As the Portuguese in Quilon offered no resistance, the only opposition, that the party met with, came from the Nayars of the Queen of Quilon, who had built a redoubt from which they fired on the Dutch. Though the firing did very little actual harm, it kept the Dutch near the shore and prevented them from advancing. The Dutch commander, therefore, decided to cut down the forest on the side and take the artillery behind the redoubt. "Immediately all our carpenters were set to work to cut down bushes and trees while the seamen were employed in levelling the grounds to make way for the Artillery." The Nayar army holding the redoubt withdrew. The fort was captured. "We continued our march," says Nieuhoff, "to the city of Koling, passing all the way a great many fine plantations, surrounded on all sides with walls, the road betwixt them being very narrow."[2] The next day, on the 10th, the main attack on the city began. Goskeled commanded the van, Roddhas the rear, and Ryklof Van Goens directed the operations. The enemy fought bravely, but was defeated. The Dutch captured the town and immediately set fire to the palace and the temple attached to it.

After capturing Quilon, Van Goens, with 30 ships, appeared before Cochin on the 1st of January 1662. Landing his troops at Ayacotta he proceeded

---

1. *Nieuhoff's Voyages.* Churchill's collection of Voyages. Vol. II—P. 215.
2. *Ibid.*

to lay siege to the fort of Cranganore, which was defended by Urband Fereira. Preparations were made for a regular siege and all the necessary material was landed from the ships. Though considerable resistance was offered and the defence conducted with skill, the Dutch were able to storm the fort, because the Chief of Paliyam, who had already entered into a treaty with the Dutch, betrayed to the Admiral the plans of the Portuguese. Then the Dutch forces moved south, and made preparations for an immediate attack on Cochin. At Vaipin, which was an island belonging to the Paliyam Chief, they established their headquarters in a Roman Catholic Church, and erected temporary defence works. From these an attack was first made on the Cochin palace which was completely successful. Adrian Van Rheede,[1] an ensign, burst into the palace and took possession of the person of Rani Gangadhara Lakshmi, the puppet set up by the Portuguese on the Cochin throne. Three out of the five Tanur princes died in the fight. The Rani herself was handed over to the Zamorin as prisoner.

The next attempt was to cross the backwaters and establish the Rajah on the mainland. Before it could be done, the Rajah of Procaud, whose power had greatly increased during the last half-century, arrived in support of the Tanur princes and held the shore. Foiled in this attempt the Dutch and their allies turned to the fortress of Cochin. An attempt was made to blockade it from all sides. When the position was desperate the Viceroy at Goa was moved to decisive action and despatched a fleet of five ships. The Rajah of Procaud also came up with reinforcements. The siege was raised, and the Dutch withdrew temporarily.

---

1 Adrian Van Rheede came of a noble family. Later, he became Baron Van Hydrecht. He deserves to be remembered for the monumental work on Indian Botany, *The Horticus Malabaricus* which he was instrumental in producing.

The Dutch returned with greater forces as soon as the monsoon was over. With the help of the Paliyam . Chief and the Prince of the dispossessed branch, the Dutch established a blockade. Help came to the Portuguese from the side of the Rajah of Procaud, but after a heavy engagement the Nair contingent of that ruler was defeated. After two months, spent in artillery bombardment and preliminary skirmishes, an assult was decided upon. For 8 days and nights the attack continued unabated. Desertions thinned the ranks of the Portuguese and a close blockade was maintained from the side of the sea. In this hour of peril; the Portuguese inside the fort acted with great heroism. Though reduced to extremity, and with no hopes of relief from Goa, they held on to the very last. But their position was hopeless. A final attack made simultaneously on three points, though resisted with vigour by the Portuguese, ended in success. The Portuguese commander surrendered. Arrayed in black and solemn mourning clothes, and followed by his Captains, the Portuguese commander, who had fought hard and revived even in defeat the memories of Pacheco and Albuquerque, marched up to the Dutch Admiral and handed over the keys of the town to him. With this act of surrender the Portuguese flag ceased to fly over Kerala. Cranganore was handed over to the Zamorin in accordance with the treaty. Over the fortresses at Cochin, Cannanore and Quilon the flag of the Portuguese had given place to the flag of Holland. The ruins of a fine fortress, a small population of topasses and a Bishopric at Cochin are all that is left of the glory of Vasco da Gama and Albuquerque. It vanished as suddenly as it arrived, leaving behind nothing but the family names of a few Eurasians to remind one of the days when the Portuguese held the mastery of Indian trade and to keep alive that memory.

CHAPTER XII

PORTUGUESE POLICY IN KERALA-GENERAL

It is customary to speak about the "Portuguese Empire" or "Portuguese Power" in India as if it were something distantly alike, and predecessor to, the British Empire. This feeling is reflected in the writings of most European writers. The Portuguese, themselves, held that they were the Lords of India; and, following them, European writers have, almost without exception, echoed this view. One writer in the *Journal of the Asiatic Society* even worked out a parallel between British power and the "Empire" of the Portuguese in India.[1] But all such views are coloured and do not in any sense agree with historical facts. The Portuguese never had any "Empire" in India. They had a few coastal towns, and their authority never extended beyond a few miles of their naval bases. The only territorial possession of any considerable extent over which they ruled was Goa.

As against the rest of the European Powers they had a monopoly of Indian trade for about a century; of this we shall speak later. But even this monopoly of trade, based as it was on naval supremacy, was never accepted by Indian Powers. The sea power of the Zamorin was not effectively broken, as the preceding pages have shown, till the capture of Kunjali's fort in 1599. By that time the Dutch had already entered the arena and had become a serious rival on the sea. Thus, in no sense is there any justification for the facile statements commonly made about a "Portuguese Empire" in India or even an effective Portuguese Power as a factor in Indian politics.

---

1. Reade in the *Journal of the Royal Asiatic Society*, 1898, p. 589.

So far as Kerala was concerned this was undoubtedly the case. The hundred years' war with the Zamorin, which was essentially a bid for land power, failed miserably with the capture, by that ruler, of the fortress at Chaliyam. The Portuguese commercial monopoly and political authority did not affect the area between Cannanore and Cranganore, and nowhere did it extend beyond the ports in which they had built fortresses of their own. Such fortresses existed at Cannanore in the land of the Kolathiri Rajah of Chirakkal, at Cranganore, at Cochin, at Procaud and at Quilon. In these places, and especially at Cochin, something like political suzerainty was developed, but its extent was limited by the fact that the power of the Rajahs concerned did not extend beyond a few miles of territory.

Of all the rulers in alliance with the Portuguese, the most considerable, from the point of view of royal power as well as of wealth, was the Kolathri Rajah of Chirakkal. Though during the first few years the relations between him and the newcomers were extremely cordial, the Portuguese, by their high-handedness in disregarding their own safe-conduct given to one of the ships belonging to Mammali Marakkar, made him an enemy. In the time of Albuquerque the Rajah was forced to dismiss his Minister and yield to the wishes of the Portuguese Commander. But, as we have seen, his relations with the Commander never again became cordial. In the time of Martim Affonso de Sousa hostilities broke out between the Rajah and the Portuguese as a result of the murder, by the Governor's agent, of Bakr Ali, another relative of Mammali. A bitter war which lasted for many years was the result of Payo de Noronha's rudeness to the Kolathiri in 1558, and peace had to be purchased after the Cannanore garrison had undergone great privations. In fact, so far as the Rajah of Cannanore (Kolathiri) was concerned, he maintained his independent position and resisted with success the attempts of the Portuguese to intervene in his internal affairs. In this he was successful mainly because of that fact that, though his territory extended up to the coast, his own capital was at Chirakkal, a few miles inland, away from the reach of the guns from Portuguese ships. Thus at Cannanore, though there was a fort with considerable garrison, the Portuguese never had any political power and, whenever an attempt was made, the fortress itself was besieged and the trade of the factory extinguished.

At Cochin and at Quilon, this was not the case. In both these places the Portuguese exercised effective political authority. The position of the Cochin Rajah, especially, was that of a vassal maintained on the throne by the favour of Portugal. The crown which the Rajah wore was made in, and sent from Portugal. From the earliest times the Portuguese made it clear that the Rajah of Cochin stood to them in a position different from other Kerala princes. Even in the time of Almeida in 1505 they had interfered to set aside dynastic custom and to secure the succession of one favourable to themselves. At that time also the Cochin Rajah took an oath of allegiance to the King of Portugal. In all Portuguese correspondence the Rajah of Cochin was called on as a faithful "servant" or servitor to help both by men and by money. On the least provocation, the Portuguese did not hesitate to imprison him and to treat him with extreme incivility. Thus in 1510, Nuno Caliste Brocco, who was captain of the Cochin Fort, interned the Rajah in his palace as he was afraid that the Rajah might abdicate. He even refused the Rajah permission to retire and do religious work as was the unbroken custom of the Cochin family. Albuquerque in fact openly told the Rajah that it was the will of Portugal, and not the custom of the State, that was binding on Cochin. During the century and a half that Portuguese captains exercised their authority in the fortress of

Cochin, the Rajahs of that territory were virtually prisoners. Even the taxes, which by treaty should have gone to the Rajah, were not given to him. His temples were desecrated in spite of piteous appeals, and his own person was often insulted and outraged. In the family quarrels of Cochin the Portuguese regularly intervened. In every way the Rajah of Cochin was in a much worse position than when he was under the Zamorin.

The reason of this was that the Rajah of Cochin had no territorial possessions except in the immediate neighbourhood of the fortress. The land, on the other shore of the backwater, was held by the Anchi Kaimals, who were powerful Nayar barons who owned but nominal allegiance to the Rajah. There was no territory on the mainland which accepted the Rajah's direct authority. The chiefs and barons sympathised with the Zamorin and were in constant revolt. The Rajah, himself, was living practically as a prisoner, within a furlong of the Portuguese fort. Thus the control of the Cochin Rajah gave them no political authority, but was helpful only in so far as they were able to press forward their schemes under cover of the Rajah's prestige and authority.

The Rajahs of Procaud and Quilon were also subordinate allies. By the first treaty that Lopo Soares made with the Queen of Quilon that State received a share of customs, but the Portuguese, when they acquired greater power, refused to abide by this clause. The Rajahs of Procaud were brought under the influence of Portugal only in 1530. Their position never became so bad as that of either the Rajah of Cochin, whose nominal vassal he was, or that of the Queen of Quilon. He advanced greatly in the favour of the Portuguese, who gave him the title of "brother in arms" to the King of Portugal. The only other ruler, with whom the Portuguese were on friendly political relations was the Rajah of Tanur

—the ruler of Vettathu Nad. From this Chief they obtained the island of Chaliyam. The Rajah of Tanur was greatly supported by the Portuguese, who endeavoured to make him a Christian. One of the Rajahs, as mentioned previously, visited Goa and was received into the Church, but when the Zamorin's call came he abandoned the foreigner and marched at the head of his army to Vaduthalai.

Thus, except in the towns of Cochin, Procaud and Quilon, the Portuguese had no effective political authority of any kind. But they maintained a close and friendly political relationship with the minor Chieftains in the interior, without whose friendship they could not procure the cargo of spices which was their main concern. Their friendship was secured by a yearly subsidy in gold. The Rajahs of Vadakkumkur, Procaud, Udaimperur, Parur and Mangatt received 1800 fanams each. This subsidy kept the Rajahs in good humour, increased their sense of importance, and secured their friendship. In the time of Martin Affonso de Sousa these payments were discontinued, and this action contributed materially to the success of the Zomorin in the subsequent wars against the Portuguese. This act of Martin de Sousa, which alienated the minor Chiefs, was not so much due to any meanness on the part of that Governor as to a change of policy. From the time of Albuquerque there have been two schools of opinion on the question of Indian policy. Albuquerque held that a firm military power, based on fortresses which can be defended by the guns of ships, was necesary if the trade with India was to be successfully carried on. He had no idea whatever of any territorial empire but he recognised—as his letters make clear—that, without a military power based on fortresses, trade with India was not secure. As a further development of this idea, he carried out a policy of alliances with local Chiefs, on a footing of equality with the powerful ones like the Zamorin, and on a footing of supremacy with minor

Rajahs like the Chief of Cochin. But this policy had its opponents. In fact Dom Francisco d'Almeida had himself expressly denounced it as leading to political weakness. "With respect to our fortress in Quilon," he said, "the greater the number of the fortresses you hold, the weaker will be your power. Let all our forces be on the sea, because if we should not be powerful at sea, everything will be at once against us."[1] After the time of Albuquerque the tendency was more to emphasise this point of view. Wherever the Portuguese had a direct and definite hold on the ruler, as at Cochin and Quilon, they put forward increasing claims and asserted their direct authority. But the policy of political control over the Chiefs in the interior was given up.

The main Portuguese fortresses on the Malabar coast were built with a double purpose, to overawe the local ruler and to control the export of pepper. In Cochin, the Rajah's palace being only a few furlongs away from the fortress, the political object was completely successful. In Cannanore and Quilon also it met with partial success. The commercial purpose was made clear from the very beginning. Almeida advised King Manuel to have a "strong castle in Cranganore on a passage of the river which runs to Calicut, because it would hinder the transport that way of a single speck of pepper."[2] The fortress at Chaliyam was built expressly for the purpose of controlling the trade in the Zamorin's territory, as that island, by its position on the Beypore River, commanded the natural waterway in the southern portion of the Kingdom of Calicut. When the Zamorin expelled the Portuguese from that fort, the prospects, of trade in that area vanished with it.

Each fortress was practically a Portuguese settlement. Within the area surrounded by the walls, only

1. *Annaes das Scienciase Letters*—April 1658 (Lisboa).

2. *Annaes das Scienciase Letters*—April 1658 (Lisboa).

Portuguese and Latin Christians were allowed to stay. The native inhabitants, unless they became Christians and gave the women in irregular marriage to Portuguese soldiers, were expelled from within the fortress. Each fortress was thus a small Portuguese colony. According to the *Noticias da India*,[2] even in Cranganore there were living in 1600 a hundred married couples, of whom 40 were Portuguese and the rest converted Christians. Cochin, of course, was different. It was governed as a city—that is, had municipal and other rights, with officers of justice and revenue, misericordia and a hospital, besides numerous ecclesiastical and religious establishments. Its captain and garrison were paid out of the revenues of the land.

This arrangement, by which the Portuguese and their dependents were segregated in small areas, made a division of justice easy. The general arrangement about justice was as follows: "when any Nayar or native of the land or Moor had any strife or contention, the Nayar or native shall be tried by the local ruler, while Portuguese subjects were sent before the captain of the fortress." This privilege of the Portuguese was gradually extended to native Christians in the country of the smaller Rajahs. In the treaty with Quilon in 1544 it was laid down that Christians, when they were guilty of crime, should be sent for punishment to the Portuguese captain. Portuguese justice whether applied to themselves or to the Indian Christians, was of the most barbarous kind. In 1524 Vasco da Gama, himself, had 3 Portuguese women publicly whipped for the very inadequate reason of having come out on shore against his orders. Punishments for ordinary people were cruel and inhuman: but, so far as the nobles were concerned their privileges were kept intact. No fidalgo could be punished in India.

---

2. P. 225.

It is a matter of importance to note that this division of justice and the rigid exclusion of non-Christians from within the fortresses helped the Portuguese to exercise their authority without coming into conflict with the local rulers. If they had attempted to adminiser law to the native population with whom they came into contact, it must have immediately led to friction. But in this matter the Portuguese were wise; and even their Inquisition had authority only over Indian Christians living within the fort and near enough to be under actual control.

In relation to other states and rulers the Portuguese recognised no principle save that of strength. As Barros declares: "The Moors and Gentiles are outside the law of Jesus Christ—which is the law that everyone must keep under pain of damnation and eternal fire. If then the soul be so condemned what right has the body to the privilege of our laws? It is true that they are reasoning beings and might, if they lived, be converted to the Faith, but in as much as they have not shown any desire as yet to accept this, we Christians have no duties to them."[1] It is on this simple principle that Portuguese policy towards Indian states was based. The result was that, except in Cochin and Quilon, where the Chiefs became absolute vassals, the Indian rulers strongly resisted their encroachments and were always in open fight against their pretensions. Never were they able to gain either the confidence or the respect of the people with whom they came in contact. The popular idea, which was on the whole right, was that the Portuguese were, as a nation, treacherous, untrustworthy and barbarously cruel. The cruelties of the early adventures, especially of da Gama, were never forgotten. The action of Goncalo Vaz, who disregarded an official safe-conduct and captured Mammali Marakkar's boat killing all the crew and sewing them up in sails, is but a single example of

1. Barros 1. 6. 1.

the kind of atrocities which have disgraced the Portuguese name in India. *Kerala Pazhama,* a native Chronicle of the 17th century, gives a graphic description which reminds one irresistibly of the Anglo-Saxon Chronicles which describe the devastations of Robert of Belleme, Geoffrey de Mandeville, and the robber barons. Nor were their exploits of this nature confined to the sea. Whenever there was an opportunity for plunder, they never allowed either considerations of humanity, religion or good faith to stand in their way. The plunder of the Tevalakkara temple has already been alluded to. Another example, which is particularly interesting, will show the standard of honour that obtained generally among the Portuguese in India. At Pallurithi, near Cochin, there was a temple which was held specially sacred by the Rajahs of Cochin. This temple was credited by rumour to possess untold wealth. The Rajah of Cochin was the closest ally and friend of the Portuguese on the West Coast and knowing that the Governor was thinking of organising an expedition to plunder it, he expostulated with him and got his word of honour that no such attempt would be made. But the Governor, though himself desisting from it, authorised his subordinate to attack the temple, and an expedition organised under his own personal care left for Pallurithi. It was unsuccessful in its immediate object. This incident, especially as it is but one of many similar acts by the Portuguese, may be taken as showing the general unscrupulousness of the Portuguese in India.

How far they set honour and scruple at naught, can be seen from the practice[1] followed by one of the captains in issuing safe-conducts which consisted of words to the following effect:— "The owner of this ship is a very wicked Moor. I desire that the first Portuguese captain to whom this may be shown may make a prize of her." The treachery of Bastiao

1. See also note on pp. 89—90.

de Sousa in murdering Bakr Ali at the Cannanore beach, where they had met for negotiations, was the cause of a bitter war. The history of the Portuguese in India is full of incidents of this kind. Albuquerque, himself, was not much better in this respect, as he confesses to have persistently requested the heir apparent of the Zamorin to poison that King.

Devastation of land and property was systematically followed in the campaign of coastal raids by which the Portuguese attempted to revenge the defeats inflicted by the Kunjalis. At Cannanore alone, on one occasion in 1564, the Portuguese soldiers felled 40,000 palm trees.

Of the organisation of Portuguese government in India much need not be said. In their Kerala settlements, the political organisation was, even for that age, surprisingly ineffective. There was no territory to be governed in Kerala; and hence the only system they developed was a peculiar combination suited for purposes of trade and military defence. The towns were under the command of a captain—that of Cochin being appointed direct from Portugal. He worked under the orders of the Governor who, after Albuquerque's time, resided at Goa and was responsible for the defence and ordinary administration of the fort. In Cochin, as we have already pointed out, there was an officer of Justice and one of Revenue. The major part of the customs of the port of Cochin belonged to Portugal, and its collection and administration were the duty of the Controller of Revenues, who was also appointed from Portugal. This position was held for some time by that remarkable man, one of the few honest Portuguese officials who came out to India, Affonso Mexia who did a great deal to put the finances of that town in order. This office of the Treasurer of Cochin was later on found to be of little use, as the Kerala trade began to languish as a result of the hostility of the local Chiefs. Cosme Annes, writing to the King in 1549, declared that, "the office of the treasurer of Cochin is of no further use than an unavoidable expense, causing further damage to the exchequer of Your Highness."[1] It is characteristic of the Portuguese that, till 1510, there was no auditor at all at the factory. Affonso Albuquerque protested strongly against this state of affairs and wrote to the King: "It appears to me, Senhor, that it is not right to have such a standing as you have at Cochin without an auditor for house and factory. Your business has so increased that it cannot be trusted to men who say 'I will render an account when I go to Portugal' and meanwhile would have in their possession two or three thousand cruzades or even more."[2] As long as the great Governor was in India he was able to enforce discipline in financial as well as in ordinary political administration; but his fight—not wholly successful—with Antonio Reall and the rest of the corrupt gang which controlled Cochin trade, showed that even under his rigorous rule the Portuguese administrative system was corrupt and inefficient.

This obvious inefficiency in the organisation of government was emphasised by two factors which seem most strange to modern eyes. One was the right which subordinate officials had of corresponding direct with the King and high officials in Portugal. Every mail took to Lisbon slanderous letters from almost every official of importance in India in which accusations were freely made against superior officers leading often to sudden changes of policy and much scandal. Albuquerque was so disgusted with this that he wrote to the King about Antonio Reall, his subordinate in Cochin: "You recommend Antonio Reall to me—considering how he has abused me calling me, thief, Moor, coward and the confidence you place in him, it is I who want a recommenda-

1. *Corpo Chronologico,* Part I. Maco 83. Document 60.
2. *Cartas,* Letter dated 16th October, 1510.

tion to him." "What reigns here," he says in another letter, "is the wish to acquire authority before Your Highness by representing to you the defects of others."[1] In a letter written by one of the subordinate officials to the King appears the following passage about the Governor: "I make known to Your Highness that Lopo Soares came to India in an evil hour."[2] This system of private correspondence by officials continued to the end, and much of the trouble between the officials in India was due to it.

More than even this, there was no sense of loyalty among the officials even as against the enemies. The officers at Cochin were always intriguing with the local Chiefs. Not a few of them were said to be in league with the enemies of Portugal. Gaspar Gonsalves openly tells the King that his "esteemed fidalgo of the Household, Antonio Reall of Cochin was leagued with the robbers."[3] Lorenco Moreno, another officer at Cochin, got an officer of the Rajah of Cochin to write to the King of Portugal praising his qualities and recommending him for promotion. Naturally discipline was most lax; and as fidalgos could not be punished in India there was almost complete disorganisation when the Governor was a weak or timid man. Even in the time of Albuquerque personal quarrels played a great part in Portuguese history as the struggle between d'Almeida and him proves. Desertion to the enemy was a common affair, and fidalgos of note, not infrequently, took service with Indian rulers after committing some crime for which they would have been punished if they had returned to Lisbon. The case of Goncalo Vaz Coutinho is of particular interest as it sheds much light on the discipline of Portuguese officers. Countinho belonged to a well-known and powerful family in Portugal. In India his life was a career of crime

1. *Cartas* 1st April, 1512.
2. *Gavitas Antigas,* Maco 6 Document No. 51.
3. Ibid.

for which the Governor imprisoned him along with some others. Coutinho bribed one of the officials and walked out of prison in daylight with his other friends and straightaway joined the army of Adil Shah who was fighting against Portugal.

When discipline was so lax, and officials were fighting against each other, it was clearly impossible to build up an administrative system. Even if some Governor like Albuquerque or Joao de Castro wanted to improve discipline and bring into existence an efficient system of Government, the right of private trade and the great privileges of the Church would have made reform impossible. These two may be said to be the distinguishing characteristics of the Portuguese system. The permission to engage in private trade was given to all officers, and the result, as we have pointed out earlier, was that each man engaged only on his busiess leaving the King's affairs to look after themselves. Even the soldiers were allowed to trade after serving 9 years, without which inducement few men would have come out on service. The effect of this was disastrous. The perquisites of office were in fact the only consideration which made officers accept appointments. The Governorship "of India" was the easiest way to mend a ruined fortune, and, with one or two exceptions, most of the Governors who came out to India amassed enormous wealth by every possible means.

The vested interests of the Church were even more powerful than those of the officials. Of this we shall speak later on.

It should be clear from what has been said that nothing in the nature of a financial or administrative system was developed by the Portuguese. In fact, compared to that of the Portuguese, the Government of the Zamorin or of Adil Shah was better organised and more efficient. But we should not forget that Europe, at the end of the 15th century and during the course of the 16th, was only slowly evolving out of the feudal system. Organised Government, such as we know it now, existed nowhere in Europe. The indiscipline of the Portuguese officers was but a faint echo of the rebellious attitude of the baronage in Europe. There was no such thing as national patriotism in the 15th century when Frenchmen were fighting in alliance with the English against their King, and Englishmen claimed to be French rather than English. The Portuguese were thus in no way different from other European nations. The only difference was that at the time that other European peoples developed their political systems and organised their national life, Portugal had the misfortune to fall under the yoke of foreigners.

But on one thing Portuguese policy was definite from the very beginning. "Let it be known for certain," wrote d'Almeida, the first Viceroy, "that as long as you may be powerful at sea you will hold India as yours, and if you do not possess this power little will avail you a fortress on shore."[1] From this policy the Portuguese never departed. To maintain the command of the sea, the Portuguese captains were prepared to take the most heroic measures. Their imperialism, if we may use a modern term, was a system of naval bases extending from Ormuz to Malacca from which they could command all trade, and hold to ransom the vessels of other nations. They realised that once the command of the high seas was lost to them, they could not possess the trade of India. The system of blockades by which they tried to ruin the trade of Indian States was not wholly successful, especially in Kerala, but they were able to command the main line of communication between Arabia, Egypt and India. Their important naval station in Kerala was Cochin where

1. Annals of Sciences and Letters, April 1658.

they had a well furnished magazine and the necessary equipments for the repair of ships.

One point with regard to Portuguese military policy is worthy of notice. At least from the time of Albuquerque the Portuguese decided to use Kerala men under the control of Portuguese officers in their fights with Mahommedan rulers. This policy, which was perfected later under Dupleix and Clive, came to be the basis of European rule in India. But the credit of the discovery must go to the Portuguese who used Kerala troops extensively in their campaigns. Many Malabarese even attained distinction in the service of Portugal. One individual who deserves special mention is Antonio Fernandes Chale, a Nayar convert, who held various commands and was created a Knight of the Order of Christ. He died fighting at the battle of the river Sanguiler in 1571 and was buried with honours in Goa.

Portuguese authority was not based on any great military strength. There was only sufficient garrison in each fort to defend the place; and when it came to offensive actions the Portuguese met with but little success even as against minor Chieftains. Albuquerque, who was the only Governor who pleaded for a definite military policy based on fortresses, wanted no more than 3,000 soldiers to garrison and protect the factories. He wrote to the King in a letter dated 1st April, 1512: "Furthermore do I say Senhor that for effecting treaties with India and for the establishment of factories, such as are necessary for your service .... for three years would I keep three thousand men here, well armed and with every equipment for erecting fortresses." As long as Albuquerque was in command he kept up an efficient force and strained every nerve to do so. His successor, Lopo Soares, neglected the army; and thereafter the Portuguese military power was never a menace to any Indian Ruler. The soldiers who were sent out from Portugal were a disorderly rabble who had neither discipline nor military experience. Their pay was always in arrears, and it is on record that the company that came out in 1548 had to beg in the streets for food. No soldier was entitled to receive his pay until after one year's service in India, and even then payment could only be made after unnecessary and prolonged formalities.

The Portuguese policy towards the Indian communities in Kerala is of interest. Their religious policy has to be reserved for later discussion. From the social and political point of view it may be noted that converts to Christianity enjoyed all the privileges of the Portuguese citizens, and no distinction based on colour or race was recognised. The main and central fact of their relations with Indian communities was the encouragement of intermarriage. The Portuguese had no kind of racial prejudice, and from the very beginning their relations were socially cordial. Albuquerque started a policy of encouraging intermarriage, presiding at the functions himself and giving dowries to couples so married. Lands and houses were allotted to them within the fortress walls. They were exempted from paying customs especially for silk from China and for sugar from Portugal. Even for the rest they paid only four per cent to the Rajah of Cochin. "I was in Cochin." wrote Caesar Frederick, the Venetian traveller, "when the Viceroy of the King of Portugal wrought what he could to break the privilege of the citizens and to make them pay customs as others did; at which time the citidens were glad to weigh their pepper in the night that they landed the ships with all that went to Portugal and stole the custom in the night. The King of Cochin having understanding of this would not suffer any more pepper to be weighed. Then presently after this, the merchants were licensed to do as they did before and there was no more speech of this matter, nor any wrong done."[1] The rights of married men were indeed very considerable. It should be remembered that the Portuguese, themselves, brought no women with them to India. The difficulties of the voyage and the precariousness of life in India made settled family life among Europeans impossible. The idea of regular marital connections "by the regulations of Albuquerque" became, therefore, the custom, and helped much to keep the Portuguese flag flying in their fortresses even when their military strength had become negligible.

Towards the Mahommedans the attitude of the Portuguese was one of inveterate hostility. Their one idea was to root out the trade of the Moors and to destroy the Mahommedans as a race so far possible. This was not only due to commercial rivalry, but to a hostility which the Iberian powers had inherited from their long-drawn out fight with the Moors in Spain and Africa. Whenever a Moor was captured the most barbarous tortures were inflicted on him and he was either killed or made a slave. The whole history of the Portuguese in India is nothing but a commentary on the statement of Barros that the Moors were the "Enemies of God." Towards the Hindus they had no such enmity. Their relations with Hindu noblemen and Rajahs in Kerala were very cordial from a social point of view. When friendly relations existed between the Zamorin and the Portuguese, the scruples and superstitions of the Hindu ruler were respected by the Portuguese. To the Nayars as a whole they behaved with great consideration. The policy of religious presecution against the Hindus, which was attempted in Goa, was never tried in Kerala. The relations between the Native Christians and the Portuguese were of a most complicated nature and deserve to be treated specially.

---

1. *Hakluyt's Voyages*: Vol. V. pp. 392-395.

CHAPTER XIII

PORTUGUESE RELIGIOUS POLICY IN KERALA

The Portuguese, we are told, came to India with a Cross in one hand and a sword in the other. Their own pretensions in the East were based first on the Bull of Nicholas V, dated 8th January 1454, by which Affonso V was given, by virtue of the pontifical and apostolic authority of the Pope, exclusive right to all the countries that might be discovered by the Portuguese in Africa and India. The conversion of the inhabitants of the lands so discovered was to be one of the objects of Portuguese policy. In fact Dom Joao II, who was the real originator of the expedition, had much of this evangelistic spirit in him. To the pious Kings of mediaeval Europe conversion of the heathens seemed to be an imperative duty.

Neither King Manuel, who succeeded Dom Joao, nor Vasco da Gama, the leader of the expedition, had any ambition in this direction. Vasco, in fact, had such crude notions that he mistook a Hindu temple of Kali to be a Christian church and worshipped there with all solemnity.[1] Europe knew only Islam as a religion different from Christianity. The idol of Kali was mistaken for a representation of the Virgin, and, though the service must have appeared curious, nothing therein excited his suspicion. Cabral's instructions were based on the assumption that the inhabitants of India were a sort of primitive Christians and that they only wanted instruction to become Romans in their methods of worship.[2] Cabral's fleet contained 8 Franscian friars, 8 chaplains and a chaplain major. Faria mentions that at

1. Faria y Sousa, p. 46,
2. Castenheda III. 130.

Cannanore Cabral knew of the existence of some Christians of St. Thomas under Armenian Bishops.[1] Two Christians from Cranganore, Joseph and Mathew, approached Cabral with a request to take them to Europe, and gave a description of their customs to him. Both of them were taken to Lisbon and educated in the Catholic Faith. Mathew died in Lisbon. Joseph travelled to Venice, Rome and other places, wrote his impressions of those countries and published them in the form of a book entitled "The Travels of Joseph the Indian." Vasco da Gama received messages from Christians in Cranganore who sent a deputation to him asking him to take them under the protection of Portugal.[2]

The Christians of the Syrian Church had been treated generously by Hindu Rulers who had allowed them to live without molestation or interference. Even Gouvea, the biographer of de Meneses, states, "that their privileges were most religiously guarded by native Rajahs." They lived in religious matters under their own *Metrans*. And yet, though the Hindu Rulers had treated them like this, at the very first opportunity, they hastened to disclaim their allegiance and to accept the sovereignty of the King of Portugal. Little did they imagine that by this change they were inviting on themselves a reign of religious terror and oppression which was to culminate in the Synod of Diamper. The centuries of schism and split, which have weakened the ancient and prosperous Church of Malabar may be traced to the foolish and short-sighted action by which its representatives accepted the authority of Portugal. *Kerala Pazhama* gives detailed information[3] about their visit to Gama, which account is also corroborated by Faria.[4] They surrendered their privileges

---

1. Faria p. 59.
2. Ibid p. 67.
3. *Kerala Pazhama* p. 24.
4. Faria pp. 33 and 61.

and authority to Portugal and undertook to conduct their affairs only in the name of the Portuguese King. The ancient records and insignia which their Chief possessed were also handed over to Gama. More than even this, they suggested to him that with their help he should conquer the Hindu Kindoms and invited him to build a fortress for this purpose in Cranganore. This was the recompense which the Hindu Rajahs received for treating with liberality and kindness Christians in their midst.

The Portuguese policy towards the Christians developed with their increasing authority. The newly converted Christians in Cochin and Quilon were declared to be under the judicial protection of the Portuguese. In all quarrels between a new Christian and a local inhabitant the former was to be handed over to the Portuguese.[1] The main controversy with the Queen of Quilon was about the privileged treatment, which the Portugese insisted, should be meted out to the Christians.[2] Under Albuquerque a new policy was initiated of expelling non-Christians from within the walls of Portuguese fortresses. This order led to a number of conversions in Cochin and in Cranganore.

During the lifetime of King Manuel the policy of conversion was not dictated by any religious zeal. Its purpose was merely to strengthen the Portuguese hold on the coast. But in the time of Joao III, evangelisation was taken up as a main object of policy. A Bishopric at Goa was created in 1538 and Frei Joao d'Albuquerque, a cousin of the great Governor,

1. Faria P. 61.

2. Over the St. Thomas or "Syrian" Christians the Portuguese exercised no authority. Moens in his *Memorial* says: "The company has never had any authority nor could have over St. Thomas Christians who were always subjects of the country princes. Not even the Portuguese exercised any jurisdiction over them." *Memorial* P. 180.

was sent out as Bishop. Cochin was soon raised to a Bishopric, and the Kerala coast was placed under it. The King was particularly anxious about the spread of Christianity and wrote to the Viceroy, Joao de Castro, demanding that all the power of the Portuguese should be directed to this purpose. "The great concernment which lies upon Christian princes to look to matters of Faith and to employ their forces for its preservation makes me advise you how sensible I am that not only in many parts of India under our subjection but in our city of Goa, idols are worshipped, places in which our Faith may be more reasonably expected to flourish; and being well informed with how much liberty they celebrated heathenish festivals we command you to discover by diligent officers all the idols and to demolish and break them up in pieces where they are found, proclaiming severe punishments against any one who shall dare to work, cast, make in sculpture, engrave, paint or bring to light any figure of an idol in metal, brass, wood, plaster or any other matter, or bring them from other places; and against who publicly or privately celebrate any of their sports, or assist and hide the Brahmins, the sworn enemies of the Christian profession ... It is our pleasure that you punish them with that severity of the law without admitting any appeal or dispensation in the least."[1] As the Portuguese had no territorial possessions in Kerala, except within their fortress walls, this inhuman policy had only an indirect effect. The Governor was instructed to try and convert the Rajah of Cochin who, however, was not so pliant in this matter as in others. The cunning Rajah of Tanur more than once offered to become a Christian, and in fact was formally baptised at Goa, but on his return he kept up his old customs and denied the conversion. But even in Cochin, Cannanore and Quilon none but Christians were allowed to live within

1. Jacinto Frere Andrade. *Life of Dom Joao Castro* Translated into English by Sir Peter Wyche 1664. p. 45.

the fortress. In 1567 it was decided by the ecclesiastical council that no Christian was to engage infidel doctors or even be shaved by an infidel barber.

The policy of conversion was naturally unsuccessful in Kerala where the population was under the rule of Hindu Rajahs. The narrow spirit of intolerance which animated the Portuguese was, therefore, felt more by the native Christians than by the Hindu population. The Portuguese Christians always looked upon the local Christians as heretics. Antonio de Gouvea, the enthusiastic historian of Archbishop Meneses, writing in 1609, thus states the attitude of the Catholic Church. "Voila, certes le piteux etat de ces peuples, viola le Chrestiens de St. Thomas, plongez es profondes tenebres et erreurs des le jour que l'eglise de Babylone, leur presenta le hauage plein de poison nestorien et a dure jusques a l'a notre seigneur 1599; quand le seigneur Frere Alexis de Meneses les ramena au gyron de leur mere la sainte eglise Catholique."[1] As soon as an ecclesiastical policy was clearly developed by the establishment of the Archiepiscopal See of Goa with a Bishopric in Cochin, and with the foundation of monastic Orders, an attempt was made to make the Syrian Christians conform to Roman practices. The first attempt was made by the Franciscans who founded a college at Cranganore in 1545 for the education of priests. The Kathanars, or Syrian priests who were trained and ordained by them, were, however, disowned by the Syrians. The Syrian Church in Kerala was administered by *Metrans* or Bishops sent out from Bussorah. Their influence was strong enough to resist Catholic aggression, and, as a result, in 1558 the Portuguese authorities issued an order that foreign ecclesiastics should not be allowed to enter Kerala. On the failure of this attempt the matter was again taken up by the

---

1. *Historio Orientale des grands progres de l'eglise Catholique*: Anvers 1609, p. 29.

Society of Jesus. They established a college at Vaipukotta in 1587. Instruction in this college, of which the first Principal was Antonio Morales, was given in the Syrian language. But, in spite of this concession, the attempt met with but indifferent success, and, till the time of Alexis de Meneses, the Syrian Christian community continued to be self-governing in internal matters.

In Alexis de Meneses, Archbishop of Goa, Rome had an agent suitable in every way for great political and ecclesiastical missions. Born of the highest nobility, a relation of Kings, able to defy Governments when necessary and to use them when expedient, trained alike in the methods of diplomacy as of force, de Meneses was of the type of priest-politicians whom the Holy See has produced at all times, from Hildebrand to Antonelli. Moreover, de Meneses was intensely religious. He came out as the Archbishop of Goa with no other idea than the spiritual conquest of India and the extension of the powers of the Holy See. Clement VIII in a special brief asked him to enquire into the state of the Malabar Churches. Like most men of his time, what seemed imperative to him was the "reclamation" of the heretic Christians rather than the conversion of the heathens. With single-minded zeal he set himself immediately to the task of bringing under Rome the Syrian Churches in Kerala. With this object he landed in Cochin on the 26th of January 1599. Arriving at the time when the siege of Kottakkal was going on, de Meneses's first business was diplomatic rather than ecclesiastical. He had to persuade the King of Cochin not to attack a feudatory of the Zamorin during the siege. After he was successful in that mission, de Meneses elaborated his plans for bringing the Malabar Christians within the Church. This could only be done by a regularly constituted Synod, at which, however, it was impossible to get a majority for surrender to Rome, as the native Christians were very tenacious of their beliefs. Moreover the "Syrian" Christians had found a leader of equal capacity in their Archdeacon who successfully resisted the spiritual and temporal blandishments of the Roman Church and kept his flock in allegiance to their ancient form of worship. Meneses called upon the Archdeacon to come to Cochin and submit to his authority. The Archdeacon had already applied to Bussorah for a Bishop and he was expecting a Syrian Prelate to reach Malabar in time to take up the fight. But the Bishop did not arrive on the fixed date. The Archdeacon rose to the occasion; he refused to recognise the Roman Church; and a Synod which he called at Angamali swore along with the Kathanars to uphold the traditions of the Church without any change and not to accept any Bishop but the one sent out by the Patriarch. It was also agreed that Catholic clergymen should not be allowed to say Mass in Syrian Churches, and that the Kathanars trained at the colleges at Vaipukotta should not be allowed to enter native churches.

De Meneses was furious. He denounced the Archdeacon as a traitor and heretic, and decided upon immediate action against him.

He suggested to the Rajah of Cochin that he should arrest the Archdeacon and hand him over to the Portuguese authorities. As the Rajah would not agree to this, the Archbishop pressed him to use all his temporal authority to make the Christian community bend to the wishes of Rome. After some hesitation the Rajah of Cochin agreed. He did so on the promise that de Meneses would intervene on his behalf for the continuation of certain annual gifts of money which the Portuguese used to make to him but which had been stopped. After the agreement, the minister of the Rajah went along with the Archbishop and announced in all churches that it was the desire of the Ruler that they should obey the orders of Rome.

Armed thus with the temporal authority of the heathen King, whose good offices he did not disdain to use in coercing the Christians, de Meneses went from church to church and used all possible methods to get the St. Thomas Church to accept the supremacy of Rome. A great Synod was held in 1599 for this purpose at Diamper (Udaimperoor) in one of the historical churches of the Christian community of Malabar, and de Meneses carried the day. But his success was only partial. A section of the Syrian Church refused to abide by the decisions of the Synod and continued in its allegiance to Antioch. This was the first of the great schisms in the Malabar Church.

The Church rivalled the State in authority and wealth in the affairs of the Portuguese. The Archbishops and Bishops lived in great magnificence. The property of the Churches and the Orders, and the revenue which the State, itself, allowed to them were out of all proportion to the wealth of Portuguese India. Though the Religious Orders, as well as the Church, had large revenues of their own, the State continued to support them. There was levied from the early days of Portuguese establishment in India a one per cent tax for the support of the clergy. The number of the clergy was far in excess of the number of laymen, especially as a large proportion of sodiers, who came out from Portugal on landing in India joined one of the Orders, because they were not entitled to receive their own pay till after one year of service. The expenditure on ecclesiastics had become a scandal as early as 1550. In 1552 Botelho, writing to King Joao III, the most zealous of all Christian Kings, stated: "The religious in this country desire to spend so freely and give so many alms at the expense of Your revenues that a large part of it goes in this........A great part of the revenue is thus alienated."[1]

1. Botelho's *Cartas*, p. 35.

In 1631, the Viceroy wrote that in certain areas in Travancore the Jesuits had become masters, that they did not obey his orders and that they had usurped Royal authority and jurisdiction.

Cochin was the seat of a Bishopric. Besides a large Cathedral, there were in that city monasteries of the Society of Jesus, of the Franciscans, of the Dominicans, a monastery of Augustine Monks and another of St. Pauls. There was also an ecclesiastical college. At Quilon, besides the famous Church of St. Thomas which was the cause of much quarrel, "there was a misericordia and a hospital, and the Church was represented by a Vicar-General with two religious Houses, one of St. Francis and one of the Company of Jesus."[1] In every little fort the Church flourished similarly, but at the expense of the State.

The overbearing attitude of the ecclesiastics towards the administration was a matter of complaint from the very beginning. Alone of all the Governors, Albuquerque refused to bow to their pretensions and in fact carried matters with a high hand against the priests. An incident which happened at Cannanore when he was Governor illustrates both the extreme pretensions of the priests and Albuquerque's own attitude towards them. A native Christian who had killed a Hindu had taken sanctuary in a church. Albuqerque ordered the captain, Diogo Correa, to hand him over to the Rajah, which was done. When Albuquerque left Cannanore, the priest fined the captain a heavy sum and placed the whole of Cannanore under an interdict for the high crime of obeying the Governor. Albuquerque was furious that Correa did not take stern measures against the priest and, as a disciplinary action, dismissed that unfortunate man.

One important fact remains to be noticed with regard to the religious policy of the Portuguese. That is the missionary work of St. Francis Xavier.

---

1. *Noticias da India,* p. 235.

Francis Xavier, the youngest son of a Spanish gentleman, was born in 1505 in the hilly tracts of the Pyrenees. The name of his family came from his mother, the heiress of the Houses of Azpilqueta and Xavier. His father, Juan de Jasso, was high in the employment of the King of Arragon. One of his sisters, Moddelena, who also held a post at the court of Queen Isabella, became later on the famous Abbess of the Poor Clares at Gandia. Very early in life he began to show signs of extreme religiousness and devotion to the Church. He was sent to the Paris University for study where he made the acquaintance of Pierre Lefevre. After completing his studies, Francis became a lecturer on the logic and metaphysics of Aristotle. It was while thus employed that he came under the influence of Ignatius Loyola. He and Lefevre were among the first six who, along with Ignatius, founded the society of Jesus. It was by chance that Xavier came to be sent out to India. When Joao III asked Ignatius to suggest two members of his Society for missionary work in India, the choice first fell on Simon Rodrigues and Bobadilla. But Bobadilla fell ill, and, in his place, Ignatius nominated Xavier.[1] After receiving the blessings of the Pope on the 15th of March 1540, Xavier left Rome with no other provision than his breviary. He reached India early next year and began a remarkable career of evangelisation. After a short time in Goa, he turned his attention to the Kerala coast; and his main work in India was accomplished among the fisherfolk and other low caste people of Travancore. In a letter written to the "Brethren of the Society of Jesus" dated January 1544 he describes his method of work among the untouchables, which was somewhat in this manner — "When I first came, I asked them if they knew anything of our Lord Jesus Christ. They only replied that they were Christians and that as they were ignorant of Portu-

1. *Life and Letters of St. Francis Xavier*: H. J. Coleridge (S. J.) London, Burns & Oats, 1812, vol. I p. 58.

guese they know nothing about the precepts and mysteries of our holy religion. We could not understand one another as I spoke Castilian and they spoke Malabar. So I picked out the most intelligent and well-read of them and then sought out with the greatest diligence men who knew both languages. We held meetings for several days. By our joint efforts and with infinite difficulty we translated the Catechism into the Malabar tongue. This I learnt by heart and then I began to go through all the villages of the coast, calling around me by the sound of a bell as many as I could, children and men. I assembled them twice a day and taught them the Christian doctrine and thus within the space of one month, the children had it well by heart."[1]

His piety, obvious sincerity, simple life and overwhelming faith appealed to the ignorant folk among whom he worked. Considerable success attended his mission, especially in the southern parts of Travancore where large numbers of fishermen and other low caste people are said to have become Christians. Xavier, however, did not stay to consolidate and organise his work, and left Kerala for other fields. After his departure a considerable portion of his flock seems to have returned to their original habits.

Xavier's mission is of interest, because he may be considered to be the first missionary, in our modern sense. He came to preach the Gospel, to give to the Indian world what he considered the true light. His methods were crude, but he showed an appreciation of popular psychology; and his life, spent among foreign people in the service of his Church, not as the member of a powerful community or as Bishop, but as a preacher, was indeed a source of inspiration.

---

1. H. J. Coleridge: *Op. cit* p 151.

CHAPTER XIV

THE CAUSES OF PORTUGUESE FAILURE

European writers and historians are accustomed to devote considerable space to explain the causes for the downfall of the Portuguese. It is impossible to understand the fall of Portuguese power unless the main characteristics of their hold on the East are understood. It should, first, be kept in mind that the Portuguese had at no time any Empire in India. The extraordinary habit of the Portuguese writers and historians of talking as if the few fortresses they held on the coast constituted India has misled many European writers into the belief that at some earlier time the Portuguese possessed a territorial empire. In fact the Portuguese possess even now the main centres which they possessed in the 16th century, excepting the fortresses of Cochin, Cannanore and Quilon. In Goa alone they possessed a small territory, which they still hold and govern. Their supremacy was entirely on the sea, and their fall was also, therefore, a matter of naval power.

It is, indeed, a matter of some curiosity that the Portuguese should have held undisputed mastery of the sea routes for over a century. But the explanation of it lies in the fact that Egypt, which was the natural rival of any Power claiming authority on the waters of the Arabian Sea, had been reduced to a province of the Ottoman Empire. The Ottoman naval policy was at no time directed to a maintenance of supremacy on Indian waters. The orientation of Turkish policy under Suleiman the Magnificent was towards the Western Medierranean. The Turkish admirals were fighting in order to establish their supremacy in Crete, and, under Khair-ed-din Barbarossa, they were menacing the very shores of Italy and Sicily. It is curious that, at the time when the Portuguese supremacy in the Indian Ocean was unquestioned, Barbarossa was making the Turkish name a by-word for terror to the coastal population of the Mediterranean. The European ambitions of Turkey made her neglect the question of the Indian Seas after one or two sporadic attempts. It was this alone that gave the Portuguese their power on the sea. When another nation, equally well equipped, like the Dutch, challenged their power, it fell to the ground like a house of cards. As against the smaller Indian coastal Powers they were able to maintain their maritime pretensions; but against the Dutch and the English they were powerless.

We have shown that, so far as administration was concered, the Portuguese in India developed nothing in the nature of an efficient system. From the earliest times, they showed themselves to be corrupt, inefficient and altogether unfit for the arts of government. The Portuguese soldiers were certainly brave and cared little for life. Some of their leaders were chivalrous and honourable men; but few are the names in Portuguese Indian history that could add to the military glory of Portugal. Duarte Pacheco and Affonso Albuquerque are the only two names who could bear comparison with men like Bussy or Dupleix, Clive or Goddard. Indeed, but for the pompous exaggerations of her historians, the hundred and fifty years of monopoly, which Portugal enjoyed, pregnant as it is with future history, would have been considered hardly more than an unimportant incident in the history of India.

The connection of the Portuguese with India was mainly a question of trade. What Almeida and Albuquerque desired was to turn to Portugal the whole commercial wealth of India. "The volume of Indian trade is enormous; silks, brocades, copper, mercury, coral etc.; it is almost beyond belief" wrote Albuquerque. It is characeristic, therefore, of the

Portuguese relations with India that, while their political prestige diminished and their fortresses and factories were defenceless, the trade continued to increase. The largest commercial fleets that sailed to India were sent after Philip II of Spain had become also the King of Portugal. Till the very end of the Portuguese maritime supremacy the commercial value of the Indian connection kept on rising. But it is at the same time true that the administration itself was never properly solvent. The Governors were always in lack of funds. From the time of Martim de Sousa the Government had taken to the disastrous policy of debasing the coinage. In its final stages the administration permitted dues to be paid in copper, even accepting in certain ports Chinese copper. The reason for this was that copper was useful for casting cannon; and as the fortresses were left without guns this was the only method of improvising a defence.

From the very beginning, the officers had no other object but private gain. Cosmo Annes, in a letter dated 30th December 1549, had complained that things were going from bad to worse in Cochin. A letter of Alvaro de Mendonco to the King, dated January 8th 1540, declared that the conduct of the Viceroy was so corrupt that "no one could remain here who could have a loophole for departing." The only object of the officials was to enrich themselves either by peculation or by private trade.

Officers were not regularly paid. In fact, till the time of Joao de Castro, the pay was not fixed. Even when there was a nominal salary, often it was not forthcoming. Garcia de Noronha neglected to pay the salaries of the officers; and it was not uncommon that payment was long in arrears. For Indian service salary was of course the least consideration. A system of percaloes or profits was attached to each office, which brought to the holder enormous sums. The pay and profits of each appointment were calculated with great care in 1612 by Figuere de Falcao, and this document, which may still be examined in Lisbon, gives remarkable figures. One minor captaincy, the pay of which for three years did not come up to £. 1,000, brought a profit of £. 57,000 to the holder. When the authorities in Portugal came to know of the enormous profits attached to these offices, it seemed to them to be a royal and easy way to enrich the coffers of the State. The King ordered that all these appointments should be put up for auction and sold to the highest bidder—surely a singular way of carrying on Government.[1]

This was not all. The ruling authorities in Lisbon developed the custom of sending out to India orphan girls, with patents of Indian appointments as dowry. No doubt, in modern States also, the system of providing public offices to those who undertake the obliging duty of marrying well-placed women is not quite unknown. But the Portuguese government had no qualms about it. Offices were given openly as dowries; and one lady brought with her out to India the King's order of appointment for the captaincy of Cranganore to any one who cared to marry her. Matters went so far, that the Viceroy had to represent that this procedure would lessen the revenue which the State received by auctioning the appointments; and in accordance with his representation a law was made whereby offices given as dowry were valid only for three years.

Nepotism was another vice among the Portuguese authorities. The Governors and their officers brought out to India their sons and nephews and placed them in all the offices of advantage, and pro-

1. Faciscul0 6. *Archivo Portuguez Oriental* No. 353. P. 1059.

tected them in their career of peculation. Gaspar Gonsalvo writing early in the 16th century during the Governorship of Lope Soares represented the matter to the King thus: "Your Highness should not send out as Captain-in-Chief nor as factor, nor as one for your treasury any who has a son or relative or any near relatives. Your Highness should be particularly careful about the factor who comes out to Cochin, because the factory of Cochin is the largest house that King or Prince ever had and therefore it needs a man of great sufficiency."[1] Unfortunately this excellent piece of advice was never taken.

It could be imagined what utter demoralisation would characterise an administration based on these principles. There was no honesty in public services, no discipline in the army and no loyalty towards each other. "Robbery," wrote St. Francis Xavier, "is so public and common, that it hurts no one's character and is hardly counted as a fault." As for discipline, there are some most extraordinary cases recorded. In 1539, a company of soldiers, taking possession of a fortress in Diu, turned their guns on their countrymen. Nothing was done to them, though a later Viceroy wrote to the King that he "would have seen them dead and the site of the fortress sown with salt."[2]

No nation with an administration so corrupt and based on principles so unwholesome could conquer a country; and, in spite of popular belief to the contrary, India was never an easy country to conquer. The British, with much greater naval, military and economic power, and an organisation which was the model of all imperial governments, took 100 years to conquer India. From their first intervention in

1. *Gavitas Antigas*. Maco, 6. Document No. 81.
2. Letter October 30, 1540, of Joao Castro, Investigator Portuguez.

Arcot to the annexation of the Punjab, there is a century of unceasing warfare, in which the superior organisation and military equipment of the British finally gained for them the Empire of India. And the British were favoured by the circumstance that, at the time they stood forth as an Indian Power bidding for supremacy in the land, India was divided and disorganised as a result of the decay of Mogul power. The Portuguese never had, and never could have had,anything like an empire, or even the shadow of a territorial power in India. Established in Goa, Daman, Diu and Cochin, they controlled the sea trade. But on land they were powerless. The Zamorin drove them out of Chaliyam. The minor princes, whose territories lay beyond the range of their ships' guns, defied them. In fact, Portuguese India is a myth. One might as well talk of Abyssinian India, because the little town of Janjira was held by an Abyssinian family. It is merely the pompous boast of Portuguese historians that have conveyed to Europe generally the impression that the Portuguese were in some way the masters of India. There is a Portuguese "Governor General" for the few square miles marked Portuguese on the map, and still, that territory is officially called India, or the Estado da India. Historical foolishness and meaningless pretensions could go no further. The Portuguese never lost India, because they never possessed it; they never came anywhere near to possessing it. Theirs was merely a supremacy on the sea gained by purely adventitious circumstances, which vanished with the arrival in Indian waters of the Dutch and the British.

CHAPTER XV

KERALA AT THE END OF THE PORTUGUESE PERIOD

The Portuguese relations with Kerala lasted for over a period of 150 years. Politically, economically and socially, the adventurers who followed Vasco da Gama represented a type different from those to which Kerala was accustomed. Their arrival on the scene had undeniable effects on the whole life of Kerala. It changed the course of Malabar history, introduced new factors in its economic life, and materially altered the social conditions. A survey of Kerala at the time that the Dutch drove the Portuguese out of Kerala waters would show the extent of the change which their influence had brought about.

Politically the most important result of the Portuguese establishment in Kerala was that it checked the development of Kerala into a single confederacy under the Zamorin. The whole history of the 160 years, from the establishment of a factory by Cabral at Cochin to the capture of that fort by Van Goens, may be summarised from the point of view of Kerala as a successful attempt by the Rajah of Cochin, with the help of the Portuguese, to stem the tide of the expanding power of the Zamorin. Cochin was reduced to an absolute dependency of Portugal. But, while the Cochin Rajah grew powerless as against the Portuguese Captain who could at any moment reduce his palace to ashes, he became a powerful Ruler as against the princes and chieftains of the interior. From a local chief of no importance, the Cochin Rajah, with the help of the Portuguese, rose to the position of a powerful prince, independent of the Zamorin and a rival to him in the claim of allegiance of the southern princes.

Besides this, the growth of royal power, which was a development of significance, also met with a decisive check. The policy of the Portuguese was to deal directly with the small princes and Chiefs and to conciliate them by money gifts. They made alliances with princes, like the Rajah of Tanur who was a feudatory of the Zamorin, and the Rajah of Procaud over whom the Ruler of Cochin claimed authority. By this method the Portuguese were able to safeguard their commercial interests, and at the same time see that no Kerala Ruler became powerful enough to drive them out of Cochin or Cannanore. During the 150 years of Portuguese connection the power of the smaller chiefs continued to increase at the expense of the larger Rajahs. The Rulers of coastal tracts became powerful, and began to question the authority of the suzerains, knowing well that in any contest they could get the support of the Portuguese if they could pay for it. The Chiefs who rose to power as a result of this policy were the Rajahs of Procaud, Mangat, Parur, Quilon and Tanur. Tanur, especially, played the Portuguese against the Zamorin and the Zamorin against the Portuguese, and by this means came to occupy an important position in the history of Kerala. It will be remembered that the fortress of Chaliyam was sold to the Portuguese by this ruler; that he even went so far as Goa, proclaiming loudly that he wanted to be converted, and that on his return, after all these pretensions of goodwill, quietly marched with the Zamorin to Vaduthalai to fight against the Portuguese. The increased power of the smaller Chief was a direct result of the decisive check to the growth of the Zamorin's royal power. It put back the clock of Kerala history by 200 years, and perpetuated the division of the country into small principalities, each jealous of its neighbour and carrying on interminable feuds with others. It was this state of political disunion, which the Dutch took great care to foster, that made Kerala an easy prey for Hyder Ali.

Economically, Kerala underwent even greater changes. The Portuguese introduced into Kerala a number of new products such as the cashew tree—still known in Kerala as the Feringhee tree. They introduced tobacco and its cultivation. But more than all, they created a world market for Kerala products. At the time of the Moorish trade Kerala spices were a delicacy which made a strong but not a very large appeal. The direct exportation of pepper, cardamom, cinnamon, ginger, and other Kerala produce into Europe created a great demand for them. In the course of a few years the economic situation of the country had altered as a result of this ever-increasing demand. Orta mentions that "pepper was grown from Cape Comorin to Cannanore. In Kerala it is largely consumed in the country itself. A large quantity goes to the Red Sea against the orders of the King but nothing can be so well guarded but that much will be taken westward by the Moors. Though there are some trees to the north of Cannanore they are so few that we do not take account of them." Almost every acre of ground capable of growing pepper and ginger was cultivated; and the trade which, before this time was mainly in the hands of a few big merchants became a business of the people at large. People were quick to appreciate the changed position. The Moors had merely bought what had been produced in the country. The Portuguese were anxious to get as much as could be produced, and even put pressure on Chiefs and Rulers to encourage pepper and ginger cultivation.

The Portuguese contact also introduced great changes in the cultivation of cocoanut. It would seem that cocoanut was not one of the major products of Malabar before the Portuguese came. *Unninili Sandesam,* which describes the trade of Kayamkulam, Quilon and other ports and mentions many different kinds of rice sold, does not mention cocoanuts even once as a commodity of export. For household and local uses cocoanut was grown; but there was nothing like a cultivation for purposes of trade. It was only in 1503 that the Portutugese learnt, from one of the prize ships taken off Curia Muria Islands, the use of coir as ropes for their ships. From that time coir became an important article of trade, and more for coir than for copra, cocoanut cultivation became popular. Orta says of coir in his *Colloquies*: "Of it they make the riggings and cordage for all ships. It is very serviceable for us, for it is very flexible and does not rot in salt water. All the ships are caulked with it so that it serves as linen, as oakum and as matting. These qualities make it good merchandise for Portugal."[1] To this day, coir is one of the chief exports of Kerala. Even in cocoanut trade the Portuguese connection with Africa was of help to Kerala. Seed nuts of a better and bigger type of cocoanut were introduced into Kerala by them and are even now called *kappal thenga* or cocoanuts from the ships. As cocoanut cultivation was particularly suited to the coastal tracts of Kerala, it soon became one of the chief products of the country. It is stated that at Cannanore in 1564 Dom Payo de Noronha cut down no less than 40,000 cocoanut trees as an act of terrorism.

The Portuguese had put a stop to the historic commercial connection between Kerala, Arabia and Egypt. In its place the new European trade had grown up, bringing more money and luxury into the country. The trade was more widespread, and the resulting prosperity was also not confined to ports of small communities but to the whole people. The construction of houses on European models became fashionable; and we are informed that at Cochin, Calicut, Quilon and other places there were many stately buildings. Money was plentiful; and the system of cash payments to Rulers, by which the Portuguese kept them in good humour, tended to the

1. Orta: *Colloquies* Page 141. Translation by Markham, London Southern & Co., MCMXII.

growth of greater luxury. More than all this, the old methods of Kerala warfare underwent great change. Firearms became common and helped to increase the power of the Chiefs and Rajahs. Fortifications were undertaken in a more systematic manner—both the Zamorin and the Rajah of Cannanore had trained artillery men in their service.

A hundred and fifty years of Portuguese trade had seen the growth of many new towns and the decay of old ones. Calicut continued to be the most important town on the West Coast; but Cochin, which had come into existence as the result of a great flood in 1341 and was only an unimportant village when Cabral arrived there, had risen to the position of a very important commercial centre. Its public buildings were imposing structures, and the fortress, rebuilt by Albuquerque, was one of the strongest in India. Caesar Frederick, who visited India between 1563 and 1581 described Cochin as "the chiefest place that the Portugals have in the Indies next unto Goa."[1] Baldeus mentions that the Jesuit Church and College facing the seashore had a lofty steeple......The College was three stories high. Caesar Frederick also mentions "that the Jesuit Church which was magnificently built of square stones exceeded all the rest in height and beauty." The Augustin Friars, Franciscans and Jesuits had likewise their several convents magnificently built with very pleasant gardens and walks. Captain Nieuhoff, himself, states that the Portuguese had beautified the city with many fine edifices, churches and monasteries. "In the suburbs towards the land-side were several godly churches, and a little nearer the seashore was the monastery of St. John. Here the Franciscans and Jesuits had likewise their several convents, all magnificently built with very pleasant gardens and walks. Among other steeples that

1. Hakluyts' *Voyages*. Vol. V. pp. 392-395.

of St. Paul, being magnificently built of square stones, excelled all the rest in height and beauty which is since demolished with all the other churches except one."[1] The growth of Cochin was entirely the result of Portuguese trade, and its importance dates only from the visit of Cabral.

Other towns which grew into importance were Chaliyam, where the Portuguese erected a fortress but from which they were driven out in 1570; Pudupattanam, which was founded by the Kunjalis as their capital, and Procaud, the Rajah of which became an important Chief only after his alliance with the Portuguese. But the older towns of Quilon and Cranganore lost a great deal of their importance. Cranganore, especially, became a cockpit of warfare between the Zamorin and the Portuguese, and its traditional greatness, dating back many centuries before Christ, vanished during this period.

Portuguese influence in matters of education is also worthy of notice. The colleges founded at Angamali and Cochin for the education of Malabar Christians in the Roman Faith were useful in spreading the knowledge of Latin and Portuguese. The later Rajahs of Cochin conversed fluently in Portuguese, and often corresponded directly in that language. In fact, till the establishment of British supremacy in Kerala, Portuguese continued to be the diplomatic language of the Kerala Rulers. For instance, all the letters addressed by the Zamorin to the English factor, for over half a century after the disappearance of the Portuguese from Kerala, were written in the language of Camoens.

For their own commercial and political purposes the Portuguese were forced to learn Malayalam; and the list of Kerala words at the end of

1. Nieuhoff's *Voyages*. p. 221.

the Rotiero may be said to be the forerunner of oriental research by Europeans. Francis Xavier's translation of the Catechism into Malayalam is the crude beginning of the new movement of translation from western languages which has become so marked a feature of Indian vernaculars to-day. The descriptions of Kerala left by Duarte Barbosa, Gaspar Correa and the historians must also be counted among the benefits which have resulted from the relations between Portugal and Kerala.

An influential school of history holds that the benefits, that India received from the direct contact with Europe, are of such a nature that, in spite of all the faults, the Portuguese should be considered as the pioneers of civilisation and as the forerunners of the British Empire. It may be permitted however, to question the correctness of the point of view, wrongly called historical, which thus tries to import retrospective values into events of an earlier date. Even accepting that the connection with Europe has been beneficial to India, it is open to doubt whether a century and a half of barbarous outrages, of unscrupulous plunder and of barren aggression, is not too great a price to pay for the doubtful benefits of having the way opened for other European traders. India's own direct trade was ruined, and, in its place, there was established a monopoly by alien races, which had the effect of draining the wealth of India into Europe. The Portuguese could not even claim what the Mahommedan Rulers of India could legitimately put forward in their justification, that they had a cultural contribution to make to the life of India, such as we may, even now, see in the magnificent architectural monuments at Agra, Delhi or Ahmedabad. The Portuguese of the 16th and the 17th centuries had nothing to teach the people of India except improved methods of killing people in war and the narrow feeling of bigotry in religion. Surely, these were not matters of such importance as to make it necessary for Indians to feel grateful towards Vasco da Gama or his successors. The relations between Portugal and India were barren of cultural or political results, and there is in that history nothing which any civilised nation can be proud of. A host of imaginative historians, anxious to sing the glory of their fatherland, have pictured to us the heroic story of a small nation going forth to conquer India and holding it under sway for 150 years, fighting and winning battles against great hordes and conquering heathen worlds for Christ. Europe has accepted as true, for too long a time, the myths and legends of Barros, Castenheda and Correa. The idea is wholly and absolutely untrue. The Portuguese had mastery of the Indian seas; but never had they the mastery of any area in India outside the range of their ships' guns. The battles they won were more mythical than actual; and the pompous descriptions of Portuguese historians should not make us forget that all their campaigns were nothing more than indecisive skirmishes against very minor local Chieftains. It is indeed a fine picture which writers have drawn for us—a small heroic country draining itself of its best blood in a great attempt to conquer and hold India! But the picture has not even a background of truth except in the vainglorious phraseology of the Portuguese Kings, who called their administrative representatives, the "Viceroys of India," and the few square miles of territory at Goa, the "Estado da India."

SECTION II

CHAPTER I

ARRIVAL OF THE DUTCH IN KERALA

The Dutch had for long looked with jealousy at the monopoly which the Portuguese enjoyed in the trade of the East. But the colossal power of Philip II of Spain who had also become the King of Portugal made any direct challenge to his naval power impossible for a long time. It was only after the defeat of the Spanish Armada in 1588 and the consequent blow to the naval prestige of Spain that the Dutch were emboldened to challenge the Portuguese in the Indian Seas. In 1592 at a meeting of the leading Dutch merchants held at Amsterdam it was decided to found a company for trading with India. In order to secure the necessary information about the route and gather a general idea of the conditions of the voyage Cornelius de Houtman was sent to Lisbon. The Company also had in their possession a map of the Indian sea prepared by Pitrus Plaucius, the Geographer. But the most important information available to them came from the traveller Linschoten. Jan Huyghen Linschoten went out to India as secretary to the Archbishop of Goa. He was a careful observer and a penetrating student of affairs. On his return, he was a very enthusiastic promoter of the Dutch enterprise and his advice and information were earnestly sought by the Dutch merchants. In 1595 a fleet of four vessels commanded by Cornelius de Houtman was fitted out and sent to the East. The arrival of the Dutch in Indian waters changed the whole political situation in Kerala. The Princes on the coast saw that the Portuguese who had so far held supremacy on the sea were on the defensive against the intruders whose power they could not resist. The first connection of the Dutch with the Kerala was the treaty they negotiated with the Zamorin as early as 1604. By this treaty which was concluded between "the Zamorin, Emperor of Kerala and Admiral S. Van der Hagen...........with a view to the expulsion of the Portuguese from the territories of His Highness and the rest of India" the Dutch were allowed to trade at Calicut and to build a fort for their protection.[1]

Before the Dutch evolved any regular policy with regard to Kerala, they secured an effective footing in Java and the Eastern Archipelago and the next half a century was devoted to the development of their authority in these areas and to the control of the Eastern seas. The Malabar coast, however, was not wholly forgotten. In 1642 the Dutch negotiated a treaty with "Siam Batshery vambar", the Rajah of Procaud.[2] They also visited and kept up friendly relations with other coastal rulers.

It was only after the capture of Colombo and their firm establishment in Ceylon that they were able to turn their attention to the Kerala coast. With a base in Ceylon it was possible for them to take effective action against the Portuguese. Events in Kerala favoured them. As briefly alluded to in the earlier chapter, a war of succession had broken out in Cochin in which the junior branch of the Royal family had with the help of the Portuguese usurped the throne. The dispossessed prince of the elder branch was advised by the Paliyam chief, the premier nobleman of Cochin and its hereditary prime minister, to visit Colombo and negotiate with the Dutch Company. That prince, though in bad health, did not hesitate to undertake what was then an

---

1. India Office Records: Dutch Treaties etc., Vol. I. Page 131.
2. Nieuhoff, p. 224.

arduous voyage and he was able to persuade the Dutch Company to undertake the explusion of the Portuguese from Cochin. The Dutch commander well knew that this was the golden opportunity for him. The cause of the dispossessed branch had strong and ardent supporters in Kerala. The Zamorin was on their side. The Rajahs of Vadakkumkur and Thekkumkur were also their supporters. More, the hereditary prime minister of Cochin, the Chief of Paliyam, was also secretly in league with them. An expedition had therefore every chance of success. The Dutch had been long maturing their plans for the expulsion of the Portuguese from the Kerala seas. The invitation of the dispossessed prince of Cochin afforded them a suitable opportunity. De Weert had very early foreseen that the Portuguese naval power in India was doomed once it had ceased to exist in Cochin. "When they (the Portuguese) are once turned out of Cochin they are out of India", he had declared. In 1658 when their plans were maturing Van Goens wrote as follows to the Governor-General and Council of India: [1] "We expect they will have received reinforcements by next year for which we must also be prepared in order to maintain our supremacy on the sea. It is a pity that our fleet generally reaches Goa too late. We should therefore propose that the next expedition leave Batavia about September 15th and sail direct for Ceylon, where it could be strengthened with some small craft carrying a crew of no more than 15 men which we have found very useful against the fr'gates in our last exploit."

"With these combined forces we could then make an attempt on Cochin where the Portuguese could co'lect their strongest naval forces and if we are so lucky as to defeat them the whole coast of Malabar and the pepper trade will be ours. We could have

1. Letter dated March 17th, 1658.

at Cochin a redoubt of 100 men and give the town in charge of the Zamorin on condition to sell us the pepper a fixed price." He recommended that Roothers should be appointed commander of the fleet.

On July 6th, 1658 Van Goens again wrote to Jan Matsuycker who was then the Governor-General that the Portuguese had collected 40 frigates at Cochin and that the movements of the Dutch were being watched. He stated that they could muster about 700 European soldiers in Ceylon and if another 600 could be sent from Batavia he was confident of success. His idea was to go first to Cochin. "The town, when the fleet was destroyed, could not offer much resistance."

By the end of 1658 it was clear to the Portuguese that the Dutch were bent on forcing the issue with them on the Indian seas. The Governors of India, Francis de Mello de Castro and Antenio de Sousa Coutinho jointly addressed the King of Portugal an important communication[1] in which they explained the position of affairs with the utmost frankness. They stated: "We feel it our bounden duty to acquaint you with the position of affairs in India and to inform you that unless we are properly assisted the whole of your Majesty's possessions (in India) will be lost." They pointed out that they had no money in the treasury and that as for the equipment of the fleet they had to borrow from private individuals. "We earnestly implore your majesty to send us by next year adequate reinforcements, otherwise we shall not be able to resist the enemy at all."

After the letter was written but before it was despatched the governors received the news that Quilon had fallen and that the Dutch fleet was off Cochin.

1. Letter dated 18th Dec., 1658.

Fortunately for the Portuguese the schemes of Van Goens could not be carried out in 1659, as he had hoped, because he had to send the troops he had collected to Amboina. The fight between the Portuguese and the Dutch and the conquest of Cochin by the latter have been described.[1]

As soon as the Portuguese were expelled from Cochin, Van Goens established himself in the fort and took in hand the consolidation of the commercial and political power of the Company on the Kerala Coast.

The position of the Dutch in 1663 differed materially from that of the Portuguese at the time of da Gama and Almeida. The Portuguese had to build up political and commercial relations with the Kerala chiefs who were suspicious of the newcomers and often openly hostile to them. Besides, they had also to face the power of the Mohammedan trading community who enjoyed a monopoly of commerce on the west coast. The Dutch on the other hand saw a commercial system already established and by their conquest of Cochin they stepped into the shoes of the Portuguese. They claimed all the rights which the Portuguese enjoyed in Cochin and treated the Rajah of the place as Martim de Sousa and other Portuguese viceroys had treated him. All over Kerala the Dutch took over the Portuguese system and administered it with superior efficiency and with a larger attention to profits. In a later chapter we shall discuss at some length the organisation and methods of the Dutch Company as compared with the system which the Portuguese developed.

The Dutch were also at an advantage in that the commercial power of the great Moorish houses on the coast had been completely shattered in the

---

1. See Chapter XI of Part I.

previous century. They found themselves therefore left without serious competition in the external trade of the country. The Moorish trading community was practically non-existent in Cochin and in its stead there had grown up the "Canarenes", a Hindu community from the Konkan districts who worked as the agents of the Portuguese. The "Canarenes"—or as we now call them the Konkanis—were wholly dependent on their European masters, so that when the Portuguese went away from Cochin they became equally serviceable to the Dutch.

In one thing however the position of the Dutch was not so advantageous as that of the Portuguese. From the earliest days of the Dutch connection with Kerala, there was looming in the background the comptetion of more powerful European nations—the French and the English. The English were already established at Tellichery and in 1664 the Rajah of Purakkad invited them to establish themselves there. Further south the English had also a factory at Anjengo where under the protection of the Rani of Attungal, they carried on an extensive trade in pepper. The French did not come immediately into the field but from their base in the Ile de France it was easy for them at any time to establish themselves on the Kerala Coast.

The most important fact was, however, that the Dutch inherited from the Portuguese a system of political relations with the Rajahs and Kings of the Kerala coast which gave them definite rights on which to build. The Cochin Rajah was accepted from the beginning as a vassal whose rights were derived from the Company. The very fact that they had placed him on the gadi and his authority was dependent on their support made them look upon him as a Ruler in whose affairs they had a right to intervene. The Chief of Paliyam who was the Minister of Cochin had already been taken under their protection and was the company's liegeman.[1] He had pledged his state, his subjects and his person to the Company. With the rulers and chiefs in the immediate neighbourhood of Cochin, like Mangat and Parur, and with the feudatories of the Cochin Rajah the Dutch claimed all the rights of a suzerain and overlord. With the Zamorin their relations were even older. We have noticed the treaty between Van der Hagen and that Ruler in 1604.[2] Before the attack on Cochin in 1662 Admiral Van Goens signed a new treaty with the Zamorin by which the Dutch secured the right to the exclusive purchase of pepper in Calicut territory at the market price and the Zamorin was promised in exchange the Island of Vaipeen. As soon as the campaign was over the Zamorin demanded that the position of the Cochin Rajah should be reduced to what it was before the Portuguese elevated him to the status of an independent ruler and that Vaipeen should be annexed to Calicut territories. Van Goens rejected both of these demands with the result that the relations between the Zamorin and the Dutch were no better than those which subsisted between him and the Portuguese. The important compaigns that the Dutch had to undertake, which financially ruined the Company in Kerala, were against the power of Calicut which continued to be a standing menace to the Dutch till the invasion of Kerala by Hyder Ali.

A treaty had also been concluded with the Rajah of Travancore in 1662 at Kallada. The following were the main clauses of the agreement.

Perpetual peace was established between Travancore and the Dutch Company. The native Christians were continued in the same position as under the Portuguese. The Rajah undertook to give a monopoly of pepper trade to the Company

---

1. India Office Records: Dutch Records Vol. II.

2. Treaties etc. Vol. I. page 131.

and to accept passes from the Dutch Commandeur for all vessels. The admiral undertook in exchange of these concessions to make annual presents to the Rajah of several guns and 15,000 fanams.

It was the trade in pepper that interested the Dutch most and in this they tried to establish a complete monopoly. Even before they had driven out of Portuguese, the Dutch had made arrangements about the transport of the pepper bought in Kerala. Writing in 1658,[1] Van Goens reported that instructions have already been issued to the envoy to the Naik of Madura that pepper from the Kerala Coast shall only be carried across the Bay by the Company's servants. "This condition must be insisted on and in the event of Cotcheri falling into our hands it will secure the monopoly of pepper trade to us for in the north of Cotcheri pepper is much dearer than Cannanore."

As the establishment of a complete monopoly was possible only by new and more comprehensive agreements with the Kerala Princes, the Company sent out Captain Nieuhoff who was the Factor at Quilon to negotiate with the rulers on the coast. His general instructions, from Jacob Hutstaart, were to secure from the Princes a monopoly for the trade in pepper and in opium.

The first chief whom Nieuhoff visited was the Rajah of Kayamkulam who received him with great courtesy and entered into an agreement on the lines suggested by the Dutch. From Kayamkulam Nieuhoff went to Purakkad but the Rajah was away at Kodamaloor which was the original seat of the family. Nieuhoff followed him there, travelling by boat along the canals of Kuttanad, which he compared in his book to his own native land. The Rajah received him with great cordiality and re-

---

1. Van Goens to the Governor-General dated July 6th, 1658.

minded him how as early as 1640 his family had entered into trade agreements with the Dutch. Nieuhoff mentions[1] that in 1640 the kingdom of Purakkad was ruled by a young prince whom he calls Siam Bateserry (Champakaserry) Vanbar. He was an ambitious and enterprising ruler and could not brook the interference of the Portuguese against whom he had fought successfully for three years. It was during his reign that the Dutch first began to take an effective interest in Kerala. The Rajah made a treaty with the Dutch captain in 1642 by which the East India Company was given the right of trade. The amicable relations did not however continue long as the Rajah of Purakkad supported the Portuguese at Cochin when Van Goens first attacked it. In fact it was the intervention of the Rajah that forced the Dutch to raise the siege. Now that the Dutch were firmly established at Cochin, it was in the interests of the Rajah to forget the recent past and to renew the friendly relations that existed before. Nieuhoff describes the Rajah as being "a person of about 30 years of age, very stately and well made". He accepted the suggestion of the Dutch that he should sell all his pepper to them, though he had already given permission to the English to establish a factory at his capital. But when it was further suggested that his pepper should be weighed at Cochin the Rajah objected strongly, stating that it was never the custom at Purakkad to sell through Cochin. Nieuhoff thought it prudent to yield on this issue and an agreement was signed giving the Dutch the monopoly of pepper.

Nieuhoff next visited Maruthurkulangara, the petty principality lying beween Quilon and Kayamkulam. Though small in extent, this was an important centre of pepper trade and Nieuhoff was anxious that the Mohammedans who were settled there

1. *Voyages* p. 224.

should not break the monopoly which the Dutch sought to establish. The envoy took with him the following letter of Jacob Hutstaart to the Rajah.

"ILLUSTRIOUS PRINCE."

"Nothing could be more welcome to me, than to understand at my first arrival in these parts that your Majesty had always been in a good correspondency with our company. To show your Majesty what an extraordinary value we set upon your friendship, we have sent Jonn Nieuhoff, captain of Kailong, in order to enter with you a more strict league and friendship. We hope your Majesty will give him entire credit in what he shall propose to you which I shall be ready to acknowledge on the like occasions.

God preserve and give your Majesty a long and happy life."[1]

After presenting his credentials Nieuhoff broached the question of the trade agreement which found opposition from the considerable Mohammedan community in the state. The Rajah therefore requested Nieuhoff to set down his proposals in writing. The Dutch agent submitted a treaty by which the Rajah was to undertake to forbid the importation of amfion (opium), the peeling of wild cinnamon and the exportation of pepper. The Rajah declined to treat on this footing and seeing him obdurate the Dutch modified their terms and agreed to buy all the pepper produced in the land and to withdraw the demand about the peeling of cinnamon.

After settling these contracts Nieuhoff returned to Quilon to interview the King of Travancore. The Rajah of Travancore claimed to be the head of a number of principalities which between them ruled

1. Letter dated 2nd Feb. 1664., Nieuhoff's *Voyages*, p. 224.

the territory between Quilon and Cape Comorin. On the 14th of February Nieuhoff went to Attungal to interview the Rajah who received him with courtesy but made him understand through his ministers that he was dissatisfied with the conduct of the Company in burning the palace of the Queen of Quilon. He made it clear that the trade negotiations which Nieuhoff was anxious to take up must include the question of reparations to the Queen of Quilon. While conversations were going on a messenger arrived from the Queen to inform him that the Dutch had not paid the customs due to her nor returned the cannon as they had promised. The minister of Travancore, on hearing this, asked Nieuhoff whether they would do less than the Portuguese had done.

The answer was: "If we should follow the footsteps of the Portuguese we must be guilty likewise of the same enormities in murthering, plundering, etc. things not customary among us, the intention of the Company being to maintain everyone in his right and to establish a free commerce without interruption".[1] The King of Travancore however refused to proceed further but declared that he would send his minister to Quilon to treat with Nieuhoff. When the captain returned to Quilon he found the agent of the Rajah, a general, by name Martanda Pillai, waiting for him. A meeting was arranged at the church of St. Thomas and the following agreement was reached:—

"Nobody shall import, sell or exchange, any amfion into these countries except the Dutch East India Company.

Nobody without exception shall be permitted to export any pepper or cinnamon out of this country or to sell them to anybody except the said company.

A certain price was settled betwixt both parties also; what share each should have in the customs

1. Nieuhoff p. 226 and 227.

whereby all former pretensions and exceptions should be annulled."

As the questions with regard to the Queen of Quilon were left outstanding, Nieuhoff sent a Topas by name Nicolas de Coasta to her. She refused to yield and demanded that what is hers must be paid first. As this matter was reaching a crisis Jacob Hutstaart himself came down from Cochin. Before his arrival Nieuhoff received a reply from the Queen in the following words:—

"I received and saw the contents of the letter sent to me from John Nieuhoff, Captain of Koilang, concerning the proposed treaty. I will send word in the month of March to Kottekkary where we will meet together and I shall be ready to ratify what my plenipotentiaries shall agree to. For which I ordered this letter to be written to Captain John Nieuhoff."[1]

On the 2nd of March 1664, the representative of the King of Travancore, whom Nieuhoff calls Kurup, and the Commander Martanda Pillai arrived to accompany him to the Court. The queen received him immediately on arrival in full Durbar surrounded by the officials and nobles. Nieuhoff describes her as being "past middle age, of a brown complexion with black hair knotted in a knot behind, but of a majestic mien, she being a princess who showed a great deal of good conduct in the management of her affairs." A treaty was signed and the queen to show her appreciation of Nieuhoff's efforts to promote good relations between her state and the Company invested him with the Veera Sringala.[2]

After concluding these treaties the Dutch settled down to trade. As they had no intention to pursue

---

1. *Voyages* p. 230.
2. Veera Sringala is the highest "order" given by Malabar Rulers. It means literally the Bangle of Heroism.

the Portuguese policy of general warfare on the coast beyond the enforcement of their monopoly in spices, the military establishments which they had taken over were a great encumbrance. Hence orders were issued to bring all the fortresses on the coast to a narrow compass.

In 1665 Nieuhoff received orders to draw the city of Quilon within smaller limits and fortify it on the land-side with one or two demi-bastions. He proceeded immediately to demolish "all the houses, churches and trees and what else stood in the way". The foundation of the new fort was laid on the first of July 1665.[1] The same policy was followed in Cochin, though not immediately. The garrison was reduced to one half at Cannanore. At Cranganore also similar reforms were effected. In fact from the very beginning, the Dutch never forgot that their main business was to trade and not to exercise political authority; and with the business of trading they occupied themselves without any loss of time.

---

1. Nieuhoff, Page 263.

CHAPTER II

PLIGHT OF THE COCHIN RAJAH

The success or failure of this policy of detailed agreements with the minor princes on the coast for a monopoly in the trade in Kerala spices depended entirely on the Company's ability to control the Rajah of Cochin and to use his position in support of their claims. The total subordination of Cochin was essential if the internal trade which flowed into that port was to be controlled by the factory established on the little island by the shore. Van Goens, therefore, set himself to consolidate his position in Cochin. The pretender to the Cochin throne whose cause the Dutch had supported died before he could be crowned; but his nephew Veera Kerala Varma was placed on the throne. The very ceremony declared the altered position of the Cochin Ruler. The crown bore the arms of the Dutch East India Company, and Van Goens himself seated on a throne, placed it on the head of the prince. A new treaty with Cochin was signed by which the Dutch were confirmed in the possession of the areas previously in the occupation of the Portuguese, and the Cochin Rajah expressly accepted the protection of the Dutch and placed his state under them. He also guaranteed them a monopoly of pepper and cinnamon and undertook to prohibit the entry of opium into Cochin. The Dutch Company also received the right of constructing a fort at Cheppuram, another near Alleppy and a third one at the Cochin Harbour. Justice, so far as coastal Christians and half-castes were concerned, was to be divided as it was during the time of the Portuguese.

As the Rajah of Procaud had supported the Portuguese with vigour in the first attack on Cochin and as it was mainly due to his timely naval action that the invaders had to retire, the Dutch were naturally angry with him. A small force was moved against him but no battle took place. On the other hand as the *Padappattu* says:—

> "they met as if they were old friends and as if there was never any quarrel between them. And an alliance was formed as of old with the Portuguese."[1]

Following Van Goens, Jacob Hutstaart was for a short time the chief of the Cochin establishment, but he did not remain long. The first commandeur who took up the Cochin post was Ludolf Colster. During his time attention was mostly devoted to the establishment of relations with the other states such as Purakkad, Mangat, Quilon and Vadakkumkur and to the development of the newly secured trade. For the time the Dutch showed no aggressive intentions except with regard to the English factors at Purakkad. Even before the Dutch reached Purakkad, the Rajah of that place, Deva Narayanan, had invited the English to establish a factory at his Capital.[2] In 1665 they established a small factory there, not so much for trade as for maintaining a footing in the area. Two factors by name Grigby and Harrison were sent down and their instructions were: "Should the factors be forced to leave, they must draw up a protest against the Dutch charging them a great sum annually."[3] According to Grigby the Dutch had in 1665 between Cochin and Quilon 6 watch houses. Taking advantage of a quarrel between a small Dutch landing party and some Moors at a place a few miles south of Purakkad, the commandeur of Cochin came down and established another watch house. When war broke out between England and Holland,

---

1. *Padappattu*—Srimulam Malayalam Series, Trivandrum. p. 46.
2. *British Factories in India*, 1665-1667. Oxford 1925. p. 90.
3. *Ibid.*

the English factory with its guns and ammunition was captured by the Dutch.

Till Hendrick Van Rheede came to Cochin as commandeur in 1673 no definite policy was adopted by the Company towards the Rajahs. Van Rheede was a young officer of noble stock who had distinguished himself at the siege of Cochin. Goens was so highly impressed with his ability and resourcefulness that he recommended him for the post of commandeur at Cochin. As soon as he arrived in Cochin, Van Rheede made it clear that the Dutch Company was not satisfied with the trade of Kerala but desired effective political power. He forced the Rajah of Cochin to make a family settlement which curtailed the authority of the ruler and made him entirely dependent on the Company. The Civil List of the Rajah was settled at 3,000 fanams, of the Elaya Rajah (heir apparent) at 1,500 fanams, and of the other princes in proportion. The junior princes were to take no part in the administration which was handed over to the management of the Paliyam chiefs. This settlement also laid down clearly that no adoption to the Cochin Royal family was to be made without the consent of the Dutch commandeur. A treaty was also made between the Dutch and Eroma (Eravi Varma), the second prince, and Godarma (Godavarma) the fourth prince, on February 23rd 1674 by which the princes promised "that no chiefs will hereafter be elected kings of Cochin but such as are the descendants of the five lawful families of which three are extinct and only two are existing". Not content with this, Van Rheede, on 3rd December 1774, negotiated a treaty with the principal nobles of Cochin i.e. "the thirty thousand Nayars of Karappuram, the three hundred of Badathala, the three hundred of Kandamthurithy, the Meloor Madathil Kymal, the three hundred of Bappeen and those of Paliyattu" by which the contracting parties agreed "for the happiness of the Kingdom of Cochin in general and for their individual welfare respectively to form a league against all those who are the enemies of the Company and of the Kingdom of Cochin."

The settlement was naturally much disliked by the princes who rose in revolt against its provisions. The main body of Cochin nobles who resented the intervention of the Dutch in these matters sided with the princes. Civil war broke out and the Rajah himself left his palace and retired to the interior. The Dutch authorities were doubtful of their position especially as the Rajah had withdrawn to the interior and a letter from the Governor-General at Batavia dated 8th September, 1687 was received expostulating with him and requesting him not to stay away but return to the protection and safety of Cochin. The commandeur was not disheartened by these developments. On the other hand, he utilised the weakness of the Rajah to get him to sign another agreement dated 21st May, 1678.[1] This provided that the Company will be allowed to exercise authority without the intervention of the princes—the junior members of the family, that all persons without exception who oppose the Company will be punished, that the princes will not enter the town without the permission of the Rajah, that the Chief of Paliyam will do the needful in communication with the Rajah for the welfare of the State and that all the actions and resolutions of the Rajah and his minister will be subject to the approval of the Commandant of Cochin.

This agreement virtually handed over the Cochin state to the Dutch. The Paliyam Chief who was the Company's bondsman was to rule the state, in communication with (not under the orders of) the Rajah. The princes were strictly excluded from all influence. The Rajah himself was reduced to a cypher. Besides all these there was a curious clause which stipulated that the Nayar nobility should not be exempt from punishment.

1. Dutch Records: Treaties Vol. I. p. 386.

The earlier agreements had been strongly opposed by the Nayar Chiefs and they had sided with the princes in attempting to get the agreements repudiated by the Rajah. This new treaty further enraged the nobles against the Dutch and they openly took up arms with a view to depose the ruler. Matters went so far that the Dutch Company found that if the Rajah whom they had placed on the throne was to be maintained as a pillar of their system, the only method left them was to interfere openly and take over the management of affairs. The Rajah's officials who were inimical to the Company were also creating trouble with regard to the customs duties at the port. With a view to end all the trouble Martin Huysman, who was the commandeur of Cochin at the time, entered into a new agreement with the Rajah on the 3rd May, 1681. The Rajah was asked to accept a Dutch official as his minister and one of the Canarese subordinates of the Company as his treasurer. The Chief of Paliyam was to be the Prime Minister, but the affairs of the State were to be regulated according to the advice given by the Company's official. The commandeur was only waiting for an opportunity to take over the complete management of the Cochin State and such an opportunity soon occurred. The Chief of Paliyam died leaving a minor as heir to the estate. The vacancy to the prime ministership which thus arose was utilised for the nomination of Captain Hendrik Reins to that post to be held in the name of the minor Chief of Paliyam.

With both the treasury and the Prime Ministership in the hands of the Dutch and with the Paliyam Chief a minor, Cochin became less a dependency than a mere proprietary estate of the Dutch Company. The Rajah became a nonentity and the Company claimed the right of appointing even local officials and it was strictly laid down that no appointment made without the permission of the Company was valid. These high-handed measures did not in any way lead to the pacification of the country. On the other hand even the Rajah surreptitiously encouraged the rebels and for a time the position of the Dutch in the fort became highly precarious. The commandeur Van Dielen who knew of the preparations of the nobles and the attitude of the Rajah kept Van Rheede, the Commissar-General, fully informed of the projects and the Company was seriously afraid that the high-handed policy of the Commandeur had undermined its position in Cochin itself. From this position they were saved and their authority further consolidated by the unwise action of Veera Kerala Varma whose decision to adopt from the Chaliyur family plunged the country into a civil war and helped to consolidate the position of the Dutch.

In 1681 Veera Kerala Varma, on the advice of Martin Huysman, the commandeur of Cochin, and of the Lord of Paliyam decided to adopt into the Cochin family two princes and four princesses from the Chaliyur Branch. This was not welcome to the Nayar nobles as the Chaliyur Branch had always been the dependents of the Dutch and under the lead of Ayinikkuttil Nambidi and the Treasurer, Perumbalam, they agitated against the proposal for adoption from Chaliyur, and suggested the adoption of princes from Vettathunad. This faction which was anti-Dutch had the support of the Rajahs of Mangat, Parur and Manakkulam and the Madampies or barons of Karappuram. When the Chaliyur adoption was actually made in 1689, these noblemen gathered their forces in Mangat and resolved on deciding tht issue by force. The Rajah was by this move thrown into the hands of the Dutch Company. But even then the position of the Company was weak as the Rajah had not the support of the people of Cochin. None of the leading nobles of Cochin, except Ittinnan Achan of Paliyam was on the Rajah's side, and to champion his cause meant a land campaign of an arduous nature. On this occasion both the Company and the Rajah turned to the Zamorin. For his help in the

Dutch conquest of Cochin the Zamorin had received only Cranganore and his further claims on Vaipeen were not accepted by the Company. Yet it was to him that the Company and the Cochin Rajah turned at this moment of crisis. The Zamorin who was then reigning was Bharani Thirunal who was born in 1640 and ascended the throne in 1684. He was a ruler of remarkable ability and was naturally unwilling to come to the help of the Dutch but the Brahmin ambassador of the Cochin Rajah was able to persuade the Nayar Chiefs that as Cochin had again accepted the authority of the Zamorin there was no necessity to keep up the age-long quarrel. The Commandeur also visited the Zamorin at Cranganore.[1]

Forgetting for once the historical role of the Zamorin, which was to resist foreign aggression and to support the popular cause in Cochin, which policy successive Mana Vikramans[2] had followed with unfailing fidelity, Bharani Thirunal agreed to help the Company and the Cochin Rajah to defeat the Vettathunad faction. He was promised for this help the land of Chetwai and all military expenses. The Zamorin's army took the field immediately and joining the forces of Paliyam and of the Company marched forward to meet the rival army encamped near Alwayi. The Dutch forces were commanded by Hendrick Van Rheede who was Commissar-General. The opposing armies met at Alwayi, and the Vettathunad forces commanded by the Rajah of Mangat were defeated and dispersed. The war was carried into the enemy's territory but soon the Dutch retired with the plunder of the rich lands of Alangad and Parur. The Zamorin received Cheatwai which he had so long coveted.

---

1. *Mamankodtharanam*, p. 39.

2. Mana Vikraman is the name which the Zamorin adopts on succeeding to the throne.

But in getting Chetwai the Zamorin had lost the historic leadership of Kerala. The fall of the Calicut Rulers may be traced to this campaign when for the first time in their long history they joined hands with the foreign powers and their vassal, the Rajah of Cochin, in order to put down a popular anti-Dutch rebellion. In the next serious campaign aginst the Dutch in 1717 the Zamorin was fighting not as the leader of Kerala and the head of its popular forces but merely as a powerful king. The war of Vettam succession was thus an event of utmost importance in Kerala history. It consolidated the power of the Dutch at Cochin by making the Rajah completely dependent on the Company and by breaking the power of the anti-Dutch nobles. It saw the reversal of the traditional policy of the Zamorins, who so far had been the champions of the popular cause against the autocratic pretensions of the Cochin Rajah and the aggression of the foreign traders. By allying himself with his hereditary enemies, and those who were historically the enemies of Kerala freedom, the Zamorin lost at one stroke the singular position which two centuries of war in the cause of Kerala had earned for him.

The rivalry and feud between Cochin and Calicut were by no means at an end. The Zamorin, now well established at Chetwai and Cranganore, continued to encourage Cochin feudatories to create trouble in the Rajah's territories and to support the different factions in the country. Though nominally there was peace, the Cochin Ruler was particularly angry that the Zamorin had not evacuated the territory occupied by him during the late war. The argument of the Calicut government was that the agreed contribution to its military expenses in support of the Cochin Rajah had not been paid. Desultory warfare went on in which the Zamorin was generally successful, especially because strategically he was so placed that Calicut armies could always be moved with ease into the Cochin territory while his own domains were free from attack. The Dutch who were anxious to maintain peace with the Zamorin took up an attitude of neutrality. In fact they were not displeased with this continual warfare between Cochin and Calicut as it kept the Cochin ruler occupied. The idea of Ravi Varma who had succeeded to the gadi of Cochin in 1693 was to embroil the Company with the Zamorin but the instructions of the Batavian Government and the policy of Hendrick Van Rheede who was Commissar-General were to avoid further complications with Calicut.

In 1694, the relations between the Rajah of Cochin and the Company became very strained. The Company's Indian Agent, Bavan Prabhu, was a corrupt official in the pay of the Zamorin and he sided with the young chief of Paliyam, Ittykkanachan, who had come of age and was intriguing with the Dutch against his own master. The Rajah was powerless especially as Isaak Van Dielen, the commandeur who was inclined in his favour, died a few months after the Rajah's accession. In a letter dated January 22nd, 1694, the Rajah complained bitterly of the attitude of the new Paliyam chief and of the irregularities of Bavan Prabhu, the Indian trade agent of the company, in refusing to account to the government for the customs and duties of the port. He also accused the Prabhu of being in the pay of the Zamorin. To this complaint the Government of Batavia gave an evasive reply and told the Rajah that full instructions had been given to Adrian Van Maten, the new commandeur, and that the Rajah should consult him on all occasions. The company in fact was anxious for peace with the Zamorin and took no heed of the complaints of a prince whose importance rested solely on their support. The activities of Bavan Prabhu and the Paliyam chief were in no way interrupted. Nor did the Commissar-General or the commandeur take up an attitude which was favourable to the Rajah. The unhappy prince sent a further petition in June 1696. In it he complained that though the Commissar-General, who was instructed to discuss matters with him, arrived at Cochin, he did not stay to have an interview with the Rajah but proceeded to Calicut where he saw the Zamorin and entered into friendly relations with him. Bavan Prabhu was also with the Commissar-General and this further enraged the Cochin Rajah. That the Company should not have supported him in his fight with the Zamorin was in itself galling to him but that they should, when hostilities were actually going on between the Cochin Rajah and the Zamorin, go to Calicut and ostentatiously display their friendship was a matter which he could not suffer.

We get a glimpse of the state of Cochin finances at the time from this letter to the Supreme Government at Batavia. The Rajah complains that owing to the civil strife beginning with the last days of the Portuguese the state treasury has been left bankrupt. The only sources of revenue left to him were the mint, the customs, the profit on the private sales permitted on his behalf by the Company and the percentage on pepper. Of these the mint was run as a joint enterprise by the company and the Rajah, and as the Dutch claimed from the state treasury a large sum of money, the profit from the mint was only credited to the account. Owing to the hostile attitude of Bavan Prabhu practically nothing was realised from the customs and duties and the treasury was therefore bankrupt. The Dutch kept on pressing vigorously for the payment of their debt and at this crisis the Rajah Ravi Varma died to be succeeded by Rama Varma. With him a new agreement was made by the Company. This was negotiated by Hendrick Zwaadekroon in 1698, and it finally set the seal of servitude on the Cochin principality and made it merely an appendage of the Dutch Company.

By this time, however, the general monopoly which the Company had hoped to establish had broken down. The whole basis of the theory of compulsion was that the selling of pepper to other nations was contraband which was to be put down by the use of the Company's whole force. Unless the Company was able to inspire that degree of fear which would force Kerala rulers to proceed against their own merchants, this policy was bound to fail. This is in fact what happened. Zwaadekroon's memorial[1] shows how little the power of the Company was feared by the Rajah of Kayamkulam who traded openly with the pirate William Kidd, though the Company had negotiated with Goda Varman, the Rajah of that place, so late as 1592, a treaty for exclusive trade in consideration of 500 gold fanams and the right of sending out a vessel of 75 or 100 candyles.

A great portion of the pepper produce of the country used to reach the English. The Governor-General writing to the Company's authorities at Amsterdam as early as November 17th, 1669 stated that "immediately after the conclusion of the peace with England the Agents of the English Company have again taken up their residence at Calicut......... .... We are much afraid that from the district of Thekkumkur and Vadakkumkur a large quantity of pepper will find its way overland to Calicut which will make this article dear."[2] All this reacted on the position of Cochin on whose ruler the Company had to put the screw mercilessly in order to make their settlement paying.

---

1. Dated 31st May, 1698.
2. Dutch Records at the Hague—Vol. 29 DCCCXLI Page 6.

CHAPTER III

THE DUTCH WAR WITH THE ZAMORIN

The Zamorin's position had been considerably strengthened by the accessions of territory in 1663 and 1691. In 1663 the Dutch, agreeably to the treaty with Van Goens, handed over Cranganore to the Calicut ruler. In 1691 the Zamorin secured Chetwai for the support he gave against the Vettam faction. The two natural ways of attack on Cochin from the North were from Cranganore and from Chetwai and controlling these the Zamorin kept the offensive always in his own hands. Chetwai especially was of great importance because it lay in the domains of Payencherry Nayar, a feudatory of the Zamorin and a nobleman of considerable power and influence. The Ruler of Calicut built on the Cochin frontier a line fortresses of which Pappanety, Kattur, Mapranam and Oorakam were the most important. Besides this, the Zamorin was in close alliance with the chiefs of Mangat and Parur whose principalities bordered on Cochin in the north and with Thekkumkur and Vadakkumkur, the two powerful Nayar rulers occupying territory to the south of Cochin. Placed in this advantageous position, it was no more than a recognised sport for the Zamorin Rajahs to attack Cochin when they felt so inclined. So far, the Dutch had preserved an attitude of neutrality and had shown anxiety for friendly relations with the Zamorin. In 1694 though there was possibility of a serious war between Cochin and Calicut, the Company maintained the attitude of a passive spectator. But the relations between the two Rajahs did not improve especially as the Cochin Rajah was anxious to get back Mapranam and Chetwai. Matters came to a crisis in 1700 and the Dutch, who were anxious not to be embroiled in war, asked the Zamorin to send his representatives to discuss the outstanding questions. They also invited the representatives of the Rajahs of Purakkad, Vadakkumkur, Marta and Parur to meet in Cochin and help to settle the matter by arbitration. But the Zamorin would not agree to this and on the 19th February 1701 he invaded Cochin territory. The Dutch Company decided to support the Rajah of Cochin and took the field with a large force. Nor was the Zamorin without allies. Purrakkad and Parur declared for Calicut and the Zamorin by promising an adoption into his family from Thekkumkur got the support of that important state. The Purakkad Rajah carried war into the Cochin territory in Karappuram and thus created a diversion which helped the Zamorin a great deal. The Dutch Company finding itself attacked from the north and south decided to buy off the Rajah of Purakkad and separate negotiations were entered into for that purpose. The crafty Brahmin chieftain after securing many advantages for himself retired from the fray.

But the war against Zamorin was not progressing satisfactorily. The Cochin Rajah complained to Batavia that the Dutch Company were not serious in their efforts to support him and he claimed, by virtue of his treaties, full co-operation in the campaign from the supreme government. The reply of the Governor-General, Jan Van Horn, dated 15th November 1705, is of interest as indicating the lines of Dutch policy in Kerala. The Cochin Rajah had tried to arouse the fear of the Dutch by stating that the Zamorin was negotiating with the French Company for a settlement at Calicut and that if the Dutch did not support the Rajah "with soldiers, with ships and ammunition" his authority as well as theirs will cease to exist for ever. To this the Governor-General replied thus: "I do not know how much treasure and how much blood had been spent by the Honourable Company to aggrandise your family. But I know one thing. Our advice to put the affairs of the State in order has been uniformly disregarded by your Highness. Your Highness has lent your ears to the selfish counsels of Chetties, Nambudiries and Pattars; still the Company are not averse to give support to Cochin agreeably to our treaty but they will not at all times send their soldiers to fight your Highness's battles. For the last 50 years Malabar has been a source of large expense and little gain." But the Company at the same time seriously discussed whether it was not desirable to recapture the important line of fortresses on the Cochin border and render the Zamorin's attack on Cochin impossible. After serious consideration the Company decided on actively supporting the Cochin forces in their attempt to recover Mapranam. In a letter dated 27th October 1707 the Company claimed Cochin to be a protected state and gave the Zamorin to understand that attack on Cochin would be considered as a hostile act against themselves. The real reason for this action was not any particular friendship for Cochin but the negotiations that the Zamorin was carrying on with the English for the establishment of a factory in Calicut. The Zamorin's reply to the letter was of a conciliatory nature and the commandeur invited the representatives of all parties for a conference at the fort in Cochin. The conversations, though friendly, did not end in anything definite. The war between Cochin and Calicut continued and though pressed by the Rajah to help him the Company refused.

In the meantime things were taking a new turn at Calicut. At the Zamorin's court there were two parties. The Zamorin himself was a peace loving man who was desirous that this war should come to an end. But the great chiefs of the army, especially Dharmoth Panikkar, the heir apparent himself, and most of the nobles were in favour of continuing the war. The Mamankam festival[1] was approching and as the position of the Zamorin as the leading King in Malabar depended on his taking the initiative in that matter he decided on peace and entered into definite negotiations. By the treaty which resulted from these negotiations the Zomorin handed over Chetwai to the Company. The Nayar Lord of Payenchey became a feudatory of the Dutch and the Cranganore Rajah also was given over to their protection. The Cochin Rajah gained considerable additions of territory.

This treaty did not find favour with the Calicut nobles, especially with the heir apparent and the Commander-in-Chief, Dharmoth Panikkar. They pointed out that in giving over Chetwai and Cranganore to the Company the Zamorin had disabled himself from taking the offensive in any future war and that if the Dutch Company began building a fort in either of these places it would be a standing menace to the kingdom of Calicut. Though the Zamorin recognised the validity of these arguments he was forced to remain quiet for a considerable time. But when it was found that the Dutch were not content with merely wresting those strategical areas from him but were actually fortifying Chetwai, he was naturally incensed and entered into negotiations with the English. Besides this, the Cochin Rajah anxious always to embroil the Zamorin with the Dutch handed over to the Company the legal title to some pieces of land which had long been in possession of the Zamorin. The Dutch took over the place and began erecting a strong fort in spite of the vigorous protest of the Zamorin.

---

1. The Mamankam was one of the great national festivals of Kerala, Originally it was a national assembly for the election of an Emperor for all Kerala. In its later days, the Zamorin assumed the control of this festival though the traditional forms of an imperial election were still kept up.

The Zamorin was enraged at this high handed procedure.[1] The war party at his court utilised this for pushing forward their views and they found a friend in Robert Adams the energetic, if rather headstrong, English factor at Tellicherry. The English factor promised all help with munitions and money and encouraged the Zamorin to act vigorously. Adams had strong reasons for taking this course. Not only did he desire that the Dutch power should be weakened by continuous fights with the Zamorin but he realised that special opportunities for pushing up the English influence would offer themselves if there was war between the two powers. Besides, Chetwai was a source of considerable income to the English Company as in that place they had established a branch house and carried on trade in opium which was a prohibited commodity in Cochin.

The Zamorin was not anxious to proceed by force. He protested at Cochin against the hostile acts and warned the Company of the disastrous consequences that would follow if they persisted in that course. But the commandeur took no notice. He ordered that the construction of the fort was to be proceeded with in as great haste as possible. There was no option now but war. But the Zamorin was still averse to a general campaign against the Dutch and wanted only the reduction of the two forts that were being constructed. In spite of the advice of the heir apparent and Dharmoth Panikkar it was decided that there was no necessity to proceed against the Dutch but merely to take by force the area, legally belonging to Calicut where, on the pretended conveyance of Cochin, the Dutch Company were building their forts.

The following is the description given by Visscher of the capture of the fort by the Zamorin. "The

1. Visscher—Letter IV.

fort was almost completed and he saw that the time for his attempt was come. He was encouraged by learning that the garrison consisting of 48 men were lodged outside the half finished fortress and that none of the requisites had been provided for its defence. This showed the greatest want of foresight in the Commandant who had received intelligence of the intended attack and ought therefore to have increased his garrison and ordered his men to keep within walls and to be alert. The Zamorin perceiving his advantage crossed the river at night with 600 men who were soon followed by more, and all was effected so quietly that at about 4 o'clock in the morning of 22nd January 1715 they surprised the soldiers who were sleeping in their huts before the fort."[1] In the face of this clear statement, the version of Hamilton, who was not in Kerala at the time, that the Zamorin first introduced some of his men under the disguise of labourers and that the surprise was successful only because the disguised labourers killed the sentinels, signalled to the ambuscade and attacked the half built fort, could not be true. If such was the case Visscher, who was chaplain in Cochin itself from 1717-1722, would certainly have mentioned it as the cause of the Dutch failure.

The action in any case was completely successful. The two Dutch lieutenants who were in charge of the operations were both, according to Hamilton, diverting themselves at cards at tables in a grand room about half a mile away. The moment the Zamorin's soldiers occupied the fortress the Dutch retired to a mud turret at a distance. The captain made no attempt to recapture the fortress but ignominiously retreated to Cochin leaving the place in the hands of the Zamorin. He was immediately arrested, deprived of his commission and sent to Ceylon for trial. The commandeur of Cochin,

---

1. Visscher—Letter IV.

Barent Kettel, made the necessary preparations and with a large force backed by heavy artillery left Chetwai. He was met on the way by a detachment of the Calicut force under the Rajah of Mangat and a sanguinary action took place. Both sides lost heavily with the result that the Dutch army was not able immediately to attack the fortress. In the meantime, the Calicut general entrenched himself in a secure position and brought down heavy artillery. Kettel was in a difficult position. He had either to attack with the small force at his disposal or retire without fighting. His communicaions had become unsafe and the force which he had brought was insufficient to undertake a major operation against a fully equipped army. Retreat was even more dangerous. The communication by the backwater was threatened by the Rajah of Mangat. The commandeur decided to attack. On February 1 an attempt was made to storm the fortress, but the attack, though made with vigour, was easily repulsed with heavy loss to the Dutch. The Commandeur and what was left of the force returned to Cochin.

With Chetwai abandoned the Dutch position at Cranganore became precarious. The Rajah of the place hastened to return to his old allegiance and the Zamorin proceeded to erect a fortress at Pappanety between Chetwai and Cranganore with a view to resist any future attack of the Dutch on Chetwai. In December 1715 reinforcements were sent from Batavia with orders that Chetwai must immediately be recaptured. Commandeur Kettel, anxious to retrieve his failure, put himself to the task with energy and on January 11th, 1716 an attack was made. Even that patriotic chaplain Canter Visscher who was regaling his relations at home with the heroic deeds of his countrymen in the East had nothing good to say of this expedition. Says he: "Owing partly to some misunderstanding among the officers and partly to the faint-heartedness of Captain Pluis, the second in command, who trembled at the sound of cannon, the attempt failed. For, when the besieged beheld our men advancing, they were so terrified at their numbers that they rushed out of the fort on the opposite side. Those of our troops who were stationed there, mistaking the cause of the sally and imagining it was an assault upon themselves were seized with a sudden panic and fled in disorder. The fruitless result of the expedition created universal consternation which was increased by the rumours which began to fly about mostly originating in the apprehensions that the allied princes were about to desert us." [1]

The loss of Chetwai and the failure of two successive attempts to retake it constituted the greatest blow that the prestige of the Dutch arms had so far suffered in India. It was a disaster that spelt the ruin of their trade and the disapperance of their political influence. The council at Batavia realised that unless their prestige was regained, every one of the small chieftains would turn against them and defy them with impunity. Urgent orders were therefore issued to concentrate on Kerala as much troops as possible. In September, 1715, no less than 1570 men were sent to Cochin. In 1716, 1500 more were sent. The force was well supplied with arms and ammunition. This was probably the largest European force concentrated in India before the rise of British military power.

The Dutch established a blockade of the Calicut coast. On the 15th June 1716 a vessel flying the English flag laden with munitions of war but carrying also English passengers was captured by the Dutch. It must be said here that the policy of the Dutch Company towards the English on the Kerala coast was never friendly, as we have seen in the Purakkad case. "Every means must be employed and effort made", wrote the authorities at Amsterdam in a

1. Page 17.

letter, dated 14th May 1667, "to have the English expelled from the land of the Zamorin............ It will never do to have that nation settled so near us"[1]. From November 1669 the English Company had established a factory at Calicut. The English factor at Tellicherry who had general control over the English establishments on the coast heartily reciprocated the sentiments entertained by the Dutch. The capture of the English ship gave Robert Adams the opportunity he wanted. He claimed from the Dutch restitution and compensation. The Dutch commandeur did not answer his communication and Adams sent another insolently worded protest and accused the company of grossly ill-treating the English passengers captured with the ship. On the 14th July, Barent Kettel made a counter-protest saying that in allowing munitions to be imported into Calicut, Adams was acting in an unfriendly spirit and the Dutch had every right to capture ships belonging to the Zamorin even if they were flying the English flag. Adams was not to be suppressed in that manner. He replied that even if the ship belonged to the Zamorin the Dutch had no right to capture it as long as it flew the English flag. This bitter controversy, interesting in itself to show what sides the English Company took, did not interfere with the course of action. An army had by this time been collected from all parts of Dutch India. Hendrick Zwaadekroon who was commissioner for Kerala in 1697 and who as such had earned a great name with the princes was offered the command, but he refused. The Council then made William Baker Jacobs, who held the position of Councillor Extraordinary, Commander-in-chief.

Jacobs arrived in Cochin on the 16th November, 1716. Barent Kettel was recalled and Johannes Hartenberg was appointed in his place. Jacobs made

---

1. Dutch Records at Hague Vol. 29 CCXLI. (India Office).

no secret of the immense preparations the Company had made to carry on the war to a successful conclusion. He addressed an official letter to all the kings and nobles of Kerala declaring that he had been sent out to puinsh the Zamorin and humble his power. Jacobs did not know how a boasting Marcheal of Portugal had undertaken to do the same two hundred years before and had met with his death at Calicut, and that a greater man than he, Affonso Albuquerque, had to confess that, in spite of all his efforts, the power of the Zamorin remained unbroken because it was based on the loyal allegiance and the willing co-operation of the Nayar nobility. However, Jacobs announced his intention with much flourish.

The Dutch commandeur marched on Chetwai. He took with him the whole of the formidable force which had been mobilised at Cochin during the last year and a half. The army under his command contained besides the Nayar force supplied by the Rajah of Cochin, 3226 Dutch soldiers and 193 lascorins. The attack on Pappanety was personally conducted on the Zamorin's side by Dharmoth Panikkar and by Jacobs on the Dutch side. A most sanguinary battle took place in which the superiority of the Dutch artillery soon became evident. It was clear that the fortress could not withstand effectively the cannonade of the Dutch batteries and the Calicut force after a stern resistance evacuated it by the evening. The Zamorin also withdrew his forces from Chetwai.

The campaign, however, did not end with this. Desultory fighting continued and after some time the armies again met for a decisive battle at Oorakam where a powerful Dutch force of over 25,000 men consisting of 20,000 Cochin auxiliaries and 5,000 Dutch soldiers overtook a portion of the Zamorin's army. The battle continued for the day but the result was indecisive. The Zamorin's forces withdrew from the field and negotiations were opened for a treaty.

The Dutch on their side were not anxious to continue the war. The war had cost them already two million guilders and had strained their military and financial resources to the utmost extent. Their gains in the campaign were comparatively small. They had, it is true, defeated the Zamorin in pitched battles, but his army was intact and his territory inviolate. So far the campaign had been conducted in Cochin territory and on dispute soil. The Zamorin was also weary of warfare and was prepared to negotiate a suitable peace. But the Dutch demanded heavy indemnity which the Zamorin was not prepared to pay. The negotiations thus dragged on. In the meantime, through the intervention of the Raja of Cochin, the Company entered into agreement with some of the marcher barons who had so far supported the Zamorin. Of these the most important was the Chief of Punnathur, who agreed to desert his king and abide by the orders of the Company.

After considerable time spent in fruitless negotiations a definitive peace was made with the Zamorin (1717). The Zamorin agreed to pay the nominal indemnity of 85,000 gold fanams. The Dutch also insisted that Dharmoth Panikkar, who was according to Governor Moens "the chief firebrand of the treason of Chetwai" should be dismissed and that his property in Chetwai should be forfeited to the Company[1]. The Company and its servants were given the right of trading within the territories of the Zamorin. The Company withdrew its claims on

1. This property is situated at the northern limits of Pappinivattam in the neighbourhood of Tripporayar temple and consists of 50 acres of sowing land and 63 pieces of garden land. The revenue from this is called in campaigns documents as the Revenue of D'Hertmuttu Panikkal.

Punnathur Nambidi. Payenchery Nayar whose lands were situated in the area between Cranganore and Chetwai was recognised to be a vassal of the Company. Pappinivattam (Pappanety) was given over in full sovereignty to the Company. Chetwai was formally taken possession of on the 10th April 1717.

Thus though the compaign ended in favour of the Company, the benefits derived did not by any means justify the enormous expenditure or fulfil the objects with which the Dutch began the war. The Zamorin's power was not materially crippled, nor was he "punished" in any manner. Though the Company annexed Pappanety, and the fortress at Chetwai, the enormous expenditure of two million guilders, which the campaign entailed and the interference with trade to which it led, became more a punishment to themselves than to the Zamorin.

All the indemnity which the Dutch received from the Zamorin was the insignificant sum of 85,000 fanams equal to about Rs. 30,000. The Cochin Rajah and the Dutch were soon to find that neither the strength of the Zamorin nor his power for offence had in any way been lessened by this.

CHAPTER IV

INTERNAL INTERVENTION

After the peace with the Zamorin, the Company felt that their position was established securely and that they could now stand forth as the overlord of the Kerala Coast. So far as they were concerned this claim of overlordship meant mainly an enforcement of the pepper monopoly and the right to purchase it at their price. They had put forward political claims only in Cochin. In that place they stood in the position of a feudal overlord. The Rajah of Cochin had become their bondsman by successive agreements which we have traced in a previous chapter. Johannes Hartenberg had even forced the Cochin Rajah to agree that "all the Rajahs, princes and nobles of the kingdom shall lay their complaints and disputes before him so that he is constituted arbitrator between them by which means he becomes acquainted with their differences." Even the Civil Lists of the Cochin Rajah and of the princes were settled by the Dutch. By the treaty with the chieftains of Karappuram negotiated at Aryat on 6th April 1710, the Dutch secured very large powers of invention in that area. But elsewhere the position of the Company was only that of merchants who had a monopoly of trade. At Purakkad and Quilon they had strong establishments which helped them to dictate to the Rajahs but in neither place did they have any effective political power.

With the defeat of the Zamorin at Chetwai the vision of the political conquest of Kerala dawned on the Dutch. They were finding that the English at Tellicherry, Calicut and Anjengo, and the French lately established at Mahe were successfully breaking through their monopoly and getting a considerable share of the pepper trade of Kerala. The only way of tightening the hold on pepper was to reduce the other princes of Kerala to a position similar to that occupied by the Rajah of Cochin. The Zamorin whose influence had so long stood in the way of the Dutch was for the moment rendered powerless to act in an aggressive manner. Nor were occasions wanting which gave the Dutch opportunities for effective interference. The Rulers themseves invited such interfernce.

In May 1710 the Cochin Rajah addressed a letter to the Batavia Company[1] in which he complained that as a result of the open contempt in which he was held by the commandeur no one in the state paid any heed to him. "Considering the relations that exist between the company and the State I suffered with good grace all the humiliations in the belief that a remedy will soon be forthcoming." He appealed to the Governor-General to secure the succession of his immediate nephews in the Chaliyur branch to the Gadi after his time. He stated: "They seem to be fit to be brought up to the status............ The friends and allies of my family hope that these boys would be adopted and request us to that effect. If they are not taken into this family no one can help them......... Those from Vettom being inimical to me and to the Company could not be trusted. The three princes at Ainoor are not in my opinion fit for the Stanam (title). Moreover some of them have been adopted into the Murianattu Nambiar family and are therefore said to have lost caste. They are quite unfit. If they are adopted the state will be ruined by selfish people." On these grounds he recommended that the Company should permit him to bring into the Cochin family three more princes from Chaliyur.

Soon after the Calicut war was over, de Jong was sent from Cochin to Purakkad, Kayamkulam,

1. Recently published from the records of Paliyam by the state archaeologist of Cochin.

Madathumkur and Quilon, ostensibly to make new contracts but really to make the Rajahs understand the new position of the Company. But even without such official notification the Rajahs were able to draw their conclusions when the Company interfered on the ground of illegality in the adoption made by Murianattu Nambiar.[1] Claiming the rights of a Kerala overlord the Dutch declared the adoption made by the Nambiar to be invalid and threatened to proceed against him if he proved contumacious.

But in all these the Dutch had calculated without their host. The Zamorin was soon in a position to take up the leadership of Kerala and in 1728 he suggested to the Thekkumkur family the adoption of a princess to Calicut. This would have meant a definite check to Dutch intrigues in that area and it would also have isolated and enfeebled Cochin. Vadakkumkur and Thekkumkur belonged to the same family and their open alliance with the powerful ruler of Calicut meant nothing less than the annihilation of Cochin. The Zamorin however did not stop with this. He was moving in the direction of a Kerala confederacy against the Dutch and their vassal the Rajah of Cochin. The Dutch resident at Kayamkulam, Johannes Batta, reported in 1729 that the Zamorin had sent Olas (letters) with a Brahmin ambassador by name Padmanabha Pattar to the King of Kayamkulam asking him and the Rajah of Thekkumkur to attack jointly the Rajah of Cochin from the South in order to facilitate the Zamorin's policy.

De Jong's overbearing attitude towards the princes had raised a host of enemies against him, and the Zamorin's combination was an ominous portent of the discontent in Kerala. The Dutch realised this and recalled de Jong from Cochin in 1730. A combination between the Chieftains of the north and

1. Press List No. 134. Letter to Batavia.

south of Cochin would have crushed the political power of the Dutch which was centred at Cochin and ruined their trade especially as Cochin itself did not produce in any considerable quantity the articles that the Dutch wanted. So de Jong's policy was for the time reversed and a conciliatory attitude was taken up towards the allies of the Zamorin in the south.

There was another reason for the change. A new complication had arisen in the question of succession to the Mangat principality, which affected the Dutch directly. The domain of Mangat lies to the north—east of Cochin and comprises of the present taluk of Alangad and the lands adjacent to it. Its position is such that it covers the only important land frontier of Cochin if the little Brahmin principality of Idappalli is left out of consideration. The Chiefs of Mangat were Nayars and owed allegiance to the Zamorin, whose generals they claimed to be. They were lords of 16,000 Nayars. The Cochin Rajah had also vague claims of overlordship which the Mangat Nayars never accepted willingly. It was the Chief of Mangat who led the Zamorin's forces on the occasion of Barent Kettel's attack on the captured fort of Chetwai in 1716. In 1730 there were only two members in this family, the Chief himself, and the heir apparent who had been adopted from the family of Murianattu Nambiar in 1728. But as the perpetuation of the line demanded the adoption of a Rani—the Mangat family being matrilineal—the Rajah decided on adopting a lady from the house of Koratty Kaimal, another Nayar lord of equal standing. The heir apparent objected to this and put forward the claims of his own sister, a lady from Murianattu Nambiar's family. Matters came to a crisis in 1733. The prince rose in revolt against the Chief and in this action he had the support of the Dutch who supplied him with arms and ammunition. The Dutch Company were by no means desirous of peace in Mangat and it suited their purpose better to see that state weak and disunited. The Rajah of Cochin supported the cause of Koratty and clandestinely helped the Chief against the prince. The whole matter was referred to the arbitration of the Dutch commandeur and the Rajah of Cochin. As a result of their mediation an agreement was reached on the 8th July.

The award was in the nature of a compromise. The Chief was to adopt the sister of the heir apparent as the first princess, and the lady from the Koratty Kaimal's house as the second princess. The debts incurred by the prince were to be paid off, but the prince was to return the state treasures in his possession and surrender to the Chief his arms and ammunition. A further clause stated that no future adoption would be valid which did not get the previous sanction of the Cochin Rajah and the Dutch Company. The prince refused to accept the award and to give up the guns in his possession. The civil war therefore continued and the position necessitated constant vigilance on the part of the Company.

Nor were affairs elsewhere going any better. The Rajah of Vadakkumkur was assassinated in 1733 by the heir apparent and a civil war had broken out there also. The prince next in succession asked the Dutch to mediate in the quarrel. In 1734 Tattassery Thalachennor or chief was murdered in the Trichur temple. The Rajah of Kayamkulam was at war with the chief of Maruthurkulangara, and there was continuous warfare between the neighbouring chiefs of Parur and Mangad. The hand of the Dutch Company was only too apparent in all this.

The Dutch had also at this time to face considerable trouble in North Kerala. The English who had established themselves at Tellicherry came to an agreement on the 2nd November 1730 with the Regent of Kolathiri, who at that time was at war with the Rajahs of Cannanore, by which the Company received a monopoly of trade in Iruvanad, Dharmapatam and Randathara. The English trade was greatly increased by this. At this time Ikkeri Naik who was at war with the Kolathiri also invaded Kerala and came up to Valarpattnam. The Dutch suffered greately from this attack but held aloof from the combination of Kerala princes orgnised by the Regent with the help of Stephen Law who was the English factor at Tellicherry. But when the expedition against the Canarese began to progress satisfactorily the Dutch joined it on the understanding that the English will do nothing to intercept their trade to the north of Cannanore. On the 1st April 1736 the Canarese forces were attacked and routed and their General Gopalji slain. The Dutch, however, did not persist in the campaign and fell out with their ally the Regent of Kolathiri. The reason was that the Dutch wanted the prince to sell them 1000 candies of pepper at a fixed price. The Kolathiri had maintained even in the early days of his connection with the Portuguese that the sale of pepper was not his business but that of private merchants. Finally in January 1737 the prince agreed to sell 1000 candies of pepper at Rs. 56 per candy and the Dutch agreed to help him in the war.

The French at Mahe were also intervening in political affairs. War broke out between the Iruvanad Nambiars and the French in 1739 and the latter had the worst of it. In 1739 and 1740 French arms suffered numerous reverses in North Kerala. This was but the prelude to a greater effort. In November 1741 de Labourdonnais arrived with two ships at Mahe and attacked Kadathanad and defeated the Rajah's forces. But peace was concluded satisfactorily to all parties and the French and the English settled down amicably. This was a further blow to the Dutch.

Elsewhere the policy of intervention continued. The Company itself did not interfere in the fights between the princes for the simple reason that it would have been a costly pastime for a trading corporation. They got the Rajah of Cochin to do this work for them and that Chief under the illusion that his power would increase by such intervention was never loath to play the agent provocateur for the Dutch. Their policy on this matter was no secret. In a letter dated 8th October 1735 the Supreme Government at Batavia directed the commandeur at Cochin that care should be taken that the Zamorin and the Rajah of Cochin do not become friends; that incidents which would lead to the continuance of unfriendly relations between the two states must always be created. This policy they carried on with the different princes and noble families of Kerala with the result that all of them were continuously engaged in warfare thus becoming more and more dependent on Dutch help. Circumstances looked so favourable at that time that the Company decided on territorial conquest on a small scale. So far they had confined their military commitments principally to Cochin. When, however, they saw how well they had succeeded in spreading anarchy in Kerala the vision of standing forth as one of the chief Kerala powers came to them. In the secret letter to Batavia dated 12th May 1741[1] it was communicated that the decision was taken to annex Anji Kaimal and Maruthurkulangara. Portions of Vadakkumkur were also to be conquered and the strip of territory from Colachel to Cape Comorin was to be occupied. In fact ever since Van Imhoff's arrival in Eastern waters visions of this nature were floating before the Company. Van Imhoff was, like Albuquerque, a born imperialist. Gustaf Wilhelm, Baron Van Imhoff, belonged to one of the most distinguished families in the Netherlands. He came out to Kerala

---

1. M. S. No. 335.

in 1725 at the early age of 20. In 1732 he was sent again as councillor extraordinary, and in 1736 he became ordinary councillor. In 1737 Van Imhoff arrived in Cochin to report on Cochin accounts. The unsatifactory financial position of the settlements on the Kerala coast had long been a source of concern to the Supreme Government and they had on numerous occasions suggested that the authorities at Cochin should not interfere in political affairs and should retrench their expenditure. Van Imhoff after a thorough examination of the situation came to the conclusion that compulsion should be used to get the Rajahs to fulfil strictly the commercial terms of their agreement and sell to the Company at stipulated prices the whole quantity of pepper. This was no easy matter. It meant an increase in the military establishment of the Company. Van Imhoff also conceived the idea of conquering portions of Kerala and holding them as direct estates. There was an important reason which convinced him of the necessity of this action and that was the growth of British trade in Kerala. We have seen how, as soon as the Dutch were firmly established in Cochin, they got the English expelled from Purakkad and every method was used to dislodge them from Calicut. The Zamorin, however, encouraged the English to stay. The influence of Robert Adams at Calicut and the increasing trade of the British factory at Anjengo were political complications of considerable magnitude. Robert Adams was a forceful individual, more of a political adventurer than of a commercial agent. He gained very considerable influence over the Zamorin and his intervention was felt seriously by the Dutch in the wars with the Ruler of Calicut. "In consideration of the assistance given at Calicut and money given to my servants" the Zamorin gave Adams additional privileges in 1710. For the help in the campaign against the Dutch he received a concession to build a fort at Chetwai. With nothing at his disposal but his own very considerable wits he built up a great political reputation for his country. He made the Zamorin friendly to the English and the trade of the Dutch suffered greatly by this. As, however, the treaty of 1717 restored Chetwai to the Dutch, Adams had to retire to Tellicherry.

At Anjengo in the South, the English were established more firmly. In 1684, the Rani of Attungal allowed the Company to settle for trade, and in 1690 permission was given to build a fort. The local nobles did not approve of this grant and in 1697 they combined to attack the fort while the Rani herself gave support to the factors. In 1694 the Tellicherry factory was established in the territory of Kolathiri. In 1708 the Tellicherry fort was formally made over by the Vadakelemkur or the Northern Regent of Kolathiri.

In 1721, the factory at Anjengo suffered a great disaster. The factor who had been invited to Attungal to present his annual Nazzur went with unnecessary military display and the Nayar Chieftains suspecting an invasion attacked him and cut his escort to pieces. In 1723 Alexander Orme concluded a treaty on behalf of the English East India Company with the Rajah of Travancore. The Rajah wanted to erect a fort at Colachel for which the English Company was to supply the artillery and munitions. The treaty also declared that the Rajah was to be in league and united in good friendship with the East India Company. It is interesting to note that this is the first treaty negotiated by the English East India Company with an Indian State. As a result of this treaty the Company's position on the coast improved and their trade in pepper and spices developed greatly. They supplied artillery and munitions and received pepper, cardamom and other spices in exchange.

The growth of the English trade in pepper and piecegoods and the slow but sure rise in their political importance and the arrival of the French at

Mahe made the Dutch realise that the game of playing off one ruler against another could now be played by the Kerala rulers against the European Companies. The English could be set against the Dutch: the French could be set against both. For this reason, as also for the political complications in Java, the Dutch were unable to act vigorously at the time when they could have asserted their political authority. Instead of this they tried the game of nibbling interference and created against themselves a host of enemies through the length and breadth of Kerala.

CHAPTER V

RISE OF TRAVANCORE

Up to the accession of Martanda Varma in 1729 Travancore was only a minor principality and did not count as a factor in the general politics of Kerala. Though the Trippappil family is undoubtedly ancient as is witnessed by the fact that one of its members attests the copper plate grant of Vira Raghava Chakravarthi, its influence in Kerala politics in the days of the Portuguese and in the first fifty years of the Dutch connection was very little owing to the sub-division of its territory and the internal squabbles of the different branches of the family. Travancore was but one of the five branches into which the Trippappil family was divided. The others, Deshinganad or Quilon, Elayadath Swaroopam, Attungal which was ruled by the eldest princess of the family and Nedumangad were often at war with each other and with Travancore. The principality itself extended only from Edavai to Thovala. The southern portion of this territory both climatically and to some extent ethnologically belonged to the Tamil districts, and its political and cultural affiliations were more with Madura and Trichinopoly than with Calicut, Cochin and Quilon. There was also another and more immediate reason for the negligible influence of Travancore before the 18th Century. In Travancore, more than anywhere else in Kerala, the feudal nobility had reduced royal power almost to a vanishing point. By a settlement made in 1050 A.D., the Government of the Sripadmanabha Temple at Trivandrum which owned most of the lands in the country was handed over to a council consisting of eight hereditary Brahmin priests and the Rajah. The Rajah, however, was to have only half a vote. This ecclesiastical commission was given full authority to collect the revenues and administer them. The councillors or Yogakkar divided the area owned by the temple into eight districts over each of which they placed a nobleman entrusted with the collection of revenues. In course of time these noblemen known as the Lords of the eight Houses—Ettuveetil Pillamar—usurped all secular authority. With the encouragement of the Temple Yogakkar they partitioned the territory. The Rajah became a mere figurehead. During the reign of Rajah Aditya Varma who ruled from 1661 to 1677 the feudal anarchy in the State took a most violent form. The palace of the Rajah was set fire to and later on the ruler himself was poisoned. As there remained only a Rani named Uma Amma with her six minor children, the nobles succeeded to all the power in the State and paid but nominal allegiance to the Ruler.

When this state of anarchy was at its height a Moghul soldier of fortune appeared in the South with a small force of cavalry. Meeting with no opposition he advanced on Trivandram and established his authority in its neighbourhood. The Rani herself retired leaving the capital to the invaders. The nobles who had usurped the royal power made no attempt to organise opposition. The Rani, however, rose to the occasion and invited the help of a prince from Kottayam in North Malabar, Kerala Varma by name, renowned alike for his prowess in the field as for his literary and artistic accomplishments. He was not slow to respond to the desolated Rani's call and organising a small force from the adherents of the family drove out the invader and freed the country again. His success seems to have turned Kerala Varma's head. He began to assume royal powers, and the nobles resenting this usurpation had him assassinated in his palace.

The next few years saw the culmination of this state of anarchy. The Rajah himself was a fugitive and the nobles had everything their own way. It was at the height of this anarchy that Martanda Varma was born (1706). While he was but fourteen he vowed like Philip Augustus of France that he would re-establish royal power in the state and put down the might of the nobles. From that time, even while he was only a prince, twice removed from succession, he set himself with single minded devotion to the task. Soon the Pillamar discovered that they had to deal with one who was as ruthless as they were and more determined than they. Naturally, all their power was directed towards his destruction. For many years the prince was a fugitive, chased from place to place, escaping from the clutches of his adversaries only through the steadfast loyalty of the peasants. His experiences at this period taught him that if the anarchy which reigned in his state was to be put down, it could only be done with the help of a powerful military organisation. It was soon clear to him that if he depended on raising a local militia for this purpose he could not succeed because the Nayar system of military organisation was based on service to the immediate feudal lord and not to the sovereign. So in 1726, while still heir apparent to the thone, Martanda Varma advised his uncle to take what was the most important decision in the history of Travancore, to offer his allegiance to the new Moghul Governor of the Carnatic and solicit his help for the extermination of the refractory feudatories. With this object the Rajah left for Trichinopoly accompanied by a few leading officers of the State and paid homage and allegiance to the throne of Delhi, which, in spite of the wars tha followed Aurangagib's death, was still tho Empire of India—in the person of its Governor of the Carnatic. He agreed to pay a tribute of 3,000 rupees to the Nawab of the Carnatic who in exchange took him under his protection. In the eyes of the Moghul Governor, the Rajah of Travancore was no more than a petty Zamindar and the "treaty" concluded between the Nawab and the Rajah speaks of Rama Varma as a Zamindar of Malabar. But what was lost in dignity was more than compensated by the effective force put at his disposal. The Rajah returned to Travancore with an army under Venkitapathy Naiker. This army with which he hoped to crush the nobles and establish royal authority was to be paid by the Rajah and was to remain under his orders.

Martanda Varma succeeded to the throne in 1729. Though only 23 years old he had learnt both warfare and statecraft in the school of adversity. With the help of the Carnatic troops he set himself out first to crush the nobles. But he soon found that these soldiers of the Nawab would not take their orders from him and were in the position of his masters. They arrested and imprisoned his minister and in other ways showed that they owed no allegiance to him. Nothing daunted, Martanda Varma set to work at once to hire another body of mercenaries. Within the short time of a few months the Rajah collected an army of Maravas from the Tamil country with which he replaced the forces lent by the Nawab. But even with this new force Martanda Varma did not find matters easy. Sri Padmanaban Thampi, the son of the late Maharaja, claimed the throne and appealed to the Nawab of Arcot as the Suzerain. The Nawab as well as the Travancore nobles supported his claim. An army was sent against the Rajah who, however, was able to bribe the commander and get him to retire. The Thampi and the Pillamar, thus betrayed by the commander of the Trichinopoly forces, were left alone to face the wrath of the Rajah. But even unaided, the strength of the nobles was such that Martanda Varma did not dare to attack them openly. In 1733 the Thampi who was the head of the faction was assassinated while on a friendly visit to the Rajah and the nobles were also surrounded and arrested at the same time. Clemency was not one of the virtues of Martanda Varma and the vengeance he exacted was of a nature that struck terror through the whole of Kerala. Forty-two of the proudest nobles were sentenced to be hanged and their women and children were given away in slavery.

This was the first and the most important blow struck against the Kerala political system. With it went the feudal conception of Kerala polity. The old idea was that the Nayar lords could not be punished even in case of treason. In fact, as pointed out in a previous chapter, the Dutch Company made it a condition in their treaty with Cochin that the Nayar nobles who rebelled against the State should be punished. Though the Company had demanded it, the Cochin Rajah had been unable and perhaps unwilling, as too revolutionary a procedure; to punish his noblemen who were constantly in revolt against him. Martanda Varma swept away those notions of chivalry and exterminated without scruple the families that had so long dominated the state. He wished to found an autocratic state of the kind which was in existence at Trichinopoly and at Tanjore. The conception was entirely foreign. The instrument used for its realisation was equally foreign being the mercenary army of Maravas recruited on the East Coast.

With all internal opposition crushed with so little difficulty Martanda Varma turned his attention northwards. The area immediately to the north of his own state was partitioned between the Rajahs of Quilon and Peritaly (Elayadath Swaroopam). Martanda Varma had already found occasion to intervene in their affairs on the ground of adoptions against his interest. The Quilon Rajah had in 1731 decided on an adoption from the family of Kayamkulam. Martanda Varma demanded that this adoption should be rescinded and on refusal attacked Quilon with a large force. The fort of Quilon was very ably defended by Atchuta Variar who was the chief minister of the Rajah. Though Variar fought with great gallantry he had to yield to superior strength. Quilon was annexed and the Rajah was interned at Trivandrum as a state prisoner. This was the first occasion in which a state was thus dealt with in Kerala history, for until this time, the custom was merely to reduce the ruler of a conquered territory to the position of a subordinate chief and leave him in the enjoyment of his territory.

This annexation of a historic principality naturally spread consternation in the rest of Kerala. The northern princes immediately organised a confederacy to liberate the Quilon Rajah and instal him again on the throne. The minister of Kayamkulam, Easwara Pattar, went to Cochin to persuade the Company to take the leadership in this alliance. But the Dutch authorities in Cochin had not yet recognised the full significance of Martanda Varma's policy. The quarrels betewen Kerala chiefs were by no means unwelcome to them as they only strengthened the Dutch hold on all of them. The new warfare-meant to conquer and to annex—had not entered into their calculation, nor had they counted on the force of the military system which Travancore was slowly introducing in the place of the inefficient feudal hosts of traditional Kerala warfare.

The Northern Alliance which the Kayamkulam Rajah negotiated met with some success, in spite of the lukewarm support given by the Dutch. The Rajahs of Kayamkulam, Procaud, Vadakkunkur and Cochin agreed to support each other in a war against Travancore the object of which was to re-instate the Rajah of Quilon on his throne. The Rajah of Maruthurkulangara who was not in the coalition was to be attacked and the forces of the allies were to invade and reconquer Deshinganad. The Rajah of Quilon who was interned in Trivandrum successfully escaped and reached Kayamkulam. A strong force was placed at his command and he immediately marched on Quilon. The Travancore garrison commanded by Arumugham Pillai put up a stout resistance but was obliged to retreat. The allied forces gained another notable success against the main body of Travancore forces led by Martanda Varma himself. The Quilon Rajah was safe again on his throne and the allies carried warfare into Travancore territory.

Martanda Varma had retreated merely in order to remedy the defects in his military organisation and had no intention of giving up the fight. He reorganised his army, especially the new cavalry, procured more efficient weapons and trained and drilled his forces to a point up to which no other Kerala prince had gone. The English merchants at Anjengo and Edavai sold him new and improved war material. When the military reorganisation was complete Martanda Varma took the field again. He divided his forces into two armies and simultaneously attacked Kayamkulam and Quilon. The campaign against Quilon met with immediate success; but at Kayamkulam, the Travancore army was again defeated. Every time the forces of Martanda Varma came out in open conflict, they were heavily defeated and driven back. By an accidental shot the Rajah of Kayamkulam was killed on the battlefield in 1734, but his brother who succeeded him carried on the campaign. Martanda Varma was forced to own defeat and retire.

Defeated ambition again turned to foreign aid to achieve its purpose. For the second time in his short reign Martanda Varma tried to raise a corps of foreign mercenaries with whose help he could conquer Kerala chieftains. Ramayyan—an intriguing and unscrupulous Brahmin who had gained the confidence of Martanda Varma—was deputed to arrange with the Polygars of Tinnevelly for a Marava force. Ramayyan secured the services of Ponnam Pandia Tevan, a Marava chief, who brought with him one thousand horse. With the help of this new reinforcement Martanda Varma made another attack on Kayamkulam. Though he gained some minor advantages in the campaign, the military power of Kayamkulam remained unbroken and a treaty was made by which peace was re-established and the Rajah of Quilon was reinstated on his throne. But the Travancore Rajah had no intention of remaining at peace. In 1734 he annexed Elayadathu Swaroopam a principality lying to the east of Quilon. The unfortunate Rajah of Quilon also died in this year and this precipitated a third war with Kayamkulam.

On the death of the Quilon Rajah, the chief of Kayamkulam claimed the territory by virtue of adoption and immediately took possession of it. Martanda Varma, who had already protested against this adoption and refused to recognise it, claimed the territory for himself. War seemed imminent, when the Dutch Company, who had already begun to feel nervous at the restless ambition of Martanda Varma, intervened. Commandeur Maten sent an envoy to Martanda Varma remonstrating against the annexation of Elayadathu Swaroopam and warning him against attacking Kayamkulam. Martanda Varma, who at this period of life seems to have been absolutely ignorant of the position and power of the Dutch and had not introduced these unknown factors into his calculations for the conquest of Kerala, was surprised at their action. His experience of European merchants was practically confined to the English at Anjengo who did not interfere in political affairs and whose only interest lay in trade. He did not evidently realise at the time that the Dutch claimed political suzerainty over some portions of Kerala and were preparing to enforce it by arms in the coastal region. Martanda Varma's ignorance on this point was useful on this occasion. He sent a reply to Maten in which he asked the Dutch Company to mind their own business and not interfere in the politics of Kerala. This reply naturally incensed the Dutch. The internal difficulties of the

Dutch in Java made an immediate attack on Travancore impossible and this gave Martanda Varma his opportunity to make extensive preparations for the new war with Kayamkulam. Ramayyan, who had in the meantime become Prime Minister and Commander-in-chief, marched against Kayamkulam in 1739. The Dutch considered this to be a proper time for intervention. Van Imhoff, the great Governor of Ceylon, was then at Cochin and he decided to take immediate action. The treasury in Cochin, was, however, not in a state to undertake any great military responsibility. So as a first step Van Imhoff decided that the princes and chiefs who were bound by agreement should be forced to yield the full quantity of pepper and those who were unable were to be mulcted of large sums. Van Imhoff also decided that Marta and certain provinces of Vadakkumkur should be conquered and annexed to the Company's territory. In the meantime a messenger was sent to the Rajah of Travancore asking him to reinstate the princess of Elayadathu Swaroopam but Martanda Varma was in no mood to listen. Van Imhoff himself undertook a journey to the court. He was received with every courtesy but all his diplomacy could not shake the resolution of the Rajah. Van Imhoff threatened and cajoled in turn; but Martanda Varma proved obstinate. They were, indeed, well-matched. The Dutch Governor was a man of extraordinary personality, great courage, and in every way a leader of men. He was determined to gain his point by methods of peace, and failing them, by methods of war. By long experience of diplomacy and warfare in the East, Van Imhoff knew the price he would have to pay for a prolonged campaign in the Travancore hills, away from the range of his ships' guns. But he knew also that if he allowed Martanda Varma to defy him on a matter on which the Dutch were bound alike by their treaty obligations as by their own interests, then the Company would have every petty chief in Kerala against it. Martanda Varma was also equally obstinate. Of his courage and resourcefulness the Dutch had already ample evidence. He did not realise the might of the Dutch on the seas; but as his reply to Van Imhoff proved, he was well aware that he had all the advantages on his side in a prolonged campaign of guerilla warfare conducted from an impregnable base on the hills. War between two such adversaries was therefore inevitable.

Van Imhoff's plan of campaign was well conceived. He decided upon attacking Travancore simultaneously from the north and the south. A powerful force, well equipped with artillery, was to land at Colachel from Ceylon and conquer the area between the Cape and the port and march northwards. From Quilon another force was to attack Trivandrum, while the Rani of Elayadathu Swaroopam, reinstated in her state, was to attack Martanda Varma from the east. As a price of her reinstatement the Company received Vechoor. Martanda Varma did not wait for the campaign to open. He recognised that the weakness of Van Imhoff's plan lay in the untrained levies of the Rani and therefore directed his attack against her. The forces of Elayadathu Swaroopam were completely routed and the Rajah re-occupied the territory. In the meantime the Ceylon forces landed at Colachel. The Rajah who had expected to finish his northern campaign in a short time in order to be ready for this invasion found himself in a hopeless position. The Dutch forces soon fortified their base at Colachel and from there systematically conquered the area to the south of it. Martanda Varma was forced to abandon his northern campaign and proceed south to meet this new menace. But it was a hopeless situation that faced him. The Dutch had established themselves firmly in the littoral from Cape Comorin to Colachel and were advancing on Padmanabhapuram which was one of the chief cities in the state. In this state of despair Martanda Varma turned to the new power which had risen in the Carnatic—to the French at

Pondicherry under M. Dupleix. Negotiations for an alliance were entered into with the French, who were only too glad to get this opportunity to interfere decisively in the affairs of Kerala. But before the new alliance could be of use the fortune of the war turned in the Rajah's favour. Martanda Varma even in this most desperate plight had not abandoned his hope or given up the struggle. He had enlisted and trained a new army which was fully supported by an efficient arm of cavalry and with this force he attacked and totally defeated the Dutch at Colachel (10th August 1741). The Dutch abandoned their positions and evacuated Colachel itself, leaving many persons wounded and 24 Europeans as prisoners. A quantity of muskets fell into the hands of Martanda Varma when the fort was occupied by him.

The battle of Colachel was, in its effects, a disaster of the first importance to the Dutch. It is true that the struggle itself, like that of Plassey, was hardly anything like a big battle. But it put an end to the Dutch dreams of the conquest of Kerala. It was the first great blow inflicted on the Dutch arms and its moral effect was so great that the Dutch never recovered from it. They were too powerful on the sea to yield immediately; but from this time, except for unimportant diplomatic skirmishes with Travancore, the Company was reconciled to the position of mere traders without political pretensions.

So far as Travancore was concerned the battle of Colachel may be said to be the most decisive factor in its development. It removed the main obstacle in the way of its triumphal march towards the north and made the conquest of Kayamkulam and other states possible. As long as the Dutch barred the way and declared that they were the allies of the minor states, Martanda Varma was cooped up within his narrow boundaries. But the victory of

Colachel made such an intervention impossible. It also increased the prestige of Martanda Varma with the rest of the Malabar princes. Till 1741 his arms had achieved no great victory. His fight with Kayamkulam had been indecisive. At Quilon "the gallant old Rajadorai Atchuta Variar" had held him at bay. Nowhere had he made any headway. But this victory showed the Kerala princes that Martanda Varma had not only the ambition but that he also commanded the power to conquer the rest of them.

Of the 24 prisoners taken at Colachel there were two lieutenants Eustachio D'Lannoy, a Fleming and Doncaud, a Frenchman, whom the Maharaja selected for employment in his army. After his experience of the East Coast Martanda Varma had realised the value of cavalry as an arm of his military force. The war with the Dutch taught him the superiority of trained infantry over the feudal levies of Kerala. He employed these two officers to organise for him a standing army trained and armed on the western model. D'Lannoy[1] was useful for the Maharaja in the construction of an arsenal and the provision of an efficient magazine. These activities put the state of Travancore on a new footing and made it possible for it to expand northwards.

In the course of 12 years Martanda Varma had suppressed rebellion in the State, uprooted the elements which had so long rendered the kingdom impotent, annexed Quilon and Elayadam, defeated the Dutch and established unquestioned power from

1. De Lannoy's tombstone can still be seen in Udaigiri fort. It bears the following inscription:—

Hic iacet Eustachus Benedictus de Lannoy qui tanquam dux generalis milittiae Travancotidis praefuit a/e per annos XXXVII ferme summa felicitate regi inserviit cui omnia regna ex Caimcolum usque ad Cochin vi armorum ac terrore subject. Vixit annos LXII menses V et mortuus est die Junii MDCCL. XXVII. Requiescat in pace.

Kayamkulam to Cape Comorin. Now he also organised an efficient standing army and created for himself an instrument which was powerful enough for the purpose of welding Kerala into a single state. Within this short time he had also undertaken numerous reforms, some of a very expensive kind—like Nanjinad irrigation works—and made the state not only the most powerful but the most progressive of the Kerala kingdoms.

CHAPTER VI.

EXPANSION OF TRAVANCORE

After the defeat of the Dutch at Colachel Martanda Varma was free to attack his enemies in the North. The only serious enemy who was powerful enough to hold up his advance was the Rajah of Kayamkulam. Supported by a powerful and well disciplined army, Martanda Varma marched against that state. The three previous campaigns undertaken against that state had not the effect of breaking its military power and Martanda Varma found that the Rajah was ready to win or die but would never yield. Of all the minor principalities to the south of Calicut, Kayamkulam alone had the tradition of heroism, which for centuries had resisted all attempts to encroach on its territory or to curtail its independence. The new attack on Kayamkulam developed into a desultory campaign. The Dutch who felt the disgrace of the defeat of Colachel gave every help to the Rajah of Kayamkulam who counter-attacked Travancore territory and laid waste the lands of Marta, (Maruthurkulangara) a state which Martanda Varma had already annexed. In 1742, the Dutch fort of Quilon was attacked by the Travancore soldiers but there they suffered a crushing defeat at the hands of the gallant old "Rajadorai Atchuta Variar".

The armies of the Kayamkulam Rajah advanced from Quilon into Kilimanoor, a town of considerable importance, not far from the capital itself. The Kayamkulam forces captured the fort and made preparations for advancing further south. But at the height of his misfortune Martanda Varma showed courage. He mobilised all available troops within striking distance of Attungal, recruited a new army and spent his last penny in equipping the forces at his disposal by arms and ammunitions procured from the English at Anjengo and from the French at Mahe. Martanda Varma was fighting clearly with his back to the wall. If he lost the battle he stood to lose everything. The Kayamkulam army with their Dutch allies could, if victorious, march straight to Trivandrum. But never did Martanda Varma's courage shine better than in adversity and the blind goddess favoured him. He surrounded Kilimanoor and besieged the Dutch and Kayamkulam forces within the walls. After a siege of 68 days the Travancore forces carried the fortress by assault and the commandeur of Cochin and the Rajah of Kayamkulam retreated to Quilon. But the defeated army was not given time to reorganise. Martanda Varma was quick to press an advantage and the allied forces of the Dutch and Kayamkulam Rajah were chased to the walls of the latter's capital. Defeated again in open conflict, the Rajah signed a separate peace and became a tributary of Travancore and ceded to Martanda Varma more than half his territories.

With Kayamkulam under him, Martanda Varma's career of conquest met with no serious opposition. Vadakkumkur and Thekkumkur were immediately attacked and after a short campaign annexed to Travancore. A more serious campaign was necessary to subdue the Rajah of Purakkad. As soon as Kayamkulam was annexed, Martanda Varma entered into negotiations with the prominent leaders in the Purkkad State with a view to weaken its defences. That state was one of the mainstays of Dutch power on the coast and the Rajah of the place was a loyal ally, first of the Portuguese and then of the Netherlands Company. If the Dutch power was to be broken on the coast, it was necessary that the Rajah's dependence on the Company must first be destroyed. The Minister of the Raja, the Bhattathiri of Thekkedam, and the general of his forces, Mathur Panikkar, visited or sent delegates privately to Martanda Varma. But before hostilities were actually begun, the Dutch Company sent a message that they were prepared to negotiate for peace. The continued warfare in Kayamkulam, Quilon and Vadakkumkur had caused much loss to the Company's pepper trade. Not only were they involved in considerable military expenditure which burdened a depleted treasury but even the ordinary trade of the Company suffered owing to the conquest by Travancore of Quilon, Kayamkulam and Vadakkumkur. Naturally, therefore, the Company was anxious for peace and made direct overtures. The minister Ramayyan and Talavady Kochumoosad were sent by the Raja as plenipotentiaries to meet the Dutch representatives, Ezekiel Rabbi and Captain Sylvester Mendes, at Mavelikkaray. But as both parties put forward claims which the other would not accept, the negotiations came to nothing. The Dutch were not yet so completely defeated as to be forced to surrender their dominant position, and Martanda Varma had gained too much political sense to allow them to meddle again in Kerala political affairs. The Company wanted to be considered a political power; Martanda Varma would negotiate with them only on the basis of their being a trading agency.

Negotiations were started again a few months later only to be broken off and desultory conversations were kept up as neither side cared to carry on actual war. The reason of this peculiar diplomacy was that Van Imhoff was in the Indian seas with an imposing armada and whenever he came near the Kerala coast, Martanda Varma took up a conciliatory attitude. But the Dutch, if they thought they could intimidate Martanda Varma by a demonstration of imposing naval strength, were totally mistaken.

Though the Dutch did not embark on direct hostilities, they did not hesitate to build up another coalition against Travancore. The Rajah of Kayamkulam, who found the conditions imposed by Martanda Varma too irksome for his independent spirit, was easily persuaded to take up the leadership of this new confederacy which included the Rajah of Thekkumkur and Purakkad. A new war broke out and Martanda Varma's forces marched north in 1746. Kayamkulam was taken and the territories belonging to its ruler were permanently annexed. Now Martanda Varma was free to turn against Purakkad. The Purakkad Rajah of that time, according to Gollenesse, was a young man of about 35, of great intelligence and some ability. His state was difficult to attack and conquer as it was a marshy area. Also, his army was highly trained and well equipped. The Travancore army was opposed by the Rajah's forces at Tottappalli—the southern extremity of his state and in the battle that ensued the Purakkad army remained victorious. But the crafty Brahmin Minister, Ramayyan, was equal to the occasion. He entered into negotiations with the general of the enemy's forces, Mathur Panikkar, who was bought over to the Travancore side. For this betrayal the Panikkar was rewarded by grants of title and money. After thus buying off the main portion of the Rajah's troops, the Travancore forces again attacked and turned the Purakkad lines. The Rajah himself was taken prisoner and sent to Trivandrum.

From out of the six Dutch establishments south of Cochin, Quilon, Marta, Kayamkulam and Purakkad thus passed under the control of Travancore. The agreements which the Dutch had made with those chieftains for the monopoly of pepper trade became valueless and the Company soon recognised that with a hostile Travancore their trade in pepper and cardamom would continue to fall. Kerala in fact had become a serious financial drain to the Dutch Company. The area to the north of Cochin which after the successful war with the Zamorin in 1717 was yielding excellent results in pepper trade had again become a cockpit of warfare. The Zamorin invaded Cochin in 1742 and took possession of the great temple of Tripporyar. After a great deal of desultory fighting in which the Cochin Rajah suffered much loss, the Zamorin, taking advantage of the Company's difficulties with Travancore, attacked Chetwai. The Payencherry Nair, a former feudatory of the Zamorin, whose allegiance was transferred to the Company by the treaty of 1717, joined the Calicut forces. The whole area of Chetwai was reconquered. Thus, attacked from both sides, the Company decided that peace with Travancore was an immediate necessity. The draft treaty submitted by Travancore was ratified in 1753 (15th August) though its provisions had in the main been accepted and carried out in 1748. This treaty which practically destroyed the political power of the Dutch in Kerala deserves careful study. The main clauses are that the Travancore Ruler undertook on any pretext not to receive or encourage other European powers in the territories subject to him provided that the factories of the English at Anjengo, Vizhinjam and Edawai were allowed to continue; if any other European power attacked the Raja the Company would give full support by land and by sea.

Martanda Varma undertook to deliver to the Company 1,509,999 lbs. of pepper every year at the price of Rs. 65 per candy: The English Company should receive only as much as they are entitled to by the treaty of 1727. But it was also agreed that the Travancore Rajah would sell to the Dutch at the cheaper rate of Rs. 55 per candy pepper from countries which he had conquered or will in future conquer. The most important clause, so far as Travancore was concerned, was that the Dutch undertook not to interfere in favour of any one with whom Martanda Varma and his successors were at war. The Company also undertook to sell war material at cost price to Travancore.

Two important facts will be noticed with regard to this treaty which places it on a different footing from all the previous treaties concluded by the Dutch.

First, the Dutch Company surrendered all pretensions to political authority and undertook not to intervene in favour of any prince attacked by Travancore. The extent of this surrender will be realised only when it is remembered that the cause of the war between the Company and Travancore was an attempted intervention by the commendeur of Cochin in Quilon and Elayadath Swaroopam. The Dutch Company had always claimed that except in the case of the Zamorin of Calicut they had the right of intervention and that they were the final arbiters in all disputes. We have seen how they insisted that they should be consulted, and their permission taken, for adoption in the families of Mangat and Parur. In Cochin they had gone even so far as to declare themselves direct suzerains. With most of the states they had treaties of alliance which put on them the burden of defending the Rajah from external aggression. Their surrender of this claim was therefore a betrayal of their allies who had put their trust in them. By this, the Dutch Company handed over the petty Rajahs of the coast to Martanda Varma whose military power, based on a Marava force recruited from Tinnevelly, was irresistible in their eyes.

The disastrous implications of this clause were pointed out by the Cochin Rajah in a formal protest which he lodged with the Supreme Government at Batavia. He complained that the Company had "sacrificed an old friend and ally besides other Malabar Kings and broken all contracts. When from the very beginning our ancestors tried to bring some kings under their sway and obedience the Honourable Company continuously interfered; by observing this rule this kingdom got divided in so many parts and has, therefore, become unable to check its powerful enemies. Now that the king of Travancore has become a powerful king he has been able to coax the Honourable Company under promise to observe everything by means of which he bids fair to bring the other kings under his sway. But we believe he will shortly try to subjugate the Honourable Company also and besides it will have to put up with all kinds of affronts in one way or another."[1]

The second point of importance is that this treaty contained no clause about special protection for Christians. Ever since the first Portuguese treaty made with Quilon the European traders had taken the Latin Christians of the coast under their special protection. These people were tried and punished by the Company and they had their special privileges guaranteed. This extraordinary system was the cause of much trouble and when Martanda Varma refused to include it in the general clause, the Company, having had to yield on even more important points, was not strong enough to resist.

There is no doubt that the first of these two exceptional conditions dealt the death below to the Company's position on the coast. The stipulation that the Company shall recede from all engagements which they may have entered in with other Kerala princes whom the King of Travancore may choose to attack and that they will on no account interfere in their disputes or afford them assistance or shelter was indeed too humiliating a surrender to have been made for nothing. The Dutch had suffered no crushing military defeat under the pressure of which they were compelled to sign this clause. Though the compaign had gone against them, their military position was safe and unassailable. What was then the motive behind so fundamental a surrender as this clause implied? The fact was that the Dutch had lost the pepper trade as a result of the war

1. Quoted in *Cochin State Manual*, Govt. Press, Ernakulam, pp. 108-109.

and were anxious to secure it again. In 1726 they had exported 1,952,979 lbs. of pepper. In 1746 when they were at war with Travancore the quantity had been reduced to 541,189 or almost to 25 per cent. This was a grievous loss and the Batavian government realised that if their trade was to be reestablished in Kerala, it could only be done by one of two methods: either by reducing the king of Travancore to a tributary chief or by coming to an agreement with him. The first course was found to be impracticable. There was, therefore, nothing more to do than to accept the best terms for their trade. The Company besides securing from the ruler of Travancore an agreement to sell annually to it 1,500,000 lbs. of pepper at Rs. 65 from his ancient territories, also got better terms for pepper from the territories to be conquered by him. From the point of view of trade they gained greatly; for during four years 1756-1760 they collected 10 million lbs. of pepper or an average of two and a half millions a year.

The treaty clearly ended the Dutch political power. Even in the matter of trade the benefits secured by the treaty for the Dutch proved to be temporary. When the Travancore Rajah had conquered the petty chiefs and extended his territory up to Cochin, he denounced the trade clauses of the treaty and when reminded of his obligations to sell the Company pepper at a fixed rate he gave them the crushing reply that as they no longer had any political power they were only merchants and as such he would be glad to give them permission to buy in the open market.

With the Dutch neutrality thus established by the treaty, Martanda Varma was in a position to advance towards the North. That was easy enough. Thekkumkur and Vadakkumkur were conquered and the boundary of Travncore extended from Cape Comorin to the Periyar river. But the people of Kayamkulam, Purakkad, Changanachery and other northern principalities, so long accustomed to independence, and the feudal nobles, so long masters in their own houses, rose up in revolt against this invasion of Tamilians. The Travancore conquest was not really the conquest of one Kerala State by another. It was the conquest of Kerala States by a ruler who had made himself strong by the help of Marava mercenaries. The Rajah of Purakkad escaped from his internment, and took up the leadership of this movement. He was joined by the other dispossessed rulers of Vadakkumkur and Thekkumkur and received also the assistance and active support of the Cochin feudatories. The Cochin Rajah himself had become nervous about his position between the Zamorin and the Maharajah of Travancore and therefore joined the alliance. Martanda Varma had forseen this probability. He had already launched upon a diplomatic offensive against the Rajah of Cochin by encouraging the factions in the Cochin family which were against the Ruler. In the Cochin family there are two titles, Perumpadappu Muppil or the head of the family who is the eldest member of the ruling and non-ruling branches combined, and the Ruler who is the head of the ruling branch. In 1748 these two dignities became separate as the eldest member who claimed the title, Perumpadappu Muppil, belonged to the dispossessed branch. The Rajah, however, refused to recognise the title. The disinherited prince escaped to Trivandrum and sought the help of Martanda Varma, who was not slow to recognise the diplomatic value of this claim. He took the prince under his patronage and notified the Cochin authorities through the Company that any settlement made without his concurrence would not find acceptance.

The chronicles of Trippoonittarah mention that there was another cause of conflict between Cochin and Travancore. Martanda Varma had taken possession of the rich and ancient temple of Tiruvalla which was under the control and sovereignty of the

Cochin Rajah though it was situated in what had become the Travancore State. Naturally the Cochin Rajah was incensed and he thought that the new combination gave him an opportunity of humbling the proud Rajah of Travancore. The Vadakkumkur Chief kept back from the alliance as a result of his connection with the dispossessed Cochin princes. But the coalition looked formidable. The Cochin army was commanded by Palliyil Idikkela Menon, the Paliyam Chief being a minor at the time. The campaign went against Cochin, though no serious engagement took place and the Rajah agreed to the terms suggested by Travancore. Cochin agreed to pay an indemnity, to accept the dispossessed princes and to surrender to them the land of Karappuram extending from Cochin to Alleppey. The rulers of Cochin and Travancore met at Mavelikara in 1753 to negotiate a treaty and Martanda Varma was able to get these and some more important clauses agreed to by the Rajah of Cochin. It was agreed that all the pepper in Cochin—excepting 500 candies—must be sold to Travancore, that the rights of the temples at Tiruvalla and Haripad should be surrendered to Travancore, that the rights of the Princes should be settled after consultation with the nobles, and that Travancore should be given an indemnity of Rs. 25,000.

This treaty, however, was not ratified. The escape of the Rajah of Purakkad and the rebellion of the peoples of the newly conquered territories seemed to the Raja of Cochin to afford a new opportunity for taking his revenge. The nobility of Cochin was particularly anxious to stop the progress of Travancore. The Dutch also secretly supported them. In a letter dated October 9th 1756 the Government of Batavia wrote to the Cochin Commandeur remarking that it was not possible to accept quietly the march of Travancore to the north and that he hoped action would be taken to ensure the success of the northern allies. A powerful Cochin army led again by

Palliyil Idikkela Menon took up its position, near the present town of Alleppey. The Cochin hosts were reinforced by the subjects of the princes of Kayamkulam, Purakkad and Vadakkumkur. This was in fact the last great fight undertaken by Cochin—the last field where the Cochin flag flew. The great noble families of the States were all there, Komu Achan,—the new heir of Paliyam, a brave and handsome youth of 18, but even in that early age giving the promise of highest distinction in war and statecraft, the personification of the feudal chivalry of latter day Kerala—, the chief of Kodassery, the Kaimal of Panamukkam, the Changaramkoda Kaimal, the president of the 30,000 of Tottachery and the rest of the great families of Cochin, forgot their ancient rivalries and took up their position besides Palliyil Idikkela Menon in an attempt to stem the tide of Travancorean aggression in which they saw not only the ruin of their own position but the conquest of Kerala by a prince whose main sources of strength were an alien bureaucracy of Tamilian Brahmins and a mercenary army of Maravas. But against the discipline and training of the Travancore forces their patriotism counted but for little.

The Cochin army reached Purakkad by sea and took up its positions in December 1753. A small force also marched through Karappuram and joined the Cochin army. The Travancore forces immediately cut off their communications from behind and de Lannoy's artillery threw their whole army into confusion. The flower of Central Kerala chivalry fell on the field. Among those who were captured were the heir of Paliyam, the third Kaimal of Panamukkam and the Chief of Kodassery.

The victory was systematically followed up. The whole of Karappuram was conquered and the Travancore army reached within two miles of the Dutch fort. The Rajah of Cochin sued for peace and the Dutch Governor strongly supported him and promised to act as an intermediary. But though the army of Cochin was defeated the people of Purrakkad, Thekkumkur and Vadakkumkur were not so easily reconciled to the new Ruler. They rose again in revolt. The whole country north of Kayamkulam took up arms against the exactions of Ramayyan and the unchivalrous attitude of Martanda Varma towards the princes. The position of Travancore was precarious; but Martanda Varma in his desperation was utterly unscrupulous and totally devoid of all sense of patriotism. In order to put down the discontented populace he did not hesitate to invite the assistance of Hyder Ali who was then the Mysore Commander at Coimbatore. This policy of invoking foreign help to build up his personal greatness was at the root of Martanda Varma's policy from beginning to end. It is this fact which takes away from him any claim to greatness as a Kerala King. The fact that he should have thought of invoking the aid of Hyder Ali to put down the discontent of his own subjects is the measure of his political sense as well as of his patriotism.

Fortunately for Travancore this remedy, more disastrous than the disease, was not found necessary. The people showed a greater appreciation of the crisis than the King and peace was restored. But it is important to remember that much of the later misfortunes of Travancore arose from this foolish and unpatriotic act of Martanda Varma. Hyder Ali's assistance once sought was not so easy to shake off. He wrote to Martanda Varma that he was ready to march on the disaffected population of Travancore, but as the rebellion had quietened down the Raja declined Hyder Ali's assistance. The Mysore commander demanded compensation and considered the excuses of Martanda Varma specious. The attack of Tippu on Travancore at a later date and the disasters that followed it were the outcome of this invitation.

The weakness of the Cochin Rajah and the loss of the Company's political power afforded the Zamorin the opportunity he was long waiting for to recover the areas he had lost to the Dutch. The reigning Zamorin was a prince of great ability and foresight. He was anxious to make the best use of the opportunity to recover Chetwai and in 1755 he attacked the Company's outposts at Pappinivattam. It will be remembered that by the treaty of 1719, the Zamorin had given up to the Company his feudal rights over the Velost Nambiar and Pazhayancherry Nayar. The lands of these noblemen were also attacked and reconquered. The whole of the southern lands bordering on the backwater soon returned to the old allegiance. The Zamorin garrisoned the fortress well, strengthened the bastions and erected a new outpost at Pullikkarai with the object of cutting off the communication of the Dutch garrison at Chetwai with the sea. The fort at Enamakkal was surrendered to the Zamorin and the guns were taken to Pulikkarai for strengthening it. Chetwai was invested with 8000 soldiers. Calicut forces also occupied Parur and in May the Zamorin himself occupied Trichur. In October the outpost at Mulloorkarai was occupied.

The Zamorin then attacked the territories of the Rajah of Cochin. Having obtained the submission of Mangat and Parur the Calicut forces marched into Cochin from that side. Another army attacked from the side of Chetwai. The frontier on this side was controlled by the Enamakkal fort which was powerfully garrisoned with men and heavy artillery. But the commander of the fort had already surrendered it to the Zamorin without firing a shot. With Enamakkal in hand the whole of north Cochin lay open to the Zamorin. The feudal lords of the area offered no resistance and the rule of Calicut was firmly established. With his base in the heart of the enemy's territory the Zamorin advanced on Paliyam and occupied the domains of that chief.

In the short period of nine months the Zamorin had conquered practically the whole of Cochin and recovered the possessions lost by his predecessors to the Dutch. The Company tried hard by diplomacy as well as by force to get the Zamorin to withdraw from Chetwai. Commandeur Cunes himself went to Cranganore and the Cochin heir apparent reached Tiruvanchikulam with an army. The chief of Paliyam commanded the main army. The effort so made to relieve Chetwai ended in defeat. The Dutch force was compelled to retire, abandoning its artillery. With the field cleared of the Dutch soldiers, the Zamorin immediately attacked Cranganore. With a view to surround the territory of that chief the Calicut forces occupied Parur and then began to advance steadily on the fort of Cranganore. When matters came to this crisis the Dutch authorities in Cochin took fright and decided on determined resistance. But with the forces at their command no resistance was possible. The garrison in Ceylon was also below strength and as a result commandeur Cunes was helpless to take any effective action. In this plight he requested the lords of Chetwai to join hands with the Rajah of Cranganore and stop the onward march of the Zamorin. But these nobles instead of playing the commandeur's game decided to throw in their lot with the Zamorin and the Company was made to realise that they had ceased to possess the status of even a third class political power in Kerala.

The Zamorin's attack on Cochin almost annihilated that Kingdom. The Ruler of Calicut first secured the submission of Mangat and Parur. From there he consolidated his rule over the area immediately bordering on Travancore.

But at the height of his victory the Zamorin died on the 5th of May 1758. He was one of the greatest kings that royal line produced and in his time the glory of the Manavikrama Rajahs was redeemed. He was succeeded by a prince who was anxious for peace. It was feared that Hyder Ali would take an early opportunity to invade Kerala. The Zamorin was anxious to conserve his forces to resist this invader. The Zamorin was also getting anxious about the expansionist policy of Travancore. It was clear that, if matters were allowed to take their course, the fight for Kerala supremacy would have to be fought out between Travancore and Calicut. It was necessary for this purpose that the Dutch should remain neutral and with this object in view the Zamorin made a treaty with the Company.

The progress of Travancore from the south made the position of Cochin equally impossible. Travancore had already occupied Karappuram and the territories lying immediately to the south of the capital. The Cochin Rajah was left with but a bit of territory but even over this the Travancore ruler began to put forward claims. It was at this time that Martanda Varma died (1758). There is no doubt that for all his shortcomings he was a great Ruler. Undoubtedly he was unscrupulous, cruel to the point of inhumanity and unmoved by a sense of patriotism. He showed himself during the whole of his career entirely devoid of a feeling for Kerala Dharma and the basis of his statecraft was the utilisation of foreign help for subduing the chieftains opposed to him and to strengthen his own position; the second time he went to the extent of inviting Hyder Ali to come to his help in North Travancore. His cruelty towards the family of Ettuveetil Pillamar and the murder of the Thambis show that he attached but little value to fair play towards his enemies. Apart from these, from the point of view of Kerala history Martanda Varma's policy was disastrous in another way. His attempt was to sweep off the whole Kerala polity and establish in its place an autocracy of the type which prevailed in Madura under the Nayaks and in Trichinopoly under the Nabobs. This autocratic state was to be supported by the twin pillars of a mercenary army and an alien bureaucracy, both hostile to the population of Kerala and unsympathetic towards its institutions. The Travancore state was in fact a Tamilian conception and its advance towards the north was the victory of Tamilian over Kerala culture. Martanda Varma in the interest of his dynastic ambition surrounded himself with scheming Tamilians of whom Rammayyan was the supreme type and with ambitious adventurers like de Lannoy.

Even with these limitations it can hardly be denied that the results achieved by Martanda Varma were of a nature which gives him a position in the front rank of Indian statesmen in the 18th century. When he came to the throne his state was one of the smallest in Kerala. Royal power was practically non-existent. There was no money in the treasury. The army obeyed the commands of rebellious nobles and his own life was in constant danger. In Kerala politics the Dutch Company put forward pretensions of suzerainty and claimed the right to intervene in all affairs. In a few years' time he chnged the whole map of Kerala, The Dutch Company was forced to abandon its proud position and had to be content with that of mere traders dependent on the goodwill of the Travancore Ruler. The minor principalities from Cochin to Quilon were all conquered and annexed and the rule of Travancore established firmly over them. An efficient and trained army was raised which gave to Travancore a predominance in Kerala affairs which no State had enjoyed before. Great irrigation works, roads and canals of communication were undertaken and carried out. Charitable institutions were founded. These results could not have been achieved except by a man who possessed rare foresight, strength of will, energy and decision. He was, thus, with all his faults, the greatest Ruler of the Travancore line.

CHAPTER VII.

ECLIPSE OF THE DUTCH

Among the prisoners taken at the great battle of Purakkad was the young heir apparent of Paliyam, Komu Achan. He was sent to Trivandrum where he was kept in honourable confinement. Being of noble presence and high accomplishments the young prince became a favourite at the Trivandrum Court. His stay at Trivandrum helped to open his eyes to the new situation in Kerala and made him realise the strength of the forces operating in favour of Travancore. He realised first of all that the strength of Travancore as against the other Kerala princes lay in the fact that the unruly feudal nobility which considered warfare a hobby and changed sides to suit the occasion was crushed by Martanda Varma and in its place a trained army disciplined in the modern manner was raised and maintained directly by the state. He also realised that in the establishment of the central power of the state as against the pretensions of minor principalities lay the sources of Travancore's greatness.

The scales fell from his eyes also in regard to the Dutch. At Cochin the Dutch still looked a formidable power. They had their forts and their ships, But only the dilapidated facade of the edifice of Dutch power now remained. Its weakness was not visible from Cochin. From Trivandrum it was evident. To Komu Achan this came as a revelation. The tradition of his family, as well as that of Cochin Rajahs, was an alliance with the Dutch against the encroachment of the Zamorin. It was now clear that the Dutch were powerless to resist the Zamorin and Komu Achan quickly grasped that Cochin would soon vanish into nothingness unless a valuable ally was secured. The chief of

Paliyam, Kunjunnattachan, died soon and Komu Achan returned to Cochin as the hereditary Prime Minister of the State and the ruler of his own fief.

From the first he had decided on his policy. He saw that for Cochin the only course of safety lay in an alliance with Travancore in its fight against the Zamorin. With this object he worked both at Cochin and at Trivandrum. He induced Martanda Varma to visit the Rajah of Cochin at his capital in November 1756, but the Cochin Rajah would not agree to cede any territory. The negotiations proved abortive. But Komu Achan was not made of the stuff which gave up a policy merely because it did not prove successful in the first instance. In 1757 the Cochin Rajah visited Trivandrum and a general alliance of friendship was then negotiated. When the Zamorin's attack on Cochin carried everything before it and Trichur and the areas around it were under the effective occupation of the Calicut ruler and nothing but a slice of territory was left for the Rajah of Cochin, Komu Achan succeeded in cementing a new alliance with Travancore. The chief of Paliyam came to Trivandrum in 1760 and negotiations were opened for a permanent treaty of alliance between the two states. The main clauses of the treaty were that Travancore would send an army to drive the Zamorin out of the territories belonging to the Rajah of Cochin as a price of which the Cochin Rajah would renounce all his claims over Karappuram, and would cede to Travancore Alangad and Parur. If territories not belonging to Cochin were conquered from the Zamorin such conquests were to go to Travancore. The treaty was solemnly ratified before the altar of Sthanumurti at Suchindram.

Rama Varma, the new sovereign of Travancore, was anxious to continue the ambitious policy of his uncle. A gifted scholar and poet, a liberal patron of all arts, a musician and actor of renown, the

Rajah was also gifted with rare insight in political matters and combined high statesmanship and knowledge of foreign policy with a desire for active reform within the state. Unlike Martanda Varma he was a prince in the true tradition of Kerala chivalry. Kind hearted and refined, he stood out among the princes of his time as an exemplar in many ways. His fame spread to many countries. He is the Rama Rajah of whom the French, English, Mysorean and Carnatic correspondence speaks. Though averse to war, he had inherited the ambitious policy of his uncle which had as its object the unification of Kerala under one flag. The offer of alliance with Cochin [1] opened out a new line of action for him and he was not slow to take advantage of it.

The Travancore army marched forward under the command of the chief minister, Martanda Pillai. A small force was also sent by sea to Ernakulam. The plan of campaign was extremely well conceived. Trichur, in many ways the most important town in Cochin and its religious capital, was under the occupation of the Zamorin. The objective of the Travancore forces was to capture it, because the Zamorin's prestige in Cochin depended on his possession of this important town. Besides this, the strategic position of Trichur on the nodal point was such that it commanded all the routes and cut the territory of Cochin into two unequal portions and confined the Rajah to his coastal tracts. On arriving at Parur the Travancore commander on the advice of General de Lannoy decided upon a direct attack on Trichur from two sides. For this purpose the army was grouped in two divisions, one under Martanda Pillai and the other under General de Lannoy. The plan was to make a converging attack on Trichur, the minister marching directly on it while the General

1. For the text of the correspondence see Appendix II.

was to capture Chetwai and attack it from the north. ...

The Zamorin's forces at Trichur were caught within the blades of this pair of scissors; but from this difficult position the ruler of Calicut extricated himself by ordering his garrison at Chetwai to fight desperate rear-guard actions in which every inch of territory was contested. In the meantime the Zamorin himself after a pitched battle which ended indecisively retired with his army intact. The Calicut forces evacuated Cochin territory and the Zamorin made peace with Travancore. The Travancore Rajah was glad to agree to an immediate peace. That the Zamorin in spite of the fact that he had suffered no heavy defeat sued for peace, was due to the exigencies of external policy. The growth of the Mohammadan power in Mysore and the aggressive intentions of Hyder Ali towards Calicut had made the fight with Travancore seem like a domestic quarrel. The clouds were gathering thick on the eastern horizon and the Zamorin was not slow to realise that the threat to his independence which the European fortress at Cochin meant and which had caused him 250 years of warfare with the Rajah of Cochin had ceased to be of importance and that the new source of danger arising from the military power of Hyder Ali was likely to succeed where Marshal Countinho, Affonso Albuquerque and Van Rheede had failed. The Ruler of Travancore also was gifted with sufficient foresight to realise the dangerous character of the new portent. Besides Rama Varma was himself involved in frontier trouble with the Governor of the Nawab of Arcot at Madura. Yusuf Khan, a rebellious subordinate who had himself been sent from Trichinopoly to displace another rebellious Sirdar, attacked Kalacaud in the territory of Travancore and took possession of it. The attitude of the Nawab of the Carnatic was also doubtful as he was in correspondence with the Zamorin and encouraging him to continue the war with Travancore. A treaty was therefore negotiated by which the Zamorin agreed to pay Rs. 15,99,99 as indemnity and to withdraw from Cochin territory.

This was the last war between Cochin and Calicut. In the same year as this treaty was signed, 1762, Hyder Ali had attacked and conquered Mangalore, Bednore and other important points on the West coast immediately to the north of Kerala. The Mysore storm broke over the whole of Northern Kerala within the next few years sweeping away before its advance the military power of the Nayars and the political institutions of Kerala. With the treaty of 1762, the last page in the independent history of Kerala may be said to have been written. With this date the Nayar hegemony of Kerala may be said to end. So far the history of Kerala had been the history of the Nayars. But in 1762, the military power of the Nayars is broken finally in Travancore and in Cochin, and within a few years it was completely wiped out in North Kerala.

The position which existed up to this time may be described in the following words of Logan: "I would call attention to the central point of interest in any descriptive and historical account of the Malayali race—namely the position, which was occupied for centuries on centuries by the Nayar caste in the Civil and Military organization of the province—a position so unique and so lasting that but for foreign intervention there seems no reason why it should not have endured for centuries to come. Their functions in the body politic have been wisely described in their own traditions as "*the eye*", "*the hand*" and "*the order*" and to the present day we find them spread throughout the length and breadth of the land, but no longer—I could almost say alas!—preventing the rights (of all classes) from being curtailed or suffered to fall into disuse".

This bulwark against the tyranny and oppression of their own rulers secured for the country a high state of happiness".[1]

Alas! that hegemony which looked so secure was finally broken.

The expansion of Travancore was the first direct blow to the Nayar predominance. The Travancore state was founded as a military autocracy on the ruin of Nayar power. The instruments by which Martanda Varma annihilated the Nayar nobility of his state and conquered the Nayar kingdoms to the north of his state were essentially foreign. It was with foreign mercenaries that he expanded his territory and it was with an essentially Tamilian bureaucracy that he governed it. Martanda Varma never forgot—and his successors too cherished the tradition to the end of their rule—the troubles that the Ettuveetil chiefs had given to his house for over three centuries and in the new State that he founded he took good care to see that the Nayar nobility had no position and no power. In the home provinces of the Rajahs of Travancore the Nayar nobility had been systematically annihilated. In the conquered areas the ruling families were reduced to poverty and their nobles soon discovered that power and prestige no longer belonged to them. It was a purely bureaucratic state that Martanda Varma founded and his officials were mainly recruited from the small Tamilian minority in the south. The dominion of petty Kerala sovereigns and princes had come to an end, as Fra Bartolomeo observed at the time.

The example of the ruler of Travancore and the success which attended the dispossession of the nobles and their exclusion from political authority were not lost on the Prime Minister of Cochin. The chief of Paliyam, Komu Menon, who was instru-

1. Logan-*Malabar*, Vol. 1, 1887, Preface p. III and IV.

mental in negotiating the treaty with Travancore, had learnt statecraft in the school of Martanda Varma. After the success of the campaign against the Zamorin, Komu Menon took in hand the problem of organising the State of Cochin on the model of Travancore. Cochin as we had occasion to point out was never really a State. The Rajah's territorial authority was confined to a very small area while even the districts lying adjacent to his palaces and temples were in the hands of Nayar chiefs. This was one of the chief causes of the weakness of Cochin as these chiefs often changed sides and supported the Zamorin. Komu Menon realized that if Cochin was to be organized into a state the reduction of the power and territorial influence of these feudal barons was necessary. With the object in view, Komu Menon had inserted a clause in the treaty with Travancore that the Travancore Rajah would help the authorities in Cochin in their efforts to reduce the power of the nobles. As soon as the war was over the leading noblemen like Mankata Rajah, Chengazhi Nambiar and others who had helped the Zamorin were brought before the Rajah and made to realize that the days of political power were gone for them. Komu Menon proceeded also to confiscate and disinherit many minor noble families who had taken arms against the Rajah. By systematically enforcing this policy over a period of three years Komu Menon was able to establish the Rajah's power in Cochin on a sound and stable basis. But here also the establishment of the bureaucratic state meant the destruction of the Nayar power. But it took a different form. The Nayar nobility disappeared from Cochin history. No more do we hear of Anchikaimals, Kodassery Kartavus and Chengazhi Nambiars. But the bureaucratic machinery was predominantly Nayar and therefore in the place of the baronial families there arose a new class of Nayar officialdom dependent on the pleasure, and upholding the power, of the Rajah.

During these years between the treaty of Mavelikkara and the invasion of Kerala by Hyder Ali, the political power of the Dutch had practically ceased all over Kerala. In the course of the northern expansion of Travancore, all that the Dutch commandeurs asked was that their immediate possessions should not be attacked. Martanda Varma annexed Karappuram over which they had definite and well established rights and they were unable to protest. His successor annexed Mangat and Parur, two states in whose affairs the Company had long interfered even to the extent of forcing the Rajahs to accept its unquestioned suzerainty. The Dutch were powerless to intervene even in this. The glory of Van Goens, Van Rheed and Van Imhoff had departed and the Dutch flag flew over Cochin merely on sufferance.

CHAPTER VII.

DISAPPEARANCE OF THE DUTCH

The story of the Mysorean invasion of Kerala will be dealt with in the succeeding section. Here the subject is alluded only to complete the history of the Dutch settlement on the coast. In 1766 Hyder Ali made himself master of the kingdom of Chirakkal. In the same year he took Calicut, the Zamorin committing suicide by setting fire to the palace. The Dutch were alarmed at these unexpected developments and were afraid that Hyder might turn his attention towards them. With a view to placate him, Breekpot who was the commandeur of Cochin sent his commissioners to Calicut with presents to compliment Hyder on his success and to find out what his attitude was towards them. The Dutch submitted that their rights in Mapranam and Chetwai should be respected and that the Rajahs of Travancore and Cochin as the allies of the Company should not be attacked. Hyder received these proposals and in his turn suggested a trade agreement on the following conditions:

> That the Company should enter into an offensive and defensive alliance with him;
> That in his southern campaigns the Company should provide him with 1,000 European soldiers;
>
> That he was prepared to respect the Company's rights in Chetwai and Mapranam subject to his right to march through them.

He agreed to spare the Rajahs of Cochin and Travancore provided Cochin paid him an annual tribute of 4 lakhs and eight elephants and Travancore 15 lakhs and 30 elephants. The commandeur was not in a position to accept these extensive commitments and therefore he replied that the matter would have to be referred to Batavia. The Company, however, communicated the terms to the Rajah of Travancore whose reply to this humiliating proposal was the erection of defence works on the northern boundary of the State up to Cranganore.

The dilatory reply of the Dutch met the situation for the time as Hyder was called away from Kerala by the news of a Maratha invasion. In 1773 he again turned his attention to Kerala. He annexed the territory of the Zamorin and placed it under his own officers. The Mysorean Governor at Calicut immediately began to press the claims which his master had inherited from the Zamorin. The principality of Cranganore was formerly subject to Calicut and the Mysorean general lost no time in demanding that the Rajah should pay a tribute and accept his authority. Moens who had become commandeur of Cochin in 1771 claimed that Cranganore was a fief of the Company and tried to intervene in order to save that principality from Mysorean attack. But Sirdar Khan, Hyder's general, refused to listen to the expostulations of the Dutch and the Rajah was forced to yield.

In 1776 Hyder demanded of the Dutch free passage to attack Travancore. Moens replied that no answer had come from Batavia. Hyder knew that this reply was dishonest because it was over 10 years since he made that condition which Breekpot had referred to Batavia. Furious at this double dealing of the Dutch Sirdar Khan invaded Cochin territory marching through areas over which the Dutch claimed rights. In August 1776 Sirdar Khan captured Trichur. The Company could do nothing to protect its ally and vassal and in its anxiety to retain the trade looked on unconcerned while the Rajah of Cochin was being humiliated.

Now it was their turn. Chetwai was formerly a portion of the Zamorin's territory and Sirdar Khan now claimed accounts and arrears for the administration of that area. The Company did not know what to do. They had tried to placate Hyder, had sent him presents and had allowed the Rajahs of Cochin and Cranganore to be despoiled. The position of the Company was humiliating but as the Dutch were unable to oppose Hyder by force of arms they sent him an account which showed that the Zamorin was in arrears. Without waiting for further correspondence the Khan crossed the river a little to the south of Chetwai and took the Dutch officials prisoners and demanded the payment of 20 years' revenue. From there the General invaded Pappanetty and after having reduced it and taken up his headquarters at the Dutch Residency, he wrote to the commandeur complaining that he had not received any reply to his letters. He then invaded Cranganore and laid siege to the Company's fortress there.

The Company had by this time lost all its territorial possessions. Chetwai and Pappanetty passed to Hyder without the Company striking a blow in its defence and Cranganore was also reduced. Besides this, the Khan also demanded 20 years' revenue for the lands of the Zamorin which the Company had held. Now there was no option for the Company. They had either to abdicate and withdraw ignominously or resist Hyder's demands by force. Moens approached the Rajahs of Travancore and Cochin with a proposal that they should ally themselves with him to resist Hyder. It was clear that what the Mysore King wanted was to reduce Travancore. Moens had therefore some hopes that the Ruler of Travancore would declare himself openly for an alliance. But Rama Varma knew that the Dutch in Cochin had not sufficient strength to be of any help to him and replied that as he had allied himself with the English and the Nawab of the Carnatic he could only act in concert with them. So he declined the alliance adding, however, that he would be willing to concert defensive measures.

Thus thrown back upon their own strength the Company asked the Colombo Government to send them reinforcements immediately. Aya Kotta was fortified and proper defensive arrangements were undertaken. It was feared that the Mysoreans would attack Cranganore from the sea. On the arrival of the reinforcements for the Dutch, the Mysorean did not open the attack on Aya Kotta.

Moens, satisfied that his honour had been saved, was now anxious to open negotiations with Hyder. A letter which had arrived from the Supreme Government at Batavia was, therefore, despatched to Seringapatam with suitable presents. In reply Hyder stated that he had only feelings of friendliness towards the Dutch and was willing to enter into an alliance with them. To this the commandeur sent an evasive reply. He pretended anxiety to be on friendly terms but was actually planning to recover what the Company had lost to Hyder. An expedition was sent to Cranganore early in 1778 which re-occupied that principality and attacked Pappanetty. The expedition advanced so far as Chetwai but there it met the Mysore forces and suffered a heavy defeat, entailing the loss of some guns. The Dutch troops retreated to Cranganore with their morale badly shaken. Fortunately for the Dutch war broke out between the English and Hyder which prevented him from actively pursuing his schemes in Kerala.

For the rest of Hyder's life-time the Dutch were safe. But Tippu who succeeded his father in 1782 was not inclined to give up the claims which Hyder had pegged out in Kerala. In 1788 Tippu proposed to the Dutch commandeur at Cochin an offensive and defensive alliance. But the Dutch as usual were cautious and nothing came of the proposal. Then he proposed that the Company should sell him the fort of Cochin, Cranganore and Aya Kotta. The fortress at Aya Kotta was the main obstacle in his projected attack on Travancore lines. These lines had been constructed in 1764 by the Travancore Raja on the advice of General de Lannoy. The Flemish soldier who had considerable engineering skill had noticed during his northern campaign in support of Cochin, how open the new boundary of Travancore was to any attack from the north. Therefore he designed a long and defensible line which is thus described by George Powney, the English East India Company's Agent at Trivandrum in a letter to the Governor of Madras dated 17th February 1790. "They run from West to East commencing at the sea on the island of Vaipin and continue to a broad river called Chinnamangalam on the opposite bank of which they begin again and extend to Annimally or Elephant mountains where they terminate on the top of one of them. The lines consist of a ditch about 16 feet broad and 20 feet deep with a thick bamboo hedge in it, a flight parapet and good rampart and bastions on rising grounds, almost flanking each other. From one extreme of the lines to the other they are only assailable by regular approaches from the north."

For the attack on these lines the possession of Aya Kotta fort was indispensable and it is with this object in view that Tippu offered to buy that fort from the Dutch. But the commandeur, instead of acceding to the request, immediately approached the Rajah of Travancore and by an agreement dated 31st July 1789 sold the forts of Cranganore and Aya Kotta to him. The agreement reads as follows:

"The Illustrious and mighty king of Travancore Wanjie Walla Martanda Rama Varmar having sent his first State Minister and Dalava his Excellency Krishna Poole to the Hon'ble John Gerard Van Anglebeck, Counsellor in ordinary of Netherlands India and Governor of the forts and possessions of the illustrious and mighty Netherlands East India Company on the coast of Kerala, to purchase from the said Company and receive over the fort of Cranganore and the outpost of Aya Kotta with the plantations and fields belonging thereto and they having agreed on the terms have concluded the sale on the following conditions.

The Dalava Krishna Poole for his master bought, and Governor Van Anglebeck has on account of the Company sold to the King of Travancore for the sum of three hundred thousand Surat silver rupees the fort of Cranganore and the outpost of Aya Kotta; with the cannon and thereto belonging ammunition as they at present are as also the powder but no firelocks, cartridges and other articles and moreover the following plantations and gardens.................

The Mosquito Island rented to Bellote duzepo Palio for		300	Rupees
The garden of Telio Barky rented for		115	„
Do.	Ascentio de Roza rented for	190	„
Do.	Naga Shetty rented for	164	„
Do.	Hendrick Mayer rented for	230	„
Do.	Bapoo Probu rented for	64	„
Do.	Allewyn rented for	810	„
Do.	Dama Mussa rented for	1220	„
Do.	Arkell Iltopoe rented for	119	„
Do.	Tronotoe Barky rented for	115	„

The purchase and sale is concluded with this condition that the King of Travancore shall not prevent the passage past the fort, either to boats belonging to Company, or to King of Cochin and his subjects but all the same should they be empty or laden with rice, paddy or goods of any denomination whatever, as also rafts of wood and bamboo etc., etc.; in a word all goods whatever without exception are to be allowed free, without molestation to pass and no new duties to be charged thereon.

The king promises expressly that the firewood, which must be brought from above Cranganore, shall not be prevented on any pretext whatever and no new charges laid thereon, but on the contrary will assist in forwarding the same to Cochin.

The Lepers' House at Palliport with its adjoining buildings, gardens and other grounds belonging thereto, is to remain in the Company's full and free possession.

The Roman Churches at Cranganore and Aya Kotta having for a long time under the Company are to remain so and the King is not to trouble himself with the Priests; the Christians are to remain vassals of the Company and must not be burdened with any new taxes.

The Priest's House at Palliport, which the Governor built and presented to the Church is to remain to the Church and no new taxes will be laid on them.

The inhabitants retain their houses, gardens and plantations which are now in their possession and as long as they remain Christians are like other Roman Catholic vassals of the Company, and must not therefore on any pretext whatever have any new taxes lain on them, but they are to be held answerable to pay unto the King whatever they formerly paid to the Company.

The king promises to pay a sum of fifty thousand rupees ready money, before delivering over the above-mentioned forts and ground and the remainder being two hundred and fifty thousand rupees to be paid in the four next following years at equal periods and to be carried to the credit side of the pepper account yearly to the amount of sixty-two thousand one hundred rupees for the fulfilling of which for the merchants David Rahaboy, Ephrain Cohen and Anta Setty bind themselves as bonds-minor legal debtors. All this is agreed to in the city of Cochin in the year Koliang 974 the 19th of the month Karkadagom or the 31st July 1789."

For this piece of double dealing Tipu's wrath would have fallen on the Dutch but for the complications arising from his attack on Travancore and the third Mysore War which it precipitated. By the treaty of 1792 Tippu lost his Kerala possessions and the Dutch had nothing more to fear from him.

The possessions of the Dutch had already been reduced to the Cochin fort and a few acres near Quilon. With the conquest of Kerala by the British the position of the Dutch, as traders, suffered and Cochin ceased to be of any importance. But even as a relic of the days of Van Goens and Van Rheede they were not destined to hold it for long. The war between England and France caught Holland in its toils and the alliance of the Batavian republic with Revolutionary France gave the British Company an opportunity to demand the surrender of Cochin. To enforce this demand a force under Major Petrie marched down from Calicut. But the Dutch Governor Van Spall refused to yield. A force was therefore landed to the south of Cochin. This consisted, besides one regiment of European soldiers, of a battalion of sepoys, and a strong force of artillery. As soon as fire was opened Van Spall sent his proposals for surrender. Though many conditions were made Major Petrie refused to agree and the commandeur rather ingloriously accepted the terms offered to him.[1] Major Petrie agreed to give the garrison the honours of war. The officers were allowed to retain their swords. The garrison marched out in military formation and deposited their arms upon the esplanade and returned as prisoners of war. The request that they should be repatriated was refused by Major Petrie who bluntly stated that the garrison will be disposed of as the commander-in-chief may direct. With this, the Dutch flag ceased to fly on the Kerala Coast (20th October 1795). The formal cession took place by the Convention of Paris in 1814 when the alliance with Revolutionary France which had been so disastrous to the Colonial Empire of Holland, was broken by the defeat of Napoleon.

---

1. For the text of the treaty see Appendix III.

CHAPTER IX

DUTCH POLICY IN KERALA

The Dutch policy in Kerala was governed by the single consideration of maximum pepper trade at minimum expense. The original idea with which the Dutch started was a monopoly in pepper trade by agreements with the Chieftains and Rajahs whose territories lay to the south of the Zamorin's kingdom. These contracts which were negotiated with the Princes immediately after the conquest of Cochin, all contained a clause that pepper should be sold only to the Dutch Company. Such an agreement was clearly difficult to enforce without political power backed by a considerable army. That was, indeed, what was attempted until the rise of Martanda Varma and the treaty of Mavelikkarai which crushed the political authority of the Company.

The policy of the Company falls distinctly into three periods; (1) from 1664 to 1697, (2) from 1697-1717 and (3) from 1717-1754. During the first period the Company maintained a considerable military establishment and kept up the pretence of great power. The attempt at that time was to enforce rigorously the pepper contracts with the rulers. The authorities embarked on a forward policy in Cochin and reduced the Rajah of that place to utter dependence. They claimed the right to interfere in every matter concerning the administration of the State and even in the internal affairs of the Royal family. Nor were their pretensions any less in Cranganore whose Chief was declared to be a bondsman of the Company. At other places where the seat of the Ruler was not within the range of the Company's guns their claims were not taken seriously. But in the lands of the petty lords round about Cochin, in

Mangat, Parur and Idappalli they interfered, claimed and enforced political control.

This policy was found to entail vast expenditure on military establishments. If the authority of the Company was to be felt and feared, military posts all over the coast could not be avoided and this would naturally lead to incessant trouble. Defiant Chieftains would have to be punished. The military posts must always be in a satisfactory condition for defence against local inhabitants. In spite of these the major princes may take no heed. This is exactly what happened. Though the Company's military estabilishemnt cost a great deal, it produced no satisfactory results. The monopoly in pepper trade could not be enforced. The Rajahs were openly selling to outsiders, and the Chief of Kayamkulam, in whose territory there was a military post of importance, was harbouring Captain Kydd and selling pepper to him.[1] The failure of the policy of enforcing by arms the pepper contracts was so clear that in 1697 the Company decided to reduce the garrsion and withdraw from a number of outposts it had built. The Resolution said:

1. "That the fortifications of the city of Cochin, which by the large garrison it required and the continual reparations to be made in consequence of the great extent of the walls were too expensive for the Company to maintain, should be reduced by one-half.

2. That one of the present fortifications of Cannanore, the Portuguese tower, only should be preserved with a garrison of 20 or at the most 25 Europeans.

3. That in Cranganore the ancient interior works should be preserved with a garrison of 20 Europeans which is judged a sufficient

1. Straveninus, Vol. III. p. 235.

number for the purposes of the Company there.

4. That it is likewise judged advisable at Quilon no more should be retained than the old Portuguese tower or as much of the present works as may be thought necessary, for the interests of the Company with 15 or 20 men to which number the establishment should be reduced; and that the remainder of the fortification of the 3 last places should be removed or demolished.

It was further thereby determined that all military outposts should be withdrawn except Paponetty, Proca and Cali Coylang (Kayamkulam) should be maintained as residences or factors in order to keep an eye over what might be going forward all along the coast."[1]

Similar reductions were made in all naval and artillery establishments of the Company. The vessels were reduced to one small yacht, two sloops and three small row boats. In fact, the Company never attempted to enforce the Portuguese policy of completely restraining navigation and never claimed to be the sole lords of the seas. Such a claim was impossible as the English and French and other European nations were keen competitors on the Kerala Seas. Besides, the Dutch had a considerable fleet at Colombo which was always available for use in Kerala. Artillery on the coast was fixed at 95 pieces of iron, six pieces of brass, and ordnance with two motors.

This extensive reduction in the military establishment of the Company was undertaken because "the ostentation of a great power which cost the Company such large sums of money had not the

---

1. Straveninus, Vol. III: P. 235.

effect of producing on the native princes that degree of awe and apprehension which is indispensably necessary for the carrying on of an extensive trade". But these retrenchments undertaken in the interests of larger profits did not help the affairs of the Company. Almost immediately after this, war broke out between the Company and the Zamorin which really came to a close only in 1717 after an extended campaign involving the use of a considerable European army. In this period, between 1697 and 1717, the Company's policy was to reduce military establishments, but they were forced to carry on a defensive and later on an offensive war against the King of Calicut who was not included in their political system.

Even after the conclusion of peace with the Zamorin the military charges grew to such an extent that the Supreme Government at Batavia issued strict injunction (by their secret despatches dated 30th September 1721) not to continue hostilities against the princes on the coast. They went even to the extent of saying that the Company should not interfere to support the Rajah of Cochin if he were attacked by the Zamorin. After 1717, the policy of the Company, as we have traced elsewhere, was one of increasing intervention in the affairs of the smaller princes. The prestige which they had gained by the defeat of the Zamorin was of help in bringing the petty Chiefs under control. With the Madampies or petty chiefs of Karappuram they made a treaty at Aryat in 1710, but the policy of intervention in the internal affairs of the chiefs developed only after 1717. Gollenese even went to the extent[1] of suggesting that the principalities of Vadakkumkur and Perittally should be conquered and held directly by the Company. But of its feasibility he himself was not certain and his proposal was there-

1. See Chapter III.

fore couched in the following equivocal terms. "However should the Company have a great force at any time in India and occasion permit us to push the matter energetically my opinion would be that it would suffice to make ourselves completely master of the states of Perittally and Vadakkumkur." Van Imhoff who visited Kerala in 1739[1] was even more imperialistic and wanted the Company to "punish" the princes who were defiant.

The rise of Martanda Varma foiled their plans. Their whole policy of internal intervention and the claim to political power were given up by the treaty of Mavelikkarai. The Company by the famous 9th Article of the treaty receded from all engagements with the Princes whom the Travancore Rajah chose to attack and agreed to interfere on no account in their disputes nor in any respect to raise any objection to the enterprises of the King. After this, the only object of the Company was to trade peacefully and to keep whatever little power they had in Cochin and its environs.

An attempt has recently been made by an English writer to prove[2] that the Dutch were sovereigns in Kerala from the beginning and had seriously entertained the idea of conquering the country. There is indeed no basis for such a claim. It is true that the Dutch Company was accepted as one of the Kerala powers and in Cochin they claimed superior authority on the pretext of which they intervened in the affairs of the petty states on the coast. But the whole territory of the Zamorin was completely outside their influence; the Rajahs of Travancore even before the time of Martanda Varma were more friendly towards the English Company than towards the Dutch; while the princes in the interior never even had dealings with them. Even the more power-

1. Madras Records page 72.
2. Mr. Galletti's *Dutch in Malabar*, p. 25.

ful coastal chiefs like the Rajah of Kayamkulam did not consider the Company to be anything like a superior power. The power of the Company was in fact confined to Cochin and to such small states like Mangat and Parur which could be bullied and intimidated from the Capital. They were in fact exactly like one of the minor chiefs in Kerala and never at any time were they "the Paramount power in Kerala" as Mr. Galletti pompously declares. An ambitious man unacquainted with Kerala conditions like Van Imhoff may have thought it possible to conquer portions of Kerala, but the authorities in Batavia recognised after some experience that wars only serve "on the one hand to reveal the impotence of the Europeans against the Natives of the country if they have to be brought to reason by force of arms, on the other[1] hand to impose a great and unbearable burden on us rather than to bring to the Company something substantial proportioned to the great hazards, inconveniences, burdens and crosses which it has brought on itself by the Wars". Even Gollenesse when he suggested that Perittally and Vadakkumkur might be conquered did so in full realisation of its impossibility. The Dutch were never, and did not at any time attempt to be, the paramount power in Kerala. All that they claimed politically was authority over Cochin and its dependencies and at Quilon.

The Dutch policy in Kerala had to fight against the rivalry of other European nations all over the coast. The English had established a factory at Purakkad in 1664, from which they were sent away by the Rajah as a result of the agreement with the Dutch. The English were prepared to pay a higher price for pepper and buy it in the open market, and therefore their competition soon became very keen. The Dutch policy from the beginning was directed

1. Moens p. 106.

towards a "blockade from the land" by prohibiting the Rajahs from selling pepper to the English. "Every means should be employed" wrote Their High Mightinesses in a letter dater Amsterdam, May 14th 1667, "and every effort made to have the English expelled from the land of the Zamorin. The present time of war is a suitable occasion to achieve this. It will never do to have that nation settled so near us."[1] As the Zamorin could not be persuaded to expel the English, the Dutch attempted to prevent merchants from selling pepper to the English. This also was unsuccessful and was given up in 1669. "Although last year we prevented any pepper from reaching the English from Cannanore, we know that they have received large quantities. Therefore we need not trouble ourselves to buy pepper at Cannanore at such high prices for the sake of preventing other nations."[2]

In 1669 the Dutch and the French established themselves again in Calicut. The Zamorin was very friendly especially towards the English and helped them to attract to his port much of the pepper that was produced in Vadakkumkur and Thekkumkur. This competition rendered the pepper very dear for the Dutch and they attempted to intercept the land route by persuading the Rajah of Cochin to attack the chiefs through whose territory the trade was carried on.[3] In 1690 the English were established at Anjengo and diverted to that factory the pepper, cardamom and cloth trade of Travancore. The real competition between English and the Dutch began, however, only with the arrival of Robert Adams in 1716 as the Chief of the Calicut factory. Robert Adams was a masterful man and he soon became a great

1. Dutch Records at the Hague-Letter dated May 14th 1607.

2. Letter Amsterdam, August 25th 1669.

3. Letter of November 17th 1669, from Governor-General, Volu. 29, D. CCC. p. 6.

favourite of the Zamorin. As we have seen, he received from the Zamorin the right to establish a trading centre at Chetwai and in return helped that ruler greatly in the war against the Dutch. The English were thus well established at Tellicherry, Calicut and Anjengo, with the result that the Dutch had no prospect at any time of having the pepper monopoly or political predominance in Kerala. Naturally, they hated these intruders and did not fail to intrigue with the Rajahs to their deteriment. But as the English kept strictly aloof from political complications, their trade prospered while that of the Dutch declined.

Other European powers who had interests on the Kerala coast were the French and the Danes. The French were established at Mahe in 1725. The Danes had for some time close relations with Calicut, for in 1756 the Dutch Commandeur complained about the Danes supplying the Zamorin with arms and ammunition.

Though, in the days of the monopolitistic pretensions, the Dutch Company looked upon the European nations as intruders, with the decline of their political power and the increase in the stability of the English Company after the union of the two rival companies, the Dutch attitude towards them changed greatly. Though there was never any cordiality, the Dutch ceased to look upon the English and the French as those who were unjustly interfering in their business. The English Company, in many ways more far-sighted, while keeping itself strictly outside political entanglements, was not loath to supply arms and ammunition to all those who fought against the Dutch. Thus the Zamorin in his various campaigns against Cochin, and Travancore in its prolonged and successful wars against the pretensions of Gollenesse and Van Imhoff were able to depend upon the English factory at Calicut and at Anjengo for an uninterrupted supply of arms and ammunition.

There is another point with regard to the Dutch policy in Kerala which is worth notice. Kerala was only an unimportant part of the Dutch interests in the East. It was subordinate not only to the supreme government at Batavia but to the government of Ceylon. Naturally it was not able to pursue a forward policy and often its schemes could come to nothing for want of adequate support from Ceylon and Batavia.

The failure of the Dutch policy in Kerala was due to a variety of reasons. The first and the most important cause was the rise of Travancore as a powerful military state. The Company after its first effort to impose its will by the pretence of great military power had given up the idea in 1697. Their methods of action after that lay in working through the instrumentality of the Rajah of Cochin and the Christian population over whom they claimed special rights. They also asserted a right to maintain the balance of power in Kerala. The rise of Travancore demonstrated the hollowness of their military pretensions and destroyed the balance of power on which they depended for their trade. All the minor chieftains in whose affairs the Company had habitually interfered for over half a century, the Rajahs of Mangat, Parur, Vadakkumkur, Purakkad, Desinganad, Maruthurkulangara, Perittally and Attungal disappeared all of a sudden from the map and were absorbed into one single state. In the territories of the Zamorin the Company had no power at any time. In the territories of Travancore, extending to the very borders of the town of Cochin, the Company's power was destroyed by the growth of Travancore. Even the special right of jurisdiction over coastal Christians which the Company enjoyed at Quilon, which was a useful method of interfering in the affairs of states, had to be given up.

The final and total disappearance of the Dutch from the mainland as also from Ceylon was due to a cause over which they had no control—the rise of the British power in India. In 1795, when Cochin was taken away from them, the British had already become one of the leading powers in India. The fight with England, as a result of the Napoleonic wars cost Holland much besides the little settlement in Cochin. Otherwise it might have continued for another century and a half as a picturesque survival like Mahe, Daman, or Chandernagore. Its political importance was lost in 1753 but it disappeared as a Dutch possession only 40 years later.

A second cause of the failure of the Company's policy was the presence of other European nations whose commercial interests were opposed to those of the Company. This position helped the states to organise opposition on effective lines. The armies of the rulers had improved a great deal since the time of Vasco da Gama, and the companies which de Lannoy trained for Martanda Varma were in no way inferior to the soldiers whom the Dutch were able to put in the field. Their supply of arms and ammunition was guaranteed by the presence of the English and the French on the coast and the Dutch could not in the 18th century compete with either of these nations for naval supremacy. The Dutch position on the coast was altogether untenable and the growth of Travancore power abolished it altogether.

What is important to note is that the destruction of Dutch power in Kerala was in no way due to the inefficiency of the Company or to the disorganisation of the Company's administration. Their officers from Hutstaart to Moens were with few exceptions men trained in administration and highly competent both in business and in government. The system of councils and superintendence by commissaries sent out from headquarters kept the administrative machinery always in good trim. Every action was duly deliberated upon, communicated in writing to superior authorities, who kept a watchful eye on all proceedings. The system of letters to the supreme government at Batavia was extremely useful because every step taken had to be defended to a body which was closely in touch with administrative details. It was a bureaucratic system, and it had all the virtues of bureaucracy without its disadvantages. As the business of the Company was mainly commercial, its strict methods of work, which reduced it to a soulless machinery did not have the evil, which is inherent in bureaucratic government, of divorcing the officials from the people.

Unlike the Portuguese again, the Dutch Company was never in difficulties about its finance. The Company was primarily a trading corporation and never for a moment were its officers allowed to forget that important fact. Any undertaking which involved unnecessary expense was ruthlessly vetoed whatever other benefits might follow from it. The accounts were kept with scrupulous care, pay was never in arrears, and the economical management of all establishments was insisted upon by the authorities. All these present a most striking contrast to the affairs of the Portuguese in India which was always on the verge of bankruptcy owing to inefficiency of the financial administrators. So far as the Dutch were concerned, their superiority in this matter over all the other powers, Indian as well as European, was amply clear from the very beginning. That is what made their settlements in Kerala prosperous even when their political authority had disappeared. It was a standing order of the Government that every retiring chief should leave a memorandum on the state of Kerala for his successor. This was an exceptionally good plan as it ensured continuity of policy and provided a source of authoritative information for successive administrators. As Moens points out in the preface to his memoir "the affairs of Malabar are so inextricably bound up and mutually connected that if you would wish at the outset of your administration to meddle with an affair of little importance (no matter what good object you may have in view) it may sometime or other cause a derangement which on account of your not being acquainted with the particulars, could not have been anticipated." This useful system prevented the Dutch from falling into many of the grave errors into which successive Portuguese captains of Cochin fell through their ignorance.

The Dutch connection with Kerala was not marred by massacres, and other acts of inhuman cruelty which characterised the Portuguese. The only occasion in which the Dutch soldiers desecrated a temple was in the case of a pagoda belonging to the Punnathur Nambidi—in the war against the Zamorin. But even this outrage was committed by Balinese soldiers against the orders of the Dutch commandeur. In their wars against Kerala rulers, they never set fire to towns, or felled fruit-bearing palms or took as captives women and children as the Portuguese did. The barbarities which the Portuguese captains prepetrated on the sea against the Moors were unheard of in the time of the Dutch. In fact, they prided, and with reason, on their humanity. When Captain Nieuhoff was asked by the Rajah of Travancore as to whether he would do less than the Portuguese did, he retorted, that if he wanted to imitate the Portuguese he would have to murder and pillage which was against the policy of the Company. As a result, the Dutch were never so unpopular on the coast as the Portuguese had been. Many of the Dutch captains were actually popular with the Kerala rulers with whom they maintained the most friendly intercourse.

The Dutch were staunch Protestants and their hatred of the Portuguese intensified their religious bigotry, but as a whole they were liberal and tolerant and after the first years of destructive zeal they did not interfere with the Catholics. But immediately on the conquest of Cochin, their religious zeal carried them to the extraordinary length of pulling down even the magnificent Jesuit library. Tavernier narrates the incident thus: "You must know that at the taking of Cochin, the Jesuits had in that city one of the fairest libraries in all Asia, as well as for the great quantity of books sent them out of Europe as for the several rare manuscripts, the Hebrew, Chaldaic, Arabic, Persian, Indian, Chinese and other oriental languages. During the little time that the Jesuits were in Ethiopia they had copied out all the books to Cochin. But to tell of what became of this library, General Van Goens made no convenience to expose it to the ignorance of his soldiers, so that I have seen soldiers and seamen tear several of these beautiful volumes to light their tobacco."[1] Even Canter Visscher says: "This town formerly contained handsome churches but they have either been demolished or converted into magazines."

After their first zeal was over the Dutch followed a liberal policy towards the Catholics. The Jesuits who had to leave when the Dutch conquered Cochin were allowed to come back. They were allowed freedom to govern the diocese and were "even permitted to settle down within the territories of the Company, to be precise, at Ambalakkad, a village 3 hours beyond Cranganore." At this place the Jesuits had a college where free instruction was given. In 1676, 3 Carmelite fathers obtained permission to come to Cochin. The purpose of their visit was to appoint a coadjutor in place of

1. Quoted in Whitehouse *Beginnings of Light in a Dark land*, Page 132. Madras Records 13.

Alexandar de Campo who was greatly advanced in age. They had instruction to appoint some one to whom the Company had no objection. The Company did not desire to have Portuguese Bishops resident in Cochin and therefore chose Mathias de Campo. But this was not acceptable to Rome. The relations between the Dutch commandeurs and the Roman Bishops continued, however, to be cordial.

The Roman Catholics in Cochin and in Quilon were specially under the protection of the Company. In this matter the Dutch continued the policy of the Portuguese and utilised the privileges of the Catholics for the increase of the political power of the Company. They were, as noticed before, under the jurisdiction of the Company's officers. But as the strict operation of the clause would have meant immunity for the Latin Catholics living inland a later treaty (1664) stipulated that those remaining inland should obey the Rajah's government.

The Latin Catholics who were subject to Cochin were not slow to take advantage of these privileges. They defied the Rajah's government and depended on the Company for protection. They evaded the Rajah's taxes. The explanation that Governor Moens gives in his memorial is this: "As the Christians (paraya converts) are much despised by the heathens they should have to suffer humiliation and would be ill-treated if they were not protected by the Company". The commandeur did not limit his intervention in the case of Christians who were badly treated. He interfered in order to maintain the rights of free worship. "Besides the above." says Moens, "the Christian subjects (meaning the new Catholics) have the privilege that they only pay half the taxes to the king". It was natural that this right should give rise to constant disputes. The Company claimed that they had jurisdiction over all Catholics while the Rajah insisted that the treaty of 1664 gave them right only over the converted fishermen of the coast. Gradually as the authority of the Company diminished the Rajah's rights over these Christians increased.

The friendly policy of the Protestant Company towards the Catholics was much appreciated at Rome. Pope Clement XIV conveyed his thanks in a special Brief which he addressed to the vicar apostolic of Malabar in the following terms:—

"Greetings to Our Reverend Brother; our beloved Son, Stephen Boyd secretary to the congregation for the propagation of Christians has communicated to us in detail the attention paid and the trouble taken by the Dutch Governor for the safety of the Christians who are there yonder. And as such Christian acts of kindness undoubtedly concern us greatly, and as on their account, we are indebted to him, so it is our earnest desire that least our feelings of gratitude for the same be made known and clear to his man. Therefore, to show our gratitute we have hereby to recommend to your reverence, to assure him of our grateful sentiments in the most forcible and the most striking manner and at the same time to testify that we feel ourselves so much more indebted to him for what he has done as we flatter ourselves that he will continue in this way to lay the Christians and us under further obligation."

Given at Rome the 23rd July 1772 in the 4th year of our papal reign: Stephen Borgia.

The Company treated the Roman Bishops with much ceremony. The Bishop of Verapoly on arriving at the settlement when Moens arrived "was fetched by two councillors in a carriage and taken to the residence of the Chief where the so called[1] bodyguard was lined up under the command of an

1. Moens p. 157.

officer and as the Bishop passed, both this and the main guard presented arms and made the salute with the spontoon. As he ascended the steps a salute of nine guns was fired from the walls of the town."

The Dutch had originally ideas about converting the low[1] class Catholics of the coast to their own religion. But Gollenesse confesses 'to his sincere regret' that "the Reformed Doctrine has made little progress in spite of all careful fore-thought and regulations concerning schools and education of children and instructions regarding the penetration of popish superstitions". The Dutch always maintained an ecclesiastical establishment, but they do not seem to have been able to influence the Catholic population in their ways of thought.

So far as the Syrian Christians were concerned the Company had no authority but the Commandeurs gave them steady support in their fight against Rome. As Moens says; "we have after the conquest of Cochin not only favoured the revolt of the Eastern Christians against the usurpations of Rome but also assisted them in getting out new Bishops from Syria, by placing at their disposal the ships of the Company. The administrators of this coast and the preachers of the reformed community have not only kept up a correspondence with St. Thomas Christians about maintaining the rights of the Eastern churches against the Bishops of the Roman Catholics, but have also displayed much zeal in attempting to unite them with the Protestant church."[2]

Towards the Hindus the Dutch policy was tolerant and liberal. Unlike the Portuguese the Dutch were not consumed with a desire to convert the

1. Gollenesse Memoir p. 80.

2. Moens, p. 180.

heathen. The Dutch uniformly respected the scruples of the Hindus. In a treaty with the Vadakkumkur Rajah, signed on the 29th September 1740, they undertook "not to molest Pagodas or cows." They went even so far as to insist on the due performance of Hindu ceremonies. The Company once demanded that certain Nampudiris should appear before the Commandeur and explain their worshipping at the pagoda of Chembukovil which was against ancient usage.

From all that has been said, it is clear that the Dutch on the Kerala coast formed in many ways a tolerant and civilising influence and their policy, in trade, administration as well as religion was based on sound and liberal ideas. They had no desire to exploit the people who came into contact with them, or to oppress them. Their one object was to carry on trade in such a way as to yield the largest amount of profits and ideas of glory, and desire for heavenly merit by converting the heathen and plundering his temples never entered into their calculations. Their intentions were friendly and the hundred years of their connection with Kerala constituted a period which was in many ways beneficial to the growth of civilisation in Kerala.

CHAPTER X

DUTCH ADMINISTRATION AND TRADE

(1) ADMINISTRATION

Unlike the Portuguese, the Dutch had from the very beginning an elaborate and highly efficient administrative system. They transplanted their own democratic organisation, developed at home, into their settlements in the East and even the smallest factory had its councils, committees and courts. The Portuguese administration was more or less a feudal system. It knew no discipline. The king and the high officials in Portugal interfered even in the minor details of administration, and every Portuguese factor in India had the right of direct communication with the court at Lisbon. The Dutch method differed from this. The "Dutch methods" were so superior to the colonial systems then in vogue that it was the ambition of the English Company to copy them and to develop a system as much like the Dutch Government in the Indies as possible.

The Dutch Company was governed by a body of 17 directors, elected from among the principal bodies interested in the East India trade. These bodies were organised into Chambers which were autonomous in matter of accounts, internal government etc. But the government of the settlements was a matter for the 17 directors, who through their subcommittees carried on the correspondence, issued directions and generally administered the affairs of the Company.

The settlements in the East were governed by a Governor-General in Council whose capital was at Batavia. The Council or their High Nobilities, as they were called, consisted of 9 members, four of whom were Governors of the outlying settlements.

The head of the Administration was the Governor-General; but next to him in importance and in authority was the Director-General who was the head of the commercial affairs of the Company. The Council represented the different interests of the Company and was practically independent of the authority of their principals in Amsterdam.

The Dutch establishment in Kerala was governed by the Commandeur and Council of Cochin. In the beginning there were five main outstations: Quilon, Kayamkulam, Purakkad, Cannanore and Cranganore. Thengapattanam was a residency. They were under Captains but their military force was reduced to a minimum. The Council of the Commandeur consisted of members of his political department and the Chief Military Officer on the coast. The number varied, but up to 1741 it was generally 9. The Chief Administrator who was the second in command was in special charge of the commercial affairs of the Company.

The service of the Company was divided into political, ecclesiastical and military. As the purpose of the political administration was commercial the functions of the political officials included those of trade. At the head of the political service stood the Governor or Commandeur, and in minor stations, Resident or Captain. Below them was a hierarchy of officials from apprentice to upper merchant. The pay of the officials was not large. A Governor received 200 gilders while a Commandeur received only 150-180. But this was only the nominal pay The officials were allowed commissions and perquisites which made the Governorships of the Malabar coast lucrative appointments. Article III of the Regulations declared that the Governors and Directors, and seconds in governments, directorships or commanderies, but no inferior chiefs or servants, shall be allowed to take what they want for their own use out of the Company's warehouse upon paying 50 per cent. advance upon European and 30 per cent. upon Indian comodities, spices excepted. The Commandant of Malabar was to have one per cent upon all goods imported and exported by private persons to be reckoned upon the sales of the former and the invoices of the latter. The Commandeur and the second in command were also permitted private trade. At the time of Moens this privilege was compounded and the Commandeur and his second received 5 per cent. on sales of merchandise and 3 per cent, on pepper bought. Of this sum the Commandeur was to get four-fifths and the second one-fifth..

The military establishment in Kerala was very small. It generally consisted of a Captain, one captain lieutenant, four lieutenants and six ensigns, 4 officers for Indian troops and 3 officers for artillery. The actual strength of the military force in peace time never exceeded 2000 of whom less than a half were Europeans. At the time of the war with the Zamorin and later on with the Travancore Rajah large reinforcements were brought from Colombo and Batavia, but generally speaking the military strength of the Dutch was negligible. The naval strength was no greater and it bore no comparison to the large squadrons which the Portuguese always had on the Kerala coast. At Cochin there was a maritime officer but his squadron consisted only of one small yacht, two sloops and three row boats. A large squadron was not necessary for the Dutch for, from the first, they had decided[1] "not to obstruct any more by measures of constraint and harshness the navigation of the Malabars and their trade in the productions of their country". Besides the Dutch had a naval base at Colombo from where they could, if necessary, control the Indian seas.

Besides these essential organisations, the Dutch in Kerala had also many subsidiary institutions

1. Stravonines, Vol. III, p. 237.

meant to secure the welfare of their factors. They had an excellent medical service, a fairly large number of skilled European workmen, for the repair of arms, for employment in the ship yards, etc.

The administration of justice was a matter in which the Dutch took special pride. The Memorial of Moens gives a description of the courts, from which we could see the workings of the Dutch Judiciary in India.

"The Court of Justice here," says Moens, consists of the Second in Council and Chief Administrator as President with most of the members of the political Council and some other members of the services as members; which court as everywhere in India (i.e. Dutch Indies) decides and grants executions both in criminal and civil matters in the name and on behalf of their High Mightinesses.

We have here a subordinate court also named the civil court or the court of small causes consisting of one of the members of the political Council here as president and some officers of inferior standing as members."

In the Commission given to Governors, Directors and Commandeurs it is among other things specially ordered that care should be taken that right and justice be administered among the people both in criminal and in civil cases. The Chiefs of Settlements used to preside in Courts of Justice as well as in the political councils but this naturally led to miscarriage of justice and to corruption. The evils of this system came prominently before Their High Mightinesses in the case of Peter Veeyst who utilised his position as Governor of Ceylon and Chief Justice of the Court to personal ends leading to the judicial murder of innocent people. This Governor, it must be said to the credit of the Dutch, was tried and publicity executed at Batavia in 1732. After this scandal the Second in Council in each settlement was given the presidency of the Courts of Justice.[1]

Moens complains that there were but few men in the Eastern settlements who had studied law. There was no proper system of pleading and advocacy in courts. The Government lawyer (the advocate fiscal) had to plead both pro and contra and as Moens points out every "Fiscal is not of a sufficiently well balanced temperament to plead the cause of the accused with the same zeal as he employs to substantiate his own cause."

In criminal cases there were two kinds of procedure, the extraordinary, where strict proof was not required and ordinary cases where the rules of evidence and procedure were rigidly adhered to. The criminal cases affected the people of the country more than Europeans but the proceedings were entirely in Dutch and were conducted with the help of interpreters. Moens had an idea of training a number of Dutch people as interpreters. In fact he apprenticed Gerrit Van Waardenburg and Jacob Goliath to the second interpreter at Cochin for the purpose of learning Malayalam.

The Company administered justice over the low caste Christians of the coast. By the treaty of 1663 it was specially laid down that the Christians "are under the jurisdiction of the company and if they committed a crime are punished only by the Company. The Company also exercised an appellate jurisdiction in cases affecting the Konkanis. The Konkanis were nominally under the Rajah of Cochin but they had the right of complaining against the Rajah to the Company. "It is necessary," says Moens, "every now and then to make good our claim to the supreme authority reserved to us over them." As the

1. P. 243 Selections from the Records of the Madras Govt., Dutch Records No. 13.

Konkanis have most of their dealings with the people of the State this was a great encroachment on the judicial authority of the Rajah.

(II) TRADE AND REVENUE

The commercial policy of the Dutch differed from that of the Portuguese in many important respects. The circumstances of European trade had so considerably changed in the period between the 16th and the 18th century that the policy of complete monopoly which the Portuguese followed with success had been rendered impossible. The English and the French were established on the coast and carried away a great deal of the Kerala trade. At Tellicherry and Calicut the English established their position at the same time as the Dutch established themselves in Cochin. In Anjengo they built a factory in 1690 diverting into that factory most of the trade in the area south of Quilon. In 1725 a French squadron, which carried as one of its junior officers a young man by the name of Mahe de Labourdannais, appeared on the Kerala coast and established a factory. Thus the advantage which the Portuguese had in being the sole European naval power on the Indian waters was denied to the Dutch from the very beginning. They had therefore to adjust their policy on the basis of this open competition.

The desire of the Dutch was to establish by contract with Indian rulers a monopoly in the goods they wanted to buy. In the agreements that Nieuhoff made with the Rajahs south of Cochin a clause was invariably inserted that "Nobody without any exception shall be permitted to export any pepper or cinnamon out of this country or sell it to anybody except the said company." With all Kerala Kings, except the Zamorin and the Rajah of Chirakkal the Dutch had these agreements. The Rajahs accustomed to and accepting the Portuguese idea of monopoly did not demur at the demand of the Dutch. But they soon found that there were others who were prepared to buy their products at a higher price and despite agreements and treaties a considerable portion of pepper trade began to flow into other channels. The Dutch stigmatised the selling of pepper to other nations as contraband trade, and they attempted at first to put it down by force. But such a policy would have involved heavy expenditure, for which the Batavian authorities were not prepared, and military resources which they could ill spare. As Stravonines himself says "these attempts (to put down forcibly contraband trade) were as little productive of the effects proposed as they were expensive; for the princes themselves were not able to restrain their subjects from carrying on this trade with other nations, by which they made double the advantage they did in selling us."[1]

As the Company found out that in the altered circumstances "the ostentation of great power had not the effect of producing on the native princes that degree of awe and apprehension which is indispensably necessary for the carrying on of an extensive trade", they reduced their forces which further encouraged the princes in their policy of defiance. In 1698, Zwaadekroon in a memorial dated 31st May complained that the Company was so little feared by even the Rajah of Kayamkulam that he was openly trading with the notorious pirate, William Kidd. From the beginning the Dutch made no attempt to insist like the Portuguese that all trade on Indians seas should be carried on only in vessels permitted by them. The sea-borne trade was to be free and the Company gave every facility for navigation.

Thus the trade of Kerala was not so profitable to the Dutch as it had been to the Portuguese; and

1. Stravonines Vol. III, p. 272.
Also see—'Secret considerations' De Jong—25th October 1757.

the charges were proportionately heavy. They had to conduct 3 wars with the Zamorin and one with Travancore, even before the arrival of Hyder Ali in Kerala. The most serious military effort that was made was against the Zamorin in 1717. But even after that the charges did not go down. With the new plans of conquests ambitious commandeurs developed after the treaty of 1717, the military expenditure and charges increased. Though on the basis of this added prestige they were able for a time to maintain their monopoly of pepper trade, it again ceased to yield satisfactory returns when the campaign against Travancore developed; and the conquest by Martanda Varma of the petty chieftainships up to Cochin made direct trade impossible in those areas.

The Company's trade in Kerala was divided into two departments; investments for Europe, i.e. goods bought in Kerala for sale in Europe, and goods sold in Kerala. The stock merchandise which the Company sold in Kerala consisted of sugar, Japanese bar, copper, tin, lead, silk stuff, camphor, vermillion, quick-silver. The Dutch Company had also a monopoly for the sale of opium and great profits were realised from this because it was the custom to exchange this for pepper. But Zwaadekroon[1] discontinued this method of forcing opium upon people. It was fortunate for Kerala that the great demand for opium in Java did not permit the Dutch to flood Kerala with it and after 1700, the sale of opium though large was not of sufficient importance to be considered a big item in the trade of the Company.

Of all the goods bought by the Company from Kerala pepper was of course the most important. The breakdown of the monopoly in pepper trade led to competition and Zwaadekroon, when he was Commissary for Kerala, recommended that pepper should

---

1. Selections from Madras records—Vol. XIII, p. 70.

be sold by the Company at the comparatively low profit of 25 per cent. This would have made competition impossible, because others buying direct from the Kerala market would have had to pay a higher price than that which was secured to the Company by agreement and the trade would not have yielded a profit. But Their High Mightinesses in Amsterdam disapproved of this excellent proposal and the premium was raised to 50 per cent in 1725 and later in 1733 to 100 per cent. This policy was on the face of it suicidal. When the Company was selling pepper at twice the price it bought, their private competitors as well as the English and French companies found it possible to pay a higher price on the market and still realise a reasonable profit at a price below what was the official price of the Dutch Company. This meant the quantity which came into the warehouse of the Company decreased year by year. Gollenesse advised that the whole system should be given up and a system of conquest should be undertaken especially of Perittally and Vadakkumkur. But this as we have seen ended in miserable failure, the Company after a conflict with Travancore withdrawing from all its positions and yielding up its political authority to Martanda Varma.

The Company soon accommodated itself to the new conditions and began to collect according to agreements where such a course was possible or by paying the market price where it was necessary. The Travancore Rajah was bound by treaty to sell to the Dutch 150,000 lbs of pepper at Rs. 65 per candy of 500 lbs. from his hereditary possessions and 10,000 lbs. from his newly acquired territories at Rs. 55. As the English paid the Rajah Rs. 80 per candy and the Danes at Colachel still higher rates, he never supplied the Dutch with the full quantity stipulated. Moens in fact[1] complains that the Company gets only whatever is left and in times of

1. P. 113.

drought, etc., it gets but little. It should have been clear that such a policy was bound to fail, because if the Dutch had not the power to enforce their contracts the Kerala princes would naturally sell the produce to those who could pay the best price. Out of the 2000 candies which the Travancore Rajah had promised he supplied at an average only 73 candies!

When collection according to contract ceased to be regular the Company was, like other private traders, forced to buy on the open market. The Company paid as much as Rs. 100 per candy in the market and often-times 120 to 135 when buying from Indian vessels. Moens mentions that during his term of office he bought 764, 667 lbs from private traders.

Next to pepper the most important trade when the Company first established itself on the coast was in cotton cloth made in South Travancore. The fine cloth made in Eraniel and Kottar has been famous for many centuries and the Portuguese carried on a very flourishing trade in it. When the Dutch Company expelled the Portuguese from the coast, Captain Nieuhoff who was the Chief at Quilon observed that Kottar was a centre of great traffic. The Company bought the piece goods from the traders through their agents. An effort was also made to secure the services of some expert dyers from the East coast and settle them near Cochin. The attempt was not a success and the industry died out. But the Kottar piece-goods continued to be a large and important item of trade and found a ready market in the other colonies.

Cardamon was always one of the chief products of Kerala. The Dutch Company traded in it a great deal at the beginning but in course of time its importance diminished as other competitors arose in the field. The best cardamon grows in North Kerala where the English and the French paid such heavy prices that after a short and unsuccessful competition the Dutch practically gave up the idea of trading in it. They attempted to secure only the grain produced near Cochin in the territories of Kodassery Kaimal and the Rajah of Punjar. With the Kaimal they quarelled and the cardamon from that source ceased to be available. The Rajah of Punjar refused to enter into a contract unless the Company secured for him "a small piece of land called Condasider" belonging to the Kutal Manikyam Devaswam at Irinjalakuda.

Kerala indigo was much in demand but though the plant grew wild in the country, only so much was produced as was required by the people. The Dutch on finding that it was of a superior quality introduced scientific cultivation of the plant in Mangat and Anjekaimal. Seed was sent for from Surat at the time of Gollenesse who encouraged the local people to take up its cultivation. It was also introduced on an extensive scale in Vendurtty, Chetwai, Pappanetty and Cranganore.

The import trade of Kerala was also to a large extent in the hands of the Dutch Company. The main objects in which they traded were opium, sugar, coffee, Chinese silks, Japanese copper and arms and ammunition. The Company either imported direct or bought from Indian merchants who traded with those ports. They purchased generally by exchange. The trade in opium for which the Dutch were anxious when they came to Kerala ceased to be of importance because it was found possible to sell the drug at much higher price in Java and the Archipelago than what it fetched in Kerala.

Besides the revenues derived from trade the Company directly administered, or farmed out, some areas and derived much revenue out of them.

The most important estate was that of Dharmoth Panikkar. This was part of the estates belonging to Dharmoth Panikkar's family which by the treaty of 1717 passed in full proprietary right to the Company. It was situated in the northern limits of Pappinivattam (Pappanetty) and consisted of 437 paras of sowing land (about 50 acres) 63 pieces of garden land and 22 slaves. The Company generally leased out these lands. These were in the possession of the Company only up to the time of Hyder Ali's invasion.[1]

The Pazhayanchery Nairs in 1755 offered to give the Company 492½ gold fanams (Rs. 190), 523 parras of rice. In 1764 they raised it to Rs. 341.

The Dutch held besides this, land round about Cochin, containing, according to Moens' memorial[2] 42089 cocoanut trees in the fruit-bearing stage, 500 acres of paddy land and 19,716 salt pans. There were altogether 9 islets and 69 gardens. Considerable income was derived from this. Other sources of income consisted of tolls and duties and the export of slaves. Every ship other than Dutch entering the ports of Cochin, Quilon or Cranganore had to pay port dues but of this half went to the Rajahs of the place. The export of slaves was a profitable concern: and the revenues derived from tobacco and from the sale of arrack formed another item of importance.

Malabar was always an "expensive" settlement from the point of view of the Company. Not that the Dutch did not make large profits. Even without counting the profits of the pepper trade in Holland the actual trade carried on in Kerala showed considerable profit. But the Company was never satisfied with less than 100 per cent profit. The profits in pepper, which was sold in Europe at four times its purchase price were enormous but the Company did not calculate it as Kerala trade The difference between the factories in Kerala and those in Ceylon

1. Moens p. 134.
2. Ibid p. 207.

and Java was that the Kerala settlement involved considerable military expenditure. The Company was always at war with the Kerala princes and had within a hundred years to fight at least four major campaigns. Prolonged warfare exhausted the financial resources of the Company and destroyed its prestige. In the intervals however the Company made handsome profits. In 1770-1771 the expenditure amounted to £208,507-17 sh. while the income was £325,687-17 sh. This state of uncertainty in the profits of the Company arising from the political conditions of Kerala caused the more conservative section of Dutch opinion in Holland to demand the evacuation of Kerala or at least the restriction of operations to the trade in pepper. But with the conquest of Northern Kerala by Hyder Ali and later on the fight between Travancore and Mysore even the pepper trade lost its value to the Dutch, so that when they yielded up Cochin to the English, the trade and revenue of that port had ceased to count in the trade of India.

CHAPTER XI

KERALA AT THE END OF THE 18th CENTURY

From the conquest of Cochin in 1663 to the break-down of Dutch power lies a century which in many ways is the most important in Kerala history. During the course of that hundred years the whole political character of Kerala underwent a change. From the time of Cheraman Perumal to Martanda Varma, the political face of Kerala had remained the same. The division into petty principalities was traditional and even the Zamorin at the height of his power had not interfered with that arrangement. When the Dutch conquered Cochin there were in existence four "Kings" and 46 petty chieftains. The kings were the Rajahs of Chirakkal., the Zamorin of Calicut, the Rajahs of Cochin and Travancore. Between Cochin and Travancore lay the 70 madampies of Karappuram, the Rajahs of Idappalli, Vadakkumkur, Thekkumkur, Punjar, Purakkad, Kayamkulam, Maruthurkulangarai, Deshingnad, Perittally, Attungal and Vadayattu Pillai. At the end of the period all these states had been conquered and, what was more, annexed to Travancore. There was nothing new in one state conquering another. But annexation was new and against all the traditional ideas of Kerala polity. But Martanda Varma cared nothing whatever for Kerala ideals and annexed his conquests and reduced the chiefs to absolute poverty. By 1763, the political divisions which lasted for nearly two hundred years were practically complete. Cochin and Travancore and the Zamorin territory (later on British Kerala) stood out as the three divisions and the rest had disappeared to make room for the three.

There was some destiny that had decided against the unification of Kerala. Twice there was such a possibility and at each time, some unexpected foreign intervention prevented the consummation of that ideal. In the 15th century the Zamorin's power was steadily growing towards the south and there was every possibility of a unification of Kerala under the rule of the Zamorin. But the appearance of Vasco da Gama shattered that dream to pieces and checked the advance of the Zamorin at the ford of Idappalli. The next occasion was when the Travancore army marched up to Cochin to attack the forces of Calicut. But before Martanda Varma's dream of a united Kerala could be realised a new eruption, this time from the Mysore side, dashed it to pieces and cut up Kerala into three political divisions.

The annexation of the smaller states and the division of Kerala into three kingdoms instead of fifty principalities had two important results. It crushed the power of the Nayar nobility; and the feudal anarchy that reigned from one end of Kerala to another vanished never to return. Secondly, it marked the growth of royal power and of the modern centralised bureaucratic state. Travancore, as we noticed before, was transformed by Martanda Varma into a military state based on a standing army and governed by a civil service which had but little to do with the people. The Nayar nobility had no voice in the administration and the Rajah's officials whose powers had enormously increased were recruited either from Tamilians of low birth and no standing or from among Nayars who were in no way connected with the old noble families. It is true that for sometime to come the administration, especially in the outlying districts, was crude and inefficient. But that did not in any way affect the military character of the state or its authority vis-a-vis the population. Before the time of Martanda Varma rebellion was the recognised form of protest and Kerala law did not allow either confiscation of property or even capital punishment in the case of nobles. But after the firm organisation of Travancore, rebellion as a political weapon and warfare as a national habit disappeared from Kerala history.

That policy was followed with great success in Cochin by Paliath Komu Achan, the greatest name in the annals of that state. He reduced the nobles and took away their feudal privileges. This was all the more remarkable in his case, as Paliyam was the most important of the feudal nobility of the state. Komu Achan did not hesitate to sacrifice the interests of his order for the good of Cochin and his firm hand converted what was a nominal suzerainty over warring chieftains into an effective political authority.

This transformation marked the end of Nayar predominance in Kerala. From a privileged order which through its local chiefs controlled the affairs of Kerala, the Nayars in Travancore and Cochin became merely the chief community in these states. Their political power as a community was completely broken. In the territories of the Zamorins and Kolathiris their influence continued for a few more years. The invasion of Hyder Ali swept away much besides Nayar political power before it. And with the annexation of Kerala by the British by the treaty of Seringapatam, the policy which Martanda Varma had initiated in Travancore and Komu Achan followed in Cochin, was carried with relentless vigour. The second half of the 18th century thus witnessed the destruction of the political predominance of the Nayars and this is the most capital fact in the history of Kerala during the last 400 years.

Economically Kerala underwent great change, during the Dutch period. The raising of the Portuguese blockade, and the consequent freedom of commerce permitted by the Dutch led to a revival of Kerala trade. Ships from the Red Sea, Mocha Gujerat, and even China came to Kerala ports. The competition of the other European nations was also an incentive to commerce. The major rulers, especially the Zamorin and the Rajah of Travancore zealously encouraged trade and did everything in their power to increase it. This naturally led to a great activity at the various ports, especially Cochin, Colachel and Calicut.

The Dutch did much to improve cultivation and to introduce new products. Both cocoanut and rice the Company itself cultivated extensively. In the small scattered properties of the Company there were no less than 49,000 fruit bearing cocoanut trees. In fact, Baipeen was so closely planted that according to Moens its military value became greatly diminished. They introduced better methods of cocoanut cultivation and improved seeds. In Vendurty alone, they had 4,990 trees. In Kalikad, an island lying between Kayamkulam and Quilon they had 5,462. Even now in the areas formerly cultivated by the Dutch the cocoanuts are better in quality. Following their example, the entire coast took to cocoanut cultivation, especially because both coir and cocoanut oil were in great demand. Rice cultivation also derived much encouragement from the Dutch. But much of the rice that was consumed in Kerala was imported from Canara.

The Dutch introduced indigo cultivation into Kerala. Though this plant is native to the soil in Kerala its commercial cultivation had not been undertaken before. The Dutch thought that much profit could be made by an extensive cultivation of indigo and for the purpose seedlings were brought from Surat and they were sown in Mangat country and in Ernakulam and attempts were made to continue the cultivation in earnest. The seeds were distributed in Vendurty, Chetwai, Pappanety, Cranganore and Varapoly, and the Mukkavas were entrusted with the cultivation.

The Company also tried to cultivate a good many other Kerala products. Both by their improved methods and by their scientific system, the Dutch attempts at cultivation improved and the coastal people took to plantation of cocoanuts for the purpose of trade and this introduction of commercial economy was highly beneficial to the population.

They also introduced many industries. Salt farming became one of the main industries of Kerala. The Company itself owned 19,700 salt pans and following them the Indian rulers introduced this industry which was very profitable. Another industry which the Dutch introduced and which took root in Kerala was that of dyeing. The community of dyers first came to Kerala from Tuticorin and was brought by a Canarese merchant, Babu Prabhu. About 50 years later in the time of Gollenesse another community of dyers was encouraged to settle in Kerala and they received plots of ground for houses and were given other conveniences.

The revival of industries and the opening of ports led to a large increase in trade. The ports all over the Kerala coast naturally showed signs of prosperity. Cochin especially was until the end of the 18th century a very important port. James Forbes states that in 1770 Cochin was a place of great trade and presented a striking contrast to Goa; a harbour filled with ships, streets crowded with merchants, and warehouses stored with goods from every part of Asia and Europe, indicating the industry, the commerce and wealth of the inhabitants. The following is the description of the city of Cochin under the Dutch given by Francis Day.

"The Dutch Cochin fort according to Stravonines was nearly semi-circular and about a mile and a half in circumference. On the land-side were six large bastions and a cavelier to the eastward; an irregular work on a large scale on the waterside, a substantial loop-holed wall terminating at its eastern extremity in a ravelin before the cavelier: a wet ditch ran round these works whilst before it was a covered way and glacis."[1]

The north or river-side was defended by batteries whilst a stone wharf or more properly speaking a plain wall was erected on the river face.

"The sea a west face protected by a ravelin, the east by morasses and by a strong wall, and the west by walls and a wet ditch. There were small gates one to the west, the Bay Gate, another to the east called the New Gate and one to the north the River Gate. Along each side of the wider streets and ramparts were portia trees, Thespesia populena, left by the Portuguese and under their grateful shade, the inhabitants of an evening lounged or promenaded. A small but elegant public garden was kept inside the fort and a larger one near the Governor's house; in the vicinity of which the richer classes possessed bungalows.............. The pieces of artillery in the fort consisted of 95 of iron, six of brass and two mortars .... The buildings in the fort were the commandant's house on the north-west bastion and the only one built on the Dutch models. The Governor's house was half a mile to the south divided from the fort by a long sandy plain."[1]

The trade of Cochin-without including the business transacted by the Dutch which probably formed at least 90 p.c. of it—amounted to 5 lakhs. The total trade must have been much over half a crore and this, in terms of the rupee of to-day, was indeed a very considerable figure.

The other important ports on the coast, besides Calicut whose trade was in a flourishing state up to Mysorean invasion, were Colachel and Quilon. The Travancore government founded a new port at

1. Day: *Land of the Perumals*; 1868—p. 125-6.

1. Ibid. 126.

Alleppey for foreign trade and it soon developed into an important centre of commerce. Quilon, Anjengo, Colachel, and Tengapatanam which were the main ports in the south, all of which except the first developed into important trading centres only after the decline of Portuguese power, exported mostly coir, cotton cloth, tamarind and jaggery. Kottar, which was a very ancient centre of piece-goods trade, maintained its predominance as it does to-day. Nieuhoff mentions it as a place of great traffic and Van Imhoff also found it to be a place of importance.

In the 18th century, most of the inland towns and the local capitals of chiefs like Purakkad declined greatly as a result of the Travancorean conquest. We do not hear any more of the famous market of Kayamkulam, or about the trade of "Proca". The centralised administration of Travancore which established a state monopoly in all possible goods, diverted the trade from these ancient ports. As a consequence, the economic centre of gravity shifted from the centre of Kerala to the south. It was to the south of Quilon that new towns arose and new ports, except Alleppey, became of importance. The most rapid rise was that of Trivandrum. At the beginning of the 17th century, it was but an insignificant town unknown to history except for its famous pagoda. At the end of the 17th century, it became the capital of the Travancore Rajahs, then practically prisoners of the Ettuveetil Nobles. But with the rise of Martanda Varma, Trivandrum became practically the capital of Kerala. Martanda Varma was a great builder. He planned the city and had it rebuilt to suit its altered position. The ancient pagoda was pulled down and the noble structure which now commands the city of Trivandrum was constructed, as a lasting witness to the King's architectural tastes. Wide roads were laid down and port facilities were developed, though the coast is shallow and not suitable as the site for a harbour. In fact, by the time of Martanda Varma's death, Trivandrum had usurped the place which Calicut had held all through Kerala history as the chief centre of Kerala. In the time of Martanda Varma's successor, Sri Rama Rajah Bahadur, Trivandrum was further beautified and made a much greater trading centre. His famous Prime Minister, Raja Kesava Das, pursued a particularly enlightened policy with regard to trade and built just outside the fortress walls a commodious bazaar where foreign merchants were encouraged to come and seltle down. For the trade of the northern districts, Kesava Das built a new port at Alleppey where better natural harbour facilities existed. Alleppey was laid out as a modern city, with wide streets and large bazaars. As it was situated on the southern end of the Vembanad backwater, it had excellent and cheap transport facilities for collecting up country produce for export. Alleppey continues to be a flourishing port even to-day and is next to Cochin the chief centre of Kerala trade.

Economic and political changes of this nature gave rise to far reaching changes in national character. In the course of the last fifty years of the 18th century, the population of Cochin and Travancore became peaceful cultivators of land instead of maintaining their livelihood by warfare. Swords and shields were thrown away and the Nayars took to ploughing the soil and improving their land. In national habits also there were remarkable changes. Tobacco became a universal habit in Kerala. The Jaffna leaf had become almost a necessity with every person in Travancore, even more than food and drink. Their habit was to chew tobacco with betel leaf, a habit which still persists all over Kerala. Its prevalence among all classes of people made the demand for it imperative. Of Jaffna tobacco, Travancore used to take 3/5ths of the entire quantity. For a long time the Travancore price was the standard price of the article on the market. The use of opium also was prevalent at the beginning of the Dutch period. Nieuhoff states: "They use amfion very greedily. They take the quantity of the bigness of a pea. This they either mix with arrack or chew alone sometimes, till they fall asleep. Some of them are accustomed to use amfion every day: Some every two or three days." But the use of opium declined greatly during the century. The Dutch had stipulated by contract for a monopoly of the supply of opium, but they gave up the trade in it as they found the demand in Java much greater and consequently the profits also much higher. After about 1730 opium was scarce in Kerala and its use became exceptional.

Intoxicants were freely used. The favourite drink of the people was cocoanut toddy. The satirical poets of the age always accused the non-Brahmin castes of being addicted to drink. It is also known that many distinguished Brahmin scholars did not disdain this drink, though it was prohibited by their religion. The observant Nieuhoff noted that the Malabaris "distil a spirit called Arack out of the liquor but it is not near so good nor wholesome as our brandy" which no doubt is a matter of opinion. Foreign liquors also acquired some popularity, mostly among Syrian Christians but the use of brandy and wines owing to the prohibitive cost did not affect the masses.

Another important change in national habits was in clothing. When the Portuguese first visited Kerala, in fact, till the first quarter of the 18th century, even the upper classes of society wore only a loin cloth of muslin. The ordinary people used coarser country stuff. As a result of Mohammedan influences from Trichinopoly, the higher classes began to wear clothes in the north Indian fashion, long achkans and pyjamas and turbans on the head. This was the official costume of the Travancore and Cochin courts till recently.

It is natural that the eventful 18th century should have witnessed considerable change in the condition of the various sections that constituted Kerala society. The spiritual predominance of the Nambudiries continued unquestioned. Their position as Jenmies and as the sacred caste suffered no alteration. In Travancore, Martanda Varma was able to assert his royal authority over them in matters affecting the state, but only at the cost of abject spiritual surrender. The punishment that was meted out to him for taking away the temporal authority of Brahmin rulers like those of Purakkad and Tiruvella was a penance of 56 days and religious ceremonies to be conducted by Nambudiries at great expense to the state.

The position of the Nayars, as noticed before, underwent an almost revolutionary change. No longer was Kerala the free field of Nayar ambition. Their territorial authority was extinguished by the conquests of Martanda Varma, the policy of Komu Achan and the invasion of Hyder Ali. But they continued to be the most influential community as a result of their extensive landed possessions and local prestige. Their kalaris fell into disuse and the organisation of the kara existed only for social purposes. The Nayar aristocracy deprived of military and political power, lived entirely on its old traditions and the Kaimals, Kartavus and Panikkars maintained their dignity and their style for a considerable time longer merely by the force of tradition. But the days of their unrestrained power were gone never to return.

Of the condition of the Syrian Christians during this period, there is ample material for a detailed history. For our purpose it is sufficient to summarise here the religious schisms that affected the growth of this important community. The Latin Christians on the coast, as we have already said, were subject to the Company, but the Syrian Christians were not. Governor Moens says emphatically: "The Company never had any authority, nor could have, over the St. Thomas Christians, who were always subject to the country princes. Not even the Portuguese exercised any jurisdiction over them, although they did their utmost with the consent of the king of Cochin, to make these Christians accept the doctrines of Rome and acknowledge the hierarchy of the Pope."

The Syrian Christians at the time of the Dutch conquest were much divided among themselves. The Synod of Diamper had theoretically united the Syrian Church with Rome and brought the Christians of Kerala under the authority of the Pope. Even before the Portuguese flag ceased to fly over Kerala, revolt had broken out in the community. In 1640 they approached the Jacobite Patriarch of Antioch, the Patriarch of the Copts and the Nestorian Patriarch of Babylon to send a prelate. In 1644 a Syrian Bishop by the name of Ahballa was sent out to Kerala by the Patriarch of Antioch but the Portuguese came to know of it and interupted him on the way and it was widely rumoured that he was thrown into the sea with a stone round his neck. On hearing this a considerable section of the community met at Mattanchery and decided to break away from Rome. They elected their own Bishop Mar Thoma Campo who maintained a precarious position until the Patriarch of Antioch sent in 1655 two Bishops, Mar Basilus and Mar Johannes, who established the authority of the Patriarch in Kerala. But a hopeless schism divided the Church. A great majority remained faithful to Rome, and the Bishops who were sent out from Antioch did not find it very easy to carry on their duties or even to organise their flock. Besides this fundamental difficulty, even the non-Roman Christians were not united in points of doctrine. There were two parties, one Nestorian and another Eutychian or Jacobite, who were fighting theological battles among themselves. The Jacobite Bishop Mar Thoma invited the Patriarch of Antioch to send three Bishops in order to strengthen the anti-Nestorian party but their arrival was the cause of further strife among the Jacobites. As soon as the Bishops arrived Mar Thoma turned against them and denounced them as heretics and though the commandeur supported the Syrian Bishops nothing could be done to force Mar Thoma to accept them. The Bishops and the commandeur turned to Martanda Varma in the same way as Alexis de Meneses had turned to the Rajah of Cochin and invoked his help. Martanda Varma recognised the Syrian Bishops and Mar Thoma was forced for the time to yield an unwilling obedience. But as soon as Martanda Varma died, Thoma represented the matter to the new Maharajah and again refused to recognise the Syrian Bishops whom he denounced publicly as heretics. This controversy continued for over 30 years and weakned the Church.[1] It was only in 1773 after the death of Mar Thoma, who was succeeded by his nephew, that Governor Moens was able to reconcile both factions and restore peace.

The Syrian Christians like the Nayars were mostly cultivators of the soil and their economic condition was then as now fairly prosperous. Moens noted that "the houses of these Christians are not mixed up with those of the other Malabaris, but they have separate quarters where they live among themselves. They do not mix or intermarry with newly converted Christians of lower castes or classes. The majority of them belong to the Nayar caste or class of nobles and for this reason they, like Nayars, carry a sword in the hand as a token of their dignity."[2] Their priesthood at that time was not particularly educated, except in the case of the Catholics

---

1. Richard Collins: *Missionary Enterprise in the East*; H. S. King Co. 1873, p. 77.

2. Moens, p. 178.

for whose benefit the Jesuits had established excellent colleges at Verapoly. But the influence of the Kattanars with their flock was very great as Alexis de Meneses and later on the bishops from Syria discovered to their cost.

The Mohammedan community lost its importance in the politics and trade of Kerala with the fall of the Kunjalis. There were important families here and there, but in the general affairs of the country they ceased to count till invasion of Hyder Ali. A hundred years of warfare with the Portuguese had reduced them to insignificance in Kerala and when the Dutch were installed in Cochin and gained control of the Kerala trade they did not meet with any effective competition from the Mohammedan merchants. The days of Mammalis and Kuttialis were over. The Moorish population on the coast and the families inland became merely another section of Kerala population. From this insignificant position they again rose to some importance in the territories lying to the north of Cochin at the time of Hyder Ali's invasion.

The position of the untouchable castes remained much the same during this period. It would not, however, be correct to assume that though the Thiyas suffered from social disabilities their position was altogether unimportant. They were an important factor in the life of Kerala and were utilised for military purposes by the Company. There were many scholars of considerable standing among them, and one of them, Itty Atchutan, was among the valued collaborators of Henrick Van Rheede in compiling the monumental work, *Hortus Malabaricus*.

The eighteenth century witnessed a remarkable revival in Malayalam literature. The Rajahs of the time were great patrons of literature, especially the last Rajah of Purakkad and the Travancore Rulers,

Martanda Varma and his successor Rama Varma. In the court of the Rajah of Purakkad lived the great Kunchan Nambiar who is justly esteemed as one of the greatest of Malayalam poets. When Martanda Varma conquered Purakkad, he carried off with him the poet as his richest booty and installed him at Trivandrum. In the reign of his successor, who was one of the most accomplished scholars of his time in India, the Trivandrum court became justly famous all over Hindustan as the centre of scholarship, culture and wit. A nod from the Rajah of Travancore, says a Sanskrit sloka, is more valuable than a lakh of rupees from any other Rajah. Moens, who had occasion to talk with the Rajah, states that he conversed fluently in English, read the papers and periodicals published in London, Calcutta and Madras and was generally well informed in European affairs. He was a poet of great distinction and in his court resided Kunchan Nambiar, Unnayi Warriyar and other great writers of Kerala.

Education was fairly widespread during the 18th century. Kerala always had an efficient system of village schools at which elementary education was imparted free to all comers. Kerala was the home of Sanskrit scholarship in the 18th century and the kavyas, dramas and grammatical works in Sanskrit produced at that time in Kerala will bear comparison with the work produced at any time after the golden age of Sanskrit. Medicine especially was studied extensively. For Christians there were special institutions maintained by Carmelite friars near Cranganore. For a certain number education was given free in Latin and Syriac. The students were taught, besides these languages, theology, mathematics and geography.

While the economic results of the contact with the Dutch were undeniably beneficial to Kerala, on its cultural side it was altogether barren. It is noteworthy that the educational and other institutions which continued to have influence over a section of Kerala population, were maintained almost entirely by the Catholic Orders. It was neither Portugal nor Holland but Rome that attempted to bring education to Kerala. The Dutch founded neither libraries, nor colleges, nor were they interested in any thing except their trade. But they were diligent observers and their memoirs, accounts and letters form one of the main sources of our knowledge of Kerala. Besides this, an indirect contribution of higher importance to the culture of Kerala was the compilation of *Hortus Malabaricus* under the direction of Henrick Van Rheede which together with Orta's *Colloquies* may be said to constitute the first attempt at scientific research concerning India. The accounts left by Linschoten, Nieuhoff, Stavonines, Baldeus and others also form an indirect contribution to Kerala history, on which is based most of our present day information of the condition of Kerala in the latter half of the 17th century.

The 18th century marked definite advancement in various directions in Kerala. Trade and commerce improved greatly and became stable. The economic condition of the masses also improved leading to much higher standards of living. Political organisation also underwent great changes. A new state with different ideals and ambitions came into existence and the old feudal anarchy disappeared over a large part of Kerala. In all this, except in the stabilisation of trade, the Dutch had hardly any part. It was in spite of their active opposition that Travancore annexed the smaller lords between Cochin and Quilon. Nothing would have suited the Duthc better than that feudal anarchy should reign in Kerala. Thu s if the 18th century saw Kerala making rapid advance it was in no way due to the presence of the Dutch. Their position was limited and their activities circumscribed. Within the limits they imposed on themselves, their activities were directed, it must be admitted, to the betterment of Kerala.

With the conquest of Cochin by the British even the last relic of the connection of Hollanders with Kerala vanished. Their political power had ended a full half-century before.

It cannot however be said that their contact with Kerala was barren of results. They actively promoted industry, introduced artisans into the country and, at least in one very important case, took great interest in Indian learning. Van Rheede's *Hortus Malabaricus* would by itself make the Dutch connection with Kerala memorable, while the activities of Gollenesse, Moens and others to improve the cotton fabrics of Kerala and to introduce better systems of dyeing and printing entitle them to the gratitude of Malayalees.

Unlike the Portuguese, the Dutch never claimed that they had conquered India or any portion of it. As their pretensions were less and their desire to do profitable trade evident, they caused less friction and created less trouble than the Portuguese. The Portuguese from the time of da Gama appointed governors and viceroys to govern the East. The Dutch were satisfied with commandeurs and factors. Their connection with Kerala was not marred by any of those atrocious deeds of barbarism which made the Portuguese name a bye-word in the East. Calculating, matter of fact, and well trained in the doubtful art of diplomacy, the Dutch presented a striking contrast to the arrogant and incompetent Portuguese whose finances were always on the brink of bankruptcy but whose pretensions were never less than those of universal dominion and empire.

The end of the Dutch was inglorious. That was hardly surprising. A full half century before the end came they had lost all the vestiges of political power. The rise of Travancore and the invasion of Hyder Ali had made them impotent on land. The absolute mastery of the Indian seas which the English gained, after the great Suffren withdrew from the Indian waters, and the authority which the English East Indian Company came to possess on the mainland with the end of the 18th century, rendered the position of the Dutch totally dependent on the favour of the British. After the Treaty of Mavellikkara their attitude towards Kerala princes was one of nervous neutrality. With the invasion of Hyder Ali it changed into one of servile subservience towards the Mysore power. When the power of Tippu was destroyed in Kerala and the British Company annexed the broad domains of the Zamorin, the Dutch settlement in Cochin was merely an unimportant trading centre. Its conquest by the British came in the natural course of events and was not marked by an heroic defence as the Portuguese even in their decadence had put up against Goens. The continuance or disappearance of Cochin as a Dutch settlement had come to mean little for Kerala. If the British had spared it, the port would have continued like Mahe, a foreign possession of no importance—a historical and picturesque survival of an interesting period of history.

SECTION III

CHAPTER I.

KERALA AND MYSORE

The conditions which had for so long a time helped to isolate Kerala from the rest of Peninsular India and turned it seaward, underwent an unexpected change with the establishment of a powerful military state in Mysore. The rise of Hyder Ali to the command of the Mysore forces and later his assumption of ruling authority in the state were events of great significance to the history of South India and the second half of the 18th century in Kerala is dominated by the personality of the two Mysore Rulers, Hyder and Tippu.

Hyder Ali was appointed Foujedar of Dindigul in 1752 by Nuneraj, the Commander-in-Chief of Mysore. His command extended to the boundaries of Palghat. Komu Achan, the brilliant but erratic ruler of that principality, was being pressed hard by the Zamorin, who had attacked his territory and annexed a portion of it. The Rajah turned for help to the Mysore commander who was then only an unknown officer, dependent on the favour of the Dewan in Mysore. The invitation was promptly accepted. Hyder Ali, at that time no more than a local commander, was not actuated by any desire of conquest, or military glory. He looked upon the invitation of the Palghat Rajah solely as an opportunity of replenish the treasury with a view to take advantage of the developments in Mysore itself. The pay of his own corps was in arrears: besides, Hyder had obtained the services of French artificers and had begun to organise a regular arsenal and artillery. All this required heavy expenditure which he could not ask the Mysore Government to provide.

Before Hyder could lead his troops to Kerala, information reached him of critical developments at the capital. A quarrel had developed between Devraj, the Dewan and Nuneraj, his brother, who was in charge of the army, and the assignments which had been made to the army commanders were revoked by Devraj with a view to weaken the authority of his brother. In order to set these matters right so far as his own appointment was concerned, Hyder had to leave immediately for Seringapatam. Mukudam Sahib, Hyder's brother-in-law, was therefore ordered to proceed to Palghat with 2,000 horse, 5,000 infantry and 5 guns. Until this time, infantry was the only arm of warfare seen on the Kerala coast. The organisation and equipment of Malabar infantry had undergone a great change since the Portuguese first landed in Calicut; but except in Travancore where de Lannoy had disciplined them on European models, the armies of the Kerala rulers retained the characteristics of feudal hosts serving under their immediate lords. Hyder's infantry, on the other hand, was a compact, well-organised and highly disciplined force under officers who had been trained under French commanders. Besides, cavalry was altogether a new and unfamiliar arm in Malabar warfare. The maritime European nations with whom the Kerala rulers had to fight for over two-and-a-half centuries never used a cavalry force.

Mukudam Sahib's force, though small, was an effective and mobile body eminently suited for the purpose he had in view. Arriving in Palghat, he secured the co-operation of the Raja's Nayars and the Allies immediately attacked the Zamorin who withdrew from his campaign against Cochin to face this new enemy. The Calicut forces, unaccustomed to Mysorean warfare, retreated before the enemy, closely pursued by Mukudam Sahib to the coast. The Zamorin, realising that Hyder was not interested in territorial aggrandisement, but desired only monetary compensation, temporised with Mukudam and an agreement was reached by which the Calicut ruler undertook to pay 12 lakhs of rupees to Hyder and to return to the Raja of Palghat the territories conquered from him. On this understanding, Mukudam withdrew his troops after receiving the first instalment of the contribution and after leaving an agent to collect the balance.

The intruder having departed, the Zamorin and his advisers believed that they were safe from further troubles and negotiated direct with the Mysore Government for the payment of the contribution agreed on. The Ruler of Calicut naturally desired to evade the payment and sent secret emissaries to Devraj, offering to pay the money to him if he would recall the Mussalman soldiers and send his own agents to receive it. Devraj, whose advisers, especially Hari Singh, a Rajput adventurer in Mysore employ, were hostile to Hyder Ali did not view with approval the efforts of the Foujeder of Dindigul to make himself too powerful, agreed to the suggestions of the Zamorin, and claimed that the contribution was directly payable to the Mysore Durbar, Hyder Ali being compensated to the extent of three lakhs for the extraordinary expenditure incurred by him on the expedition. Devraj sent Hari Singh and his Rajput Corps to collect the 12 lakhs which the Zamorin had promised to pay.

Before Hari Singh could realise any part of this money, news reached him that his patron Devraj had died of dropsy at Seringapatam. He therefore returned in all haste to the Capital to safeguard his own interests, well realising that the accession of Nuneraj to sole power would mean his humiliation. On his way, while camping near Dindigal, he and his forces were surprised by Mukudam, Hari Singh losing his life in the affray that ensued.

The Zamorin was well pleased with the result of his diplomacy. He had escaped the payment of 12 lakhs and secured the withdrawal of Hyder's forces. He thought that the confusion into which the Mysore Court was plunged after the death of Devraj and the constant attacks of the Mahrattas on the northen frontier of Mysore would keep Hyder fully engaged, leaving Malabar in peace. Judged by ordinary standards, he had every justification for these conclusions: but, unfortunately, events did not turn out as he anticipated. The confusion in the Mysore Court soon cleared itself, leaving Hyder the sole and undisputed master of the kingdom under the nominal authority of his Raja. The Mahrattas were engaged heavily in the North and this also provided Hyder with a period of comparative security necessary for the consolidation of his power. In fact within the short period of five years, Hyder had evolved order out of chaos, enlarged the boundaries of his state, created an efficient military organisation and established himself as the most formidable military power in Southern India. Kerala rulers had indeed cause to tremble.

The Malabar coast had also come to mean something new and vastly important for him. The power of his new military state was dependent on the unobstructed supply of arms, ammunition and equipment, besides horses for his cavalry regiments. It was also necessary for him to maintain close contact with the French. Free and uncontrolled access to a port was, therefore, essential for the success of his policy. As Pondicherry was far away and could only be reached through the territories of Mahommed Ali of the Carnatic, who was not only his inveterate enemy, but one whose object was to embroil him with the English, Hyder had to depend upon Mahe on the Malabar coast. The control of the line of communication between Mahe and Mysore became of vital importance to him, and it is the recognition of this essential fact that made him turn his eyes once again towards Kerala.

The political conditions of Northern Kerala from the boundaries of Cochin to South Canara were of a nature which facilitated foreign intervention. There were five rulers of importance, none of whom was powerful enough to meet Hyder, but who, without any realisation of the fate awaiting them, were in a perpetual state of war among themselves. Counting from the North to the South, these states were Koluthunad (or Chirakkal or Kolathiri), Kottayam, Kadathanad, Calicut and Palghat. Besides these, there was Ali Raja of Cannanore, the Mahommedan prince who carried on a perpetual feud with his suzerain, the Kolathiri, and who saw in the rise of Hyder a great opportunity for himself. The position was further complicated by the jealousies and rivalries of European settlements along the coast. Of these the most important were the English factory at Tellichery, the French station at Mahe and the Dutch settlement at Cochin. The English and the Dutch had each a factory at Calicut. The English factory at Tellichery, which was in close and intimate touch with the Rulers of Kottayam, Chirakkal and Kadathanad, also held the Dharma Pattanam island and deported itself as a minor power on the coast, carrying on political intrigue mainly in the interests of a monopoly in the pepper trade.

By 1763, Hyder, by his conquest of Bednore, had extended the new state of Mysore to the very boundaries of Malabar and had thus come into close contact with the North Kerala Princes. The Nayak kings of Ikkeri, originally governors of Vijayanagar, had achieved independence with the break up of that empire. The Portuguese trade brought them great prosperity and the Nayaks were treated with respect by the neighbouring rulers. In 1737 Somasekhar Nayak, the thirteenth ruler of the dynasty, attempted an invasion of Chirakkal, but had to withdraw after an unsuccessful campaign. But the frontier quarrels continued with the Rajas of Nileswaram, a branch of the Chirakkal family, and so late as 1750, Ikkeri forces attacked Nileswaram, but were driven back by the Regent of Chirakkal.

On the death of Buswappa Nayak in 1755, the regency of the state of Bednore passed to a Rani, who in order to maintain her own power murdered her adopted son. This happened in 1757, but in 1763, while Hyder was reducing Chitteldrug, a young man claiming himself to be the Prince said to have been murdered, presented himself in the camp and requested Hyder to re-instate him on the throne of his ancestors. Hyder gladly undertook this new conquest and in March 1763, he took the capital, Bednore, and imprisoned the Rani and her ministers. Hyder now claimed to have discovered the imposture practised on him by the youngman and had him also confined in jail. The State of Bednore was created a separate Province, but it was not annexed to Mysore. It was treated as the personal domain of Hyder and different from the territories of the Raja of Mysore whose Minister Hyder claimed to be and whose State he was ruling in the Raja's name. This conquest brought Hyder to the boundaries of Malabar and provided him with opportunities for legitimate intervention in the affairs of the Nileswaram and Chirakkal Rajas arising out of their previous connections with the Nayak rulers of Bednore. Hyder, on assuming the authority of the Nayaks of Bednore, immediately demanded of the Raja of Nileswaram that certain frontier fortresses which the Bednore chiefs had claimed should be restored to him. The Raja of Nileswaram refused this demand in May 1763. Hyder, who had put forward the demand for the purpose of picking up a quarrel with the Raja, immediately began his preparation for a general advance on the southern country.

factors were torn by their friendship and loyalty to the rulers and the possibility of serious damage to their commerce. It is hardly necessary to add that commercial considerations prevailed over political loyalty. The chief of the factors therefore agreed to remain neutral, provided the commercial privileges of the Company in those territories would be guaranteed by Hyder.

After securing the neutrality of the factory, Anant Row turned his attention to political affairs in Kerala. The attitude of Ali Raja and his desire that Hyder Ali should conquer Kerala for his (Ali Raja's) benefit, have already been alluded to. Anant Row discovered an exceptionally good opportunity for his master's intervention in the quarrel that was then going on as usual in the Chirakkal family. The Prince Regent of Chirakkal was being opposed and openly thwarted by one of the junior members of the family, Capu Thampan. The Thampan had taken the field with his followers and was defying the authority of the Raja. Ali Raja, with the encouragement of Anant Row, now sided with the Thampan and proceeded to commit aggression on Chirakkal territory. The Raja asked the Tellichery factors to mediate, but Ali Raja, being assured of the support of Hyder, would not agree to mediation. Ali and Capu Thampan were defeated by the Chirakkal forces, but the Thampan refused to agree to any terms and kept up a guerilla warfare.

Early in 1766, Hyder arrived at Mangalore. His ostensible object was to collect from the Raja of Chirakkal a sum of money owing to the Nayak Rajas of Bednore and also to enforce against the Zamorin the promised contribution of 12 lakhs which was still outstanding. Ali Raja met Hyder at Mangalore and requested him to take up the Thampan's cause against the Regent, and it was with these professed objects that Hyder crossed the border in February 1766.

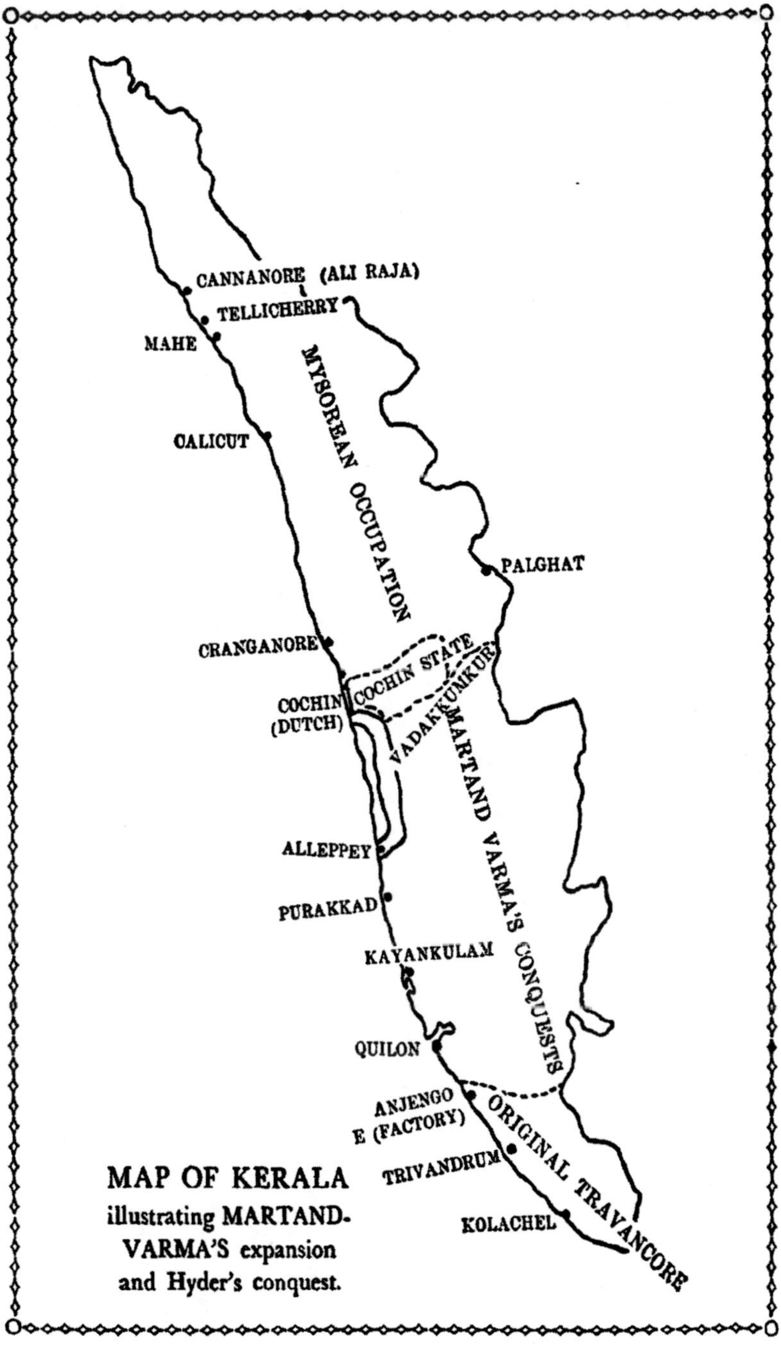

MAP OF KERALA
illustrating MARTAND-VARMA'S expansion and Hyder's conquest.

Hyder had with him according to Dutch sources an army of 40,000 men, including 10,000 cavalry and four pieces of cannon. He also took with him provision for four months. A powerful fleet under the English renegade Stannet moved along the coast. The Navy consisted according to Peixoto of 93 vessels, a few ships fitted out for war, with guns and a large number of small craft. The main purpose which it was to serve was to transport heavy material, facilitate the crossing of the numerous rivers which made military operations on the west coast difficult and if necessary to enable landings to be made behind the lines of the enemy.

The first engagement took place at Baliapatanam, where 500 Nayars offered obstinate resistance; but they were dispersed by artillery fire. After this engagement Chirakkal surrendered without a serious fight, the princes taking refuge in the Company's settlement. Hyder who was encamped at Chirakkal, naturally protested against what he considered the unfriendly action of the factory, but the Chief evaded responsibility. As the Mysore commander was not yet prepared to attack the British he left Tellichery aside and moved south into Kottayam: after a feeble opposition, Kottayam also surrendered.

The English factors, though alarmed at the rapid progress of Hyder's invasion, were unable to act owing to the orders received from Bombay to preserve a conciliatory policy. They, however, deputed a Konkani Brahmin, Ramji Prabhu, as an accredited agent with Hyder Ali to watch their interests.

From Kottayam, Hyder Ali moved towards Kadathanad. From his experience of Chirakkal and Kottayam, he had thought that no opposition would be offered to his advaace. But the Kadathanad Nayars decided to put up a strenuous resistance. The country of Kadathanad is separated from Kottayam by the Mahe river and Hyder on reaching the river found himself opposed by a powerful army determined to oppose his crossing. Finding it impossible to force a crossing against a well-entrenched army, Hyder ordered his fleet to enter the river, which it did to the navigable point. Then he drew up his infantry and artillery as if to cross the river after forcing the enemy to retire by a bombardment. In the meantime, he moved the cavalry cautiously up to a higher point and when the tide was low, crossed it at full gallop as the velocity of the current was greatly diminished by the ships which had anchored up in a line against the current. The Kadathanad Nayars were taken on the flank and forced to retreat in disorder. Hyder gave immediate orders of pursuit to his cavalry and the carnage that took place is thus described by a Mahommedan historian:—

"This order being executed with the utmost strictness nothing was to be seen in the roads for the distance of four leagues round but scattered limbs and multilated bodies. The country of the Nayars was thrown into general consternation which was much increased by the cruelty of the Mapileys, who followed the cavalry, massacred all who had escaped, without sparing women and children; so that the army advancing under the conduct of this enraged multitude, instead of meeting with resistance, found the villages, fortresses, temples and in general every habitable place forsaken and deserted."[1]

Hyder met with very little organised resistance after this. He moved south after securing his communications by block houses and entered Kurumbranad. There he was met by the Zamorin in person, who had been given a safe conduct to visit the camp on the 11th April 1766. Hyder received the Zamorin with every courtesy, and with marks of high distinction. The terms of the Zamorin's submission were

1. *History of Hyder Ali Cawn*, Thacker & Co. P. 69.

discussed and settled and it was agreed that the Calicut territory should be left undisturbed on the Zamorin accepting Hyder's suzerainty and paying a military contribution of 4 lakhs of Venetian sequins. Hyder Ali, accompanied by the Zamorin, moved towards Calicut. In the meantime, however, a mobile column which had been detached reached Calicut and demanded its surrender. The garrison evacuated the fort at night. Misunderstandings arose out of this, as the Zamorin legitimately concluded that Hyder was breaking his agreement, while the Mysore ruler, knowing the previous conduct of the Zamorin, was not inclined to trust him about the money without an effective territorial guarantee.

When the time came for meeting the financial demands, the Zamorin and his ministers began what Hyder considered to be dilatory tactics. Besides the heir apparent with the main forces of Calicut was offering stout resistance in the South. In spite of every effort of the Zamorin the Prince refused to yield and opposed Hyder's generals. Realising that the time at his disposal was short as the monsoon was approaching, Hyder kept the Zamorin and the Ministers under restraint in the hope that by this method he would be able to collect the money without delay. The pride of the Zamorin was deeply hurt by this enforced confinement which prevented him from fulfilling his daily religious duties. He was also afraid that Hyder might further humiliate him, or perhaps force him to accept Islam. In this plight, he took what he considered heroic measures in shutting himself up in the Palace and setting fire to it. The rest of the Zamorin's family together with the Brahmin dependents escaped to Travancore by sea.

Forbe's *Memoirs* give an interesting version of this tragedy:

"Hyder Ali, after taking Calicut, sent a complimentary message and desired to see the Zamorin:

but was refused. He however admitted Hyder's head brahmin to speak to him and carry his answer back to his master, then waiting at some distance from them. After this interview Hyder, instead of sending rice sufficient for the daily food of 1200 brahmins (who were daily fed in the palace) ordered only enough for five hundred. The second day he diminished the allowance for a sufficiency of three hundred; and on the third day they only received enough for one hundred. All further supplies were afterwards refused; nor did the conqueror take any notice of the Zamorin's complaints and applications. The unfortunate prince after fasting three days, and finding all remonstrances vain set fire to his palace and was burned."

The problem of Calicut thus settled itself. Hyder, being the master of the ancient territories of the Zamorin and the inheritor, therefore, to all the claims which the powerful arm of the Manavikrama kings had maintained through ages, was now in a position to contemplate the conquest of Cochin and Travancore. At Calicut, he was visited by the agents of the Dutch Company to whom he proposed a defensive and offensive alliance. The Company requested him to desist from attacking Cochin and Travancore, to which he demurred, but finally agreed on condition that both those states accepted his suzerainty and paid him suitable tributes. From the Cochin Raja he demanded 4 lakhs of rupees and 8 elephants and 15 lakhs and 20 elephants from Travancore. The Raja of Cochin, knowing the weakness of the Dutch East India Company and their inhability to defend him, agreed to the terms and became a feudatory of Mysore. Rama Raja of Travancore refused to accept the terms offered to him on the ground that he was under the protection of the East India Company through the Nawab of Arcot. He, however, undertook to pay a reasonable contribution if Hyder would re-instate the Zamorin on the throne of Calicut, a demand which was supported also by the Raja of Cochin.

It may seem surprising that both the Rajas of Travancore and Cochin should not only press for the re-instatement of their erstwhile enemy and, in the case of Cochin, its hereditary enemy, but offer to pay Hyder in cash with a view to persuading him to do so. The reason for this seemingly surprising act is fundamental to Malabar polity. As has been pointed out in the first part of this book, it was a conception totally opposed to all Kerala ideas that a sovereign could be dispossessed of his kingdom. It was only Martanda Varma, the Travancore king, who broke this tradition, mainly because he was under the influence of non-Kerala ideas. His successor, Ramaraja, became in fact the embodiment of Kerala Dharma and was naturally anxious to maintain the traditional state system of Kerala. To him as to the Raja of Cochin, a Kerala without the Zamorin was inconceivable. They looked upon their own hereditary fights as family quarrels. Also the establishment of the Zamorin's power in his territory contributed to their own safety. The annexation of Kerala by Hyder would have brought the Mysore troops uncomfortably near the Travancore boundary and naturally the Raja was prepared to pay for the maintenance of a buffer State between Hyder Ali's dominions and his own.

As the monsoon was fast approaching, it became necessary for Hyder to make preparations for his return to the East coast. Before he could begin the march to Dindigal, he had to make arrangements for the government of the country and for its pacification. The whole of Kerala north of Cochin was placed under a Civil Governor named Madana, who, according to Kilks, was an experienced revenue officer. For the pacification of the country, Hyder had blockhouses constructed at important points where he stationed small bodies of troops. Three thousand men from his regular infantry were left as a striking force at Calicut and with them were associated the levies of Ali Raja. A garrison under Syed Raza Sahib, numbering another three thousand, was left at Madakkara and after making these dispositions Hyder retired to Coimbatore before the fury of the monsoon fully burst on him.

The complete conquest of Kerala up to the boundaries of Cochin had taken Hyder Ali hardly 4 months. Within that time the ancient kingdoms of Chirakkal, Kottayam, Kadathanad and Calicut had fallen to him. The opposition had been sporadic and ineffective and Hyder retired with the feeling that he had annexed a rich and fertile province to his state at little cost; that he had given Mysore a coast line, together with free access to French and English ports. But events were to prove how sadly he had miscalculated.

The ease with which Hyder had overrun the country and the rapidity with which all opposition to him broke down can be explained only in terms of the political organisation of Kerala. North Malabar, which Hyder attacked, was not an organised state as Travancore was in the south. The states in that part of the country, except of course Calicut, were petty principalities and even in the case of the Zamorin, the military strength of the Rulers depended on the martial character of the people more than on organised armies. The defeat of the Rajas and the easy subjugation of the country did not however mean the conquest of the people. The lack of political unity was both a strength and weakness in this case. The defeat of the army did not involve the conquest of the country, as the basis of defence was not unified leadership. It is most unlikely that any combination of forces which the Malabar rulers could have called together would have been able to resist Hyder's veterans effectively; and defeat in a pitched battle would have made further resistance impossible.

A further reason to which importance should be attached is the use of cavalry by Hyder. We have direct and authoritative evidence about the extraordinary effect that cavalry had on the Nayars. Ruxots who was with Hyder in his march of conquest states: "The Nayars are more afraid of 5 men on horseback than of 500 sepoys. Many a time more than a 100 armed Nayars ran away before a single horseman. In the Malabar kingdoms there were no horses, nor were they ever invaded by horse". In all countries and in all ages, where the horse is not familiar, its first appearance on the battlefield has been of decisive influence. The conquest of the Inca kingdom of Peru is an outstanding instance.

Even while Hyder was preparing to leave in the confident hope that Malabar had been conquered, the Nayars all over the country were organising a national resistance Accustomed to the rigour of the Malabar monsoons and to its flooding rivers and ravines, they realised that the Mysore army could be most successfully harassed and driven out during the time of the torrential rains which are characteristic of Malabar. Hardly had Hyder reached Coimbatore than the monsoon set in and the Nayars everywhere rose up as a man. The Kottayam and the Kadathanad Nayars headed the rebellion (24th June 1766). The rumour that the despised Ali Raja had been appointed Civil Governor for Chirakkal made everyone realise what was in store for them if the Mysore troops were allowed to remain, and inflamed their patriotic ardour. Their plan of campaign was indeed simple. They attacked and captured the blockhouses with which Hyder had covered the country. The swelling of the rivers had isolated these posts and made any relief, or even communication with each other, impossible. After thus reducing the blockhouses, the Nayar forces invaded Calicut and Ponnani: it was only then that Raza came to know of the position. Afer sending word to Hyder, who was in Coimbatore, Raza marched with all available forces for the relief of the garrison at Ponnani. The sufferings which the Mysore troops underwent on this march were indescribable. The monsoon had made rivers unfordable and covered vast stretches with water. No provisions could be had and sickness broke out in his camp. The Nayars harassed at every stage, cut off the supplies, attacked the rearguard and kept up a steady guerilla warfare. Raza Sahib, sorely tried, valiantly marched forward, but was caught at the confluence of two rivers near Ponnani. He could neither advance nor retreat. Entrapped in this dangerous position, Raza did not know what to do. He determined to await the arrival of Hyder.

As soon as Hyder heard of the rebellion he re-entered Malabar with a force of 10,000 infantry and 3,000 cavalry, besides 300 Europeans newly arrived from Pondichery and 12 pieces of cannon. Taking with him only 8 days' provisions, and throwing away all unnecessary clothing, this army by forced marches followed Raza Sahib. The unexpected appearance of Hyder forced the Nayars to defend themselves and Raza was left in safety.

Hyder met the Nayar forces at Vettat Puthiyangadi. The Nayar forces occupied a fortified position with a moat in front. Hyder drew up his forces opposite the village. His dispositions were as follows:—The right wing consisting of 4000 of his best troops was under a Portuguese commander. The centre consisting of another 4000 troops was commanded by him personally. The left wing, which consisted of topasses, was under an English officer. The cavalry together with Hyder's bodyguard of noblemen and 300 Europeans were held in reserve.

After a considerable artillery preparation, which had but little effect on the entrenched position of the Nayars, orders were given to the Portuguese commander to attack the village. The troops advanced steadily, but halted before the ditch and opened musketry fire on the enemy. The Nayars returned the fire with deadly effect as the Mysorean troops had no cover and were placed at close range to the entrenched positions of the Nayars. For two hours the Mysorean soldiers held their ground in the face of the fire, though they sustained very heavy losses. No progress was made and if Hyder had not the courage to order the withdrawal of the troops, the day would have gone against him. At this moment, the French commander of the European reserve offered to cross the ditch and carry the village, and Hyder agreed to the suggestion. With Hyder's bodyguard and the European reserve, this officer advanced to the ditch and waded through it in spite of enemy fire: a remarkable achievement. Once across the ditch, the Mysorean troops were able without difficulty to carry the village and drive out the Nayars. Hyder now gave his orders for a general advance and the day, which began so badly for the Mysoreans, was turned into a decisive victory. The French commander was given the title of Bahadur on the spot and was created a mansabdar of 10,000 horse by Hyder.

Hyder's revenge on the Nayar population was merciless. He divided up his army into detachments and gave orders to lay waste the country and by fire and pillage to strike terror into the hearts of the people. The atrocities which his soldiers perpetrated were such as to merit Burke's harrowing description of the ravages committed by Hyder's army in the Carnatic. The admiring Mahommedan author of Hyder Ali Khan Bahadur gives the following description of the state of Malabar after Hyder had taken his revenge for the rebellion:—

"Wherever he turned he found no opponent, nor even any human creature: every inhabited place was forsaken and the poor inhabitants who fled to the woods and mountains in the most inclement weather had the anguish to behold their houses in flames, their fruit trees cut down, their cattle destroyed and their temples burnt. The perfidy of the Nayars had been too great for them to trust the offers of pardon made by Hyder: by means of the Brahmins he despatched into the woods and mountains to recall these unhappy people, who were hanged without mercy and their wives and children reduced to slavery whenever they were found in the woods, by the soldiers of Hyder, severity and mildness being both ineffectual in making them return to their homes."

Hyder, however, realised that unless the spirit of the Nayars could be broken, there would be no peace in Kerala and his conquest would never be effectual. With this object in view he issued an order depriving the Nayars of all their social privileges, denying them the right to bear arms, which they alone were entitled to carry and declaring them outlaws whom any man might kill. The untouchables were asked not to salute the Nayars. It was soon realised by Hyder that this would only make the submission of the Nayars more difficult, as more than everything else they cherished their caste privileges. Certain modifications to this edict were, therefore, made and all Nayars who became Mussalmans were promised re-instatement of full privileges.

With Manjeri as his headquarters, Hyder then organised a systematic Nayar hunt. The mountain fastness of their country gave the Nayar population ample protection, but those who were caught were hanged without mercy. Later on, Hyder decided upon a more ingenious method The captured

Nayars were collected in concentration camps and orders were issued to transport them to Mysore and settle them in colonies in the less populated areas. According to Wilks, of the 15000 thus transported, only 200 survived the experiment.

The military measures taken were more successful. He strengthened the garrisons and ordered that when the rains were over, the blockhouse should be reconstructed. A new fortress was built at Palghat in order to provide the Mysore forces with a safe base for operations. After taking these measures, Hyder withdrew to Coimbatore by the autumn of 1766.

Hyder was now called north to deal with a Maharatta invasion under the redoubtable Madhava Row. The Kerala Rulers who had only waited for the departure of Hyder rose again in rebellion. Again the centre of trouble was Kottayam country. Hyder's force met with disaster, the Kottayam Raja defeating it in a pitched battle. The blockhouses were again attacked and destroyed and Hyder's authority was confined to the town of Calicut.

Events outside were helping the Nayars. Hyder Ali, as result of the intrigues of the unscrupulous Nawab of Arcot, was forced to declare war on the British and this event was a matter of great interest to the Kerala rulers, as it brought the factors of Tellichery directly into the conflict on their side. It became possible to secure arms and ammunition and to organise resistance from a central point. The Bombay Government by whom the affairs of the Company in Kerala were regulated, sent a naval force which captured Mangalore and put out of action Hyder's own fleet. Three ships were sent down to Tellichery to strengthen the operations planned from that centre against Ali Raja of Cannanore, the ally of Hyder. The factors organised a small force which, with the help of the Nayars and the Rajas of Koluthunad (Chirakkal) and Kottayam marched against Cannanore. But the Bombay Government disapproved of this action and the force, after a futile siege, had to be withdrawn. That Government, however, instructed the factors that all combinations of Kerala powers against Hyder Ali were to be encouraged. In the meantime Hyder was also not idle. A light force under Tippu, which had been sent to defend Mangalore and give aid to Liak Ali Beg, the provincial commander, was despatched to the coast. But it was not able to prevent the fall of Mangalore. On the 20th January 1768, Hyder himself, with a considerable force, appeared on the west coast. Tippu, who on effecting a junction with Ali Beg, found that his forces were insufficient to attempt effectively the reconquest of Mangalore, had withdrawn a few miles and established a land blockade of the town. This apparent inactivity gave the English garrison a false sense of safety, and when Hyder appeared before the gates early in May, they were stricken with panic. As Wilks says:

> "The impression was disgraceful in the last degree to the British Arms; a wretched defence terminated in embarking the garrison, consisting of 41 artillery, 200 European infantry and 1200 sepoys in a most unsoldierlike manner; shamefully abandoning the sick and wounded, consisting of 80 Europeans and 180 sepoys and all their field pieces and stores."[1]

The capitulation of Mangalore, Hyder's first outstanding victory against the British, came as a discomfiture to the Kerala chiefs, but the season was too late for Hyder to take his revenge on Kerala. He had to march across the peninsula and meet his enemies in the Carnatic.

The Kerala chiefs were, therefore, able to continue their operations against his officers. Practical-

---

1. Wilks: *History of Mysore*, Second edition, Vol. I p. 608.

ly every single blockhouse had been taken and all outward symbol of Mysore authority destroyed over the length and breadth of Kerala.

Hyder's Civil Governor, Madana was shut up at Calicut and the small garrison there was hard put to maintain itself against the constant encroachment of the enemy. Hyder realised that the Nayars were a difficult people to conquer and Kerala an uneasy place to govern. He decided that the effort must be given up, at least for the time and instructions were therefore issued to open negotiations with the Kerala chiefs for the peaceful restoration of their territory. Hyder made three conditions for the withdrawal of his troops and the surrender of his annexations. He insisted (1) that compensation should be paid to him for the expenditure incurred by him in the conquest of Kerala (2) that Ali Raja of Cannanore, his co-religionist and ally should be left undisturbed, and (3) Palghat with its fortress should remain in his possession. These terms were agreed to and in December 1768, Hyder's forces after a troubled occupation of 2 years, during which the commander Assud Khan Mihtru, had himself fallen in action and a large number destroyed by the Nayars, recrossed the Ghats, to the intense relief of the Kerala rulers.

Hyder's first effort to conquer and hold Kerala thus ended in failure, but the Ruler of Mysore was not the man either to forget or forgive, and he abided his time to wreak vengence on the unruly Nayars whom he despised as heathens, and hated as his inveterate enemies.

CHAPTER III

HYDER'S SECOND ATTEMPT ON KERALA

The Kerala Rulers were not left for long to enjoy the fruits of their dearly bought freedom. The death of the Peshwa, Madhava Rao in 1772, gave Hyder Ali the peace he desired and in 1773 he decided upon the reconquest of Kerala. In December that year a strong Mysore force under Srinivasa Rao Birkee and Said Sahib descended through the Tamarachery Pass. Realising the impossibility of open resistance, the Kerala Princes bowed before the storm and offered their submission. Hyder had, however, decided upon making permanent arrangements for the government of Kerala. His instructions in this behalf were given to Srinivasa Rao before the latter left Seringapatam. As soon as the country was reconquered and the Mysorean sway established, Srinivasa Rao took over the duties of civil governor while Said Sahib returned to Mysore leaving Sardar Khan as commander-in-chief with the necessary garrison.

The Ruler of Cochin had, as mentioned before, accepted Mysore suzerainty. In 1773, Srinivasa Rao requested the Raja for a contribution of 4 lakhs of rupees towards military expenditure, which was paid without delay, and the relations between the Cochin Ruler and Mysore continued to be friendly. In 1776, however, a dispute arose over a tract of territory known as Talpatti Mel Vettam. This tract was a part of Zamorin's country which, in the confusion that followed the Mysore invasion, had been occupied by the forces of the Raja of Cochin and annexed to his territories. Srinivasa Rao demanded its surrender and arrears of revenue collected by Cochin. The Cochin Ruler was evasive and after some futile negotiations, Sardar Khan marched on Trichur via

Kunnamkulam and occupied it on the 18th September, 1776, The Commander was most anxious to annex Cochin but when the Raja proposed that he would abide by the decision of Hyder Ali he agreed to it. The Raja sent Komi Achan and Iswar Pattar to Seringapatam and Hyder Ail, after hearing them, modified his demands and agreed to spare Cochin on payment of a lakh of pagodas and 4 elephants as Nuzzur and an annual tribute of 30,000 pagodas. It is mentioned as a remarkable fact that though the Mussalman army was encamped on the temple precincts, not a single door of the buildings attached to the temple was found unlocked.

Cochin thus escaped the fate of the rest of Kerala. From the territories to the north, the leading princes and nobles once again escaped to Travancore, where they found ready shelter and active help for their plans. Rama Varma, the reigning Raja of Travancore, was one of the most remarkable personalities of his time. Succeeding his celebrated uncle Martanda Varma in 1757, he found himself heir to a military State which had but recently brought large areas under its sway. The population of the conquered countries was discontented. The dispossessed princes were still in a position to create trouble. His own inclinations were far from martial. A poet and scholar of renown in Sanskrit, author of a standard work on dancing and dramatics and devoted to music and kathakali, he was more fond of the arts of peace than of war. His knowledge of European languages and familiarity with the affairs of the West are attested to by Father Paulinos with whom he had many intimate talks. But a man of peace as he was, Rama Varma or Ramraja as he is styled by European historians was determined to maintain the independence and integrity of his State.

He had the good fortune to be served by a Minister of outstanding ability. Raja Kesava Das had risen from the ranks of the State bureaucracy which Ramaiyan Dalawai had instituted. He was gifted with an intellectual curiosity which made him learn Portuguese and English. Energetic, ambitious and far-seeing but thoroughly loyal to his master, Kesava Das realised from the beginning that Mysorean pretensions would have to be resisted if necessary by force of arms. Finance was the main problem. By a system of State monopolies in pepper, cardamom and other products he was able to collect sufficient funds to enable him to undertake the necessary preparations. Nor did he neglect the diplomatic side of the struggle. In fact during this period, Kesava Das may well be said to dominate the Kerala scene.

The exiled and emigre Kerala Princes were afforded shelter and welcome in Travancore. They were provided with funds to carry on their activities. An atmosphere of cordiality prevailed with the Dewan keeping minute and most detailed accounts of every penny advanced and every service rendered.

The Raja of Travancore was animated not only by a generous desire to help the refuges, but he recognised their political value in creating trouble for Mysore forces, if Hyder Ali should try to carry out his own design of attacking Travancore. The Mysore generals also realised that their hold on Kerala would never be safe so long as Travancore provided an asylum for the dispossessed chiefs. Besides, ever since Hyder's first decent on Kerala, the Travancore Raja was making elaborate preparations for the defence of his territory. On the 20th June 1766, the Travancore lines were extended to the very boundaries of the Dutch settlements. The army was strengthened, roads constructed, and arms and ammunition collected with a view to meet any possible attack. The interval between the first conquest of Kerala and the annexation 10 years later afforded Travancore the most invaluable opportunity to put itself in a position of diplomatic and military preparedness.

The first object of the Raja was to strengthen the bonds of the alliance subsisting between the English East India Company and himself through the Nawab of Arcot. So far, in the view of the Madras Government, the Travancore Raja was no more than a feudatory of Mahommed Ali. The Raja realised that unless his direct relationship with the Company was recognised and he himself taken under its protection, the alliance with Mahommed Ali, who was but an impotent puppet, was unlikely to bring him timely succour as against the military power of Hyder. Negotiations were, therefore, opened with the East India Company. The Company also desired a close alliance with the Raja and as early as 1762 the Bombay Government had written to the Court of Directors[1] suggesting the desirability of assisting the Raja with warlike stores and recommending the surrender to him of Tinnevelly for the sake of trading concession—a proposal which was prevented only by the opposition of the Presidency of Madras. Therefore the Raja's efforts to bring the Company into closer relationship with him, met with decided success, and when the second Mysorean invasion of Kerala leading to the anexation of the principalities and the establishment of Mysore Government in that area took place, Travancore was in a position to defy the blandishments of Sardar Khan and watch with some sense of equanimity his designs and actions in the Northern regions.

As soon as Sardar Khan took up the military government of Kerala, he sent emissaries to the Dutch Commandeur of Cochin requesting free passage through Dutch held territory to Travancore.

1. Letter Dated 10th April, 1762—India Office Records—Home & Miscellaneous No. 433: "Note on our connection with Travancore."

The Dutch Company was placed in a position of great difficulty. Travancore was not only their ally, but the state from which the largest portion of their trade came. The Commandeur's reply that the matter could only be decided after reference to Batavia, which was the capital of the Dutch East Indies' Empire, did not carry conviction, as the same reply had been given 10 years before. The Mysore authorities had anticipated this reply and decided upon their course of action accordingly. They claimed from the Dutch the surrender of Chetwai and Cranganore as belonging to the kingdom of the Zamorin and Sardar Khan mrched at the head of a powerful army of 10,000 men to enforce this demand. The details of the negotiations that followed have already been dealt with in the previous section and are not repeated here. The diversion caused by the fight between the Dutch and Hyder's forces saved Travancore once again from the threatened invasion.

From 1775 Hyder's policy in Kerala underwent a change. The system of direct government through officers sent from Mysore which was at one time contemplated was given up as impracticable. Hyder, therefore, tried to utilise the Kerala princes as his agents for government. The first experiment in this policy was the nomination of the Regent of Koluthunad to the government of his ancestral domains in Chirakkal. This policy, which was cautiously extended to the whole coast, met with some success and from 1775 to 1778 there was comparative peace in Kerala. But the Nayars were unwilling to accept the authority of the Mysoreans and in 1778 rebellion broke out again.

The Rajas of Calicut, Kadathanad and Kottayam, joined together to throw off the yoke of Mysore and the Company's agents on the West Coast as usual encouraged them. War had broken out between England and France and the Company was therefore anxious to drive the French out of Mahe. Hyder, to whom Mahe was the window to Europe, was unwilling to see that port also under British occupation and, therefore, instructed the Raja of Chirakkal to help the French with all his forces. The Regent of Chirakkal inmediately moved at the head of a Nayar force to the help of the French garrison. Hyder sent a further contingent from Coorg. In spite of many efforts, the Zamorin and the other Rajas could not be persuaded to help the French, though at the beginning they were equally unwilling to be dragged into the fight on the side of the East India Company. The English Company also, realising the strategic importance of Kerala in the inevitable contest with Mysore, was anxious to impress the Kerala Princes with their power. They concentrated a very considerable naval force in Kerala waters and in the month of February (1779) collected a powerful army under Captain Walker. On March 2nd, Col. Braithwaite with a European battalion landed on the Kerala coast. This was reinforced two weeks later by 3 companies of artillery under Major Clifton. Seeing the active preparations of the British, the Zamorin and the Kottayam Raja now came out into the open. The Company supplied the latter with arms and ammunitions to attack the Chirakkal Raja (Koluthunad Prince) who was attempting to blockade Tellichery from the land side. Attacked thus from both sides, the Chirakkal Raja was forced to retreat and Mahe fell to the British on the 19th March (1799).

As soon as their objective was gained by the conquest of the French port, the Company left the Zamorin and the other Kerala princes to their own resources and withdrew from the contest. The argument of the Company was that they were at peace with Hyder Ali, and any help rendered to his rebellious vassals would led to complications with Mysore, for which they were not prepared at the time. The Kerala Rajas were, therefore, abandoned to Hyder

Ali's mercy. The Raja of Chirakkal, who was the main support of Hyder's policy on the coast, was actively helped by Bulwant Rao in crushing the insurrection of the Kottayam Raja who was again forced to flee the country. Raja of Kadathanad, who had refused to join in the attack on Tellichery, was deposed and a younger prince who was in favour of the Mysoreans was given possession of the State.

But the Kerala problem remained unsettled. The expenses of holding the country were very large and no revenue was coming in as the Nayars had preferred to abandon their lands, rather than yield to the conqueror. A further attempt to settle the country was, therefore, decided upon and Sardar Khan entered into negotiations with the Rajas of the North, especially the Ruler of Kottayam, who was the firm ally of the East India Company and, therefore, a thorn in Hyder's flesh. Sardar Khan's next attempt was to besiege Tellichery itself.

In the meantime, war had broken out between Hyder and the English and a major factor entered into Kerala politics. The English again entered into negotiations with the Kerala rulers especially the Zamorin and the Raja of Travancore, who were invited to join in an alliance to crush Hyder's power on the West coast. The position of the Company at Tellichery was serious as Sardar Khan with the support of the Chirakkal Raja had closely invested it. The only chance of safety for the town lay in the support of the Raja of Kottayam, who though deserted by the Company in the time of his need, stood staunchly by his friends at this crisis. He attacked Sardar Khan from the rear and Major Abington, with his troops reinforced attacked and crushed Sardar Khan's besieging forces.

This was the signal for another general uprising all over the country. Calicut fell to Major Abington on February 13th, 1782 and all over the coast the

Nayars rose and destroyed Hyder's garrisons and blockhouses. In the short space of a fortnight, Mysorean power had totally ceased to exist in Kerala except at Palghat. But Hyder was not the man to be daunted by defeats. He quickly changed his plans: reduced his force in the Carnatic and despatched a powerful expeditionary force under Mukudam Ali to reconquer Kerala. Mukudam entered Kerala via the Palghat Pass with a force of over 7,000 troops and marched towards Calicut. The British forces in Calicut were under the command of Col. Hunberstone, who had taken charge from Major Abington. Reinforced by a considerable number of the Zamorin's Nayars, Humberstone moved south and met Mukudam's forces at Tirur Angadi. Mukudam, though an experienced officer, took up a position which had the disadvantage of having a deep river in the rear. Humberstone attacked vigorously and drove the Mysore forces out from their position. Retreat was difficult and Mukudam himself together with a large number of men was killed.

Humberstone now conceived the idea of reducing Palghat which from the beginning had been the impregnable base of Mysore power on the coast. He began to make extensive preparations for it. Taking up his headquarters at Trittala he collected his stores and provisions at that place. Humberstone knew that the reduction of Palghat would not be an easy affair and was determined not to attempt it without full information about the country and the possibilities of defence. This he undertook himself. Leaving his battering train and heavy equipment under the protection of a battalion of sepoys, he marched with six 6-pounders, two 9-pounders and the remainder of his force to "reconnoitre the country and the fortress of Palghatchery." He met with no serious opposition but his examination showed him that the fort was not easy to storm and was capable of standing a long siege. Humberstone while wise in his judgment about the strength of the fortress, had underestimated the mobility of the Mysore forces. On his way back to headquarters after the reconnoitering expedition, he was attacked from the rear and had to leave behind all his provisions.

The defeat of Mukudum opened the eyes of Hyder to the seriousness of the danger threatening him from the Kerala coast. Immediately he decided to send a much stronger force and, if possible, conquer the area once for all. A powerful expeditionary force was prepared and put under the charge of Tippu himself, and the Prince was given as his adviser Lally, the great French General. This force was more or less kept concealed on the Coimbatore side on the pretext of a campaign on the east coast; but its real object was to sweep down upon Kerala as soon as Humberstone had so far advanced into the interior as to render a retreat difficult when the rivers were flooded. It was this powerful force which suddenly made its appearance on the rear of Humberston's troops, who had now no option but to fall back. To fight an action against such superior numbers under the command of experienced generals in a hostile country, far away from the coast would have been foolhardy, but retreat was equally dangerous as the outbreak of the monsoon had flooded all the streams in the country and made them difficult to ford. But Humburstone managed to escape by a forced march of 30 miles and reached the coast where he handed over charge to Col. McLeod at Paniani. Tippu soon overtook him there and encamped his forces two miles outside the town.

Col. McLeod, who had been sent by Sir Eyre Coote, took up his position and after some preliminary skirmishes awaited Tippu's attack. The hostile forces remained in this position for a week, and it was only on the 29th that Tippu decided to attack. The battle was indecisive, both parties remaining in their position after the combat. On the 12th December, news reached the Mysore camp that Hyder Ali was dead and Tippu hastened to the capital to be crowned as Sultan.

The withdrawal of Tippu gave the English Company, in alliance with the local Rajas, an opportunity to destroy the Mysore authority on the west coast. But the Bombay Government who were responsible for the Kerala campaign, were unaware of the retreat of Tippu, and lost the chance. They recalled McLeod and appointed in his place General Mathews, who in his desire for a spectacular achievement, diverted his forces (together with the forces under McLeod) for an attack on Bednore.

Though the Bombay Government did not realise the importance of the Kerala campaign, the Madras Council being more in direct contact with Mysore, was alive to the danger of allowing Tippu to remain in undisturbed possession of the West Coast. Recognising the importance of the fort of Palghat, which was the base of the Mysoreans for all action in Kerala, and which by its natural position commanded the only pass into the Kerala province, they decided to use this opportunity to attack and take possession of it. The fort of Palghat had been rebuilt by Hyder with the assistance of French advisers. It was strategically at the centre of Mysore dominions and commanded the route to Coimbatore, Kerala and Cochin. Fullarton, who was in charge of the expedition to reduce the fortress marched from Palni through the Anamalai forests. The fort surrendered after a siege, and Fullarton put the Zamorin in charge of the territory surrounding it. There was again a chance of taking the whole country between Palghat and Calicut. But Fullarton decided to march on Coimbatore and from there if possible to proceed to Mysore, leaving the Zamorin to hold Palghat with 4 battalions of troops to be lent by the Raja of Travancore. Before these could arrive, the Zamorin abandoned Palghat and Tippu's forces quietly reoccupied the great fort which had been conquered with such difficulty.

CHAPTER IV

TIPPU AND KERALA

In 1784 peace was signed with Tippu. The Kerala Rajas whom the Company had encouraged to revolt against Tippu were left to his tender mercies, the first Article with unconscious irony declaring 'the Rajas or Zamindars of the Kerala Coast' to be the friends and allies of Tippu. The Tellichery factors were not slow in pointing out the injustice of this action, especially in regard to the Raja of Kottayam, who had been a steadfast ally of the British during all their troubles and who had never yielded to Mysorean authority. But these expostulations of the Company's own officers went unheeded and the Kerala Princes were left unprotected in the Treaty.

After his own affairs in Mysore were settled, Tippu took in hand the problem of Kerala which had baffled even his father. Hyder had recognised that Kerala could only be conciliated and not held down, and just before his death he had appointed as governor of the province Arshad Beg Khan, whom Wilks describes as "a Mussalman of rare talents, humanity and probity." Arshad Beg had instructions to use all the methods of conciliation and restore peace in the country, and in this work he was eminently successful. He introduced regular revenue laws assessing the lands reasonably. He formed an estimate of the produce and calculating an average amount imposed a tax on each tree. For every cocoanut tree the tax was ½ a fanam (A fanam was equal to 1/5 of a Bombay rupee). Young trees and old ones were exempted. Mr. Srunee calculated that the average yield of a tree was 1 ⅛ of a fanam, so that the assessment was about 2/5ths. This system brought the land back under cultivation and Arshad

Beg had reason to be proud of his work. But Tippu as soon as he ascended the throne decided to try other methods. He separated the Civil and Military functions and appointed as military governor, Meer Ibrahim, a headstrong and inexperienced officer who in a few months undid all the good work of Arshad Beg and brought the province again to the verge of rebellion. He broke all the treaties with the Princes, imposed new exactions and generally infuriated the Nayar chiefs. Even the Mopla notable Mancheri Kurukkal turned against Mysore. The position became so serious that Arshad Beg had finally to complain about the highhandedness of his colleague, and invite Tippu to come to Kerala and see the effects of the new policy himself. Accordingly, at the head of a large army, Tippu descended on Kerala via Tamarassery Pass in January, 1788. He marched on Calicut without meeting any opposition. There he took in hand seriously the question of changing the entire structure of Kerala society.

Tippu, unlike his father who was a plain soldier, was a born reformer. Like his contemporary, Joseph II of Austria, he felt it to be his kingly duty to reform every institution and rearrange society on a definite plan. In fact he had already established a Ministry of Administrative Reorganisation which issued under the Sultan's direct orders minute instructions in regard to every department. To Tippu it seemed that no part of his dominions required reorganisation so urgently as Kerala. The social system of the country with its peculiar marriage customs and the matrilineal law of inheritance seemed especially barbarous and uncivilised to his narrow mind. The low position of many communities and the caste tyranny of the Nayars particularly shocked him. He has himself left a description of his impression of Kerala which is particularly interesting as affording an insight into the mind of the Mysore Ruler.

In a letter to Budr-uzzuman Khan and others dated the 6th March 1789, Tippu Stated.

"Seven months ago our special retinue proceeded in splendour for the purpose of settling the country of Furkhy (Calicut). When calling together all the Nayarmars, and Mapilars, we made enquiry respecting the state of the receipts and disbursements of the ryots; and having ascertained the same, remitted a third part of the amount which they had been accustomed to pay to the Sircar, delivering at the same time to every one of the rulers or chief men of the country, a Hukm-nameh (or mandate) to the following effect. "Your tribute has been reduced to one third part. You must (therefore) apply yourselves, diligently and faithfully to the promoting of cultivation; and, paying your rents regularly to the Sircar, always attend obediently upon our aumils. Moreover, as among the tribe of Nayarmars, the woman has no fixed husband, or the man any fixed wife; but the whole, with the exception of mothers, sisters and daughters, cohabit promiscuously together like the beasts: now this not being (a) good (custom) it is fit that you should desist from so hateful a practice; and that every man, taking to himself a wife, and keeping her in his house, do not suffer any other person (or stranger) to come before her." In short a great many other matters of the same improper nature were set forth in writing (on this occasion) and at the end of the Hukmnameh was written: "In the course of the last twenty-five years, you have slain near a hundred thousand of the Sircar's soldiers and repeatedly committed excesses. Now (or henceforward) you must desist from these proceedings; but if you should ever again be guilty of the like, or engage in war or tumult against the Ahmedy Sircar, we will, with the blessing of God, the Helper, act by you according to the book of God; and carrying into execution, the commands of God and of the Messenger of God will confer upon your whole nation the honour of Islam, and place, (or enroll) every individual of you in Ahmedy ranks." This was given in writing: after which, having laid our strict injunctions on the whole (body) our special retinue shed splendour on the royal residence (Seringapatam).

"Four months after this, (settlement) these base wretches, spreading confusion around and setting sedition on foot, broke out universally into (a fresh) rebellion; and engaging in frequent hostilities with the Foujdars stationed among them, reduced the latter to great straits. Immediately upon learning of the whoreson behaviour of the infidels, our special retinue again moved in the direction of Furkhy (Calicut) with a view to fulfilling the commandments of God; and of the Messenger of God, as contained in the Koran, and delivered twelve hundred years ago. The Jehads which (in consequence) took place at that period, may be learned by reference to ancient books. Since then no person has undertaken a Jehad, till now that we through the divine favour and with the aid of the holy prophet, have embarked in the present one, with which no other good work can compare; nor can any claim so high a reward."

The letter proceeds to state that the holy war now pursued had already led to the spontaneous profession of the true faith by great numbers of the infidels and their families; and it concludes with inculcating the positive duty of all Mussalmans, "to take up arms for the advancement of Islam; and by expatiating on the favour which they will by so doing, acquire with God, with his prophet, and with the Mahomedan world at large."

The foregoing mandate was directed to be read to the whole of the Mussalman population of the place, who were to be assembled for the purpose, on the next ensuing Friday after its receipt in the public mosque, where, besides the customary devotions of the day, a special thanksgiving was ordered to be rendered to the Almighty, for the Sultan's recent successes and prayers to be offered up for a continuance of the same. The service was appointed to be closed with a discharge of twentyone guns, and the distribution of fifty maunds of sugar among the people (i.e. the true believers).

It was not religious bigotry that made Tippu issue this amazing proclamation. He was firmly convinced that in asking the Nayars to give up what he called their obscene habits he was undertaking a mission of civilisation. It is the narrow reformer's mind, anxious for the moral and material welfare of the people and not the fanaticism of a bigot desirous of converting the Kafir that speaks in this proclamation.

As the monsoon had by this time started, Tippu retired to Coimbatore. Already on the verge of rebellion, owing to the exactions of Meer Ibrahim, the Sultan's proclamation added fuel to the fire and the whole country rose in open revolt. The Sultan, therefore, was forced to return and in January, 1789, Tippu again descended by the Tamarassery pass. He arrested and put Arzhad Beg in jail presumably for not giving full effect to his orders, and allowed that venerable man to die in disgrace. On arrival in Kerala the Sultan found that the Nayars had taken to their mountain fastnesses where pitched battles were altogether impossible. The thickly wooded forests afforded the Nayars full protection against large scale military operations which Tippu had planned. Baulked of his intention of "honouring" the whole community with Islam, the Sultan organised what was a veritable man hunt. He divided up his army into small detachments with orders to scour the country and enforce his social reforms on the unwilling Nayars, and on refusal to convert them to Islam at the point of the sword. To such lengths did his zeal for social reform carry the Mysore ruler.

The Sultan himself with a strong force surrounded at Cootipur a body of Nayars, who after offering a spirited resistance, surrendered to superior numbers. They were all circumcised the very next day and this achievement was held up as an example for other detachments to emulate.

The Kerala Princes, allies and enemies alike, soon began to feel the presence of the Sultan. The Koluthunad Raja (Chirakkal) who was in the time of Hyder the tool of Mysore policy, was the first to suffer. He was invited to Tippu's headquarters and strong in the conviction that he was the pillar of the Mysore State in Kerala the Raja arrived in camp with a suitable retinue and with numerous presents. Tippu received him with honour and treated him with consideration for a few days. Knowing the desire of the Sultan to plunder the Hindu temples, the Raja, according to the Sultan's own memoirs, offered 4 lakhs of rupees and plates of gold on condition of sparing the temple itself, to which Tippu replied that he would not spare the temple for all the treasures of the world. The Raja was formally given permission to depart but before he could reach his capital Tippu announced that a conspiracy had been unearthed in which the Raja was implicated, and ordered his party to be attacked. In the fight that took place the Raja himself was killed. The dead body of the Raja was mutilated and exposed to public gaze. Tippu gloated over his own atrocities in the memoirs which he left. The fate of the Chirakkal Raja decided the attitude of the Zamorin. In 1788 Tippu had restored the Zamorin to a part of his dominions and embarked on a policy of conciliation with that Ruler in the hope that the Zamorin's claims could be used for his own schemes of aggression. The Zamorin was not unwilling to be friendly with Tippu, but the Sultan's treatment of the Chirakkal Raja and the orders for the conversion of resisting Hindus made him realise that peace with Tippu was impossible and the Ruler of Calicut again headed the general rebellion and escaped after its suppression to Travancore.

After celebrating the marriage of his son Abdul Khalic with the daughter of Ali Raja of Cannanore, Tippu marched by slow stages along the coast to Chowghat, with a view to impress the population with his military power. There he issued final orders for the reorganisation of the province, separating the fiscal, civil and military arrangements. The lands were to be resurveyed, fruit trees numbered, and the lands of the rebellious people were to be confiscated and added to the royal domain. A permanent army of occupation was left in Kerala to overawe the population and to suppress any possible revolt. After making these arrangements, the Sultan retired to Coimbatore.

CHAPTER V

RESISTANCE OF TRAVANCORE

The Ruler of Travancore, Rama Varma, known to history as Rama Raja, had watched with growing nervousness the conquest of Kerala by Hyder Ali and the establishment of Mysore power on his own borders. As mentioned before, the Raja realised that the support of Arcot had ceased to be of practical value to him and that if he was to put up an effective resistance to the aggressive designs of Mysore, the help of the British East India Company, which was the only military power in the south of India strong enough to resist Tippu, was absolutely necessary. The Dutch power had utterly vanished and the English Company had established effective authority over the Carnatic Suba. In the war against Hyder Ali, Travancore troops fought on the Company's side and rendered very meritorious services. The Madras Select Committee wrote to the Court of Directors on the 13th March 1779:

> "The Raja of Travancore afforded the troops sent to attack Mahe a free passage through his country and amply supplied them with provisions."

On the 27th of March 1782, Lord MaCartney reported to the Select Committee that the Raja's conduct in supporting the Company, in spite of other advice from the Dutch, deserved "the highest encomiums."

Colonel Humbertone wrote to the Raja as follows:

> "I am well informed how steady and sincere an ally Your Majesty has ever been to the English Nation. I will relate to the Governor-in-Council the great friendship you have shown

> and the services you have rendered to the English interests in general and to the army that I commanded in particular."

Also it was the support of the two Travancore battalions at the battle of Pannini, as McLeod himself reported which enabled him to save his own troops in a desperate position making it possible for him "later to penetrate to Biddenore and thereby save Carnatic." The help of Travancore during this period was of the utmost importance. The Raja's case for inclusion in the Mysore treaty was, therefore, particularly strong.

In the instructions to Messrs. Callander and Ravencroft, the Commissioners deputed by them to assist in concluding a treaty with Tippu in January, 1784, the Bombay Government after directing them to include the Kerala Princes, which they did not seem to press very strongly, added with regard to Travancore as follows:

> "The Raja of Travancore, being an ancient and faithful ally of the Company and having given them the most decided marks of his attachment by very active assistance against Hyder Ali in the late war, you must stipulate for a clause in the treaty including the Raja as an ally of the Company."

Colonel MeLeod, writing to the Madras Select Committee, also bore witness to the help rendered by Travancore in the following terms:

> "The King of Travancore has always been the most faithful friend and ally to the Hon'ble Company. Last year, two of his well-disciplined battalions fought with me at Pannini and by that means enabled me to save the army which afterwards penetrated to Biddenore and thereby relieved the Carnatic. This Prince should have been in posses-

> sion of Paliccachery (Palghat) which would have given his dominions full security and have proved a notable check upon Tipoo."

The Raja was included by name as an ally in the Treaty, and Tippu undertook not to molest Travancore. But the Mysore Ruler did not give up his intentions on Travancore. Ramaraja had given asylum to all the discontented Kerala Rulers from the Zamorin downwards, and helped them to continue their fight against the Mysoreans. Also, he had bought from the Dutch the forts of Aya Cotta and Cranganore, which, though belonging to the Dutch Company, were in the territory of the Cochin Ruler, who was a feudatory of Mysore. More than all, Tippu knew that, as long as Travancore was independent, his own flank was open to attack and his position in Kerala and Coimbatore never safe. He was, therefore, anxious to come to an amicable understanding with Travancore and if such a settlement was not possible, to reduce that state also by force of arms. It was with this object that Tippu even restored the Zamorin and asked him to put forward claims and promised support for any action that the Zamorin might take against Travancore. But that plan miscarried, as the Zamorin refused to be made an instrument against a Ruler who had stood by him in the days of his own trouble.

Tippu, it must be remembered, had just grounds of complaint against Travancore. The Raja had undoubtedly given protection to all the dispossessed noblemen of Kerala against many of whom Tippu had legal claims. It was not a question of migration at the time of conquest. For over twenty years, Mysore had held the Kerala Princes under subjection, and many of them had paid homage to Tippu, and entered into contracts for revenue with him. To afford asylum to those who were Tippu's enemies was undoubtedly an unfriendly act. Secondly, the Raja had bought from the Dutch two forts, outside his own territory. While, no doubt, those forts in the hands of Tippu would have meant disaster to Travancore, and as such the Travancore Raja's action was justified on the plea of self-defence, it was undeniable that one of the forts was situated within the Cochin territory and could not be legally acquired without the permission of the Cochin Raja and his suzerain, the Mysore Sultan; the other was in Cranganore, and the Dutch Company had agreed with Sirdar Khan to pay rent for it to the Mysore Government.

Tippu tried every available method to get the matter settled amicably. He asked the Cochin Raja to intervene and negotiate; but the Travancore Ruler proved obdurate. Tippu then instructed his own envoys, Abdul Kadir and Athom Amir, to protest to the Raja, but that was also unavailing. He moved the Madras Government and drew their attention to the illegal act of their ally, the Raja of Travancore. Mr. Holland, then Governor, saw the justice of Tippu's contentions and asked the Raja to give up the fort. From the very beginning of the negotiations, the Government of Madras had pointed out to the Raja that the acquisition of Aya Cotta and Cranganore would be against their wishes, and was likely to involve them in trouble with Mysore. As soon as it came to be known that the negotiations were about to be completed, John Holland wrote on August 17, 1789, that he viewed these negotiations with alarm, and advised the Raja against the purchase. To this the Raja replied on September 3rd, 1789:

> "The arrival of your friendly letter (No. 70 of the 17th August) at this time has given me much pleasure: and I have understood the whole of its contents. You inform me that you had understood from the Information of Mr. Powney that I had nearly concluded a Negotiation with the Dutch for the purchase

of Jayacottah and Cranganore, which they hold of the Raja of Cochin; that from this circumstance you were afraid that the purchase of this territory and those forts which are dependent on the said Raja, who is a tributary of the Chief of Mysore, might be the cause of an increase of illwill in him and withdraw the assistance of the Company in the event of my entering into any dispute or troubles beyond the bounds of my own country, and pointing out the necessity of my considering well on this matter. All this I have well understood and what you have advised is highly proper; nevertheless the accomplishment of this business will no doubt give you pleasure; the real state of the commencement of this transaction is this:—That in former times the forts of Cochin, Jayacottah and Cranganoor and other places were in possession of, and dependent upon, the Portuguese. At that time, on account of some differences between the dependents of the Raja of Cochin and the Portuguese, disturbances took place between them: but the dependents of the Raja not finding themselves able to oppose them, called upon the Dutch for assistance; the Dutch thought proper at that time to lend them the aid they wanted, and assisted them in opposing the Portuguese, and having taken from them the country they possessed, kept the Fort and Places above mentioned in their own hands; for 135 years past they have remained entirely dependent on the Dutch, nor has there been any connection, nor have they in any shape whatever been dependent on the Raja of Cochin, nor has the Dutch paid a single cash to him as a yearly tribute for these places. My friend, of all the places belonging to the Dutch, Jayacottah and Cranganoor are immediately opposite to the wall of my fort. As I was under a great deal of uneasiness on account of the proximity of these places to my wall, that it should so happen that an enemy watchful for a favourable opportunity should take those two places, which, as being the high road for an entrance into my country, are the keys to the welfare and prosperity thereof—at such a time adverting to the propriety and necessity of defending my country, and the engagements for mutual assistance in case of an attack from an enemy which are subsisting, and in full force between me and the Dutch, it would be necessary that I aid and assist them; at that time the Troops belonging to the Company, who are at present here, should excuse themselves from lending any assistance and acting in concert with me, on account of their being dependent on the Dutch. My friend would also imagine that for the sake of defending the confines of others, I had drawn this trouble upon myself, and if at such a time you should remain quiet and not lend me assistance, it would, in the first place, have the appearance of a breach of engagements with the Dutch, and in the second, my whole country would be open to the depredations of an Enemy; on this consideration, therefore, for two years past I have negotiated with the Dutch for the possession of those two places; and as at this Time orders have been received from the Government of Batavia to the Government of Cochin to give them up to Me, I have paid for and received those two Places, namely, Jayacottah and Cranganoor, from the Government of Cochin, the Raja of Cochin has not the smallest connection with those places; If indeed that Raja had the least pretentions to them, undoubtedly it might, as represented by my friend, be the cause of displeasure to the Chief of Mysore; and why should I wish to purchase those two places if it was likely to be the cause of any contest or, dispute between Me and the Chief aforesaid? Never shall such an impropriety, or so inconsiderable a business be done by Me; and in everything that may be agreeable and pleasing to the Company, and for the present and future advantage, I will exert myself with all my power, nor ever think of acting contrary thereto. Mr. Powney will acquaint you with whatever more may be necessary.

Looking upon me as the well-wisher of the Company, rejoice me with your friendly letters; May your friendship constantly increase!"

When Holland received the information that the purchase had been completed, he protested and declared:—

"I cannot approve of your having entered into a tready with the Dutch for extension of territory without the consent of this Government. This very impolitic conduct makes you liable to a forfeiture of the Company's protection for you cannot expect that they will defend territory of which you were not in possession when their troops were sent to your country and which have been since obtained without their assent. I therefore think it necessary that you should at once give back to the Dutch the places which you have thus indiscreetly received from them and thereby establish your affairs precisely upon their former footing.

The Raja replied as follows:—

"Your friendly Letter (No. 75, dated the 8th of Zehudjee, 1203) informing Me that you had received Accounts from Mr. George Powney, that the Negotiation between Me and the Dutch for Jaycottah and Cranganore was nearly concluded which was the cause of your writing to me under date 17th August stating the Ideas that had occupied your Mind on the Impropriety of that Negotiation; that your Government would not lend me their Assistance or Protection on Account of any Troubles or Difficulties which I might bring on Myself beyond the Limits of my own Country, that you were under Apprehensions that if, in consequence of so inconsiderate a Business on my Part, Tippoo should determine to re-possess himself of those Places which are now in my Possession, it might be the Cause of very great Distress to me; that from such illjudged and improper Conduct, which could not at all be agreeable to you and which I had pursued without the knowledge of your Government, I subject Myself to the recall and withdrawing the Assistance of the Company; that the Company will lend their Aid or Assistance for the Protection of such Districts as were not belonging to my Country, or in my Possession and which has been at this Time obtained without the Consent of the Company, and were not mine previous to the sending the Troops of the Company, hither; that I should without delay and Hesitation give back to the Dutch these Places which I had in so inconsiderate a manner obtained, that by so doing my Affairs may be put upon their former Footing; that in every Respect, and on every Account I should be particularly careful in My Conduct towards Tippoo, and that I should pay the most particular Attention to the Advice of Mr. George Powney, who had been sent by you. This Letter was delivered to me on the 25th of the same Month by that Gentleman, and I understand the whole of its contents. As I have for a Length of Time been the Friend and faithful Ally of the Company, I am well convinced that should Tippoo entertain the Idea of going to War with me, it may be said in fact he would quarrel with the English Company. I have well understood the Advice which you in consonance with your former Friendship, have given for my Ease and Prosperity. The real situation of this Matter and the Extent of my Wishes are these:—The Forts of Cranganore and Jaycottah which I have now purchased from the Dutch, were formerly belonging to and in the Possession of the Portuguese: some time since the Dutch were at a great Expense to obtain possession of these two places and having sought a Cause of Dispute with the Portuguese and held them in their own Hands: the Dutch did not obtain these Places from the Hands of any other Person; the Raja of Cochin had not ever, nor has he any Right therein, even to the value of an Hair, to this Moment. I never so much as heard that Tippoo or Others had any Claim on these Places; How then was it possible that I should have been an Eye-Witness thereof? Previous to my purchasing Them I was particularly careful to ascertain that they were not dependent on any other Person; after which I paid the Dutch and received Them from Them. For your Information I wrote the whole of these Circumstances before I sent them You (I hope the Letter was received). At the Time that Sir Archibald Campbell sent Major Bannerman hither with one Company of Sepoys, I caused these two Places to be particularly shown and pointed out to the Major, and in a particular Manner explained to him, that should these two places still remain in the Possession of the Dutch, the whole Chain of Connection in the Management and Prosperity of my Country would be entirely broken and destroyed, and that it would be impossible for the Company's Troops to arrive there in Time to my Assistance; and that it was necessary he should write the Whole of this Account to Governor Campbell. The Major accordingly wrote to the Governor and received an Answer thereto, advising the Purchase of these two Places on every Account from the Dutch; which Letter of the Government the Major fully explained to me, from which Time I did all in my Power to make a Purchase of these two Places, and at this Time, by the Assistance of the Almighty, I have completed my Wish, namely, with the Knowledge and agreeable to the Advice of the Government, I have purchased those two Places from the Dutch. But now that you have written to me that without the Knowledge of your Government I have made this Purchase is extremely strange, and very wonderful. It was heretofore my Intention and wish, that Major Bannerman should explain all this Matter to you, but now it is evident he has not done so: in consequence, therefore, I have now written this account that will give you Pleasure. I never will undertake a Business of this Nature without the Knowledge of Government; I have constantly looked upon the Advice of the Person appointed by your Government in the same Light as the orders of the Company, and to this Moment have acted in Conformity thereto, and shall continue to do so in Future, but should there in such Advice be any Difference, or anything extravagant, I should be without remedy. I am the faithful Friend of the Company, and I considered and pondered well in my Mind that should these two Places remain dependent on the Dutch, and Tippoo of a sudden possess himself of them, that the entire welfare and Government of my Country would be done away and destroyed, that at such a Period the Pains and Trouble of the Company, who are my Protectors and Ally, would be infinitely increased, and it appeared sooner than this should be the case, that I should obtain these two Places by purchase: independent, my Friend, of this Consideration, there is not the smallest Benefit or Advantage accrued to me from the possession of Jaycottah and Cranganore, setting aside this Consideration; if the Company's Government, according to their Justice and Impartiality, should examine the Cause and Reason of my Purchasing these two Places, the Idea of not lending their Aid and Assistance could not possibly enter their Minds: and I have the Fullest Confidence, that when my Friend shall have examined well this Matter that I shall receive Directions to retain and strengthen these two Places; whatsoever Business I undertake, it is after much Advice and Consideration, and I have the firmest Hope that the Company will assist me in the best and most effectual Manner. In a word, Obdul Cawn, the Vakeel of Tippoo Sultan, who was at this Period sent to the Raja of Cochin, is now through the Means of the Raja, carrying on a Negotiation with the Dutch for the Purchase of the Fort Cochin, an Account whereof I formerly gave to Mr. Powney for your Information, and he, no doubt, has transmitted the Same to you: but my Friend will consider if Tippoo has any Intentions against Jaycottah and Cranganore, why should he enter into a Negotiation for the Purchase of Cochin? To a Certainty, so long as Jaycottah and Cranganore remain in my possession, the Dutch will never dispose of Cochin to him—

> but should I relinquish those Places and return them, they would sell them, together with Cochin to Tippoo—You, my Friend, will Consider well if such an Event should happen, what Misfortunes and Difficulties might hereafter ensue. The Intention of all this is that I am an old Friend of the Company. I have written the whole circumstances without Disguise for your Information, in Hopes that you will take the whole into your Consideration, and that hereafter it may not be said I did not fully inform you thereof: I am in Hopes that in a friendly Manner you will quickly favour me with a kind Answer to this Letter, the Receipt of which will relieve my Mind, which is full of Expectancy. What can I write more?"

When pressed again to return the forts to the Dutch, the Raja said that his action in purchasing the forts was taken on the advice of General Sir Archibald Campbell. Holland contested this point and referred the matter to Sir Archbald. General Campbell in his reply stated: "I can venture to affirm from memory that I neither countenanced nor advised the Raja in the purchase of Cranganore and Jaycottah; on the contrary when Major of Brigade Bannerman signified to me that the Island of Jaycottah which the Dutch were inclined to dispose of to the Raja, appeared to him to be the fittest situation for a cantonment on the northern frontier of Travancore country, and gave various reasons in support of it, I differed entirely from him in that opinion .... As I was positive in this idea and expressed the same sentiments in all my minutes upon the subject it is not probable I could adopt a contrary opinion without mentioning the same to the board .... I am the more confirmed in this impression, as Mr. Secretary Morton's letter mentions, that nothing appears on the Madras records to corroborate the assertion of the Raja."

It is clear from the above that the Raja's action in purchasing the forts was taken on his own initiative, probably with the encouragement of Bannerman. Tippu was not unaware of the strong objection taken by the Madras Government to the Raja's procedure, and the Madras Government had, in fact, in reply to his protest, disassociated themselves from the Raja in the matter. He wrote a further letter dated the 24th December, 1789, which is quoted below:

> "For a length of time past it had been represented to the Presence by the Fouzdars and Aumildars of the Calicut country, that Ram Raja the Talookdar of the Malabar Country, had given protection to the Rajas of Calicut, Chirkul, Kolenugger, Kirnut, Nair, & C. Thieves who belonged to the Calicut country, and indebted in large sums of this Circar, and was exciting troubles throughout the whole country (sic). When I reflected on the wisdom, ability and foresight of the Raja, I could not give credit to those reports; I, therefore, went in person to arrange those countries, and remaining near four months at Coimbatoor, I with certainty ascertained, from confidential people, and the inhabitants of the country, that without a doubt Ram Rájah is the source from whence the troubles of this country have taken their rise; that subsequent to the time when the country was subdued, and the Raja of Cochin became obedient to this Circar, he had made a boundary and a ditch in the Cochin country and at Cranganore; that he had without my knowledge purchased the Fort of Cranganore which stands on ground belonging to this Circar, and placed a garrison of his own people in it; the circumstance respecting the ditch is this—they built a place at Cranganore, and paid a yearly rent to the Circar, in the same manner as the Ryots do

for the Lands.—All these circumstances I have before twice written to you, and I also twice wrote to the Raja on this subject; after which I sent a gentleman named Abdul Cawder, with a letter to the Raja for his information, who having repaired to the Raja, made a demand on the subject of the above-mentioned three points. I send you enclosed for your information a copy of the Raja's answer thereto, which was sent to the Presence, and copies of my letter to him and an agreement or treaty of the Raja of Cochin and Cranganore; from these you will be well acquainted with the whole circumstances. Independent of of this he still continues to keep a guard of 200 men at the house of the Cochin Raja; notwithstanding the certainty of his being a dependent on this Circar, he will neither permit a single person belonging to him to go in or out, and the letters from the Presence and the servants of the Circar, unless they have an order from the Ram Raja, are prevented from going to the Cochin Raja; from this you may form a judgment of the impropriety of his conduct, his evil disposition and want of consideration. As the bounds of friendship and goodwill are firmly established by treaty between this Circar, the Raja (King) of England, and the Company, it is therefore I have written you in a friendly manner, that you should send positive orders to Ram Raja on these three important subjects, that he should relinquish the improper ideas he entertains, and in future that he should not engage in any thing that is improper which will impair the basis of the goodwill which is between us, and no trouble whatever will be given by my Army to the country belonging to Ram Raja.

> Make me happy with constant accounts of your welfare. May the days of prosperity continue for ever!"

Tippu thought that he had successfully isolated the Raja and was given freedom by the Madras Government to enforce his demand for the evacuation of the forts.

But both Holland and Tippu under-estimated the diplomatic skill of the Raja of Travancore and his Dewan. The Raja addressed the Governor General direct and brought to his notice the threatening attitude of Tippu and the position taken up by the Madras Government. Lord Cornwallis, who was well aware that it was necessary in the interests of British policy that Tippu should in no case get control of Travancore, issued instructions to the Madras Government defining the policy to be adopted on the matter. Lord Cornwallis' attitude was that, if Travancore could prove that the places did not belong to Cochin, but were independly held by the Dutch, then the Travancore Raja was to be supported. But, if Tippu had already taken possession of the forts, by expelling Travancore garrison, then it was not to be considered a *causus belli*; but,if the war extended and the Raja's own territories were attacked, then the British Government would consider that a breach of the Bangalore Treaty guaranteeing the territory of Travancore had been committed and will be "followed up vigorously by war."

Holland did not communicate this decision of the Supreme Government either to Tippu or to the Raja of Travancore. Assured of the neutrality of the British Government, Tippu now took definite action. In December, 1789, the Mysore Sultan sent a formal demand in the following terms:

> "For these five and twenty years past, the Hamildars and Phouzdars have repeatedly represented that you have given protection to

the Rajas of Calicut, Hotgery, Kinnl Nair, Chirkul, & C and lakhs of deserters, from whom large sums of money are due to this Circar; I never thought the report was true, for I considered that you were a person who had seen much of the World, and one of the best informed of your time, that therefore, you would not behave in this manner; but having now twice turned my attention to the arrangement of the Calicut country and proceeded thither in person, from your having within these two months stationed your people in the Fort of Cranganore, which is dependent on the Dutch, and within the district of this Circar, the Dutch having formerly obtained the ground thereof from the Amildar of Calicut, on condition of their paying a rent in the same manner as the Ryots did, and which they have yearly paid; from your giving protection to the Rajas of Calicut to a parcel of thieves and lacks of public disturbers in your country; from this conduct the above circumstances appear to be true. After the reduction of the Calicut country by this Circar you built a boundary in the middle of the territory of the Cochin Raja, who for these fifty or sixty years has been a dependent on this Circar; this also is improper; It is proper that you should not give any protection to the disturbers of the public, but deliver them up to the Circar; that you should remove the boundary from the Raja of Cochin's country and your people from the Fort of Cranganore. Whatever you may chuse to do in your own efforts you are at liberty to do. Abdul Cawder will particularly explain anything to you verbally.

I have sent you a dress which I hope will arrive safe. What can I write more?"

To this the Raja replied with becoming humility, but with firmness, as follows:

"Your two letters by favour of Abdul Cawder and Mahomed Amer Choubdar, together with a dress which had been bestowed by that asylum of kindness and favour, arrived at the most fortunate time, and I was highly honoured by this unbounded kindness. I have particularly well understood what was written in your exalted letter, and also what was verbally explained to me by Abdul Cawder respecting my giving up the Raja of Chircul & C. and other persons who are largely indebted to the Circar, also regarding my removing the boundary from the territory of the Cochin Raja, and my people from the Fort of Cranganore. My Lord, the Raja of Chircul & C being driven from their own country and under great dread and apprehension, took refuge with me on account of the near relationship between us. God is my judge that I have never taken any pains to assist them, or gave them evil counsel, nor have I ever raised any disturbances in the country of the Circar until this moment, nor did I until now ever know of any enquiry or examination on the part of the Circar with respect of their remaining here; but since I have at this time, from the perusal of your dignified letter, become acquainted with the circumstances of their being so greatly indebted to your Circar. I have given positive orders that those Rajas should leave the country. Prior to the time that the Cochin Raja became a dependent on your Circar, the Calicut Raja had possessed himself of all his country; at that period I expended large sums of money to lend him assistance and restored him his country. He then granted me a place for the purpose of building the wall of my boundary in his country, by an irrevocable grant, in consequence whereof, the wall was completed there, at a very great expense, since which five and twenty years have now elapsed. This is the real state of the case; nor has there until this present time been any lett or molestation whatever in this respect, nor has there or ever will be any trouble caused to the Raja of Cochin by me. At the time of the negotiations for peace between you and the English, my name was also included in the treaty; it was well-known to the servants of your Circar that this boundary was then in being. When I received the Fort of Cranganore from the Dutch, they proved by particular writings and treaties that no persons whatever had at that time, or ever had, the smallest claim or connection with it, but that it was dependent entirely upon them; in consequence of which, I bought it of them: I have never given protection to thieves or rebels to the Circar. When you now sent me your directions to withdraw my people from Cranganore, I required a partichlar explanation of the matter from the Dutch; in answer I was acquainted that you had at this time particularly addressed them on the subject of this Fort, and that they had fully replied thereto. I, therefore, hope that when you have examined all the circumstances respecting it you will be satisfied. As I cannot act in anything without acquainting the English I have written all these occurrences to the Governor of Madras: immediately on receipt of these orders I shall fully answer everything regarding.

I have sent a dress & c. agreeably to the enclosed Paper and depend on your favour to honour me with your acceptance of them. What more than reverence!" ,

On the receipt of this reply, Tippu decided to dispossess the Travancore Government of the two forts forcibly. He refused the offer of arbitration which the Madras Government proposed, and moved his forces by the middle of December for an attack on the lines. Before taking the final step, he addressed a further communication to the Madras Government, emphasising how he had personally satisfied himself of the injuries done to him by Travancore and how his own friendly advances for a settlement had been rudely received by the Raja.

Having thus assured himself of the benevolent neutrality of the Madras Council, Tippu attacked the lines on the 29th December 1789, with a force of 7000 infantry. The engagement was sharp and as the force employed was unequal to the task, he was repulsed. He did not immediately renew the attack; if he had done so the course of history might have been different and there would have been no time for Cornwallis' Government to override the Madras Council and act in favour of Travancore. On the other hand, he sent for re-inforcements from Seringapatam troops, battering rams, guns and stores. Nor was Kesava Das idle in the meantime. He was unremitting in his efforts to secure the help of the Company, but having little hope in that direction, raised an army estimated at 1,00,000 and distributed them on the Lines which were further strengthened. On the 15th of April, 1790, Tippu returned to the attack. The events that followed are thus described by a contemporary author.

"A temporary cessation of hostilities, was the only salutary consequence that ensued from negotiation, for, although apparently of a conciliatory nature, it produced neither a foundation for peace, nor any relaxation of military preparations. To assign the causes that produced unproclaimed truce for upwards of two months, between inveterate enemies not five miles assunder, would be to put truth too much to the hazard. It is probable, that the wounds or bruises which the Sultan had received, his want of cannon, together with the inequality of the force now unedr his command to the task that he had undertaken, contributed to his apprent inactivity. During that period, however, he obtained from Mysore and Seringapatam, troops, battering guns and stores, without molestation; whilst the Raja, on the other hand, making the like use of this interval, through the influence of religion encouraged by a temporary success, assembled about one hundred thousand Gentoos, all of whom were carefully distributed on the lines.

The month of March had opened with a period to all interchange of civilities, and with the movements of considerable bodies of troops, when a party consisting of about one thousand men were sent from the lines, as well to reconoitre, as to clear away the brushwood in front of the Mellore gate. Ere they advanced four hundred yards, a body of the enemy, that had lain in ambush, attacked and drove them back with considerable slaughter, notwithstanding their being supported by a heavy fire from the ramparts. On the 4th of the month some timber cut down by the Sultan discovered a work of great extent within the distance of five hundred yards of the ramparts, and two days afterwards a battery was erected to the westward of this work, on which seven eighteen pounders had been planted. From these a cannonade of short duration served to dismount some guns and to silence the fort of Mellore; but it had no material effect on the walls. The besiegers had by the 20th extended their lines to the westward so as to embrace a space of nearly three miles; they had completed several considerable batteries; and advancing by zigzags from four different directions, they approached within fourteen feet of the counterscarp of the ditch. Such was the severity of the cannonade, and so perpetual was the discharge of the musquetry, that by the 29th of the month, of all the guns on the lines two only remained serviceable; one of them in the fort of Millore, the other in a bastion somewhat to the westward; and not a man durst appear upon the ramparts. Approached from so many different quarters protected by a fire from about forty pieces of cannon distracted the attention of the Gentoos, and, that nothing might be neglected to complete their consternation. another battery had been erected at Bagvady-Cottah, about ten miles to the westward of Mellore. To render these operations still more successful, the Sultan, as the memorable siege of Mangalore during the former war, had constructed mortars from which were thrown showers of stones and large billets of wood. Having completed their works, the Mahomedans instigated by superstition, or some other unknown motive, observed a listless inactivity for the space of ten days. From whatever cause this extraordinary conduct took its rise, it suggested to the besieged the idea of an enterprise which was productive of serious consequences.

At three o'clock in the afternoon on the 9th April two parties consisting of about one thousand five hundred men each, sallied from the lines. The one advanced against the western Zigzag, the other from the Mellore gate hastened to attack in front of that quarter. The former division advancing with a good countenance was discovered and fired upon by a small party that the enemy had concealed in an advantageous post. This sudden check, though not the sole cause of immediate victory, contributed considerably to bring about the defeat that ensued. The assilants took post in one of the enemies lines; but, the batteries having by this time taken the alarm, opened with such a heavy discharge of round and grape, that with the assistance of the troops on duty in the trenches, they were compelled to withdraw; not, however, until they felt the bayonets of their opponents. The eastern division succeeded still worse. Charged from different directions by a rsolute body of Mahomeans who added discipline to other advantages the Nayars were happy to regain their lines. To warfare of this nature they had been but little accustomed. The result proved the temerity of the attempt, for a loss of one hundred and thirty men not only dispirited the besieged, but, in proportion to the terror with which they were struck, it confirmed the confidence of the Mysoreans.

All the batteries opened against the walls on the morning of the 12th. From this period of consistant cannonade, night and day, attended by occasional showers of rain mouldered the walls, making a practicable breach of at least three quarters of a mile in extent. By break of day on the 15th, the enemy had planted small flags on their lines as a signal for attack, and without loss of time, three distinct columns advanced to the storm. The resistance at the breach was so inconsiderable as scarcely to merit mention. Fear appeared to have supplanted the courage that the besieged had lately shown; nay, amazement, distraction and terror, seem to have made a deep impression on the whole defensive host. From a heavy fall of rain during the night, numbers of them had retired for shelter to the neighbouring cottages. Some were employed in collecting firewood, others in drying their clothes, and the few that remained in their lines, flying for protection to the extremities of the breach lurked where the ramparts were entire. The columns pressing to the centre of the opening advanced in safety. Stimulated by the presence of the Sultan, they surmounted obstacles, which, if defended with valour, would have rendered this a desperate service. They cut down the bound-hedge; passed the ditch; ascended the shattered walls, and in short, laid open a passage into the heart of Travancore. Gentoos of every description, whether Nayars, Polygars, or Sepoys, fled indiscriminately. Of the latter, two battalions that had been raised for the service of the Travancore Rajah in the Carnatic, were prevailed upon to face about and give one fire; but, abandoned by their associates, they could not be persuaded to reload. The want of experience in warfare; the want of confidence in each other; and, above all, the want of discipline, rendered every attempt to rally ineffectual. The Sultan consequently took possession of the lines, for a considerable extent, with all the cannon and ammunition without meeting any further resistance. The Travancore Minister, to whom the defence of the lines had been intrusted, in so suddenly abandoning works, where the whole force of the country was collected, and where he might have taken the advantage of ravines, nullahs and rivers, gave no proofs of judgment or courage. Ground so capable of being maintained ought never to be yielded to an enemy but in the extremity. Fortunately for the fugitives, no part of this panic had communicated to the two Madras battalions that were then encamped at Shandamungulam, under the command of Captain Knox. It was sound judgment that dictated to them the propriety of removing from thence without loss of time. After covering the runaways until they crossed the river of that name, the detachment fell back, and took post on the Island of Nepean, within ten miles of Cochin, to which station they could readily retire should such a measure become necessary. The consternation that ensued the capture of the lines surpassed credibility. Inhabitants of all descriptions forsook their occupations and crowded to the southward: and the countenance of the detachment alone prevented that part of the country from being totally depopulated.

On the 18th, the enemy made their appearance within one mile of Cranganore. They garrison fled instantly; and, as a great part of them approached the Madras battalions, the Minister detached a party of his own troops with directions that the foremost of the runaways should be cut to pieces. Such was the alacrity and steadiness with which this order was put in force, that only four victims had fallen when all the rest returned to their works. Day after day added to the consternation and distress of the Travancoreans, and rendered it the more necessary for the Carnatic troops to be on their guard. The arrival, however, of Lieut. Col. Hartley with a detachment from Bombay on the 23rd, revived the desponding spirits of the one, and strengthened the confidence of the other. It was at a period materially interesting to Great Britain, and critical with respect to the Rajah, that this junction took place, for, whilst the detachment meditated on the propriety of retiring to Cochin, the Gentoo leaders had determined to seek for safety in precipitate flight. The Sultan filling the ditches by overturning the ramparts as he advanced, had by the 26th, erected batteries against the fort of Cranganore. Protected by his cannon, he made rapid progress with his approaches; and, by the 7th May, he had demolished the defence and silenced all the guns in the fort.

No serious acts of hostility had by this time taken place between Great Britain and the Sultan on the coast of Kerala, although the usual indignant treatment of Christians marked all his actions and every step of his march. Other motives, however, besides policy contributed to induce Colonel Hartley not to attempt the defence of Cranganore. An officer of Engineers, that had been sent to examine the post, reported a total deficiency of cannon, of ammunition, of provisions; he reported also, that the enemy were not only well provided with artillery, but were far advanced in the siege, having erected batteries within three hundred yards of the ramparts. To these disadvantages it may be added, that as the rest of the lines had been completely demolished, Cranganore of itself, availed but little; nor would the parisimony of the Minister grant the usual allowance of cash to the workmen even if the defence had been undertaken. Under those circumstances it was judged advisable to evacuate the post.

Jayacotta, Paroor, Curiapilly, with various other inconsiderable forts, surrendered successively to the Sultan without opposition. The total demolition of the lines was completed by repeated explosions that laid Cranganore in ruins; and a general devastation, as well by fire as the sword, desolated the whole face of the country. The Nayars betook themselves to their strongholds in the mountains, the Travancorean troops to the extremity of their kingdom. All cultivation ceased. In short, the inhabitants exchanged their homes for the most innermost recesses of the jungle, prefering the adventitious attack of the Wolf or the Tiger to the certain and merciless persection of the Mahomedan conqueror. The approach, however, of a powerful army, already in the field, now portended, that nought to boast of this success should descend to the posterity of the Sultan.

The Raja felt helpless. There was no possibility of help coming from Madras, and the Governor-General-in-Council whom he had approached was obviously being thwarted by Mr. Holland. As soon as the news of the attack reached Calcutta, Cornwallis again wrote trusting that war had already been declared. When it came to be known that Mr. Holland had no intention of marching to the support of Travancore and was determined to disobey the orders of Lord Cornwallis, the Governor-General as Commander-in-Chief wrote to him on the 10th of February as follows:—

> "We shall forebear on this occasion to declare any decided opinions on the subjects which we shall state: but the duty which we owe to our country as well as to the late Hon'ble. Company, obliges us to call upon you for explanations of certain parts of your late con-

duct, which we must acknowledge appear to us in a very disadvantageous light.

From the general situation of the political affairs of this country, it seemed to be highly improbable, a short time ago, that Tippoo would venture to force us into a war, but upon the supposition of that event being possible, we prescribed a line for your conduct, under certain contingencies that were specified, in terms which we conceived to be so clear as not to admit of misconstruction.

We directed in our letter, dated 29th August last, that if you should receive certain information that Tippoo had invaded any part of the dominions of the Nabob of Arcot, or of the Raja of Travancore, you were to consider him from that moment as at war with the Company.

These directions were repeated in our letter, dated the 13th November and the instructions contained in both letters were also explicit that from the day on which it appeared that we should be under the necessity of engaging in a war with Tippoo in consequence of his committing actual hostilities against either of our above-mentioned Allies, the payment of the Nabob of Arcot's private creditors, and all steps for the provision of an investment in Europe at your Presidency should immediately cease, in order that these funds might, with the other pecuniary resources of the Carnatic, be applied according to the intention of the Court of Directors to defray the exigencies of war.

We likewise gave our sentiments fully in our letter, dated the 13th November on the circumstances that had been laid before us respecting the Raja of Travancore's purchase of the Forts of Cranganore and Jaycottah from the Dutch; and our orders were positive that if those Forts belouged originally to the Portuguese, and were made over by them to the Dutch, and if the Dutch hold the independent possession of them, without any reserve of allegiance, or stipulations of dependence upon the Raja of Cochin, who is a tributary of Tippoo, the transfer of them by the Dutch to the Raja of Travancore should be deemed valid and just, and the Raja's possession maintained and defended.

Notwithstanding the above instructions, you thought proper in your letter, dated 3rd of January to lay down proofs as being in your opinion founded on the laws of nations, respecting the transaction between the Raja and the Dutch. which militated against the spirit of our orders, and which we conceive it was not regularly within your province to discuss, as you are not responsible for the measure that was directed.

We were also surprised to observe, by the enclosures which accompanied that letter, that what you wrote to Tippoo in consequence of our instructions of the 13th November is only in part conformable to them; as you do not acquaint him that we had determined to assist the Raja of Travancore in the defence of the Forts of Cranganore and Jayacottah, if it should appear upon investigation that the Dutch possessed an independent right to dispose of them.

But it gave us the most serious concern to find that the letters which you sent at the same time to Mr. Powney, The Resident at Travancore and to the Raja himself, are not only silent on the above determination, which we had communicated to you, but are couched in terms calculated to discourage a faithful ally in the defence of his own country against an enemy who was within a few miles of his frontiers, and with the insolence and violence of whose character you have long been fully acquainted.

It has also come under our observation, that posterior to the time of your having received information that Tippoo had committed actual hostilities against the Raja of Travancore, by attacking his lines on the Northern Frontier of his dominions on the 29th December last, you have continued to advertise in the public newspapers for proposals for furnishing you with certain articles to a very considerable amount, of an investment for Europe; and by letters which the Commander-in-Chief has received from the Commanding Officer of the troops under your Presidency, and laid before this Board, it appears to us, that although you had issued orders for a large body of troops to hold themselves in readiness to take the field at the shortest notice, and that a considerable detachment should march from the centre for the purpose of re-enforcing the Southern division of your army, you had, after Tippoo's flagrant infraction of the late treaty of peace was known at your Presidency, informed Col. Murgrave that it was to be understood that bullocks were not to be provided for the Ordinance at Walaujabad till further orders; and we saw that restriction with the more surprise as it had been so recently verified by the military operations of the late war in the Carnatic, that a disappointment in that branch of supply would render all other preparations for active field service nearly nugatory and useless.

After having thus enumerated the parts of your late public conduct which have appeared to us in a disadvantageous light, we have to require that you will assign your reasons for withholding the information from the Resident at Travancore, and from the Raja himself that we should assist in maintaining and defending the Forts of Cranganore and Jayacottah, if it should be proved upon investigation that those Forts had been independent Dutch possessions before the country of Cochin became tributary to the Mysore Government:—for continuing to take steps for providing an investment for Europe;—and for delaying to order a sufficient number of draft and carriage bullocks, for the purpose of enabling the troops to act with vigour in the field after it was known to you that Tippoo had attacked the Raja of Travancore's lines, on the 29th December last being measures in which you seem to have acted in disregard or contradiction of our repeated instructions by which you were directed to look upon Tippoo if he should commit hostilities against either of our Allies, the Nabob of Arcot or the Raja of Travancore, as at war with the Company. We have the Honour to be, & c."

In the beginning of March, Holland was superseded and General Meadows appointed to the Governorship of Madras. In the meantime, Tippu reduced the lines, the Travancore forces offering but little resistance. The Company's forces subsidised by Travancore (10th and 13th Madras Battalions under Captain Knox) remained passive spectators, as they had no orders to resist Tippu. At Cranganore a further British force, one regiment of Europeans and two regiments of Sepoys under Col. Hartley arrived from Bombay, but they also advised the evacuation of Cranganore, which the Sultan occupied on the 8th May. The forts were demolished, but Tippu did not seriously attempt to march into Travancore. The monsoon was about to commence; besides information had reached him that Cornwallis was seriously preparing for war and negotiating with the Nizam and the Mahrattas for a joint attack. He deemed it prudent to return to Seringapatam in order to reorganise his army and prepare for an effective campaign.

Thus Travancore was again saved from conquest, though it was without the actual help of her allies. Keshava Das had effectively worked up an alliance against Tippu by playing on the fear of the British. Thus, though defeated in war, it was Travancore which came out with flying colours as Tippu had to abandon his scheme and depart for Mysore to meet the new danger.

CHAPTER VI.

EXPULSION OF TIPPU

The declaration of war on Tippu by Cornwallis and the triple alliance he organised to fight the Mysore power saved Travancore from conquest. Powerful armies had been concentrated at Tiruchirapalli and Walajabad ready to attack the home domains of the Sultan. Anxious to ward off the impending blow Tippu addressed a letter to General Meadows expressing his friendly intentions but received a reply which stated that "the English have always looked upon war as declared from the moment you attacked their-ally the king of Travancore". It was clear to Tippu that war could not be avoided. He hastened back to Seringapatam immediately with a small force of horse and foot, leaving his regular troops and heavy equipment to meet the attack on Kerala.

The attack that the British authorities had planned against Tippu was from the side of Palghat. The citadal of Palghat commands the only entrance to Kerala from the East coast. Its natural position, always advantageous, was greatly improved by the fortifications that Hyder Ali had erected. Lt. Col. Stuart who was in charge of the operations had received instructions to occupy this important place. "He (General Meadows) wishes you," wrote the Adjutant General to Col. Stuart on the 21st August 1790 "to carry towards Palghatchery as much shot, stores and grains as you can possibly find conveyance for and that you will be in Palghatcbery as soon as you can conveniently arrange matters."

Stuart started his operations against Palghat with an artillery bombardment on the 21st Sepember between six and seven o'clock. From a periodical publication of the time quoted in "A sketch of war with Tippu Sultan" the following facts are taken. In an hour's time the Mysorean guns were silenced: by four in the afternoon a practicable breach had been made and by two o'clock in the morning, after seizing the outer work the fort was called upon to surrender. The Killedar Yanin Khan surrendered. Among the papers captured in the fort was an order from Tippu which enjoined on the Killedar that he should "by every exertion of judgment and policy whether by force or by consent make a Musalman of every infidel in the district."

The fort was formally occupied on the morning of the 22nd. The door was now open to the whole of the Kerala area.

Col. Stuart handed over command to Col. Hartley who moved on to Calicut. He had with him the 75th Regiment, the 7th Bombay Battalion and a regiment of Indian grenadiers supported by 5,000 Nayars of the Zamorin. The Mysorean soldiers were entrenched in a jungle and the first engagement took place there. The Sultan's force was driven into a neighbouring village, where a severely contested battle was fought, at the end of which the enemy evacuated the village and took refuge in the Trincalore fort. Col. Hartley followed up and the fort itself was captured. Hussain Ali Khan, the commander was taken prisoner but a considerable force under Mahbub Khan escaped north. Feroke, Tippu's new fort was also evacuated.

Early in December 1790 Major-General Abercromby with a powerful force landed in Tellichery. The Rajas of the neighbouring countries who had been in a perpetual state of revolt joined him. Among them was Kerala Varma of Pazhassy, who was for a long time the leader of the guerrillas against Tippu and who later was destined till his death 15 years later to be the leader of the national revolt against British authority. Cannanore was reduced on the 16th and Biliapatam surrendered without resistance. By the end of the month Col. Hartley effected a junction with the forces of General Abercromby and Kerala had been cleared of Tippu's forces.

The Sultan's defence of the Kerala territories was in fact only nominal. The British took over the territory without encountering any serious resistance though considerable forces had been posted in different places in Kerala. The only serious engagement was the reduction of Palghat. Even there the defence was half-hearted and Col. Stuart had no difficulty in silencing the guns of the citadel.

Why was it that an area conquered with so much difficulty and held with such loss of revenue and blood abandoned in the face of a small force? The physical features of Kerala were ideally fitted for defence. The Moplas were well affected towards the Mysore regime and communications with Mysore were safe and uninterrupted. A small determined force could easily have held up the British advance. Why then was the Mysorean resistance so ineffectual?

The reasons were simple. In the first place, Tippu's precipitate flight to Seringapatam had demoralised the troops in Kerala. There was no one left in charge of the defence of the territory and therefore there was no clear plan. The garrisons were left to themselves and no effort was made to withdraw the isolated forces and form them into a single fighting force. No instructions were received from Seringapatam and individual commanders surrendered one after the other without offering effective resistance. After Palghat the campaign was only one of mopping up.

Secondly the Nayar chiefs and the local Rajas who had never been reconciled to the Mysore conquest led the civil population which rose up as a man. The leaders of the emigres in Travancore, the Zamorin and the other hereditary Rulers had under Kesava Das's inspiration sent their secret agents and organised an effective underground movement in the face of which the civil administration of the Sultan collapsed completely. The Rajas themselves, or their accredited agents came back to the country from which they had so long been forcibly evicted. It was like a flood and Tippu's officials, deprived of military power, found themselves helpless against it.

With local defence arrangements crumbling in Kerala, Tippu himself was in no position either to send reinforcements or give other support. Cornwallis, anxious to wipe off the disgrace of Yorktown, had planned a great campaign. Tippu had been attacked from all sides. The Mahrattas and the Nizam had put powerful forces into the field on the north. Coimbatore was attacked from the south and the Bangalore plateau was the scene of the major campaign. To Tippu, attacked from all sides and his homeland actually invaded by the British, the Kerala campaign was only an unimportant battle front.

The end was inglorious. From 1766 when Hyder invaded Kerala with the intention of conquest, to 1791 when Tippu's power was extinguished on the West coast, the Mysorean conquest lasted for a quarter of a century. Never had the Mysoreans a complete hold over the area they conquered. Hyder Ali had tried conciliation and a policy of friendliness towards the Rajas. Tippu had exhausted the methods of stern rule and brought the full weight of his military power to bear upon the people of Kerala. In anger and despair he had even been forced to lay the country waste, forcibly convert the Hindus to Islam and generally treat the whole country as under military occupation. But as he was himself forced to admit in his proclamation already quoted, his most stringent measures led to no result. The rich province of Kerala was a drain on his men and money. The Nayars preferred the privations of living in the jungles to being protected by Tippu. No inducements would bring them back to their fields: no blandishments would make them give up their resistance. Abandoned by their chiefs and nobles who preferred the pension of the Raja of Travancore, without support from outside, with nothing but their love of freedom to guide them, the Nayar population kept up for a period of 25 years a resistance which is unparalleled in Indian history.

The Mysorean hold on Kerala was therefore extremely weak and it depended for its strength on continuous supplies of men and material from across the Ghats. It met the fate of all military occupations—ended ingloriously at the first shock of attack from outside. It vanished overnight and the 25 years of Mysorean interlude is remembered in Kerala only with horror even today.

CHAPTER VII.

MYSORE AND COCHIN

As mentioned in the previous chapter, early in his campaign in Kerala Hyder Ali received the submission of Cochin. The then Ruler of Cochin was not in favour of surrender but the initiative in this matter was taken by Rama Varma, surnamed Saktan (the strong) who though only a junior member of the family had already given indication of a dominating personality and outstanding gifts of leadership. Against the advice of the Dutch Commandeur who wrote saying that they were expecting naval reinforcements and suggested that the royal family should evacuate Cochin and take shelter in Travancore, an advice which found favour with the Ruler *, Rama Varma was able to carry his point and persuade his government that discretion was at least in this case the better part of valour. Negotiations were therefore opened with Hyder Ali who received the Cochin delegates with distinction and shrewdly deciding that for his projected attack on Travancore a contented Cochin was worth at least an army corps agreed to leave the Ruler unmolested on payment of a substantial tribute. During the life time of Hyder this agreement was honourably kept on both sides. In the first years of Tippu's reign also, Cochin as a peaceful part of the Mysore Empire enjoyed special protection. When the trouble did come, it was not due to any fault of Tippu.

When the Mysore-Travancore relations deteriorated and the situation assumed serious proportions, Rama Varma began to discover the truth of the old

* Original in Malayalam quoted in Saktan Tampuran (pp. 163) Viswanath press, Ernakulam 1940.

proverb that he who sups with the tiger should have a long spoon. In a letter written on the 8th of March 1789 the Ruler of Cochin complained to the Dutch Commander of the heavy calls that Tippu was making on him in preparation for his attack on Travancore; of the humiliations he has had to suffer and the fear he entertained generally of Tippu's intentions. In June 1789 Tippu summoned the Raja to Palghat. Rama Varma was then only the heir-apparent. He was 37 years of age and had virtually displaced the Ruler in the administration of affairs. He had practically ruled the country for over 15 years and had established his undisputed authority in administration by setting aside senior members of the family and displacing the older officials. The Raja arrived at Palghat with customary presents and did his obeisance in Durbar. Tippu was particularly gracious towards him and Rama Varma was invested with a Khillat and presented a costly pearl necklace. In private audience the Sultan raised the question which was uppermost in his mind. The Prince was asked to put forward the claims which Cochin had against Travancore about two Taluqs and if no satisfaction was received to declare war on Travancore. The Raja was on the horns of a dilemma. To declare war on Travancore at the time was merely to become a tool in the hands of Tippu, a pawn in his policy with no chance whatever of his getting the Taluqs that Cochin had lost. Besides such a policy of active co-operation with Tippu whose activities in Kerala had sent a thrill of horror through the whole of Kerala would have been extremely unpopular with his own people. Besides, the Prince knew that Travancore had the support of the English company which would not permit the conquest of that State. If acceptance of Tippu's proposals was impossible for good reasons, a direct refusal was even more dangerous. Cochin was in no position to resist Tippu. Nor had it any other friends as the State was an acknowledged vassal of Mysore. The Raja therefore temporised. He offered to persuade the Raja of Travancore to accept the suzerainty of Tippu and to mediate on the points at issue between the two governments. The Sultan did not at this stage desire to press Cochin further and professed to be satisfied with the outcome of the interview.

Rama Varma, on return to the State, informed the Raja of Travancore of the discussions he had with Tippu and also kept the Dutch Commandeur posted with the developments. In fact the Raja's visit to Palghat was with the knowledge and approval of the Travancore Ruler. Warned of Tippu's intentions the Travancoreans pressed on with their preparations. Nor was Tippu slow to make his dispositions. He was merely waiting for the monsoon to be over. From his camp at Coimbatore he was keeping a watch on the activities of his vassal. When the monsoon was over, Tippu, with his preparations com pleted, moved slowly into Palghat He entered Cochin territory in November 1789. Though he still maintained outwardly cordial relations with Rama Varma, this time Cochin was not treated with the same consideration as before. The route from Palghat to Trichur was subjected to systematic devastation. Tippu held his court in the precincts of the famous temple at Trichur and his officers were quartered in the Mutts adjoining it. The places which had resounded with the chanting of Vedas echoed the cries of kine which were slaughtered. An army of 30,000 infantry and 5,000 cavalry had to be supported by the district.

Rama Varma kept at a safe distance from the Sultan's camp. Outwardly he was still the loyal feudatory. But he was in deep intrigue with the Ruler of Travancore.

The failure of the first attack on the Travancore lines on the 29th December saved the Raja from the Sultan's immediate anger. When in April 1790 the

Sultan had forced the Travancore lines and his army had moved into Travancore, the storm had burst for Tippu with Cornwallis' declaration of war and the Mysorean forces had to hurry back to Seringapatam. By good luck Rama Varma thus escaped the wrath of his suzerain.

During the 25 years of relations with Mysore it is interesting to note that the Mysore Government maintained the correctest relations with its feudatory. There was no attempt to interfere in the internal management of the State and the Cochin documents recently published in the biography of Rama Varma show that both Hyder and Tippu were equally solicitous of the well-being of the State and never encouraged malcontents and others who petitioned the Mysore government about the administration of Cochin. Only the prompt payment of the *peishcash* was insisted upon. General obedience to the orders issued in pursuance of high policy was expected, but some latitude was shown in this respect also. The following will show the relations in which the Cochin Raja stood.

A group of merchants from Cochin complained to the Sultan about the exactions of the Raja. Tippu wrote to the Raja as follows: "Complaints have been made to the Huzur that you are dealing harshly with your subjects and merchants The Huzur has ordered that complaints should not be made to him of the affairs of that Taluq (Cochin)."

On a representation from the Raja that certain areas included in the Chowkat taluq belonged rightly to Cochin, Tippu looked into the matter and ordered their return to the Raja. These it may be added are still included in the territory of Cochin on the basis of Tippu's firman.

Again the generous treatment of the Raja by Tippu is witnessed by his decision on a matter which was a source of great loss and difficulty to the

State. The goods that reached Cochin from Malabar were subjected to transit duties at the frontiers and the Raja represented to Mysore that he may be exempted from payment of these duties. Tippu ordered as follows:

"From your petition I have understood the situation. You have submitted that the rice imported for you is being detained at Chetwa. A firman is enclosed ordering that the rice be released. On presentation of the firman you will be allowed to carry it away. Your vakil has been allowed to return."

In fact Tippu seems to have gone out of his way to be generous to Cochin. The just claims of Cochin were always conceded. Chitrakuta, the mount to which Cochin sentiment attaches so much value was at the Raja's request ceded by Tippu. Ghulam Mohidin was ordered to give up the area to the State Arshad Beg was asked to see that boundary troubles were minimised. On a complaint that the inhabitants of border villages were being molested Rasu Ayya, one of Tippu's officers, the Amildar of Palghat, was reminded that Cochin was under the protection of Tippu.

It is obvious that from 1765 to 1789 for a period of 24 years Cochin had no complaint about the treatment it received from the Government of Mysore. Both Hyder and Tippu not only showed the greatest consideration to the Rulers, but met their legitimate grievances in a spirit of generosity. Compared to the treatment that the Cochin State had received at the hands of the Portuguese, this was indeed something about which the Cochin Rulers could pride themselves. It is permissible to assume that had the attitude of the Kerala Rajas been equally docile and their nobility and people not taken up arms in stubborn defence of their age-long independence, Kerala would also have been treated in a like manner. But the historical tradition of the Rajas of Kadathanad,

Kottayam and Calicut was wholly against any such compromise. Never had they bent their knees to others. Even the great Affonso Albuquerque had found in the Zamorin an enemy whose spirit he could not break either by diplomacy or by war. Nor were the nobles less freedom loving. The Iruvanad Nambiars whose boast it was that they were not subordinate to any Ruler and the Nayars of Kottayam vied with each other in the fight against the invader. They preferred to lose their all rather than accept the invader as their master. The tradition of Cochin was different. Two hundred and fifty years of servile dependence on foreign overlords had destroyed whatever spirit of independence it possessed. It bought its right to continue to exist as a State by accepting the suzerainty of Mysore. For Cochin it was only a change of masters. It may have been from the point of view of Kerala unpatriotic. But it paid dividends, for while the heroic rulers of Calicut, Kottayam and Kadathanad were reduced to the position of pensioners, the Ruler of Cochin enjoyed limited sovereignty for another one hundred and fifty years.

CHAPTER VIII

KERALA SETTLEMENT

The treaty of Seringapatam freed the Kerala Coast from the menace of Tippu. The State of Travancore, which had contributed generously in men and money to the war was no longer assailable by any outside enemy. The State of Cochin was freed from its humiliating vassalage. The area to the north of Cochin which officially belonged to the Zamorin, Kolathiri and other Rajas but which had been annexed by the Sultan was ceded to the British.

Lord Cornwalls, who recognised the importance of the coast and its strategic value in case of another war with Tippu, issued orders for the appointment of a Commission to enquire into to the state of the country and report on the future system of government. In pursuance of these orders, General Abercrombie, the Governor of Bombay, arrived in Cannanore and charged Mr. Farmer and Major Dow to make the necessary enquiry and settle the country. The actual negotiation as well as the detailed settelments that were arrived at fall outside the scope of this study, but a short summary is given below in order that the true posture of affairs on the withdrawal of Mysore power may be understood. Writing to General Abercrombie from his camp at Seringapatam, dated March 23, 1792, Lord Cornwallis expressed pleasure that the general had recognised the importance of the new acquisitions and expressed his anxiety to introduce and establish a new system of government. The Governor-General added that anarchy, confusion and violent animosities prevailed between the Nayars and the Moplas since Tippu's power was overturned and therefore it would be necessary to put a stop to them by the adoption of vigorous methods.

Twenty five years of Mysorean occupation had practically reduced this fertile country into a wilderness. The once prosperous kingdom of the Zamorin had been the scene of continuous warfare and military ccupation during the whole of this period. The peasantry had taken shelter in the forests. The Nayar nobility had been dispossessed and had formed themselves into bands of condottieri and the Nampudiri land holders had escaped to Travancore. Mopla fanatics roamed the country and there was neither peace nor order through the length and breadth of the land. Cultivation had been given up in many parts and what was once a flourishing garden had become practically a jungle preyed upon by the beasts of the forests and by organised bandits.

The Commissioners appointed by the Company to settle the affairs of Kerala had a very difficult task to perform. They had to settle the disputes of rival claimants, make equitable revenue settlements, pacify the country, restore confidence, and persuade the peasantry to believe in the permanance of arrangements. The very peculiar system of *tharwad* ownership and conflicting claims of different branches of the same family, the suzerain claims of the Zamorin over many of the southern chiefs, the provisional arrangements entered into by factors and military commanders during the period of war with Tippu Sultan and the intervention of the Travancore Dewan Kesava Das, who under an agreement with governor Medows had collected various sums of money from Kerala chiefs added complications to an already difficult problem. The commissioners, hawever, went into the matter systematically and began to come to arrangements with the Rajas district by district.

They started with Tellichery, the factory of which place had close connections with the Rajas of Chirakkal, Kottayam and Kadathanad. The terms which the Company arranged with them provided for the exercise of authority by the Rulers under the protection of the Company, the monopoly of pepper trade either through the Company or through merchants appointed by the Company, and the payment of regular *peishcash* or tribute to be settled when the retun from the land could be properly estimated.

Their next object was to settle with the Zamorin; but as they found that his pretensions were too high, the commissioners leased a portion of the Zamorin's territory (consisting of Payyanad, Payormala, Kilakkumpuram, Vadakknmpuram and Puzhavayi) to the Raja of Kurumbranad. Unlike the previous settlement with the Northern Rajas, these districts were given only on lease and it was made clear that the Raja was only the Company's manager.

The Zamorin still refused to come to terms, which gave the Commissioners a further excuse to deal with some other outlying portion of his territory. In the territory which originally belonged to the Rajas of Palghat there was an area which the Zamorin had taken possession known as Naduvatham. The Commissioners in coming to an arrangement with the Palghat Raja, handed over the Naduvatham area also to him.

It was now possible to take up the negotiations with the Zamorin. After prolonged negotiations an agreement was reached which provided for the hereditary territory of the Calicut Raja together with the mint and sea customs being leased to the Zamorin. The Zamorin was also temporarily vested with judicial authority over the petty Rajas, and it was decided that as a mark of the Zamorin's exceptional position the revenue fixed for the Rajas of Baypore, Parappanad and Vettathunad should be paid through him.

Trouble broke out as a result of this settlement in the Zamorin's family. The Patingare Kovilakam—or the Western Palace—the most influential branch of the family, refused to accept the settelment, and endeavoured to make itself independent. The person of the rebellious prinde had to be sedured and he either died or committed suicide the very next day after this humiliation. But the family was not reconciled to the settlement and much trouble followed as a result.

Lord Cornwallis' original idea was that the Supreme Government should be associated with the Bombay Government in the enquiry and settlement of Kerala affairs. He therefore deputed Mr. Jonathan Duncan and Charles Boddam to join in the work which Messrs Farmer and Dow had begun. Their instructions were mainly in regard to settlement of land revenue, the establishment of a plan for the administration of justice. and the regulation of the pepper trade. In regard to land settlement, Lord Cornwallis while approving for the time the arrangements made by the Bombay Commissioners stated in his instructions:

"And as the settlement for the first one year ending, as we understand in September, 1793, will probably be everywhere concluded before your arrival on the Kerala Coast, your principal attention will of course be directed to the permanent adjustment of the public revenue to take place from that period, for the first year of which series (or up to September 1794) we shall with a view to preventing interruption to the current business of the country or obstruction to the progress of its improvement, confirm as a matter of course the Jama which you and other Commissioners may stipulate for each district, but the settlement for the remaining years of each lease you and they are only to recommend and (as far as you may find satisfactory grounds) conclude with the several parties subject by an express clause to our ultimate approbation or alteration, which shall be signified as soon after your report as possible."

It was further directed that they should report on the judicial system to be established. The instructions stated: "We rely with confidence on the experience gathered on this side of India, for your being able to determine in a satisfactory manner on the number and constitution of the several courts of justice that will be necessary to ensure to the utmost possible degree the dispensation of equal justice to all classes of the society.

The Kerala settlement therefore had three aspects, (1) The liquidation of the claims of the Princes and Chiefs, and a settlement with them regarding their permanent status

(2) Revenue settlements for a considerable period in order to restore the economic prosperity of the province. This included a definite policy in regard to the pepper trade which in the words of the Governor-General in Council constituted "a very material branch of Commerce to the Honourable Company."

(3) The creation of an administrative and judicial machinery in place of the old system of Nayar States and the later system of Mysore administration.

The first was, as noticed before, carried out after much negotiations with the restored Rulers, who, though they disliked the arrangement, were in no position to resist it. The question of their sovereignty was not considered. Direct administration having been decided upon, the only points to be decided were (*a*) the compensation to be paid as Malikhana to the families whose rights had been taken away, and (*b*) the kist or tax which they were to pay to the Government for their land. Individual settlements were negotiated on these points with all the families. The detailed arrangements took very considerable time, as not only conflicting claims of different

Rajas to the same areas and to the same rights had to be settled, but the pretensions of different members of the same family had in many cases to be enquired into. On the whole, it may be said that the Commission proceeded on the enquiry with a sense of fairness and equity, the conclusive proof of which may be seen in the fact that both the families concerned and the population accepted the decisions which were the bases of the social configuration of British Malabar till the very end of the British rule.

But the same success did not attend their revenue settlements. The kists which were decided upon were found to have been too heavy and payments fell into arrears. The Nayar Chieftains, unable to meet the demands fell into debt to the Mohammedan merchants and the Brahmin money lenders. In fact, after over 25 years of continued warfare it was impossible for the land to bear the heavy burden put on it. In 1726 the direct management of the Zamorin's territories had to be assumed temporarily. Palghat and Kavalappara followed. The Company attempted to enforce the settlements strictly, but it was humanly impossible. The Commissioners had finally to report that after the lease of 1799, revenue collection had to proceed solely under the control of the Company's officers.

The Judicial Administration was also organised on the sole responsibility of the Company and its officers.

In short Malabar became a British district. Though till 1799 revenue was collected by the old Princely families, their authority was expressly excluded. They were merely revenue farmers. In 1800, even the right of collecting revenue was withdrawn. The great Kerala families, from the Zamorin downwards, who had maintained their political independence for over a thousand years were by

Executive Acts reduced to the position of mere landholders. This was not in accordance with the agreements entered into with the Rulers at the time of the war with Tippu, when the Zamorin and other Princes were assured that they would be restored to their States. It is clear that from the beginning the Malabar Commissioners had no such intention. Besides, the instructions of the Governor-General in Council directing them to organise the revenue system and the judiciary in the district, clearly proceeded on the assumption that the Kerala area which Tippu had surrendered came in sovereignty to the Company.

Legally also the point of view of the Governor-General in Council was unexceptionable. Tippu ceded the Kerala Province to the Company. His rights in it were those of a Sovereign. The Province had been under the direct administration of the Mysore officers, and the Company undoubtedly had in law authority which Tippu had exercised. Morally, however, the position was different. The Kerala Rajas had fought as allies on the understanding that their territories would be restored to them to be enjoyed as in Pre-Mysorean days. The assumption of direct administration came to them as a blow, and they found they had been deprived legally of the position which they had enjoyed for nearly a thousand years.

It may be added that no other course was possible. Forty years of anarchy had created a wide gulf between the old claims and the actual realities of the situation. More than this, as a result of Hyder's and Tippu's settlement of the land the old feudal system had completely broken down. Lands had been surveyed by the Mysoreans and taxation fixed on the basis of produce, a system which had been unknown in Kerala before. The Rajas had effectively lost their power for over so long a period that a "Bourbon restoration" which the Princes desired would have been impossible. In fact the Mysorean period had wiped out the middle ages in Kerala and changed its inherited social structure in a manner which it was impossible to revive. The *ancien regime* had ended and it was a new society, based no doubt on the old, but all the same on new principles of land-holding and legal rights that took its place.

CHAPTER IX.

POLITICAL AND ECONOMIC RESULTS OF MYSORE INVASION

Murdoch Brown, a most observant man in charge of the Company's pepper plantation at Angaracandy and who was also the tax collector and who had thereby exceptional opportunities of watching the changes that had come over Kerala is quoted by Buchanan as below. At the time of Hyder's invasion "Malabar was a country rich in money. For ages the inhabitants had been accumulating precious metals that had been given them for the produce of the gardens......... Immediately after the conquest of Malabar vast sums were extorted from its inhabitants by the military officers and by the Canarese Brahmins placed over the resources. Of these exactions Hyder received a share: and no want of a system of revenue was felt until these resources began to fail. When he found the assets from Malabar fall short of its charges, he listened to the proposals of the Rajas to become tributaries. An estimate of the revenue was made by the above mentioned Brahmins......... By this new order of things, these latter (the Rajas) were vested with despotic authority over the other inhabitants instead of the very limited prerogatives they had enjoyed by the feudal system under which they could neither exact revenue from the lands of the vassals, nor exercise any direct authority over their districts. Thus the ancient constitution of government (which although defective in many points was favourable to agriculture from the lands being unburthened with revenue) was in a great measure destroyed, without any other being substituted in its room. The Raja was no longer, what he had been, the head of a feudal aristocracy with limited authority, but the all-powerful deputy of a despotic prince whose military force was always at his command to curb or chastise any of the chieftains who were inclined to dispute or destroy his mandates. The condition of the inhabitants under the Rajas, thus reinstated in their governments, was worse than it had been under the Canarese Brahmins, for the Rajas were better informed of the substance of individuals and knew the method of getting at it. In short, the precarious tenures by which the Rajas held their station, joined to the uncontrolled authority with which they were vested rendered them to the utmost degree rapacious .... The country however was daily declining in produce and population: In so much that, at the accession of Tippu, I have reason to conclude from my own observations and from the enquiries which I then made that they were reduced to one half of what they had been at the time of Hyder's conquest .... But still greater calamities were reserved for the unfortunate inhabitants of this country in the reign of the Sultan......... The Hindus were everywhere persecuted and plundered of their riches, of their women and of their children. All such as could flee to other countries did so: those who could not escape took refuge in the forests from whence they waged a constant predatory war against their oppressors. To trace the progress of these evils would carry me too far. I mention them only for the purpose of showing, how the ancient Government of the country was completely destroyed and anarchy was introduced. The Moplays never had any laws nor any authority except in the small district of Cannanore, even over their own sect: but were entirely subject to the Hindu chief in whose dominions they resided. Tippu's code was never known beyond the limit of Calicut ...."

From this short sketch it is evident that this province at the time it was ceded, had really no form of government and required a new system to be framed for its use. The feudal system was broken, and no other kind of administration was known to the Rajas who laid claim to their respective districts, than that which they had exercised or witnessed under Hyder and which was a compound of corruption and extortion. To these men, however, the most unfit that could have been selected, was the whole authority of the Government over the nation entrusted. Two evils of great magnitude were the consequence of this measure; the extortions and corruptions of the preceding administrations were continued; while the ancient feudal institutions were revived and all the Nayars were thereby attached to the different Chieftains and then again to the Rajas. Nothing could exceed the despotic rapaciousness of these men, to oppose which there was no barrier; for it is well-known that none of these inhabitants dare complain against a Raja whatever injuries they may have sustained, assassination being a certain result of complaint. It is not surprising that under such Rulers agriculture did not flourish and that the fields newly cultivated which in some districts bore but a small proportion to the waste lands should yield but very indifferent crops.

It must be recognised that the administration of Hyder and Tippu in their own territories was in no way harsh. In fact important authorities like Col. Wellesley and Sir Thomas Munro have borne witness to the prosperity of the Mysore dominions at the time of conquest. But the position in respect of Kerala was unfortunately very different. The Mysore Rulers never were allowed to administer the country. The twenty-five years of connection between Kerala and Mysore constituted a period of uninterrupted warfare. The higher strata of society migrated to Travancore. The cultivators in the areas north of Cochin to the boundaries of Mangalore abandoned their fields and homesteads and took to the forests The country settled down to a system of merciless guerilla warfare. The economic effects of this thirty years of war can well be

imagined. Pepper cultivation on which the prosperity of the country had depended for so many centuries was given up over large tracts. The vines were themselves destroyed as the Company's Commissioners found out during their enquiry. Flourishing towns had been laid waste and commerce disappeared except in the immediate neighbourhood of European factories. In Murdoch Brown's report dated 25th June 1798 it is noted with considerable surprise that gold and silver which the country had accumulated by centuries of trade had disappeared. From the time of the Romans, the products of Kerala had a world wide market. Three centuries of the closest trade relations with Europe had brought material prosperity such as few places in India could have enjoyed. As Murdoch Brown enviously remarks: "Quantity of gold and silver in Malabar must have been immense for all the nations that traded with it paid for its produce almost solely in money and none went from it except in payment of rice." But thirty years of rapine, plunder and warfare, reduced it to extreme distress. Through the pages of the Malabar Commission's report and from the careful observations of Dr. Buchanan whose travels through Kerala and Canara constitute a mine of information we can form a picture of what Kerala, north of Cochin must have looked like when the Mysore forces withdrew.

The houses of the Rajas and the Jenmies were deserted and in ruins. In many of its famous temples even daily worship had not been carried on. Forest had encroached on the fields and a large percentage of cultivable land had been abandoned. The peasantry lived on the verge of famine. Commerce which had contributed to the fame of Kerala languished and its once famous ports were deserted.

Socially the historic stucture of Kerala society had crumbled. The feudal aristocracy deprived of its political power but maintaining its social preten-

tions became an instrument of oppression especially in the period that followed the expulsion of the Mysoreans. The Moplas after tasting political power for thirty years and strengthened numerically by the conversions never reconciled themselves to the position which Kerala society allotted to them. They were in a state of general revolt.

It was the Nayars who had suffered most. The disappearance of the Malabar kingdoms and the disbandment of troops left large classes of them without occupation. Economically they were impoverished by the decline of agriculture and commerce. Continuous opposition to the regime that was established led to their disarmament. while the continued rivalries of the petty princes left them without the benefit of local peace. The state of society in which they were the executive arm and of which they were the centre disappeared, when Hyder entered Kerala. Though in the period that followed they regained in some measure their social importance, the great authority which was vested in them as a community responsible both for Government and for defence ceased with the Mysorean conquest.

The general condition of trade in Kerala during the Mysorean occupation may be summarised as follows:

Pepper was the main article of trade. The price averaged between Rs. 105 to 125 per candy. Before 1793 Mahe which was the French port was the chief centre of trade as it was patronised by the Mysoreans. The chief merchant on the coast was Chookara Moosa of Tellichery whose trade interests were considerable.

In 1788 Tippu established a monopoly of trade. His principal factory was at Vadakarai but smaller trade offices were established at Mahe, Quilandy and Calicut. Government purchased the goods at fixed

prices, pepper for example was bought at Rs. 100/- and it was sold at market price. One consequence of this was that the Moplas who had previously a monopoly of this trade found themselves utterly impoverished. The great Mopla houses whose ships sailed previously to Surat, Mocha, Madras and Bengal were utterly ruined. The ship building business which had flourished in Kerala for centuries was also runied. Buchanan says: "since trade has been laid open only two vessels have been constructed here and the produce of the country is chiefly exported in vessels coming from Muscat, Cutch, Surat, Bombay, Goa and Mangalore."

It was cultivation that suffered most. The land was overrun. The farmers had escaped into the wilds, leaving their holdings. Large bands of people roamed about the country, pillaging and laying fertile areas waste. 25 years of scorched earth policy converted the garden of India practically into a desert. 15 years later when Dr. Buchanan made his notable journey of observation he was surprised to find that cultivation has not wholly become normal. The difference between the area under the Raja of Cochin and the villages reconquered from Tippu by the company seemed to him striking. Time after time he is forced to observe as at Mankada: "the country is very beautiful: a mixture of little hills, swelling grounds and rice fields. They are in a bad state of culture. Again we passed through a beautiful country consisting of low hills intersected by narrow, fertile valleys. Their cultivation is exceedingly neglected."

In fact the districts recovered from Mysore occupation took many decades before they again become prosperous. Depopulation, abandonment of fields, disputes about ownership and changes in taxation—all combined to ruin the area. It is only after the settlement of the Commissioners and with the growth of a new tenantry that prosperity came back to Kerala. When the Mysoreans left it after 25 years of occupation the countryside was a scene of terrible desolation.

In the area south of Ponnani which had remained under the Rajas of Cochin and Travancore the position was somewhat different. Social changes of equal significance had taken place. The authority of the Nayar land-holding classes had disappeared: the rights of the feudal nobility had been curtailed in Travancore by Martanda Varma and in Cochin by Komi Achan. A bureaucratic State had beeen organised on the basis of increased royal power and direct trading by the State had replaced the free economy of the past. But these changes were gradual, an evolutionary movement which did not inflict the misery that the Mysorean conquest involved for the northern territories. Economically Travancore and Cochin flourished. With the decline of Cannanore and Calicut, Alleppey to which Kesava Das had devoted some attention became an important port on the Kerala coast. Martanda Varma's conquests had given to Travancore large areas of great forest wealth which after the territory had been settled by the pacific policy of Kesava Das found an outlet through the new port. Cultivation was encouraged and under a beneficent peace prosperity returned which even the Mysore wars did not seriously affect.

The trade and economic policy of Travancore was a crude kind of State enterprise. A system of monopolies was introduced which from the point of view of the present day was a gross exploitation of the people. In 1757 Mr. Spencer took an account of the pepper produced in Travancore. It amounted to 11752 candies. The whole produce was considered a monopoly of the State and the cultivator was only given Rs. 30 per candy while the State sold it an average of Rs. 112 per candy. Almost all other commodities having a commercial value like tobacco, salt, teak and other valuables were also State monopolies.

The British company at Anjengo was the main purchasers of pepper, though their pretension to be the sole body entitled to purchase was never accepted by the Travancore Government till after the conclusion of the subsidiary alliance. The trade brought a steady income, a net profit of over 9 lakhs a year. The policy of Travancore was so far as possible to secure at least part payment in essential war supplies. In the period that followed the Mysorean conquest of Malabar, Travancore was practically the one source of supply and prices also naturally increased to about Rs. 130 per candy. In the general letter from the Bombay Government dated the 23rd March 1784 it is stated: "The debt due from this Government to the King of Travancore for supplies of pepper at different times is considerable and your hope of discharging it is so distant that we are precluded from asking any future aid from him in this article: he has repeatedly demanded payment of the balance but our inability to do it is manifest. We have however consistently furnished him with supplies of stores." (No. 433 Home Misc.)

Kesava Das encouraged trade. A firm believer in Colbertism he converted the State into a trading corporation. The profits of the trade enabled the State to maintain a standing army, and to make other necessary preparations for the struggle with Tippu. It was essentially a system of war finance. In spite of the system of monopolies the condition of the peasantry and general population in Travancore during this period was undoubtedly prosperous. For one thing which was undoubtedly most important the country had not been subjected to the miseries of war. The northern areas of the State which had only been recently conquered were pacified. Cultivation was encouraged. Roads and communications were built or improved. A new port, with modern facilities was established at Alleppey to handle the trade of northern areas. Gujaratis, Konkanis and other trading communities were encouraged to settle down there and a serious effort was made to divert the trade of Cochin to the port.. The Kerala ports which had come under Mysorean occupation languished while Alleppey under royal patronage became a leading emporium on the west coast.

Cochin under its able Ruler, Rama Varma, was not slow in following the ideas of Kesava Das. Every effort was made to keep up the trade on which the State had depended. Rama Varma's plans bore full fruit only after the withdrawal of Mysoreans but he was able to organise in spite of the alarums of war, internal trade in such a way as to lead to considerable economic prosperity. Cochin also was not ravaged by war, though some areas came under temporary Mysorean occupation.

In respect of the whole area of Kerala the aspect of trade changed completely by the end of the period. The expulsion of Mysoreans from the Northern area practically extinguished the competition of Europeans on which Kerala had flourished for over a 150 years. The French and the Dutch were no longer serious factors in Kerala trade A virtual monopoly passed to the British East India Company with the consequent fall in prices. The numerous ports on the coast never recovered from this, though Alleppey and Cochin were able to maintain their own as the main outlets of Kerala produce. A second factor of importance was that the Mussalman traders who had for so long maintained predominance in the trade of the country were ruined. Tippu's monopoly had that effect on the general trading activities of the Moplas as already noticed before. Shipbuilding in which they had specialised from time immemorial practically ceased to exist as an industry. Buchanan noticed that as trade was now being carried on ships from Muscat, Cutch, Surat, Goa and Mangalore, and at the port Ponnani which was the centre of ship building, only two ships had been built. The great Mopla houses which had previously traded with such distant places as Fez and Cairo and during recent years with Bengal and Madras went out of business except for particular individuals like Chowkar Moosa who under the protection of the Tellichery factors still did extensive business. In fact while Mysorean occupation gave to the Moplas great political status, economically they were ruined both by Tippu's shortsighted policy and the hostility towards them which was an aftermath of Tippu's political activities.

The period under survey is in some ways remarkable for the personalities it threw up. The resistance movement in the north produced at least one man of outstanding ability and character, Kerala Varma of Kottayam known as Pychy Raja to Wellington and his associates. Scholar, poet and soldier, Kerala Varma who was junior member of the Kottayam family organised an unrelenting resistance against Tippu. Later he led the rebellion against the British and the despatches of Wellington bear witness to the terror that his name inspired. He was the last great Kerala patriot who sacrificed his all for the freedom of his people and refused till the last to bend his knee to the foreigner. As a poet and writer he is still remembered for his great Kathakali pieces, but his true greatness lay in the unquenching love of liberty which made him choose the wilds of Kerala, while his brother princes accepted the decision of the Company to annex their little States.

In Rama Varma, the Saktan Tampuran, Cochin produced a Ruler who while less heroic than Kerala Varma showed himself a far-sighted statesman, ready to yield to the storm but agile enough to raise his head and exploit every opportunity that presented itself, a ready diplomatist, a strong ruler and a man ahead of his time in financial policy. Rama Varma's position was extremely difficult. He was an acknowledged vassal of Tippu, one who had received many notable marks of favour from the Sultan. He was at the same time a strong upholder of the rights of his State, never on friendly terms with the Sultan's officers who were desirous of interfering in his affairs. Though an unwilling instrument of Tippu's policy he went to the extent of defying him when Tippu attacked Travancore. He played a difficult game with supreme skill and came out successful in the end.

Saktan Tampuran enjoyed immense prestige in his day. He it was who shook off the authority of the Dutch, organised the independent commerce of Cochin and traded directly in his own ships. He brought order out of chaos in a State whose authority had been reduced almost to vanishing point by centuries of foreign intervention.

Though Kerala Varma and Rama Varma were notable figures the dominating figure of the period was Raja Kesava Das, the Dewan of the Maharaja of Travancore. Kesava Das rose to be the Chief Minister of the State at a time when it was in serious danger of losing its very existence. A scholar of English and Portuguese, he realised early in life that political power in India had passed to the British: that the Nawab of Arcot was only a figurehead and that the danger to the freedom of Travancore would come from the military power of Mysore. His very considerable diplomatic talents were therefore utilised for the single purpose of securing an independent alliance for his State with the East India Company. When the first clause of the Treaty of Mangalore (1784) expressly declared the Ruler of Travancore to be a "friend and ally to the English" Kesava Das won his most notable diplomatic victory. Prior to the treaty of Mangalore,

Travancore was protected as a feudatory of the Nawab of the Carnatic, a position which involved no direct responsibility on the Company. By this inclusion Kesava Das gained two major points: the complete independence of Travancore was recognised by the Company and by implication the claims of the Nawab of the Carnatic were rejected and secondly, he secured a direct alliance with the Company.

The pivotal point of Kesava Das' policy was this alliance with the Company. He realised that war with Mysore could not be avoided, and his only hope was unequivocal support from the British. We have seen how Tippu's dealings with Holland, the Governor of Madras, very nearly ruined all Kesava Das' calculations but the Travancore Minister by a direct appeal to Cornwallis was able to secure the enforcement of the treaty.

Kesava Das did not depend on his diplomatic skill alone. He raised an army which though it was unable alone to withstand the power of Tippu's artillery played a notable part in conjunction with British troops in the campaigns of the south. He organised the finance and trade of Travancore in such a way as to enable him to play a leading role in the war against Mysore. It could legitimately be claimed for him that he was the architect of the coalition which brought about the downfall of Mysore powers. He is also the first of the long line of Indian statesmen who in collaboration with the British built up the Indian State system—the predecessor of Madhava Rao, Salar Jung and Dinkar Rao.

A more notable person in many respects was his master the famous Rama Raja of whose benevolent personality, wise and humane disposition and profound scholarship many European witnesses of all nationalities have left us full account. His scholarship in Sanskrit earned the esteem of his contemporaries. Known as the southern Bhoja for his generosity to writers his court attracted the best minds of the time. Himself an author of repute the Raja was the centre and ornament of a brilliant galaxy of poets, writers and artists. To the Kathakali he was specially devoted. It may well be said that this great dance was brought to perfection by him.

It was his wise generosity that afforded an asylum to the exiled rulers and nobles of the north. The refugees numbering hundreds of thousands found a ready welcome in Travancore where many of them were encouraged to settle down. To have looked after a displaced and exiled population for 25 years at enormous cost—no doubt recovered later with meticulous care by the Dewan Kesava Das—itself entitles him to the grateful memory of all sons of Kerala.

All in all, the results of the Mysore occupation may be summed up as below:

The "feudal" system of old Kerala under which land was parcelled out among petty princes each exercising sovereignty and each contributing to the anarchy of the whole suddenly collapsed—as it had already been abolished in Travancore by Martanda Varma and in Cochin by Komi Achan.

The Mysore administration introduced for the first time a system of land taxation based on the actual produce of land. A rough settlement was made and the beginnings of a revenue administration introduced.

The social hierarchy of Kerala inherited from time immemorial broke down and out of its ruins a new middle class developed in due course.

The trade of the country was ruined and the once prosperods ports became scenes of desolation.

In short the country suffered from all the evils of hostile military occupation and the period is important only as a link between the *ancien regime* and the new era which followed the annexation of the north and the protection of the south by the British.

CHAPTER X.

KERALA CULTURE

In literature, music, dance archiecture, painting and all the other forms of artistic life Kerala during these four centuries witnessed a development which entitles it to a special place in Indian cultural life. This aspect of Kerala history is briefly surveyed here to give some idea of the cultural activities of the people during this period.

Malayalam as a language had reached a high standard of development by the 13th century, as the extensive literature alluded to in the *Lilathilakam*, a Sanskrit work on Malayalam grammar and poetics of the late 14th or early 15th century, amply proves. Of the earlier works now available to us the most famous, and from the literary point of view the most beautiful, is *Unnunili Sandesam*, a Malayalam Kavya in the style of *Meghaduta*. Researches of modern scholars have also brought to light works like *Unniyati Charitam* and *Unniyachi Charitam*, which also show a highly developed literary technique in the manipravala style, which may be described as an artificial language using a generous mixture of Sanskrit with Malayalam words. Though the manipravala style was undoubtedly artificial and gradually faded away, it had great importance in the evolution of the language as it naturalised a very large number of Sanskrit words in Malayalam and made its vocabulary richer, more flexible, and capable of dealing with the most difficult subjects. It is this uninhibited importation of Sanskrit words, ideas and imagery by the manipravala writers, which made the translation of classics into Malayalam possible at a later stage.

By the end of the 15th century, literary activity took a different turn. A family of Nayar scholars of Niranom in Central Travancore translated into Malayalam the *Ramayana* of Valmiki, *Bhagavat Purana, Bharata Mala* and other religious classics from Sanskrit. It is specially worthy of mention that one member of this school, Madhava Panikkar, rendered the *Bhagavat Gita* for the first time into an Indian vernacular. The work of the Niranom school is of special importance as it provided the people of Kerala with a corpus of religious literature in Malayalam. An equally significant development took place almost simultaneously in north Kerala in the kingdom of the Kolathiri, where under the patronage of that Ruler, Cherusseri Nampudiri wrote his *Krishna Gatha,* acclaimed since then as the greatest single work in Malayalam. Apart from the great poetic quality of work, *Krishna Gatha* may be said to have set the standard of literary Malayalam, free alike from the artificialities of manipravala and the archaisms of Tamil.

The literary revival of the period found its consummation in Thunchettu Ezuthachan (mid-16th century) the greatest fiure in Malayalam literature His version of *Adhyatma Ramayana* enjoys the same popularity that Tulasi Das's and Kambar's *Ramayana* enjoy in their respective languages. It is the bible of the Kerala Hindus. Equally, his abridged rendering of *Mahabharatam* is perhaps the most widely read book in Malayalam, both as a literary work of great beauty and as a popular encyclopaedia of ethics and morals. Ezuthachan may indeed be said to be the father of modern Malayalam.

In the 17th century the Kerala country witnessed the birth of *Kathakali* literature, though it was only in the century that followed that its dramatic form came to be fully developed and literature achieved quality and distinction. The Rajas of Travancore and Northern Kottayam were its great patrons and were themselves the authors of some of the best Kathakali pieces. The famous Ramaraja of Travancore and his nephew Aswati were themselves poets of genius and in the court of the former lived Unnayi Warrier whose *Nalacharitam*, a dramatic cycle of four plays, is still esteemed the masterpiece in this genre. The four Kottayam plays are also considered literary masterpieces and are perhaps even more popular from the point of view of acting.

It is however not these highly sophisticated works written in Sanskritised Malayalam that represents the literary genius of the Kerala people during this period. It is in Kunjan Nambiar's *Thullal pattukal* that we have the first efflorescence of popular poetry, poetry which was addressed to the masses and caught both their heart and their ear. Nambiar invented a form of dance recital, known as *Thullal*, and he wrote the poems which he himself recited. The themes were generally taken from the *Mahabharata* and the *Ramayana* but his treatment of the stories was in terms of contemporary life. He thus turned his dance recitals into effective social satire. His medium was the plain speech of the people which for the first time became a powerful vehicle of opinion. Along with Ezuthachan he is recognised as the chief educator of the Kerala people.

The period was also notable for extensive creative activity in Sanskrit. Kerala had had, for long, a living tradition of Sanskrit atleast from the 8th century A. D. and the names of Sankara, Sakti Bhadra, the author of *Ascharya Chudamani*, Leela Suka, the author of *Sri Krishna Karnamrita*, and Kulasekhara, the author of *Mukunda Mala* and numerous others bear witness to the abiding contribution which Kerala has made to Sanskrit. In the medieval period this tradition was fully upheld. The court of the Zamorin was celebrated all over South India in the 15th, 16th and 17th centuries for its patronage of Sanskrit. Uddanda Sastri, the author of *Kokila Sandesa*, *Mallika Marutham* and other works lived at the Calicut court. Another poet who was a contemporary of his, Kakkasseri Bhattathiri is known to us by his drama *Sumati Mana Vikramam*.

In Vyakarana, Tantra, Ayurveda and Jyotisha, an immense literature was produced in Kerala during this period. Also in exegesis, Kerala writers seem to have excelled for we have a Kerala school of commentary developing on almost all subjects. Among these may be mentioned Udayas' commentary on Abhinava Guptta's *Dhwanyaloka*, Vasudeva's *Marga Darsini* on Rajasekhara's *Viddha Sala Bhangika*, Chennassu Nampudiri's *Manushyalaya Chandrika* (Silpa Sastra) and *Tantra Samuchaya* of the same author. Jyotisha seems to have enjoyed special popularity in Kerala and numerous works have come down to us, belonging to this period. This subject also involved higher Mathematics and some important works like *Gola Deepika*, Vyakhyas on Bhaskariya, Uzhuthira Varier's commentary on Varaha Mihira can be mentioned as indicating the depth of scholarship which the Kerala pandits had attained.

In the field of Mimamsa, Kerala at his period held a unique position. The Rulers of Kottayam always claimed that they were the patrons of both schools of Mimamsa but the centre of Mimamsa studies was the house of Payyoor Patteris, who were the acharyas of this branch of learning. Successive Patteris of this house made outstanding contributions to the literature of Mimamsa. Of these *Gopalika*, a commentary on Mandana Misra's *Spota Siddhi* and *Tatva Bibhavana* a gloss on Vachaspati Misra's *Tatva Bindu* deserve special mention. Another member of the family Rishi by name, is the author of *Sutrartha Sangraha*, an extensive and detailed treatise on Mimamsa.

But the glory of Sanskrit in medieval Kerala was the work of Melpathur Narayana Bhattathiri. Though Kavyas, Champus, Sandesas and dramas were always popular and had always been generally cultivated and the literature produced in Kerala in these genres is extensive, it is only with Narayan Bhatta that medieval Kerala finds a poet who is entitled to be considered among the immortals of Sanskrit. Born in 1560, he lived to the ripe old age of 88 and passed away in 1648. In almost every sphere of classical scholarship he attained pre-eminence. Not only was he a poet of supreme lyrical quality, but also a grammarian whose *Prakriya Sarvaswam* is still authoritative, a logician and *mimamsaka* whose *Manameyodayam* is probably the only work on the subject which has currency outside Kerala. His *Narayaneeya* is acknowledged as one of the masterpieces of devotional poetry in Sanskrit Addressed to the Guruvayoor Deity (Krishna) the poet sings in over a thousand verses of supreme beauty the story of *Bhagavata*. Many devotees in Kerala consider it canonical and look to it for consolation and spiritual sustenance.

Others whose contributions to Sanskrit letters deserve mention are Aswati, Prince of Travancore, whose *Rukmani Parinaya* is a lyrical drama of high quality and Manorama Thampuratti, a princess of the Zamorin family, a gramarian of note, under whose patronage a veritable school of poets flourished. In fact it may well be said that in the 16th, 17th and 18th centuries, Kerala became one of the leading centres of Sanskrit study and her contribution in all spheres of Sanskrit learning at this time earns her a place of honour in the history of India's classical literature.

In the field of dancing and music also Kerala comes into prominence at this time. Even in the earlier periods Kerala had its traditional forms of dance and the heroines of most of the manipravala poems like *Unniyati Charitam* and *Unniyachi Charitam* were famous dancers. But such dancing was mainly attached to the temples. It is with the development of Kathakali that dancing slips out of the temple precincts and becomes a secular and popular art. It is at the Zamorin's court that the dance drama which was finally to take the shape of Kathakali was first evolved. Known as *Krishnattam*, it was a dance representation of Krishna's life acted in 7 days. Its first presentation is said to have been in 1654. The music for this dance, known as Krishna Giti was specially composed in Sanskrit by a Zamorin Maharaja.

Soon afterwards the Raja of Kottarakkara decided to produce a similar dance drama based on the story of Rama. This attained great popularity, both as a dance form and as a literary genre and was followed by many outstanding writers under the patronage of different rulers and is what is now known as Kathakali. The emphasis in Kathakali is on dance and hence its popular name Attam meaning Dance. From the point of view of choreography the Kathakali is the supreme contribution of Kerala to Indian culture. In its present form, it not only embodies the tradition of three hundred years but also many improvements, associated mainly with Kalladikode and Kapplingad Nampudiris. The former emphasised the dancing aspects of Kathakali while the reforms introduced by the latter may generally be said to lay greater stress on *abhinaya*.

The popularity that Kathakali achieved in Kerala may be seen from the fact that not only every court, but the house of every nobleman with any social pretensions kept a troupe of its own. Further, Kathakali performances were a *sine qua non* in all temple festivities and were almost so in all domestic celebrations. Even kings trained themselves as Kathakali actors. The heroic Kerala Varma Pazhassy Raja, the last champion of Kerala independence and the opponent of Arthur Wellesley, was himself a noted performer.

Kerala sculpture does not attain the same heights as painting, though the figure of Trivikrama in Suchindram is a notable piece of work. The following is the description of this piece of sculpture by Dr. Kramrisch: "The power of the God's step, the magnificent distortion of the leg darting upward and accompanied by the dancing gesture of the arm is as daring as the estrangement from the body of the God of the three arms and their weapons on the right side of the relief. In their rotating movement the arms seem to burst forth from behind the leg, an aggrandised continuation on the horizontal axis of the arms on the other side. This other side of the image does not take part in the cataclysmic upheaval; there the God is nothing but beautiful and young-his club and arm provide the support of his stride. The feet of the great God is rounded off at the bottom of the relief. There the rueful Bali squats at the left while on the right the King of the Asuras and Vishnu in his dwarf shape confirm their contract by the rite of pouring water over the hands of the baby-shaped God. Clouds accompany His great stride and serenely subside in ordered rows when the celestials emerge and render homage to Him. The heavenly counter-play to the great commotion which reaches to the sphere of the gods is devotional. Their movements embody music of the spheres, which pervades the pattern of the clouds."

It will thus be seen that medieval Kerala was a centre of high artistic endeavour, that in spite of continuous wars and political upheavals, the period witnessed notable achievements in every field of cultural activity. While politically Kerala remained practically isolated from the rest of India, till at least the invasion of Hyder Ali in the middle of the 18th century, in literature and fine arts it fully shared in the life of South India and indeed made contributions of a highly significant character.

APPENDIX I

A NOTE ON BIBLIOGRAPHY

For the study of Portuguese relations with Kerala there is available in India, England and Portugal, a very large mass of material. It consists mainly of large collections of State papers, official despatches and other correspondence, descriptive narratives, besides records of a more personal character like the *Commentaries* of Albuquerque and the biography of de Castro. Neither is there any lack of "histories," for the Portuguese writers of those days were not forgetful of the duty of singing the glory of their fatherland. In India also, there is a considerable quantity of highly valuable material, mostly in the form of Chronicles in the Kerala temples and royal families.

A thorough examination of the documents and papers relating to India, preserved in the various libraries and archives of Portugal, was made by Mr. Danvers of the India Office Library. He also secured for the India Office translations and transcripts of the most important of these. As a result, the India Office Library now possesses a unique collection of Portuguese manuscripts. Their value would have indeed been greater if the translation had been undertaken by someone who had a better knowledge of English than the Portuguese scribe to whom the task was entrusted. As it stands, it is often difficult to make sense out of whole passages, and often it is easier to consult the original than to go to the translation. The following are the chief collections and unpublished books available at the India Office:

I. The *Corpo Chronologico*: Transcripts 2 vols. These are translated. They consist mostly of letters addressed by Governors and other officials to the King and sometimes to important court dignitaries in Lisbon. This collection is of the utmost importance.

II. *Gavetas Antigas*: Translations 2 vols.

III. Translations as well as transcripts from the Cathedral library at Evora and the letters from Viceroys which are preserved in the Torre de Tombo.

IV. *Noticias da India*: 2 vols. This is a very interesting, though often undependable, collection of descriptions of forts and places of historical interest.

V. Biker's collection of *Treaties and Engagements with Indian Rulers*: Two volumes are translated.

VI. The *Cartas of Albuquerque*: 4 volumes are translated. At the Torre de Tombo and the National Library of Lisbon there are many valuable documents not yet available in England. Through the courtesy of Dr. Antonio Baio I was enabled to examine a good many. Unfortunately, though the material relating to India is vast, Kerala finds but little mention after the time of Albuquerque. The *Documentos Remittidos da India,* which is a monumental series of 62 volumes covering no less than 12,465 documents, hardly touch Kerala. It covers the period between 1600 to 1697. For our purpose the most important collection is the *Corpo Chronologico*. It is on this I have had mainly to depend.

In the British Museum there is an excellent collection of Portuguese MSS. besides a number of interesting portraits.

The Portuguese Academy has been for considerable time actively assisting in the publication of important documents and books relating to India. The most important publication of the Academy in this connection is the *Colleccao de Monumentos ineditos para of historia das conquistas das Portuguezes em Africa Asia e America.* The *Annaes das sciencias e leiteras* have also published some very important documents which were until then unknown.

Portuguese histories relating to India are numerous. The most important of them are the following:

(i) Joas de Barros, whose official connection with the India Office in Lisbon gives his work, which is practically a contemporaneous record, an authority which few others possess.

(ii) Gaspar Correa: *Lendas da India.* This book also is of special importance. Correa went to India in 1512. He acted as Albuquerque's secretary and the events he describes were therefore known to him personally or related to him by those who had taken part in them. With regard to the first voyage of Vasco da Gama he had the benefit of using a diary which Joam Figuera, who accompanies the Captain-General in that expedition, had kept. His *Lendas,* it is curious to note, remained unknown till 1790, and was published only in 1836.

"I laboured," says he, "with much care on the events I saw and those which had gone before enquiring of the older men who had been of this discovery and removing my doubts by means of the same men who had been present at the events; in the course of which I found some men who had come in the very ships of discovery. Also by means of some memoirs which I found in the possession of Moors and Gentiles, especially in Cannanore who wrote with surprise at seeing what they had never imagined."

The Chapters relating to the Voyages of Vasco da Gama in this book have been translated by the Hon. H.E. Stanley for the Hakluyt Society (1869).

Other histories like the works of Diogo de Couto and Castenheda, valuable though they are, do not devote much space to Kerala affairs.

Besides these volumes which are of primary importance, I have used the following books:

Andrade, J. F. *Life, of Dom John de Castro*, translated into English Sir Peter Wyche, 1664.

Barbosa, Duarte: Hakluyt Society, 1866.

Caldwell: *Comparative Grammar of Dravidian Languages*, 2nd edition, 1875.

D'Albuquerque: *Commentaries*, Translated and published by the Hakluyt Society.

Danvers: *Portuguese in India*, W. H. Allen, 1894, 2 volumes.

Da Orta: *Colloquies—Lisbon*. 1895. Edited by the Conde de Ficalho. English translation by

Sir C. Markham, London, MCM XIII.
Ficalho, the Conde de: *Garcia da Orta e sua*

Tempo Impresna Nacional.
Logan: *Malabar*. 2 Volumes. Madras, 1887.

Menon: *History of Kerala*, Ernakulam, Cochin Government Press, 1925.

Pages, Leon: *Letters de St. Francois Xavier*, Paris, 1885.

Rawlinson: *The Relation of India with Western Nations*.

Sousa Faria y: *Portuguese Asia*, translated into English 1695.

Whiteaway: *Rise of the Portuguese Power in India*, comes up only to 1545.

Zinuddin: *Tofutul Mujahideen*.

Fra Coleridge: *Life and Letters of Francis Xavier,* translated by Rowlandson.

Gouvea: *Historic Orientale des grand progres de Chretianisme,* Anvers, 1609.

Apart from these I have also had ample opportunity of using unpublished original material available in Malayalam. There is in Kerala an ancient custom of keeping granthavaries or chronicles in the chief temples and royal families. These have so far remained unpublished. Owing to the kind help rendered to me by Rama Varma Appan Tampuran of Cochin I have been able to procure copies of these documents from whichI have occasionally drawn for the details of Kerala history. There is also available, in Malayalam, an historical account of Portuguese relations with the Kerala princes, written probably in the 17th century.

There have been some competent studies by Indian scholars on this period. Of these the following are the most important:

I. *The Zamorins of Calicut* by K. V. Krishna Ayyar, M.A., L.T., Calicut 1938.

II. *Medieval Kerala* by P. K. S. Raja, Annamalai University.

The present writer's *Asia and Western Dominance,* London 1953, may also be referred to.

For the post-Portuguese period ample material is available in Dutch, English and Malayalam. In the case of the early Portuguese period the students of history have to depend almost entirely on Portuguese sources; but fortunately for the 17th and 18th century the presence of the English on the West Coast enables us to check the Dutch records from English sources.

The Records that the Dutch left with regard to the administration of their factories in Kerala are in many ways unique. Each commandeur left for his successor a memoir dealing with the affairs of the Company and in general with the condition of Kerala. This series of which the following have been published, constitute a mine of information about Kerala:

Memoir of	J. V. S. Van Gollenesse	1908
„	Adriaan V. Moens	1908
„	Commandeur Cunes	1908
„	J. G. Angelbeak	1908
„	C. Breakpot	1909
„	De Jong	1909
„	G. Weijermann	1910
„	Van Rheede	1911

The memoir of Moens, which is the most important of these, is an elaborate document, giving a descriptive account of the conditions in Kerala. The supreme government at Batavia had asked him to submit to them all available information together with a map of Kerala if procurable; and Moems therefore wrote not merely for the information of his successor but for the benefit of his superiors. The memoirs of Moens and Gollenesse have been translated and published under the title of *The Dutch in Kerala.*

The India Office in London possesses a large number of transcripts from Dutch Records at the Hague. Thirty-six volumes are available in translation and these are indeed very valuable. But the main collection of Records relating to Cochin is in the Record Office, Madras. An analytical list of these records has been published by the Madras Government under the title of *A Press list of Ancient Dutch Records from* 1657 *to* 1825.

At the Hague in the Rijkarchief there is a very great deal of material available. Owing to the shortness of my stay in Holland I was not able to make full use of these.

The following published works deal with the Dutch affairs in relation to the mainland of India.

Aalbers, J. Rijeklof *Van Goens*:

Van Imhoff: *Considerations sun letat present de la compagine hollandaise des Indus orientals, Hague* 1741.

Stellwagon: *Gustaf Wilhelm Baron Van Imhoff* (de Indische Gids) 1889.

Veth Adriaan: Van Rheede (de indische gids) 1887. Vol. III and IV.

Philip Baldeus: *Description of Kerala and Coromandel.*

Churchill's *Voyages* Vol. III, 1748.

Day, Francis: *The Land of the Perumals.*

C. Atchuta Menon: *The Cochin State Manual.*

Vischer: *Letters from Malabar.*

Menon: *History of Kerala,* Ernakulam 1924.

Menon: *History of Cochin,* 2 Vols. (in Malayalam).

Nagam Aiyya: *Travancore State Manual* (3 Vols.).

J. J. Cotton: *European Monuments in Madras.*

There is a very considerable amount of material available in Malayalam. The granthavaries or chronocles of Trippunithura, Cochin, and the Records at Paliyam are becoming gradually available to the public. So far, the private records in important families have been treated as something mysterious and students have had no access to them. The Travancore archaeological department has however published important plates belonging to the Paliyam family. Owing to the efforts of P. Anujan Achan of Paliyam some of the more important records of the leading families in Cochin are now being published. The Cochin archaeological department has also published some of the important Malayalam letters addressed by the Rajah to the Supreme Council at Batavia. It would be a very great service to the history of Kerala if at least a Catalogue of the private collections is made by the new Kerala State and published for the information of students.

Among the published Malayalam books belonging to this period which have been of use there are two which deserve special mention. They are the *Padappattu* or the "Ballad of War" and the *Mamankodharanam.* The former which deals with the war of Cochin succession leading to the expulsion of the Portuguese, is a historical narrative of great value. Its facts and chronology are exceptionally accurate. Though devoid of any great literary merit, as a historical composition it takes a high rank in Malayalam, especially for its non-partisan spirit. The book has been edited with an excellent introduction for the Government of Travancore by Mr. Oolloor Parameswara Ayyar, a renowned poet and scholar of Kerala. The *Mamankodharanam unlike Padappattu,* does not claim to be non-partisan. It is written frankly in praise of the great Zamorin who helped the Dutch and the Rajah of Cochin in the war of Vettom succession. It deals with the history of that period from the point of view of a courtier of the Calicut Ruler. This book has been edited with a learned introduction and valuable notes by K. C. Mana Vikraman Rajah of the Zamorin's family.

APPENDIX II

The translation of a Treaty of Alliance entered into by the Rajah of Cochin under his signature with the Rajah of Travancore.

Directions written by Pandel Hicomen, Mootseddy of Cochind and addressed to Puducherry Mootseddy of Travancore, dated 12th day of Dhanu of Kerala year 937, December, 1761, viz.:

In the treaty of agreement made at Trivandrum on the 12th day of Makarom of the year 933 (the 22nd January 1757) the capitulations already drawn at Mavelikkara, the 3rd of Chingom 936 (15th August 1760) for the future formation of an alliance are included. The terms mentioned therein were, that the former discords being settled it is agreed to continue for ever friends, that we shall support and assist each other both in good and bad fortune, that the mutual friendship of the parties may be preserved in the same manner already agreed on, that none of the people, who deserted from Travancore country, shall be allowed to remain in my dominions, nor be supported in any manner, that the agent of Travancore Rajah shall be allowed to purchase on the Rajah's account from the country merchants for ready money all the pepper produced within the limits of my dominions, except 500 candies annually wanted for my own trade for collecting which it is stipulated that a ceratin place shall be ascertained; it will be taken from thence by my merchant accounting first to your merchant kept for the same purpose.

Since the time of conclusion of this agreement it was agreed that the money expended on account of the trourbles raised by the Chembakasherry and Vadakkumkur Chiefs shall be recovered from them, that until the said payment is duly made the Rajah of Travancore is empowered to collect the revenues of both their districts, that I will never in future afford them any assistance, that Chembakasherry remain at Trishchmeereo according to Rajah's permission, that while he remains there I will by no means write to nor accept any letter from him nor supply him with money for his expenses nor have any interview with him, that besides this I will not keep in my country anyone that hath ill behaved towards the Rajah and that all the superintendence of both parties in the Pagodas of both countries may be kept in practice the same as before.

All the aforesaid Articles of Agreement having been made in writing, the Zamorin entered with his army into my country on which account in attention to my request the Rajah ought to assist me with money and his army in expelling my enemy from my property until the possession of it shall be restored to me, the north boundary of which on the west side being limited to the southward of Poocoida and on the east side to the southward of Chiltur as also the villages of Bella Ponatara formerly belonging to me. In recompense, therefore, of the above required assistance I give it up in writing the districts of Karappuram (except the villages named Audicadu, Chettany and Cumballon) situated to the southward of Pompolly and to the northward of Alipee as also all the districts annexed to it Paroor and Alangadoo. I do wish the Rajah may profit by them accordingly, with all the rights and profits belonging to them.

Until the Rajah's troops are called from my dominions, where they remain now for its defence, the half amount of the revenue that my people should collect from my countries I shall duly pay for the expenses of the said troops.

In case of the Rajah's troops entering into Vellapadcara country he may take the revenue of that country appointing his own men in like manner that the Zamorin formerly collected it.

If required the Rajah will support me with every assistance of troops and money until the enemies are repulsed and the countries restored to me.

Excepting the districts situated to the northward of Murinhapaya and to the southward of Varapole containing the districts within the Charinadu already possessed by the Rajah until the year 933 (1757) all the rest I will myself take charge of.

The Rajah will assist me agreeably to my design in abolishing the dignities of every rank in my country as also in the concerns appertaining to them.

All the contents herein written you may read and impart to the Rajah of Travancore entitled Culashegharaperumal.

(Sd.) RAJAH OF COCHIN.

The Translation of an Agreement entered into by the Rajah of Travancore with the Rajah of Cochin under the 12th Dhanu 937 Malabar Style.

On the 12th Makarom 932 an agreement took place between us the particulars of which had been settled by the parties of Mavelikkara. On the 3rd Chingom 929 it was there agreed that the parties should lay aside all former enmity which subsised between them and observe and cultivate a perpetual friendship with each other. In conformity to that agreement I engage that I will not protect or afford any assistance whatever to your enemies in my country. As you wish to receive 500 candies of pepper out of the produce of your country at any place you may think proper, I have only to request that your merchant or broker may receive the quantity with the consent and in the presence of my merchant, and my merchant shall advance money and receive the remainder of the pepper produced in your country as soon as this agreement shall have taken place. The Chiefs of Chempakasherry, Ambalapilly, Vadakkumkur have been indisposed towards me and you promise not to take part with them. The sums expended by me in reducing them to subjection shall be levied from them and that until the amount be paid I shall retain the possession of their districts in my own hands and you promise not to take part with them or render them any assistance. As I place much confidence in this assurance on your part, I have agreed that the Chief of Ambalapilly, etc.. shall be permitted to remain at Trichoor and during the period of their residence at that place you promise not to hold any correspondence with them by letter or otherwise, nor to afford them any supplies for their subsistence nor to have any interview with them; you further promise not to grant protection to my enemies in your country. In regard to certain privileges which you possess in my country they must be observed and continued as has ever been the custom.

All the aforesaid articles having been agreed to, you inform me that the Samoory has entered your country with his troopss, expelled your people and taken possession of it and you desire me to assist you by sending my troops at my own expense in order to enable you to recover possession of your country by expelling the Samoory's troops from that part which extends north as far as Poocoida river and east as far as Chitoor river as also the districts you formerly possessed in Vellapanad Karee. If I should assist you and put you in possession of this country in return you agree to make over to me the districts Karappuram extending to the south of Pampolly river and north of Alipie and also Paroor and Alangadoo with all their rights, etc., except the three villages Chetany, Yeado and Chambalam and you further agree to pay into the hands of my people the amount of half of the revenues in the villages formerly belonging to the Samoory in the same manner as Samoory collected them. I will send my troops to be paid by me and will use every exertion and render all the assistance in my power to defeat Samoory's troops and restore your country. You shall be put in possession of those villages which were not conquered by me in the year 988 in the districts of Charinadoo extending north as far as Turinhapaya river and south as far as Verapole river. When you wish to discharge the petty Polygars in your country, I will join you and render you all the assistance in my power. I desire that Dewauree may read and explain this agreement to the Elder Rajah Parumpadapoo. The agreement is drawn up by Sankara Coomaran by order of the Travancore Rajah.

(Sd.) TRAVANCORE RAJAH.

APPENDIX III.

Articles regarding the Dutch surrender of Cochin

Propositions of the Dutch Commandeur	Answer of the English Commander
ARTICLES	
1. All Officers and soldiers, which are of the Garrison of Cochin, will with as little delay as possible, be transported either to Batavia, or Ceylon, at the expense of the English Government in English vessels.	Cannot be granted ; about the Garrison, it will be disposed of as the Commander-in-Chief may deem proper.
2. The said officers and soldiers will take with them all their effects, without their being liable to any search, their servants, and slaves ; whilst those that are married, will likewise be at liberty to take their families with them.	Allowed, excepting with respect to slaves, a name unknown in the British dominions.
3. The Governor, the Members of Council, and all the servants of Police, and Trade, Churchmen, Military and Naval, and other servants in the pay of the Dutch Company as also all the inhabitants of Cochin, either Europeans, or natives will be at liberty to hold their persons, and property, movable and immovable, merchandise and other effects without being therein molested, or obstructed, on any account whatsoever.	All private property will be sacred.

Propositions of the Dutch Commandeur	Answer of the English Commander
Articles	
4. Among the foregoing, is also understood, regarding the liberty of the Factor, and Resident of Porca, J. A. Scheits, who is now employed here, in keeping the Company's mercantile books and he must be allowed to return to his station, to resume his office.	A resonable time will be allowed him, to settle his affairs but he must be considered as a prisoner of war.
5. The Governor, the members of Council and all the servants of Police, and trade, the Churchmen and further servants in pay, will be at liberty to take their families, male and female slaves and also their possessions, either to Batavia or Columbo, and they will be granted thereto, at the expense of the British Government, the necessary ships and transport.	This is replied to in the second article.
6. The funds belonging to the Orphan College, and the Poor House will not be confiscated or seized upon, they being money of orphans and the poor.	The funds mentioned in this article will belong to his Great Britannic Majesty in so for that he will appoint persons over them, for their management.
7. All officers, and servants, Civil and Political, of the Company, who may wish to remain at this place, as private individuals shall be granted the protection of the British flag.	All the inhabitants, who are willing to remain and to take the oath of allegiance to his Great Britannic Majesty, will in every respect, be treated as British subjects.

Propositions of the Dutch Commandeur ARTICLS	Answer of the English Commander
8. All mercantile artlcles, ammunitions, artilery, goods, arms, provisions and other articles, which belong to the Company, and are found at this place, will faithfully be made over, according to a specific statement to the commissaries that will be appointed to receive them, and the specified list, will in duplicate, be duly delivered to Major Petrie,	Everything mentioned in this article, will be faithfully delivered over to such persons as Major Petrie will appoint hereafter, to dispose, thereabout agreeably to the direction of his Great Britannic Majesty.
9. The fortifications, the Government House, all magazines, and other public buildings, belonging to the Company, will be kept as they are at present, and not be demolished.	Regarding the Fort of Cochin and other public buildings, they will be disposed of as the Commander-in-Chief or the Commanding Officer, will think proper at the time.
10. The free exercise of the reformed religion, as usual in the Dutch Church, where Divine Service is performed, will be permitted.	Allowed.
11. The Convent at Verapoly, and all other Romish Churches as also the Heathen Temples, will receive the protection, that they have hitherto enjoyed, under the Dutch Company.	The British Government everywhere protects religious exercises.
12. All Topazes (half castes) and Inland Christians as also the Banians, Silversmiths, who are subjects and vassals of the Dutch Company, will retain their property and also privileges and protections which they always had enjoyed of he said Company,	Answered in the third Article.

Propositions of the Dutch Commandeur ARTICLES	Answer of the English Commander
13. All documents, charters Resolutiens, and other papers, belonging to this Government, will without any search being made of them, be delivered over to the Governor, Mr. Van Spall, in order to be carried with him wherever he may be removed to.	All Public Documents and papers must be delivered to persons appointed to receive them but Mr. Van Spall will have authenticated vouchers of these which may in any way concern himself during his management of Cochin.
14. No one will occupy the Govt. House during (his) Mr. Spall's stay at Cochin but he will remain unmolested.	Answered in third Article
15. In case of any English Deserters being found in the Garrison of Cochin, they will be pardoned,	All deserters will absolutely be given over.
16. All public papers notarial or Secretariat deeds, which may in the least, be to the security of the possessions, belonging to the inhabitants of this place, will be respected and preserved, in the hands of those who hold that office, in order to be made use of, whenevor required.	Answered in the thirteenth Article.
17. The Auctioner of the Town the Sequester and the Curator (Trustees) will be supported in the recovering of all outstanding money, and be therein protected, by the usual officers of Justice.	All inhabitants who remain in Cochin, will be subject to British laws.
18. After this capitulation shall have been signed, the New-gate shall be made over to an English Detachment of 50 men, to which an equal number of Dutch soldiers may go out and no English one	The Gates of the Fort of Cochin will be taken possession of, by a detachment of British troops, tomorrow noon, at 12'0 clock. The Garrison will be lodged as conveniently as the circum-

Propositions of the Dutch Commandeur ARTICLES	Answer of the English Commander
may rush in, and the next day all the gates will be taken possession of by the English troops and the Garrison of Cochin will retire to a certain place, and remain their until their departure for Batavia, or Ceylon, laying down their arms, as usual, with the exceptions of the officers commanding them who will retain their swords.	stances will allow until it can he disposed of thereabout, agreeably to the Article. The officers may retain their swords.
19. All servants of the Company the Police, Military, Navy and others in pay, will be supported by the English Govt. until they are taken in English vessels, to the place of their destination, either Batavia or Colombo.	Major Petrie is of opinion that he has not the authority to enter into such an agreement. Part of this Article has been answered in Art.
20. All sick and wounded, now in the Hospital, are to be treated, and maintained, by the English Government.	Allowed,
21. The fulfilment of all the above stated articles, and the manner of capitulation agreed to, are to be faithfully observed and signed respectively, by Major Petrie, the Governor Van Spall, and the Council of this place.	Major Petrie consents to a cessation of Arms at which time, Mr. Van Spall should declare whether or not he will accept the aforementioned articles of capitulation.
19th October, 1795.	11-30 p.m. 19th October, 1795.
(Sd.) J. L. VAN SPALL, P. J. DECAN, J. A. CELLARIUS, I. H. SCHEIDS, A. LUNEL, C. VAN SPALL.	(Sd.) G. PETRIE Major 77th Regiment Commanding.

APPENDIX IV.

The list of regular Commandeurs in Cochin begins only with Van Rheede. Immediately after the capture the fort was placed under Commissioners.

Hendrick Adriaan Van Rheede	1673–77	(Baron Hendric Adrian Van Rheede (d. at Surat Dec. 15, 1691) author of the *Hortus Malabaricus*.
Jacob Lobo	1677–78	
Martin Huysman	1680–81	
Gulmer Vorsbuy	1684–1686	
Isaak Van Dielen	1687–1693	Van Dielen (d. at Cochin Dec. 25. 1693). Adriaan Van Ommen (d. Nov. 27, 1696 at Cochin).
Zwadekroon	1693–1698	
Peter Coesaart—acting	1698	
Magnes Wickelman	1698–1701	
W. Moerman	1705–1709	
Barent Ketel	1709–1716	
Johannes Hertinberg	1717–1724	
Jacob De Jong	1724–1731	
Adriaan Van Maten	1731–1735	
J. Stein Van Gollenesse	1735–1743	
Siersma	1743–1748	
C. Stevens	1748–1750	
Abraham Corneils de la Haye	1750–1751	
C. Cunes	1751–1757	
C. De Jong	1757–1761	
Godfried Wayerman	1761–1764	
C. Breakpot	1764–1769	
C. L. Snett	1769–1771	
Adrian Moens	1771–1781	
G. Anglebeck	1781–1793	
Jan Lambertus Van Spall	1793–1795	

The main Dutch Tombs on the West Coast are described by Mr. J. J. Cotton in his book on *Indian Monumental Inscriptions* Vol. III, Madras (p. 267). The reader who is interested is referred to that excellent work. A list of the more important personages is given below. The Tombstones are mainly in the Church of St. Francis, and in the Dutch Cemetery:

Isaak Van Dielen—died on the 25th December, 1693.

Commander-in-Chief of the Dutch forces on the Coast.

Adrian Van Ommen—died 27th November, 1696. Commander-in-Chief of the Coast.

Hester Dulcina de Jong—died 4th December, 1727.

Wife of Jacob de Jong, Governor of Cochin.

Gustaf and Urusula Van Gollenesse—Gustaf died on the 30th March and Urusula 3rd of May, 1739, children of Governor Gollenesse.

Abraham Cornelis De La Haye-died 5th October, 1752.

De La Haye was Governor of Cochin (1750-1).

The tombstones of the above are in St. Francis' Church.

John Adam Cellarius—died 15th June, 1796, was one of the signatories of the Capitulation of Cochin. Buried in the Dutch Cemetery at Cochin.

Wilhelm Blasser—died 2nd February, 1729. Died at the Chetwai fort of which he was Captain. A slab was discovered in the fort leaving an inscription.

APPENDIX V.

FOREWORD

by

SIR RICHARD TEMPLE, BARONET.

to the first section originally published as
Malabar and the Portuguese.

Mr. Panikkar has performed a work of value to students in providing a summary of the history of the Portuguese in Malabar. He has, however, thus confined himself to a portion only of their doings in the East, rigorously moreover keeping to this theme, and the chief value of his observations to my mind is that he gives the history from the point of view of the Indian who has been trained in historical research and is capable of bringing out the essentials of the story he has to tell. It is not a pleasant tale, but that is not his fault—rather that of his subject.

He begins by showing how it was possible for the Portuguese to accomplish what they managed to do, as, when Vasco da Gama reached the Malabar Coast the country was split up into petty principalities over whom no one had any real authority—not even the Zamorin of Calicut. So it did not require any particular political insight to play off the princelings along the coast against each other and establish foreign authority over small isolated coastwise areas. Mr. Panikkar has no high opinion of Vasco da Gama and does not class him with the great European explorers. Perhaps he is somewhat hard on him: but, no doubt, Vasco da Gama was not a "great" man in the sense that others of his time and later on were. Mr. Panikkar has indeed but little opinion of any of the Portuguese leaders excepting Albuquerque. Duarate Pacheco as a military luminary, and Affonso Mexia as a financier; and, indeed, these men did some wonderful things, considering the difficulties that surrounded them. He is right also in stating clearly that the Portuguese never had any power or Empire in India, that they never got beyond acquiring a little local authority strictly confined to small areas around the forts they built along the coast line. Yet, with the fortuitous assistance of general politics in the Near East, and not of their own superior skill, they achieved for a long period their chief object—the destruction of the Egyptian and Venetian trade with the East, and the concentration of it in their own hands on the sea. Some of their Governors saw that it was in sea power only that their chances of success and greatness lay.

In judging of the Portuguese and their actions in India, one has to recollect that they were a century nearer feudal Europe than were any of the other nations that invaded the country—a century further back in civilisation and political organisation. In fact, they had very little of the latter, as practically every Factor had a right to address the Portuguese Crown direct and write home what he thought fit-truth or untruth, praise or slander—of the Viceroy, Governor or other superior authority. Authoritative government is impossible under such conditions, and so the Portuguese officials made it. They destroyed even Albuquerque in the end. One wonders indeed that anything at all was accomplished; and the undoubted fact that trade and civilisation did flourish under them for a time supplies yet another instance, of many in history, of the truth of the dictum that human beings act better than they organise.

In their mediaevalism there was little to choose between the higher Portuguese officials and their Indian contemporaries. The insincerity, dishonesty, selfishness, chicanery and cruelty were about on a par, though perhaps, the cruelty of the Portuguese was the greater, and indeed commercial and political intercourse must have been difficult when no man's word was to be trusted on either side. Yet, as aforesaid, they did manage to carry on commerce and the dealings of everyday life. The public proceedings of the Portuguese leaders, great and small, were essentially those of mediaeval people. There was little attempt at straight dealing. It was everyone for himself from the Viceroy downwards, and every kind of official entered into private trade. The strong succeeded in their personal aims; the weak brought disaster on themselves and their following, while as among all such people, there were individuals who were sufficiently wideawake to their own interests. Life struggled on; wealth was accumulated in places; extravagant careers were lived through: great houses and towns were built: and there was much show of success. But the whole structure was hollow, and fell before the first equally well equipped enemy that attacked it. The hollowness was not the result only of the action of the representatives of the Portuguese nation in India. The home government was necessarily ignorant of the conditions, and, as has been already hinted, took the wrong course in ascertaining the truth as to the proceedings of its agents in the East. The entire system showed its inefficiency from the very top. Otherwise such men as Cabral, de Countinho. Reall, de Meneses, de Sousa and others like them, would not have been sent to high office. The position in India was thus rendered hopeless. Officials were improperly paid, or even not paid at all: the very soldiers were unpaid for a year after arrival in any case; pay counted for little, and perquisites were everything; at first, there was no accounting, and even after it was instituted it was very bad—as a matter of course the currency was soon debased; indeed, selfishness and shortsightedness at home seem to have been endless. At any rate, they led to sending orphan girls to India with appointments—even high ones—as dowries to any husband they might marry on arrival. If such things had not actually happened, one could hardly credit their possibility.

It must not, however, be supposed that no Portuguese showed any of the higher human capacities. The records of Barbosa and Correa, among others, are proof of the contrary. Albuquerque was a real administrator; Duarte Pacheco had considerable military genius, and Affonso Mexia true financial ability as well as honesty of purpose. There were besides, even in the beginning, men who understood; but they were not in supreme power. There were also men who learnt much—more in fact than for a long time did the more successful of the Europeans who followed them to India—of the natives of the country, their tribes, their habits and their religious ideas. An unfortunately bigoted and far too powerful a priesthood led the Portuguese Church in India; but even amongst them there were such true missionaries as Francisco de Xavier. The want of principle, however, in the government and organisation made the situation hopeless. Ignorance in regard to the Indians and their ways was at first complete—so complete indeed that Vasco da Gama and his men at the beginning thought that the Hindu was a kind of Christian. The Mohammedan—the Moor—they knew and hated with a true religious fervour, but Hinduism in any form was a thing unrealised. They soon learnt better; but it will be understood that mistakes were necessarily many, especially as the bigotry never diminished. Among the mistakes, perhaps the most serious, were that the country could be taken by force, that conversion to the Portuguese form of Christianity, of all the Indian population was a feasible proposition, and that the princelings with whom they came in contact were the Princes of India. The pride and self-conceit of the Portuguese, too, were unlimited. They looked on themselves as the salt of the earth, all others being completely below them; and yet they had no repugnance to a mixture of races. Their inferiority in numbers was obvious, and, from the beginning, they sought to set it straight by mixed unions, Portuguese and Indians, not realising that the population resulting would be neither Portuguese nor Indian. The mixture of races thus permitted was carried very far and permeated every class. It unquestionably helped in the fall of the Portuguese as a race in India. At the same time the mixing of European and Indian soldiers and sailors led the way to a most successful organisation, afterwards adopted with a difference by the French and English.

A consideration, like the above, of the conditions of Portuguese power in India, such as it was, explains true tales of the times that otherwise read as pure romances, and there are many such. Take for example the career of Dom Martin (1606-1643). The King of Arakan had a son who was Viceroy of Chittagong, while the Portuguese piratical adventurer, Sebastian Gonsalvez, constituted himself Ruler of the island of Sarandip. The Arakanese Viceroy felt himself uncertain in his post and made overtures to Gonsalvez, who seized the opportunity to better his own position. In the result, a daughter of the Arakanese Viceroy, born of course a Buddhist, was married, as a Christian, to the Portuguese pirate's son. This proceeding was naturally not pleasing to the King of Arakan, who sent his eldest son to deal with the Viceroy. This eldest son was afterwards a notable King of Arakan and his visit to Chittagong was the end of his brother, the Viceroy, and incidentally, in the sequel, of Gonsalvez also. But the

Portuguese priest managed to spirit away two of the Viceroy's children, a boy and a girl, to Hooghly, where they were brought up us Portuguese Christians under the names of Dom Martin and Dona Petronella. It was in accordance with Portuguese manners and policy to treat Dom Martin the Arakanese as a Portuguese gentleman of standing. He, accordingly, served for years as an officer in the Army and Navy in India, and, as it happened, with distinction. Meanwhile his uncle, the King of Arakan, died and his successor was overthrown by a usurper. Portugal also, under John IV, had recently thrown off the Spanish yoke and Dom Martin saw his chance to recover his own throne through Portuguese help. So he managed to get to Portugal, as the first Burmese to visit any European country, in a manner that is romance itself. He obtained an interview with John IV who found him a man of parts and could sympathise with him in his desire to recover his heritage. At any rate, the King equipped an expedition for him, and then, unfortunately, Dom Martin died at sea without even reaching India. So ended, in nothing, an extraordinary romantic career, which might otherwise have seriously affected Burmese history. But the point, in the present connection, is that it was made possible by the conditions of the Portuguese occupation of the Indian coasts. Dom Martin could not have attained the position he achieved under any other European power in India.

Another story of the period, which reads impossible to the modern Englishman, also illustrates the conditions of Portuguese presence in India during the early part of the seventh century. Felippe de Brito, a cabin boy and palace menial, rose in three years (1600-1602), during the chaos on the collapse of the Peguan Empire, to the Governorship of Syriam, near Rangoon, for the Arakanese, and finally to the throne of Pegu itself, with a daughter of the Viceroy of Goa for wife. Like other Portuguese of the time, he was an aggressive, headstrong man, with no idea of ingratiating himself to his people or neighbours. So in 1613 he was ousted and impaled alive, while his unfortunate queen, who seems to have been a typically proud Portuguese woman, was sent as a slave to Ava. Here again we can see that it was the condition of Portuguese administration in India and the East that made such a story possible. There are others equally astonishing.

The mention of Sebastian Gonsalvez, who may be looked on as a real pirate, induces me to remark on what is usually called piracy in the Indian seas in the sixteenth and seventeenth centuries. The Portuguese admitted the right of other European nations to the freedom of the Western oceans, but claimed, under Papal authority, to be the only lawful sailors on those in the East. Under such a claim, sailors of all other nations, using them without Portuguese permission, were pirates. This is why the Kunjali Marakkars were looked on as such, though they were in reality the admirals of the Zamorin of Calicut, They fought the Portuguese with varying success for a hundred years until they became overgrown subjects of their nominal master and were destroyed by the Portuguese through his connivance. So was every "Moor", and the commander of every ship of another European nation sailing in the East, a pirate in Portuguese eyes. In one sense indeed every ship, Portuguese or other, capable of fighting, as were most of the large vessels in the Eastern seas, was in those days a pirate craft.

Although the Portuguese invasion of the Indian coastal regions was, in the light of the above observations, only an incident in the general history of the country, it had a profound effect on Malabar. The tendency of the rule of the native princelings was towards a consolidation of power in one of them, the Zamorin of Calicut, and there can be little doubt but that something of the kind would have been the fate of Malabar had it not been for the disruptive effect of the intervention of the Portuguese. Their action prevented any such event taking place, and after the fall of their influence nothing of the kind was possible. In fact, the present condition of Malabar under British rule is largely the result of Portuguese action. Again, as has been remarked above, however badly the Portuguese ruled the people went their own way in domestic and commercial life and did an immense amount of good to the country by introducing new products, such as the the cashew (*kishu*) nut and tobacco. They also vastly improved the spices and fruits for which Malabar was already famous. Especially was their work beneficial to the cultivation of the cocoanut; and they may be said to have created the great modern trade in coir. So, although there is much to be said against the Portuguese doings in South India, it cannot be truthfully asserted that they produced no good at all.

Montreux }
Switzerland }

R. C. Temple

FOREWORD

by

SIR EVAN COTTON

to the second section originally published as
Malabar and the Dutch

In his book on "Malabar and the Portuguese", Mr. Panikkar has traced the history of the relations of the Portuguese with the West Coast of India from 1500 to 1663. He has shown that their political organisation was singularly ineffective: that outside Goa which was an easily defensible island their authority never extended beyond a few coastal towns, and that the monopoly of trade which they claimed, was never conceded by the Indian Powers. In the present volume we are presented with a survey of the Dutch connection with Malabar, which may be said to begin with the capture of Cochin from the Portuguese in 1663 and lingered on until the surrender of that place to Major Petrie in 1795, when the Dutch flag ceased to fly on the West Coast. The period is of special interest because it witnessed the fall of the Nayar power—a subject with which Mr. Panikkar, as a member of the Nayar caste, is peculiarly competent to deal.

The Nayars are the most characteristic though not the most numerous of the communities in Malabar. In its widest sense the term includes a very large number of castes which are now quite distinct. But there can be little doubt that the real Nayars were primarily a military caste. They are the feudal and military aristocrats of he West Coast. Burke, in one of his speeches on the French Revolution, classed them with the Mamalukes of Egypt; and they have been famous since the days of Marco Polo. Traces of the martial spirit, which attracted the notice of Gaspar Correa and Duarte Barbosa, and many other early travellers, survive in the *Kalaris*, a sort of combined private chapel and gymnasium, or fencing school, which are still attached to high-class Nayar houses. There is an instructor-in-arms to the family of the Zamorin of Calicut, who is known as the Dharmoth Panikkar, and whose ancestors were the hereditary Commanders-in-Chief. In modern times, however the Nayars have exchanged the sword for the pen although they still own much land, and have secured a substantial share of the professions and of posts in the Government service in the Madras Presidency. Their origin is obscure. Sir C. Sankaran Nayar, one of the most distinguished members of the caste, has expressed the belief, in conversation with the writer, that they came in the first instance from the North, and has mentioned in support of his view that the dialect spoken at Delhi contains many words which bear a close resemblance to Malayalam. They are certainly not the original aboriginal inhabitants for there can be no doubt of the large admixture of Aryan blood. Their religious beliefs exhibit a strange combination of Hindu and Dravidian cults. In this connection Mr. Panikkar has observed elsewhere (Journal of the Royal Anthropological Institute, Vol. XLVIII) that after twenty centuries of conflict with Hinduism, the Nayars cling with extreme persistence to spirit worship. But perhaps the most remarkable feature of their social system is the *tarawad*, a family establishment which consists of all the descendants from the same ancestress, counting relationship exclusively from the side of the mother. Property is owned in common and is under the control of the senior male member who is known as the *karnavan;* but the head of the family is the senior lady, and children belong to their mother's *tarawad.*

The Travancore State, which is to-day the principal state on the Malabar Coast and extends over an area of 7625 square miles, was founded on the ruin of the Nayar power. In 1762 the military hegemony of the Nayars in Travancore and in the adjoining state of Cochin was finally broken. The Zamorin of Calicut, who represents the historic dynasty which was reigning in Malabar when the Portuguese first landed on the Coast, is now merely a wealthy landholder shorn of all sovereign authority. When the great Martanda Varma ascended the throne of Travancore in 1729, his state was one of the smallest in Malabar. When he died in 1758, he had established an autocracy over the West Coast, which Mr. Panikkar describes as the victory of Tamilian over Malayali culture. Nevertheless his family claims to be, as indeed they are, Malabar Kshattriyas, and the succession is rigidly maintained through the female line. The sons of the Maharajah are of no account; the heir apparent is the eldest male of the Maharajah's *Tarawad.* It has been said that but for foreign intervention the ascendancy of the Nayars might have endured for centuries to come: and the comment is justified. Mr. Panikkar shows us how their fall was associated with the presence of the Dutch in Malabar. "The United Company of the Netherlands" was a very powerful organism. Professor Greyl, in the chapter on "The Dutch in India" which he contributed to the fifth volume of the *Cambridge History of India,* has given us an admirable account of its composition. It was made up of six "Chambers" which traded each with its own capital, but pooled their profits and losses. The Amsterdam chamber which was the most important, appointed eight out of the seventeen directors who held office for life. But the "Assembly of the Noble Lords of the Seventeen", which met three times a year, was concerned only with the general lines of policy: the executive authority rested with the several chambers which were situated in the various towns. By the charter of March 20, 1602, the Company was given the exclusive right to trade in all countries between the Cape of Good Hope and the Straits of Magellan; and in 1609 the 1st Governor-General of the Dutch possessions in the East Indies was appointed. Ten years later the famous Jan Pietersoon Coen whose name is prepetuated by one of the steamers of the Nederland Royal Mail line, founded the city of Batavia in the Island of Java on the ruins of Jacarta, and made it his headquarters.

As Mr. Panikkar has pointed out, the first connection of the Dutch with Malabar began as early as 1604, when Admiral Stevan van der Haghen concluded a treaty with the Zamorin of Calicut, who was chafing under the constant interference of the Portuguese. But it was not until October 1661 that any definite action was taken. Quilon and Cranganore were captured; and with the fall of Cochin in January 1663, the Dutch stepped into the shoes of the Portuguese. During the next century and a quarter, their policy was governed, as Mr. Panikkar observes, by "a single consideration—that of obtaining the greatest share in the pepper trade at a minimum cost." The Commandeur, or head of the administration, whose jurisdiction extended over the Malabar Coast, Kanara and Vengurla, resided at Cochin, where the fortress of Nicuu Oranje had been built in 1662. His rank was not a high one in the Dutch Colonial hierarchy; and it was speedily discovered that the establishment of a monopoly in the pepper trade could not be realised. The expenditure more than outweighed the advantages. They were never (Mr. Panikkar insists) the Paramount power in Malabar. Their political authority was confined to Cochin and its neighbourhood and to Quilon. The rise of Travancore was fatal to their military pretensions and eventually they were engulfed in the growing tide of British dominion. At the same time they were superior to the Portuguese in many respects. Their officers were competent business-men: and on the whole they were liberal and tolerant. Their one idea was trade, and Mr. Panikkar is of opinion that their connection with Malabar was in many ways beneficial. The *Hortus Malabaricus,* which was compiled at Cochin from 1678 onwards under the patronage of Baron Hendrik Adriaan van Rheede of Drakenstegn—some say by a Carmelite friar named Matthacus; others by Johannes Casearius a Protestant pastor—testifies to their zeal for scientific research. Similarly, Philippus Baldaeus' description of Ceylon and the Malabar Coast, which was published at Amsterdam in 1672, and of which there is an English translation in the third volume of Churchill's *Voyages* (1745), was the work of another minister of the Dutch Reformed Church.

Among the remarkable men in the service of the Dutch East India Company, van Rheede takes a high place. He was commandeur at Cochin from 1673 to 1677; and his tomb in the Dutch Cemetery at Surat, where he died on December 16, 1691, is one of the sights of the town. He was appointed by the Seventeen in 1684 as "Commissar General for the Western Quarters", and held the office until his death. The mausoleum, which is said to have been built with the intention of eclipsing that of Sir George Oxinden, consists of a double cupola of great dimensions with a gallery above and below, supported on handsome columns. The curious will notice that in the inscription, "Cochin" and "Souratte" are engraved in capital letters and "bombai" in small ones. It was during Van Rheede's administration of Malabar that the Cochin State was virtually handed over to the Dutch.

Of a very different type, but no less remarkable, was the Valia Kappithan or "Great Captain", Eustache Benedict de Lannoy. He was a Fleming and was originally in the Dutch service, but was taken prisoner by Martanda Varma, with twenty-three other Europeans, at the battle of Colachel on August 10, 1741, which put an end to the Dutch dreams of the conquest of Malabar. Together with another prisoner, a Frenchman of the name Doncaud, he entered the service of the Maharajah and organised his army for him. The famous Travancore lines which were taken by Tippu in 1790 were built by him, and also the fort of Udayagiri, the walls of which enclose a hill, thirty-eight miles to the south-east of Trivandrum. He died in June 1777 at the age of sixty-two and is buried at Udayagiri. Like Monsieur Raymond at Hyderabad, who has given his name to the Myseram Risala in the Nizam's Army, he is still remembered as "Istach".

What memorials have the Dutch left behind them in Southern India? Most of them are on the

Coromandel Coast—ornamented tombs at Negapatam, Pulicat (Castel Geldria) and Sadras, Porto Novo, Bimlipatam and Masulipatam (Bunder). In the extreme south, at Cape Comorin are the ruins of Dutch fortifications and a huge granite slab, nine feet in height, now used as a doorstep, originally erected in memory of a Dutch factor. Hard by, at Tuticorin, is a well-filled Dutch burying ground. On the West Coast, there are the regal mausoleums at Surat. In Malabar itself we shall find at Cannanore on the outer ramparts of Fort St. Angelo, the grave of the wife and two children (1745) of Godfried Weyerman, who was Governor of Cochin from 1761 to 1764. At Tangacherry (Tangasseri) a minute British possession of 96 acres in extent, situated on the coast two miles from Quilon, is the grave (1779) of a Dutch Commandant of Fort Thomas, which was originally built by the Portuguese in 1503, and has almost entirely fallen into the sea. There is rather more at Cochin itself. The modern Town of Cochin, or Kuchi Bunder, is in British territory. It is a busy little port, picturesquely situated on the northern end of a long sandy spit lying between the backwater and the sea at the mouth of the Cochin river. Three miles across the lagoon at the southern end is Muttancheri, which is in Cochin state territory, and is famous for its two synagogues of the White and Black Jews. On the island of Bolghotty, in the lagoon, is the British Residency, which was built by the Dutch in 1744. The Dutch tomb-tones in the church of St. Francis which are ranged against the walls with their Portuguese predecessors, date from 1664; among them are those which once covered the last resting-place of Doctor Balthasar de Meter (1666) who, according to Governor Adrian Moens, was the first Pretestant Minister to preach in Cochin, Abraham Cornelis de la Haye (1752) who was governor from 1750 to 1751, the wife and daughter (1688) of Isaac van Dielen, Governor from 1687 to 1693, the wife (1727) of Jacob de Jong, Governor from 1724 to 1731, and the children (1789) of van Gollenesse, Governor from 1735 to 1743. The church, which was originally built by the Franciscans and is believed to be the oldest in India, was converted by the Dutch into a Protestant place of worship. The old Portuguese cathedral of Santa Cruz has vanished; it was formed into a warehouse by the Dutch and was blown up for strategic reasons in 1806 by the British together with the fort and some of the quays and houses. The Military commandant's house can still be seen, but two gates, close to the English Club, mark all that is left of the governor's residence. In the Dutch Cemetery is the grave (1784) of the wife of Jan Lambertus Vanspall, the last governor, who surrendered to the British on October 20, 1795, after the firing of a single shell "planted with excellent skill in the centre of Government House". There were until recently—and probably still are—Vanspalls on the west coast, and Mr. J. J. Cotton, in his *List of Monumental Inscriptions in the Madras Presidency* (p. 261) relates that there is a tradition among them that a great fortune awaits the Vanspall who has the ability to prove to the Netherlands government that he is descended from the governor of Cochin.

The visitor to India rarely finds his way to Malabar. He misses much. The scenery is delightful: the castes and customs amply repay study; and Malabar is one of the few places in the world where the accuracy of observations made four centuries ago can be checked on the spot. It is to be hoped that Mr. Panikkar's historical researches will tempt many to cultivate acquaintance with his subject at first hand. He is one of that rapidly growing body of Indian scholars who have enriched the history of their country by illustrations from original vernacular documents. Of these there are many in Malabar in the temples and in the custody of the principal families: and Mr. Panikkar has been fortunate enough to obtain access to them. It is in this respect that his work is especially valuable: for these papers frequently throw an entirely new light upon controversies and episodes which are apt to be coloured by their presentation by foreign observers.

EVAN COTTON.
